ENTERPRISE AND ENTREPRENEURS
IN NINETEENTH- AND TWENTIETH-CENTURY FRANCE

ENTERPRISE AND ENTREPRENEURS IN NINETEENTH- AND TWENTIETH-CENTURY FRANCE

Edited with an Introduction by
EDWARD C. CARTER II, ROBERT FORSTER,
and JOSEPH N. MOODY

THE JOHNS HOPKINS UNIVERSITY PRESS: BALTIMORE AND LONDON

Manufactured in the United States of America
The Johns Hopkins University Press, Baltimore, Maryland 21218
The Johns Hopkins University Press Ltd., London
Library of Congress Catalog Card Number 75-36936
ISBN 0-8018-1717-X
*Library of Congress Cataloging in Publication data will be found on
the last printed page of this book.*

CONTENTS

ILLUSTRATIONS

TABLES

vii

ACKNOWLEDGMENTS

THE EDITORS wish to thank the Graduate School of Arts and Sciences of the Catholic University of America, the Department of History of the Johns Hopkins University, and the Johns Hopkins University Press for their generous support of the lecture series out of which this book grew. We are also greatly indebted to Elborg Forster for her exact and sensitive translation of Professor Lévy-Leboyer's essay and to Angeline Polites, Lee W. Formwalt, and Geraldine Vickers, all of the Papers of Benjamin Henry Latrobe, for their assistance in a portion of the editorial process

INTRODUCTION

THE FOUR ESSAYS presented here were given as lectures in a series sponsored jointly by the Catholic University of America and the Johns Hopkins University in the spring of 1973. Their subject, business entrepreneurship, is not a new one,[1] although recent concern with ecology and the dangers of unlimited economic growth have placed entrepreneurship in a new perspective. There is less assurance today that large-scale organization is the decisive determinant of business efficiency and innovation. Finally, a new interest in the role of technical and scientific education has added another dimension to our study of entrepreneurial behavior and, in particular, its cultural setting. While these four essays do not constitute an exhaustive treatment of these aspects of French entrepreneurship, they all offer answers to the perennial questions about which factors shape entrepreneurial decisions and what kind of people entrepreneurs are and have been in various cultures. Whatever weight economic historians may place on cultural factors, recent experience in the Third World indicates that to ignore these factors entirely can bring disaster to economic planning. For American readers especially, the French case serves as a reminder that each country constitutes a special problem and that no standard procedure of operation, however successful in the United States, can be applied without modification, or even complete revision, in other countries and other cultures.

Charles P. Kindleberger assesses the impact of the French system of scientific and technical education on the performance of the entrepreneur. Kindleberger makes no claim to having presented a quantitative analysis or having established a precise "rate of social return" from technical education in France. With tongue in cheek, he comments: "My argument, then, is based on journalistic description, qualitative statement, and a few tables whose numbers will be left untortured."

Kindleberger begins with a thorough survey of the *grandes écoles* ("leading professional schools") beginning with the famous Ecole polytechnique and including Ponts et chaussées, Mines, Ecole centrale des arts et manufactures, Ecole normale d'administration, Inspection des finances, and the Ecole Libre des sciences politiques (Science Po). He characterizes the education they provided as superb for forming theoretical and mathematical minds and for inculcating a strong sense of esprit de corps and public service. Unfortunately, the elitism that springs as much from the competitive excellence of the schools as from the upper-bourgeois milieu from which the candidates are drawn has created certain deficiencies among those who become entrepreneurs. The most important of these appears to be a professional arrogance that makes personnel relations in the firm difficult, obstructing the give and take of committee or board meeting. Another problem emerges from the long, hallowed French tradition of awarding high status to government service, especially on the highest administrative levels. One is struck by the number of polytechnicians who become inspectors of finance or members of the Council of State. Among the graduates of the grandes écoles in general, a high proportion become military engineers or civilian engineers working in public works projects, thus deflecting potential recruits from entrepreneurial functions in the private sector or even in nationalized industries.

On the other hand, there is no doubt that since World War II the number of graduates with advanced scientific and technical training has greatly increased; in large measure France has overtaken its rivals in Germany, Britain, and the United States. In absolute numbers there are more engineers than ever going into the private sector.

Kindleberger also reminds the reader that the requisite qualities of entrepreneurship vary not only with the industry but also over time. The excellence of French technical training makes the graduates invaluable in such fields as metallurgy, electronics, or the automobile industry but much less so in the distributive industries, such as department stores or food companies, where the skills of administration and personnel relations assume greater importance. Another factor of some influence is the persistence of aristocratic values that permeate the society at large. For the French scientist and technician this means stressing the unproductive creative act, the pure satisfaction of curiosity, the *gloire* of the *corps*—motives of human endeavor, which, whatever their intrinsic worth, are likely to create products that are inelastic with respect to price. In short, the mass market is of secondary interest to the technicians of the grandes écoles.

To this point, it would appear that Kindleberger has made a strong case for the inappropriateness of French technical education for modern business leadership. By the end of the essay, however, it is clear that the author believes that time is on the side of the French educational system. While it will be useful to add the "human touch" to the nation's bag of entrepreneurial skills, this attribute appears relatively less important as technology—sophisticated, theoretical, mathematical technology—plays a larger and larger role in the modern industrial world. The high value placed on theoretical training in France, he concludes, is finally "coming into its own."

If Charles Kindleberger's conclusion is "unexpected," this reaction reflects some deep-seated attitudes on the part of English and American economic historians about the performance of the French entrepreneur in the nineteenth and twentieth centuries. This is not the place to review the long academic debate over this performance; here we can simply restate two main issues: (1) Was the French growth rate (statistically) so slow as to deserve the attention it has received as an example of "sluggishness"? (2) Admitting its *relative* retardation compared with the extraordinary dynamism of Germany or England, were the reasons for this largely material (location and cost of raw materials, labor, capital, and so on) or cultural (values and attitudes of entrepreneur, labor, and consumer alike)?[2] Those who have supported the position that cultural factors are primary have had greater difficulty proving their point, if only because the tools of the "new economic history"—or even old-fashioned "check-pad quantification"—are only partially applicable to this task.[3] The psychological dimension could not easily be calibrated even if the sources (private letters, for example) were abundant (which they are not). Still, an exploration of the cultural milieu in which the entrepreneur operated is a legitimate and necessary task of the modern economic historian, ill at ease though he may feel without his mathematical tools. How then can one approach the issue of entrepreneurial psychology?

One of the most useful tools for examining entrepreneurial behavior is the case study. David Landes, who has always placed heavy emphasis on cultural factors as determinants of the entrepreneur, provides this type of evidence. Landes has long argued that the "pace and character of French entrepreneurship was set by the family firm, owned and managed by blood relations, where primary concerns were safety, continuity, and privacy." A second, related issue is the role of religion in economic performance, a debate rooted in Max Weber's famous essay, *The Protestant Ethic and the Spirit of Capitalism.* To throw light on these issues, Landes examines the personal correspondence and business papers of the firm of the Motte family, Catholic textile manufactuers of Roubaix-Tourcoing in the nineteenth century. In the process he brings the reader into intimate contact with the total milieu of the family firm.

Preliminary to his main investigation, Landes considers the material factors—location, availability and cost of raw materials, fuel, and labor—and concludes that Roubaix-Tourcoing had no special material advantages to account for its success. In fact, nature had treated these twin towns on the Belgian frontier rather poorly, especially with regard to communication and water supply. Although labor was plentiful, it was no cheaper than elsewhere in France and was resistant to mechanization. There remains, then, the quality of the employers as entrepreneurs.

What were the entrepreneur-*fabricants* like? Drawing upon the available correspondence and memoires of the Motte family and also on personal interviews, Landes shows how business and family virtues were interchangeable; energy, hard work, thrift, discipline, and family solidarity pervaded the lives of each member, mothers and daughters as well as fathers and sons. These values were fostered by the Catholic catechism and the parochial school, by family reunions and constant parental admonition. Only by reading the letters of patriarchs and matriarchs, uncles and aunts, can one grasp the full impact of the credo. Nor were all the values related to self-denial, despite heavy doses of "sacrifice," "stubborn work," and self-discipline at all times. They included the more active imperatives of "competitive effort," "achievement," and mutual aid within the family and clan. These latter components serve to emphasize the more "enterprising" aspects of the family firm and create an image quite different from that of unimaginative caution and routine.

No Weberian Protestant ethic promoted or legitimized these values, nor did Catholic Jansenism act as a substitute. Instead, Landes finds the underpinnings of these compulsive imperatives in a half-conscious

sense of competitive envy and even in minority identity, in opposition
to a neighboring industrial rival, Lille. Perhaps this is what imparted
its "drive" as well as its "ascetism" to the Motte firm. In any event, the
values seemed to work; the family firm prospered, even contrary to
Landes's own earlier thesis about the built-in conservatism of the
family enterprise. Furthermore, the Motte experience was not unique,
and served as a "role model" for other firms in the area. The Mottes
became known as the "Americans of France," not so much because of
their prosperity but because of their total absorption in the industry.
Roubaix textiles, in general, flourished during the latter half of the
nineteenth century, until World War I produced a host of new
challenges to the efficacy of the old values.

Case studies of this kind will always incur the charge of atypicality,
especially from those economic historians enamored of the firm
quantitative data of comparative factor costs and dedicated to the belief
that alternative costs are the decisive determinants of entrepreneurial
decision-making. But without the qualitative evidence offered by the
case history, the historical concept of entrepreneurship faces the real
risk of remaining little more than a simplified view of rational
"economic man." In this essay Landes has used the case study to
question both the Weber thesis and his own earlier conclusions about
the family firm. The results testify to the necessity of continued
empirical research to test the older hypothesis about entrepreneurial
behavior and break ground for new ones. Moreover, as Landes's essay
indicates, there is much to be gained by studying actual, knowable
people working with real, functioning institutions in a total cultural
context.

Maurice Lévy-Leboyer carries forward the task of reappraisal by
challenging the view that French industrial performance in the
nineteenth century was sluggish. At the time this is being written
(1974), many Americans would be happy to have a 1.9 percent per
capita annual rate of growth. Moreover, Lévy-Leboyer is convinced
that for a number of reasons—literary muckraking and social thought
in the past, insufficient or misused statistics in the present—the image
of the French entrepreneur as slow to adapt to the imperatives of
economic growth is built on a false stereotype. André Citroën, not
Louis Motte-Bossut, is the modern prototype of the French industrial
manager. The author asserts that the size of a firm is not always the
relevant criterion for measuring efficiency and that management is not
an independent variable. Beginning with these two preliminary
assumptions, Lévy-Leboyer takes "another look" at the French

business leader, his performance, and especially his adaptation to a particular economic environment.

The author begins by explaining the persistence well into the twentieth century of small (under ten employees) and medium-sized (ten to one hundred employees) firms. A conscious policy of geographic dispersion, from the mid-nineteenth century on, was a response to the need to reach the rural market and to find cheaper labor. This was followed by a policy of paternalist education to hold labor in the locale. Furthermore, Lévy-Leboyer reminds the reader that economies of scale are not always present, that labor morale is often better in small firms, and that technical innovations are more easily absorbed in middle-sized firms than in large ones, where decision-making is a cumbersome process. The decision to disperse industry into small units was, in any case, the result of "hard" market and labor factors, not the consequence of an excessive love of privacy, safety, and continuity. Turning to business leadership, Lévy-Leboyer concludes that before 1900 it was very rare for an entrepreneur of a large firm to be drawn from the ranks of the industry. Most of these men came from merchant banking and formed a rather closed elite. Social mobility was high only in small firms such as those in textiles. But conceding the elitism of heavy industry, how efficient were these entrepreneurs? Corroborating Kindleberger, Lévy-Leboyer points out the lack of market orientation among graduates of the grandes écoles and, in fact, their modest role in industry before 1920. Beginning about 1900 and accelerating in the 1920s, however, large industry (over one hundred employees) made its appearance. The author's quantitative and qualitative data makes this clear; the automotive industry in particular seemed to exhibit all the marks of Fordism, including the use of new sales techniques, consumer credit, and various supporting services. A new type of entrepreneur had arrived.

Still, the small firms held on. "Dualism" remained characteristic of French industrial growth well into the new century. Curiously, after a spurt of business concentrations, there was a leveling off after 1932, and when mergers took place they appeared to absorb less and less new capital. The preference of the entrepreneurs for "partial" rather than "total" merger is of special interest, and here the author comes close to assigning some blame to the French entrepreneur for his lack of drive. Yet, he insists, "external factors" actually left no options open. These factors included such long-run conditions as a stagnant mass market (due to demographic trends), low labor mobility and productivity, prolonged recessions, and the state policy of often opposing mergers, instead of actively supporting them.

In general, Lévy-Leboyer's essay supports those who—like Rondo Cameron—point to material factors as the primary determinants of economic growth and as the imperatives that force the entrepreneur's hand. Although Lévey-Leboyer assigns a role to "social norms" and other cultural influences, he denies that the French entrepreneur—in the twentieth century at least—is much different from his American or German counterpart. Peugot and Citroën have replaced Motte and Méline. If the small firm persists, it will do so because of external factors and not any special "family psychology" of the entrepreneur. Moreover, the small firm is not without virtues of an economic nature.

To this point we have focused on the economic consequences of French entrepreneurship, but to the social historian it is just as important to know how the entrepreneur spent his money as it is to knew how he made it. Whatever its precise ranking in the race for economic growth, for instance, nineteenth-century France was without peer in the world of art. What was the role of the French entrepreneur as a patron of the arts? What does the world of the artist have in common with the world of the entrepreneur?

Albert Boime's essay is the first attempt to establish the interconnections between the artist and the entrepreneur in nineteenth-century France. His study goes beyond the role of the entrepreneur as patron or collector and demonstrates how entrepreneurial activities, from cotton printing and book illustrating to iron architecture and railroad construction, affect the artist. In fact, entrepreneurship was an integral part of the artistic world itself, with the art dealer representing its perfect embodiment. Boime also suggests that the artists themselves were entrepreneurs, not only in their effort "to market their product" (he characterizes van Gogh as a perennial hustler) but also in their love of risk, their creativity, and the gambling instinct that Boime associates with business activity.

It might be objected that these are the very qualities that many historians find lacking in French business leadership. If they are correct, was this interest in the artistic world an outlet for the "gambling instinct" that was not released via industrial growth? Or was it only a certain type of French entrepreneur who had contact with the milieu of art? Boime's investigation shows that the large majority of collectors were bankers, with a preponderance of Protestants and Jews in their ranks. He cites Rothschild, Fould, Casimir-Perier, Laffitte, Péreire, Delessert, Seillières, and Pérregaux among the great collectors. No doubt the first generations of these families needed the respectability a private art collection bestowed. But this does not explain the passion and taste for art displayed by subsequent generations. For temperamental reasons, the artistic world may have been especially attractive to bankers and financiers (and even to department store magnates), but much less so to textile and iron manufacturers—despite the examples of Charles Dollfus, the Alsatian cotton magnate, and Eugène Schneider of the Le Creusot iron works, both compulsive collectors.

The great merit of Boime's essay is his demonstration of the variety of interrelations between what we have always considered two separate, even antagonistic, vocations. Boime claims that the artist's perennial attack on the philistine bourgeois and the entrepreneur's pejorative allusion to the utopian artist are both myths concealing a very close, mutually supporting relationship. It was a relationship that went beyond financing and promoting the artist to embrace the new industrial world being created by the entrepreneurs. This was to become the inspiration and subject matter for the artist. Social revolutionaries, dear to the romantics, were not the leaders in establishing new artistic tastes in nineteenth-century France; the entrepreneur-patrons, the bankers in particular, were the real pace-setters.

Of course, the entrepreneurs as collectors were a breed apart from those who employed the artist in the fabrication and marketing of their product. Book publishers with their lithographs and wood engravings, advertisers with their publicity posters, cotton printers, fashion designers, and a host of others obviously had regular working relationships with artists, whom they often provided with schools of design as well as salaries. It may be that the aesthetic tastes of the French consumer have given the commercial artist and the industrial arts in general a larger role than in other industrial countries; the plethora of examples Boime presents suggests this possibility. On still another level, it is no doubt true that without the railroad and other products of the Age of Iron we would not have Daumier's *Third-Class Railroad Car* or Monet's *Saint-Lazare Station*, not to mention countless other "settings," from vacation resorts to Pacific islands, made possible by entrepreneurship in the broad sense. And one does not have to be a Marxist to agree that the Barbizon School reflected the taste of the *haute bougeoisie*.

The author sees these two worlds merging in a dynamic, not a static, manner. After 1870, changes in the attitudes of the entrepreneur-patron are discernible. The collectors began to become more public minded, donating their collections to public museums. Their tastes became more universal and more avant-garde, after earlier proclivities toward seventeenth-century Dutch and eighteenth-century French masters.

Significantly, patronage itself shifted from the notables of the July Monarchy and the Second Empire to the more parvenu "protectors" of the Third Republic, men who were more like the artists themselves in social origin. As the century drew to a close, the entrepreneur-artist relationship appears less paternalistic and more fraternal, more market oriented, innovative, and public minded.

Boime's essay stands on its own as a novel effort to join the world of the artist to that of the businessman. But he also indirectly contributes to the long-standing debate among economic historians about the influence of cultural factors on entrepreneurial behavior. His detailed study supports the contention that artistic considerations—indeed, passions—occupied a large place in the entrepreneur's activities, and were surely not limited to his leisure hours. His motives extended beyond a drive for respectability and, by the end of the century at least, included a passionate desire to share in artistic creation. True, these influences ran both ways, and the artists shared more qualities with the business entrepreneur than they always cared to admit. But both artist and entrepreneur placed the unique product of imagination and improvisation in a higher order of things than the output of mass production. In the end, the entrepreneur-patrons were not unlike Kindleberger's graduate engineers: both were only marginally interested in products that were elastic in respect to price.

Albert Boime is no doubt correct when he says that people carry within themselves both entrepreneurial and aesthetic inclinations and that there is no justification, except old myths, for keeping them in mutual isolation. But one may fairly ask which "inclination" is the stronger From this and the other essays in this collection, it appears that the French entrepreneur of the nineteenth century was subject to aesthetic cultural imperatives of particular force. Perhaps only a French entrepreneur could have really understood Emile Péreire when he said to his house guests in the Fauboug Saint-Honoré, "Il y a trop d'or ici. . . . Voilà mon véritable trésor," and then exhibited his gallery of fine paintings. That the France of the mid-twentieth century has produced a new brand of market-oriented entrepreneur is most probable. But perhaps even the Péreires and the Mottes should not be too quickly dismissed as hopelessly inefficient or outmoded, especially at a time when economic growth itself can no longer be considered an unmitigated blessing.

Edward Carter II
Robert Forster
Joseph N. Moody

NOTES

1. In the United States entrepreneurial history has been a specialized field of study since 1946. Under the inspiration of Arthur H. Cole of the Harvard Business School, the Center for Entrepreneurial History was formed to encourage the writing of business history monographs and also to develop a kind of sociology of enterprise. Much of this work, together with the debates and controversies that emerged from it, is published in the journal *Explorations in Entrepreneurial History*. For an excellent review of the research trends in this country in business and economic history, see William N. Parker, "Through Growth and Beyond: Three Decades in Economic and Business History," in *Business Enterprise and Economic Change: Essays in Honor of Harold F. Williamson*, ed. Louis P. Cain and Paul J. Uselding (Kent, Ohio: 1973), pp. 15-47, and also part 3, entitled "The Role of Entrepreneurship in the Process of Economic Development," where Japanese, British, and American entrepreneurship is treated.

2. For a beginning on the debate regarding French economic growth, both its amplitude and its determinants, see David Landes, "French Entrepreneurship and Industrial Gowth in the Nineteenth Century," *Journal of Economic History* 9 (May 1949); 45-61; David Landes, "French Business and the Businessman: A Social and Cultural Analysis," and John E. Sawyer, "Strains in the Social Structure of Modern France," both published in *Modern France: Problems of the Third and Fourth Republics*, ed. Edward M. Earle (New York, 1964); Rondo E. Cameron, "Economic Growth and Stagnation in France, 1815-1914," *Journal of Modern History*, March 1958, pp. 1-13; Jan Marczewski, "Some Aspects of the Economic Growth of France, 1660-1958," in *Economic Development and Cultural Change* 9 (April 1961): 369-86; Maurice Lévy-Leboyer, "Croissance économique en France au XIXe siècle," *Annales, E.S.C.*, July-August 1968; National Bureau for Economic Research, ed., *Capital Formation and Economic Growth* (Princeton, 1955), especially the article by Bert F. Hoselitz, "Entrepreneurship and Capital Formation in France and Britain since 1700," pp. 291-337, and "Comment," by Alexander Gerschenkron, pp. 373-78.

3. See Robert W. Fogel, "The New Economic History: Its Findings and Methods," *Economic History Review*, 2d ser. 19 (December 1966): 642-56; Robert W. Fogel and Stanley L. Engerman, eds., *The Reinterpretation of American Economic History* (New York, 1971); Lance E. Davis, "And It Will Never Be Literature: The New Economic History—A Critique," *Explorations in Entrepreneurial History*, 2d ser. 6 (Fall 1968): 75-92; Harry N. Scheiber, "On the New Economic History and Its Limitations: A Review Essay", *Agricultural History* 41 (October 1967): 383-95.

ENTERPRISE AND ENTREPRENEURS
IN NINETEENTH- AND TWENTIETH-CENTURY FRANCE

TECHNICAL EDUCATION
AND THE FRENCH ENTREPRENEUR
BY CHARLES P. KINDLEBERGER

MY EXAMINATION will begin with a general description of scientific and technical education in France, a description more or less valid for the whole period since the Revolution, rather than with a detailed chronological account, although some major milestones must be mentioned. There will follow discussions of the role of technical education in entrepreneurship generally and of the special characteristics that distinguish both scientific education and entrepreneurship in France. The method used is what two young economic historians somewhat sniffily call "qualitative statement and counterstatement," better in their view than the "journalistic generalization" out of which it emerges but well short of "standard economic and statistical tools" of a quantitative sort. "The social return to technical education could be estimated and comparison made [for Britain] with German and American rates of return."[1] Given the circumstances responsible for the quality of French scientific education—its provision to one dominant monopsony employer, the state, and the family character of French firms—I doubt that such a comparison could be made. For example, to

The writer has benefited greatly from the comments and suggestions of Raina Daston, Fritz K. Ringer, Cyril Stanley Smith, John Weiss, and seminars at The Catholic University of America and Tufts University.

3

estimate the return to investment in chemical education in France from comparative wages of French and German chemists—in 1913 France had 2,000 chemists and Germany 30,000[2]—the model must be identified. If demands for chemical services were broadly identical in the two countries, and the wage rate much higher in France than in Germany, an unambiguous calculation could be made. If supply of potential chemists was broadly the same and the French wage lower, higher demand for chemists in Germany than in France would be indicated. But if, with this difference of fifteen to one in supply, there were both a mania for theory instead of practice in France and indifference among the French users,[3] both demand and supply schedules in the two countries could differ with roughly comparable wage rates—which would tell us nothing about the social return to technical education.

Even if the task of measuring exactly the contribution of technical education to growth were possible for the new breed of economic historians, it is not so for me. My argument, then, is based on journalistic description, qualitative statement, and a few tables whose numbers will be left untortured.

II

The jewel in the diadem of scientific education in France, significant for economic growth and entrepreneurial activity, was and is the Ecole polytechnique, which was founded in the days after the French Revolution as part of a wave of educational reform. This surge had its origins mainly in the Enlightenment. A reaction against the Sorbonne and the Catholic church, it was only to a limited degree a response to pressures from scientists,[4] who quickly manned it and brought it to an eminence of achievement it has never lost.[5] Competition for admission was intense, with almost three times as many applicants taking the difficult examinations, generally after a year of tutoring, as were admitted between 1794 and 1836; in 1836, six times as many. Numbers started at an average of 130 and fluctuated between 64 in 1820 and 283 in 1872.[6] The course lasted two years and fitted its graduates for the applied schools (to be discussed presently), except, of course, in times of war and especially under Napoleon I, when classrooms were virtually emptied to fill the ranks of company-grade officers.

A military institution, the Ecole polytechnique prepared its graduates especially for the artillery school at Metz and for army engineering—a diversion from the original intention of the reformers who were interested in industrial progress. Saint-Simon, the pioneer of the movement favoring economic growth that flowered especially after 1830, in 1797 took a house across the street from the Polytechnique, although it is not stated whether this was the rue de Descartes on which, among others, the institution fronts.[7] Until they had a falling out in 1801, Saint-Simon was a close friend of Monge, who, with Lamblardie, was the prime mover in the school's formation. Monge and Lamblardie were convinced that the same training was appropriate for civil as for military engineering. Before the age of the computer, when the calculation of parabolas became a trivial exercise, the employment of artillery required competence in mathematics. Mathematics and descriptive geometry were the backbone of the curriculum and, in less rigorous form, of the curricula of all French technical schools down to the primary level. Monge himself was a geometer. The 1895 list of Polytechnicians who "made their mark" in science includes 17 geometers in first place, ahead of 14 mechanical engineers, 11 physicians, 9 astronomers, 8 geologists, 7 historians and philologians, 5 chemists, and in last place I regret to say—2 economists, Chevalier and LePlay.[8] (The greatest French economist, Léon Walras, failed to gain admission to the Ecole polytechnique on two occasions, both times in mathematics, despite his ultimate designation as the father of mathematical economics.) Mathematics was taught, however, less for its utility than for its moral value. Mathematics and science were to the French elite what Latin, Greek, and Shakespeare were to the British, and this cultural difference is important for understanding the relations between scientific education and business leadership in the two countries. Descriptive geometry was called the "Latin" of the school.[9]

The prestige of the Ecole polytechnique was enormous, and became, to an extent, an end in itself. "Glory" is frequently evoked by it; in 1828 Dupin complained that a decline in the quality of professors had dried up "this source of glory."[10] The 1840 motto of the alumni Association philotechnique was "For the fatherland, for science, for glory";[11] the inscription was emblazoned over the door of the school, for the purpose, according to Detoeuf, of communicating to the students an exact account of the practical role they would play[12] Contemporaneously, the subtitle of Callot's history of the institution reads "*Ses légendes, ses traditions, sa gloire.*"

High prestige and limited entry are of course intimately associated and together produce rents for those who squeeze through the portal. These rents attract more competitors for the prize, and the competition becomes limited to those who are bright, ambitious, and at least moderately well-to-do. Roughly two-thirds of the entrants into the Ecole polytechnique in the years between Waterloo and the revolution of 1848 came from the easy classes: 29.4 percent were children of landowners; 16.2 percent, of functionaries, superior officers, and generals; 12.1 percent, of members of the liberal professions; and 10.3 percent, of merchants and industrialists, for a total of 68 percent, or 75 percent of those whose fathers' professions were known. Another 18.2 percent (20 percent of those known) were the children of lesser civil servants and juniors officers.[13] Geographically, Paris and the regions with a military tradition and with industry—the East and the North—dominated. The representation of the larger industrial cities, like Lyons, Marseilles, and Bordeaux, was not striking; rather, a second tier —Montpellier, Grenoble, Vienne, Dijon, Strasbourg, Nancy, Lille, Rouen, Versailles, and Rennes—stood out, where industry was combined with an administrative and intellectual tradition favorable to the development of an ambitious petty bourgeoisie.[14]

Few graduates went into industry in the period before 1850. Civil engineering was neglected for military engineering, and within civil engineering, public dominated private works.[15]

The applied schools, Ecole des ponts et chaussées and Ecole des mines, go back to the eighteenth century, before the Revolution, although they were reorganized during the period of educational reform. After two years at the Ecole polytechnique, a man—and more recently, also a woman—would go on to three years at Ponts et chaussées or two years at Mines at Paris. The latter prepared students for coal and iron mining, and for steel and railroad work as well. Ponts et chaussées was directed to means of communication and also to public works generally, including, in addition to the study of bridges, roads, railroads, ports, and interior navigation, instruction on (1) large public works in irrigation, draining, regulation of water and factories, distribution of water; and (2) mechanics, civil architecture, mineralogy, geology, agriculture, political economy, and administrative law. There were only twenty to thirty students a year, plus some foreigners and so-called *externes*, who entered the school (but not the Corps) otherwise than from the ranks of the Ecole polytechnique.[16]

The Corps des ponts et chaussées was in many respects the forerunner of the post–World War II Commissariat au plan. In 1792, under the convention, the corps was asked by Minister Roland to prepare an economic plan to restore economic order by providing for public works, including plantations, mines and quarries, forges and factories.[17] The famous *Etoile* design for the railroads, which tied the country to a center at Paris, came from Le Grand—the Louis Armand or Pierre Massé (both Polytechnicians, by the way) of his day—at Ponts et chaussées in 1830. The Corps was a strong force for standardization and centralization, objecting with vigor to the use of English standards in the building of the railroad from Saint-Etienne to Lyons, with its wide curves, double tracking, and tunnel under the watershed between the Loire and the Rhône.[18]

Such was the prestige of the graduates of the Ecole des ponts et chaussées that they took precedence at state functions over colonels in the army.[19]

The Ecole des mines at Paris was designed for government service, although a small stream of its graduates went into private employment, and others, like Michel Chevalier, the Saint-Simonian economist, had public careers in journalism and government. The school at Saint-Etienne for private engineers was less selective, easier to enter, and less prestigious; the one at Alais was for foremen.

There was a welter of smaller *grandes écoles* for a variety of military, naval, and specialized purposes; we will encounter them in tables 1-3 (tables are at the end of the chapter) but need not spend time on them here. Traditionally, the French, when confronted with a problem, start a school to teach its solution. At the level of skilled instruction this results in schools of commerce, watchmaking, lacemaking, silk weaving, locksmithy; schools for the blind, the deaf and so on. It applies also to the levels of higher instruction in such fields as hydrography, electricity, geography, naval engineering, and many more. But between the grandes écoles, grouped around the pivotal Ecole polytechnique, and the primary and secondary schools of the working population, the French have developed a variety of institutions: the Conservatoire des arts et métiers, the Ecole centrale des arts et manufactures, and the Ecole des arts et métiers. The last two, in fact, now qualify as grandes écoles, Centrale since late in the nineteenth century, Arts et métiers more recently.

The Conservatoire was started during the Revolution and was provided with a museum of industrial models and an excellent library. During the Consulate, courses were undertaken, largely at a popular level. By 1810 there were 300 students regularly enrolled.[20] In 1873, fourteen professors gave 559 lessons to 135,000 individuals.[21] If each student attended only one course of lessons, and each professor gave but one, the total number of students engaged would have been close to a thousand. Early in the century, Chaptal organized a course in weaving. The two most illustrious graduates of the Conservatoire were Joseph-Eugène Schneider, later of the Schneider-Creusot steel company, and Joseph-Marie Jacquart, who invented a loom for weaving complex designs in silk, based on Vaucanson's forgotten model, which had almost solved the problem, in the museum of the Conservatoire.[22] The Conservatoire was especially distinguished for its work in chemistry under Gay-Lussac, whose laboratory was a showpiece to which

German students like Humboldt, Liebig, and Kekulé came. In the heyday of French chemistry, before 1850, it was France and not Germany that had an empirical laboratory approach, but only at the Conservatoire.[23] In 1853 the first teaching laboratory in engineering in the world was established in the museum of the Conservatoire.[24]

Centrale was started privately in 1829 by a group of industrialists discontented with the numbers and qualities of engineers made available to them. D'Ocagne, writing in 1873, stated that "there the great industrialists, heads of great factories, are to be trained, whereas the Ecole polytechnique will retain the task of supplying all state services with competent persons."[25] In the 1850s, Centrale was given to the Ministry of Commerce. Instruction took three years, a year longer than at the Ecole polytechnique, but there were no applied schools to attend afterward, unless one were admitted as an externe, a seemingly rare occurrence. Like that of the Polytechnique, the first year was based on mathematics and descriptive geometry, but since the students were selected from a somewhat less qualified group of applicants, the level, while severe, was not as rigorous. From 1832 to 1870 Centrale produced about one hundred engineers a year, which led Prost to conclude that the needs were not very large.[26]

This is not the way it was seen by contemporaries, however. The perennial drive to push technical education for economic growth sought by Talleyrand in 1791 to overcome routine methods,[27] by Chevalier in 1838 to raise the quality of French goods, was extended in the Second Empire by the Saint-Simonian Louis Napoléon.[28] One spur was the competition felt in international exhibitions. The Universal Exposition in Paris in 1862 found the French section of the international jury urging more industrial education "to maintain the products of our industry at the level which belongs to them"—a somewhat delphic remark—and resulted in the formation of a special commission.[29] Five years later improvement had presumably been realized. More than 500 alumni of the Ecole impériale centrale des arts et manufactures, as Centrale was known in the Second Empire, figured as exhibitors in the Universal Exposition of 1867 in Paris, and 248 won awards, among them five grand prizes and sixty-five gold medals, and 8 exhibitors were decorated with the Legion of Honor.[30] But there is no bench mark with which to compare this performance either in time or between countries, and in particular there is no indication of how much these prizes reflected French taste and workmanship, and how much, cost efficiency.

The Ecole des arts et métiers originated on the eve of the Revolution when the duc de la Rochefoucauld-Liancourt started a school for the children of his dragoons regiment. The school was transferred from

Compiègne to Châlons-sur-Marne, and its purpose enlarged to provide good workmen and chiefs of workshops. Other followed at Angers and later (1843) at Aix.[31] In 1874, these schools were each capable of handling three hundred students but had somewhat fewer.[32] Courses lasted three years and covered such subjects as foundry and locksmithy, with, of course, a strong component of descriptive geometry. Prost notes that the old alumni of Châlons and Angers got more mathematics and science than practical education and that they were the only people able to piece out the ranks of engineers when the grandes écoles, including Centrale, proved incapable of providing the necessary numbers.[33] Monge, Berthollet, and Laplace were interested in these schools, just as the duc de la Rochefoucauld-Liancourt had played an early role in the reorganization of the Conservatoire. Outside the realm dominated by the classic tradition of religion, philosophy, medicine, and law, which were taught in the universities, scientists and educational reformers made common cause.

The universities, of course, taught science. However, they did little research. Until 1830 French science was the most distinguished in the world, as a result, says Ben-David, of momentum gained in the eighteenth-century. Leading fields were mathematics, chemistry, and mechanical engineering. Facilities were limited, and those scientists in the less prestigious posts or without a number of sinecures (the famous *cumul*) had to divert considerable attention from science to earning a living. Primarily they were teachers rather than researchers, and they taught deductively rather than experimentally. Instruction at such a place as the Collège de France was superb. But as the freedom to reform science was gained, the will to reform it declined. About 1830 French science began to rigidify. The establishment of the Ecole pratique des hautes études in 1868 served to support research, but in the absence of sufficient money, the school had difficulty offsetting the trend.[34] Pasteur's institute, created in response to his interest in practical matters like pebrine, phylloxera, and fermentation, was an exception. The prestige of the universities in science remained high despite authoritarian and doctrinaire organization. When a choice had to be made by a student who had been admitted to both the Ecole polytechnique and the Ecole normale supérieure, the latter leading to the *agrégation* and a professorial post, it was not automatic that he would choose the Ecole polytechnique.[35]

In modern times, a well-worn route to business distinction has been via the Ecole libre des sciences politiques (since World War II the Institut [or Fondation] national des sciences politiques), the Ecole normale d'administration, the Inspection des finances. Sciences Po was created after the Franco-Prussian diaster of 1870–71, to form new men, and to overcome the failure in foresight that led to debacle. Its leading spirit was Emile Boutmy, assisted by such stellar social scientists as Léon Say, Anatole Leroy-Beaulieu, and Daniel Halévy. Sciences Po dominated the competition for the *grand corps* of the state—its graduates from 1900 to 1937 included 116 out of 120 councillors of state; 209 out of 218 inspecteurs de finance; 249 out of 284 members of the diplomatic corps; and 83 out of 94 counsellors of the corps of accounts.[36] Especially after World War II, the Inspection des finances began to rival the Ecole polytechnique in providing heads of large business enterprises.[37] Bouch quotes Francois Pietri that "the Inspection des finances is to Finance what the General Staff is to War. It is at the same time an academy, a tradition, a force."[38]

Commercial schools have existed since 1825, when two silk merchants in Paris founded the Ecole spéciale de commerce et d'industrie to provide enough scientific training to enable students to direct the business end of industrial operations.[39] The initial staff included the economist Adolphe Blanqui, student of Jean-Baptiste Say, who took over as director in 1830. The Paris Chamber of Commerce bought the school in 1868 when it ran into financial difficulties. In the early period the course took three years, and the number of students was about 170.[40]

Schools of commerce spread under the Third Republic after 1870, and especially the Ecoles des hautes études commerciales (H.E.C.). The one in Paris was founded by the Paris Chamber of Commerce in 1881. Since 1955 all French universities have initiated business curricula. At the University of Paris, 50 percent of the students had law degrees and 17 percent engineering degrees.[41] A recent school patterned after the Harvard Graduate School of Business Administration, using the case method, has been started at Fontainebleau.

The Hautes études commerciales are "certainly less prestigious and less difficult than Polytechnique, Normale or ENA (Ecole normale d'administration)."[42] Wylie et al go on to explain that if he cannot get into one of the abovementioned institutions, the bourgeois student is content with the business world (which explains average French mentality with respect to commerce).[43] Nonetheless, the ranks of the graduates of the H.E.C. include some illustrious names, especially in banking: Rodolphe and Philippe Hottinguer in the classes of 1922 and 1926; André and Philippe Mallet, 1920 and 1922; and André, Jacques, and Jean-Louis Neufflize, 1895, 1902, and 1940.[44] The pattern is too uniform and consistent for H.E.C. to have represented fourth choices.

Some numbers may help put this catalogue of institutions into perspective, across all French higher education, over time—but only from 1913 to the present—and in national cross section for 1913. Table 1.4 shows the rise of total numbers of students enrolled in French higher education; the gain of scientific and technical education at the expense of law and social science, largely law; and the surprising result that, despite a tradition of technical education, France lagged behind Europe in 1913 in the proportion of its student body devoted to it.

This cataloguing of institutions of scientific and technical education may be brought to a close by reviewing the various criticisms leveled against these institutions, especially against the grandes écoles.

1. *Admission standards are so high that entrance is limited to those who can afford highly specialized tutoring.* The social and regional biases in admission to the Ecole polytechnique have already been touched upon. If a student failed the oral examination, the written examination for the Ecole polytechnique qualified him as admissible to Centrale, as in the case of Gustav Eiffel.

2. *Instruction is too theoretical, mathematical, and rigid.* As early as 1823, the British referred to the "unhappy scepticism" in France, a condition that has been justly ascribed to the study of mathematics.[45] A comparison of German and French engineers in iron mining emphasizes that while both are well-grounded in theoretical studies and unready for practical work on graduation from their advanced training, this is much truer of the French.[46] French chemists have a mania for theory.[47] Novels and aphorisms combine to deride the dangers of dealing with engineers who understand theory but have not experienced practice. Henri Fayol, a graduate of the Ecole des mines at Saint-Etienne and a successful manager of the Société de Commentry-Fourchambault before becoming an efficiency engineer and prophet of something close to Taylorism, attacked the curricula in 1900:

> Mathematics was the subject most in need of reform. Curricula demanded an intensive study of higher mathematics. Yet in point of fact, when it came to the world of practice, almost none was used. This was Fayol's own experience. When he inquired of others, he found the same thing. Engineers at work used no higher mathematics. As managers there was even less likelihood of their so doing. The young qualified engineer, instead of being fit and alert on entering industry, was physically and mentally worn out, barely capable of undertaking the simplest tasks. If those quite useless highly theoretical studies were eliminated, the man could start an employment sooner, and he would be better prepared for what lay ahead of him.[48]

3. *The system is too centralized and authoritarian.* It is hardly necessary to support the criticism that French institutions are overcentralized—a theme that has been well developed since Louis XIV and earlier. One insight is afforded, however, by Dupin's criticism in 1828

that the timetable of the Ecole polytechnique provided detailed schedules of the amount of time to be spent on each subject during the day,
down to minutes. Dupin insisted that students were not identical and
did not all take the same time to understand given material, and he
asked that some students be allowed double or even triple allotments
for some studies.[49]

Authority and centralization meant domination of branches of
science by established viewpoints, which did not welcome new ideas
from abroad in many cases and did not indulge wide-ranging curiosity
in underlings.[50]

4. *The schools themselves are cliquish and elitist, and turn out a
product that is arrogant.* Tables 1–3 and 5 bear to some degree on the
cliquishness of various schools, although differences in the type of
education required for different industries play a role that is not
allowed for. Qualitative evidence is furnished in statements of observers. Certain posts are reserved for certain schools.[51] Alumni place
on-coming graduates.[52] Companies are known by the grandes écoles
with which they deal: the leading Peugeot heir is always entered for
Centrale and IBM in France hires mainly there. Frenchmen were
sensitive to the fact when two economists of the Ecole de droit on the
Commission of the Common Market, Marjolin and Barre, were recently replaced by two from the Ecole polytechnique, Deniau and
Ortoli. According to gossip, de Gaulle, a product of the Ecole spéciale
militaire at Saint-Cyr, detested graduates of Polytechnique and would
not have them in his cabinet, although the statement becomes suspect
in the light of the favor found by Giscard d'Estaing and Bourgès-
Maunnory, both Polytechnicians and ministers in de Gaulle's cabinet,
and Jacques Rueff, another alumnus of Ecole polytechnique, on whom
de Gaulle relied for monetary advice.

Elitism is perhaps carried no further in France than in other
countries; insiders are conscious of who earns a triple first at Oxford or
Cambridge, of who is graduated first at Harvard Law School. The
French mention these distinctions more frequently. They are impressed
that President Albert Lebrun of the Third Republic entered Polytechnique in the 230th rank and was graduated first. Michel Chevalier is
not referred to without repetition of the fact that he was first at Ecole
des mines. It may be a matter of the relative sophistication of the two
novelists, or of their interest in the characters, that the hero of *Le
maître de forges* was first at Polytechnique,[53] whereas the engineer in
Porcelain de Limoges, who dies a third of the way through the book,
was only second at Centrale, "sure of his gifts and of the power of
science."[54] Detoeuf mocks the practice—at the same time that his

autobiographical account of his fictional hero mentions that he entered Polytechnique at an average rank and left at one: "It is sufficient to enter Polytechnique. As for the rank of leaving, it is useless to be uneasy, because, whatever it is, family, friends, acquaintances, will arrange at the end of several years, that you emerged first."[55]

French literature is replete with references to the arrogance of Polytechnicians, "those parvenus of instruction." Two examples will suffice. With his strong thesis and feelings, Beau de Loménie is perhaps not the most impartial observer, but he characterizes one man in the following manner: "But Loucheur, armed with all the prestige that his title as Polytechnician and the considerable profits acquired from war orders gave him in the eyes of men of affairs, furnished with the imperturbable assurance that was one of his most characteristic traits, gave two peremptory responses. . . ."[56] Richard Kuisel speaks more judiciously of Mercier, a colleague of Loucheur and one who ultimately moved into the semi-Fascist Redressement Français: "Conscious of the supposed intellectual and moral superiority of the graduates of Ecole polytechnique, he took great pride in belonging to a ruling caste which has a special obligation for social leadership."[57] It is deemed noteworthy that the self-made textile manufacturer, protectionist, and later minister of finance, Pouyer-Quartier, in addition to distinguishing himself by an imperviousness to beer and alcohol superior to that of Bismarck, with whom he negotiated over the Franco-Prussian indemnity of 1871, should, as an economic parvenu, have been sure of himself.[58]

5. *Both the system and its output concentrate too heavily on the top ranks of instruction, administration, and industry and neglect to provide in sufficient quantities for instructors, laboratory assistants, middle cadres, foremen, and skilled workers.* This "admirable corps of engineers which the world envies"[59] was taught in schools and universities that lacked middle-rank instructors, laboratory assistants, etc., and emerged into an economic world with inadequate numbers of middle-managers and foremen. On the first score, the difficulty derived from the theoretical aspect of the curriculum with its denigration of experiment and exercises. On the second, successive attempts were made to fill the gap with the Arts et métiers, specialized trade schools, and the like, but the scale of the effort was never sufficient. As in underdeveloped countries today, France in the nineteenth century had too high a proportion of highly trained theorists relative to lower ranks who would carry out their directions in production.

The position should not be distorted. In addition to the weaknesses, there were the great strengths of brilliance, superb if somewhat biased training, and dedication to the goals of economic growth spread by the Saint-Simonians. Let us now turn to see how this scientific and technical education relates to industrial enterprise.

III

In the view of some radical economists today, the function of the boss in industrial production is to exploit the workers and distort income distribution against wages and in favor of profit and rent. We take a more conventional view, and consider the functions of the entrepreneur as consisting of (1) providing inputs, (2) adopting a technology, (3) administering the production and distribution processes, and (4) selling outputs. Among the inputs are clearly capital, and in a number of instances, such as the early *maîtres de forge*, wooded land to furnish charcoal. (In England, ownership of land included mineral rights, but in France such rights belonged to the state, which accounts for the French government's preoccupation with mining, embodied in the Corps des mines.) Some mercantile skill was required in buying raw materials, especially in such industries as textiles. The marketing function was entirely mercantile. Administration called for skill in human relations, including the exercise of authority, and could possibly be broadened to include the speculative flair. None of these bears much relation to scientific and technical education.

In technology, the analysis will follow the familiar division of Schumpeter and deal with invention, innovation, and imitation.[60] Scientific and technical education can contribute to all three, but it is not their sole source.

Entrepreneurs emerge from backgrounds that rely on these functions in different proportions. Which function should be stressed will depend on the industry in question and its stage of development. Attempts have been made to characterize entrepreneurs in different schemas. "Trader, financier, speculator, and industrialist" comes close to the foregoing functional categories.[61] A different taxonomy, "business-oriented, industry-oriented, and job-oriented," fits less well,[62] although business orientation can be associated with the mercantile function, and industrial orientation can be associated to some degree with technology. Cole's division into empirical, rational, and cognitive deals with degrees of specialization as a function of historical task-differentiation.[63] The empirical businessman could run a mercantile house, bank, and textile mill simultaneously. His skills were mercantile, he possessed capital, and he was a good administrator. The rational businessman specialized in all phases of a single industry. The cognitive businessman was a job specialist in finance, marketing, or production (again the three functions, but here only one of them is emphasized) who could shift industries without changing the nature of his work.

There is a strong temptation to build a "staple theory of entrepreneurship" that would associate given industries with particular characteristics of entrepreneurship, much as Harold Innis, the Canadian economic historian, related separate commodities to different types of economic stimulation in the growth process.[64] Broadly speaking, the textile and banking industries are entered by entrepreneurs from trade; the construction and metallurgical industries, from artisanal occupations; and industries of high technology, from technical training or complex trades like clockmaking or locksmithy, or from the shop of the apothecary. The merchant may be needed more for the provision of capital than for his knowledge of the market—as in the textile industry, in which few handworkers rise.[65] There may be national differences. Early English entrepreneurs are said to have been technically oriented, whereas in Germany the merchant was at least as important as the technician.[66] Entry into the iron industry was initially often based on ownership of woodlands needed for charcoal. No generalization stands up for long. The Krupps were a merchant family. Silesian nobility went into iron and steel based on ownership of forests, but Rhenish nobility did not.[67] Sons of professional men, especially of clergymen, are frequently successful entrepreneurs. This seems to be based less on the relation between Protestantism and business—although this relationship was not unknown—than on the tension between limited means and cultural aspirations, which becomes translated into material ambition.[68]

In France, the "kings of iron," Schneider, Wendel, and Talabot, came from petty trade via bank employment (and the Conservatoire des arts et métiers), from an established aristocratic family with land and wealth, and from the Ecole polytechnique, respectively. In locomotives, Gouin was the son of a banker, and Cail an apprentice coppersmith, who teamed up with a chemist manufacturing sugar-refining machinery.

The pioneers of the automobile in France had various social (and economic) origins: small mechanic (Bouton), aristocrat (de Dion), student (Renault), and industrialist (Peugeot).[69] It might be added that Citroën was a Polytechnician, that Panhard and Levassor were classmates at Centrale, and that the families of Renault, Citroën, and Berliet were comfortable bourgeoisie, the Renaults in drapery (and manufacture of buttons), the Citroëns in diamonds, and the Berliets in furniture. Marius Berliet, who had been apprenticed in a silk mill, became interested in mechanical looms before moving on to trucks.[70] Most salient is that the genius of Renault lay in that he was "possessed of the demon of mechanics," while Citroën was "an astonishing commercial genius, with an extraordinary sense of publicity."[71] Georges Dufaud, who introduced the puddling of steel into France, was both a Polytechnician and an heir of a prerevolutionary family; but he had a strong commercial sense, being interested in the firm's reputation, its credit, the use of intelligence in discovering new outlets, and what pleases a client.[72]

Even in the technologically demanding chemical industry there is a contrast between Kuhlmann, who at twenty-one years of age taught chemistry at the University of Lille before starting the company that bears his name, and Motte, the textile manufacturer from neighboring Roubaix, who, if the account can be accepted, was called from the army in World War I by his fellow townsman, Loucheur, to run Le Chlore Liquide, which had been established to develop poison gas. Motte is reported to have said that he knew nothing about chemistry in general or chlorine in particular, so he teamed up with his brother-in-law, Edmond Gillet, of the Lyon firm that had started in silk, and moved into dyeing and then into chemicals. Between them, Motte and Gillet formed Produits Chimiques Gillet et Fils (Progil), which was later absorbed by Pechiney.[73]

Entrepreneurship thus stems from and is nurtured by wealth, mercantile skills, technological training, and administrative ability in patterns with shifting and somewhat confused emphasis; it is nonetheless likely that the staple theory of entrepreneurship is valid. The mix in entrepreneurial capacity from these sources will vary among firms at a given time in a given industry, between industries, and over time as production processes become more complex. With its strong emphasis on technical training, therefore, one should expect France to excel especially in those aspects of entrepreneurship that require such training: invention, innovation, and imitation.

Much invention comes from scientists and engineers. Musson is right in insisting that the literature on the industrial revolution exaggerates the amateur character of British inventors, calling them tinkerers and denigrating the contribution of the Scottish universities and the dissenting academies to their scientific education.[74] French science produced many inventions and discoveries: the graduates of Ecole polytechnique alone discovered radioactivity, initially produced artificial silk, smokeless gunpowder, reinforced concrete, the Houdry process for oil refining, the electric brake for trains, and designed the brilliant Caravelle. Hydroelectric power stems from a Centralian, Berguès. The remarkable Breguet family started with an inventive eighteenth century Swiss clockmaker. A son carried on the clock business in the first half of the nineteenth century; the grandson, another inventor, turned to electricity; and the great-grandson, Jacques, after failing at Ecole polytechnique and attending the Ecole supérieur d'electricité, in 1903 switched the family field once again when he became an inventor of aircraft.[75] From the scientists came the discovery of chlorine, the Leblanc soda process, and the many contributions of Pasteur to practical fields. There also were tinkerers, like Jacquart, of the Conservatoire—although he was trying to solve an artistic problem—and there were artists.

Cyril Smith's theory of technological invention emphasizes the role played by the decorative arts in discovering new processes, particularly in developing new materials and new methods of handling materials. The casting of statues uncovered new metallurgical techniques. High-temperature methods of treating materials come from ceramics. Glass-making, at which the French have excelled, has many decorative aspects, including household art objects and stained-glass windows, whose manufacture led to the development of the technique for molding lead into H-shapes to hold the glass, which technique in its turn made possible the extrusion of steel rails and I-beams.[76] Kuhlmann went to Paris to study dyeing in the laboratories of Vauquelin but was attracted to Lille to teach in a municipal course in "chemistry applied to the arts."[77]

Smith's insight has bearing on a vital economic issue: the extent to which inventions and innovations are a response to economic forces. Schmookler maintains that inventors do not make discoveries by chance but invent in response to the market; he offers powerful evidence from railroads, agriculture, petroleum refining and paper-making.[78] Further evidence could be cited from the eighteenth and nineteenth centuries that advances in instruments—especially for navigation, surveying, and optics, to limit the discussion to one field —were responsive to felt needs. The research that went on in the Royal Manufactory at Sèvres, however, in glazes, enamels and paints, can hardly be regarded as market induced.[79] Science used to create an object of beauty, science for science's sake, science and technology for *gloire*, science for curiosity's sake, science for military purposes—all serve aristocratic rather than bourgeois values. The market is not competitive. Within broad limits, money is no object.

Pitts has pointed to the essential ingredient of aristocratic values: prowess, the unreproducible act, whether at the work bench, on the field of battle, in the salon, or in the boudoir.[80] To the slogans that he cites—"Never count your change," "Never take cover," "His men adore him"—can be added, "Make it the way I want it and never mind the cost."[81]

These innovations are market induced in a sense, but the demand is inelastic with respect to price, and cost minimization is a weak argument in the function. Nor are the inventors especially interested in making money. This aristocratic attitude seems to have been characteristic of the comte de Chardonnet, the Polytechnician who invented artificial silk. Coming from the most traditional nobility of the Vendée, he saw his invention exploited by "two groups of fortune," the Carnot Société de Viscose and the Gillet group of Lyons.[82] Berthollet, who discovered the use of chlorine for bleaching textiles, had no interest as a scientist in the material possibilities his discovery offered.[83] Three generations later, Berthelot, who opened up the field of organic chemistry by synthesizing acetylene, was massively indifferent to atomic theory and atomic notation, which turned organic chemistry to practical use.[84]

Even when an inventor hopes to gain financially, it is by no means assured that he will. The Jacquard loom was taken up in Britain long before its use spread back to France. Philippe de Girard's "great invention for spinning flax" was not accepted in France until it was appreciated by the British.[85] Verguin, who in 1859 discovered synthetic fuchsine for dyeing cloth red, saw his team dispersed and driven to Switzerland by the impatience of Henri Germain, president of the Crédit Lyonnais, who was eager to make profits quickly.[86] *Lost Illusions*, by Balzac, is a cautionary tale about one David Séchard, who invented a process for making paper out of ubiquitous vegetable fiber instead of linen rags, only to have his invention exploited by the evil brothers Cointet.[87] To carry invention through to innovation requires commercial and financial sophistication, and drive. The great innovation of interchangeable parts developed in New England by Eli Whitney and the gunmakers was anticipated in theory in the first half of the nineteenth century by Réaumur and actually put into practice on a limited scale in an arsenal in Versailles before the Revolution. Persistent application of ingenuity was lacking, however, and the attempt lapsed. There is something in the ironic remark: the French invent; the British do.

Imitation calls for an attribute contrary to aristocratic values: humility. There were, as we shall see, many Frenchmen who were prepared to learn by visiting Britain, or to be taught by imported British workers. Some were aristocrats; many were alumni of the grandes écoles. Intellectual capacity and readiness to learn from equals characterize science; intellectual capacity and acquisitiveness are often found in graduates of the grandes écoles who go into industry, but readiness to learn from peers is usually missing.

Most graduates of the grandes écoles, however, go into government service or into engineering, i.e., public works, which, in staple-theory terminology, differs fundamentally from business. Instead of selling to the masses, one deals with a government or, at most, with bankers. Rondo Cameron's *France and the Economic Development of Europe* is misleading to the extent that it implies that it was French bankers and businessmen who went abroad to spread the techniques of the Crédit Mobilier. The men who accompanied the bankers were engineers —builders of railroads, bridges, canals, tunnels, ports, stations—not industrialists. De Lesseps was not an engineer but a diplomat, although the Suez project got its start from the Polytechnicians under Enfantin. The French company was directed by Paulin Talabot, the leading engineer was Voisin-Bey—so named because of a high title conveyed on him by the viceroy of Egypt[88]—and many of De Lessep's other colleagues were also Polytechnique alumni.[89] A number of speculators—a propensity for speculation is another aristocratic and anti-bourgeois attribute—were among the French who pioneered for profit establishing businesses in Russia.[90] The products of the Ecole des mines performed their engineering feats in Algiers, Spain, Russia and elsewhere outside the Hexagon. The contribution was partly finance and partly technology. They did not serve as entrepreneurs in the full sense involving finance, marketing, technology, and administration. The French genius lay in engineering, as the career of another famous bridge builder, Alexandre Eiffel, from Centrale, testifies. As noted above, Eiffel failed the oral examination to gain admittance to Ecole polytechnique. (It is ironic that perhaps the greatest of the Ecole polytechnique graduates, Henri Poincaré, the mathematician, failed to get into Normale on the ground that his showing in the oral examination suggested that he would not make a good teacher.)

I have been unable to find traces of any but two of the foreign students of the grandes écoles. One, Charles King, had the improbable educational experience of attending first Harrow in England, next Harvard College, and then the Ecole polytechnique. He was for some time a partner of Archibald Gracie, a merchant whose country house now serves as the mayor's residence in New York, and later became president of Columbia University.[91]

The more interesting illustration is furnished by Alfredo Cottau, an Italian of an Alsatian family, who was able to enter the French naval school at Toulon by virtue of having a great uncle in the French navy, went on to the Ecole préparatoire de la Marine in Paris for two years beginning in 1855, and, after a cruise, returned to his native Naples. There he worked for a time with the English engineering firm of Guppy and Company and studied bridge and road design locally before returning to Paris to study engineering. The mention of bridges and roads suggests that Cottau may have been an externe at Ponts et chaussées, but this is only an inference. After finishing his studies he worked with Ernest Gouin and Company, specializing in the building of bridges and metal roofs. He then returned to Italy, where he won various competitions, worked briefly for the government, and finally served as an engineer for a railroad. Cottau took an active part in public questions, writing in *Il Politechnico* in favor of narrow-gauge railroads to save on capital costs and coal consumption, and in building viaducts, bridges, and roofs of stations. Alsatian and Italian genes combined with French training, British experience, and Italian conditions to produce an effective, public-spirited engineer.[92]

Surprisingly, it seems that few graduates of military schools went into industry. One would have thought that the administrative capacities developed in the military—and the French army has been cited as a counterexample to the family-firm in the argument that Frenchmen prefer organizations to be small—would make a contribution to entrepreneurship. In the United States, retired army officers are a source of top- and middle-level management. And Werner Siemens founded his electrical company with the artisan Halske in Berlin after fifteen years in the Prussian army as an engineer and in artillery school, "the happiest of his life." Having won contracts to provide telegraph installations to the army, he hired another artillery officer to run the administrative side of the company, an early step in the bureaucratization of the large-scale German firms.[93] The centennial volume of Polytechnique mentions one Jacquemart, who resigned as an officer of artillery to go into the chemical industry.[94] The semifictional Barenton resigned from the artillery when he married a lady whose father owned a business. The resignation of Gouin immediately upon graduation from Ecole polytechnique has been mentioned but is different, as he had not served in the military forces. Table 1 notes only fifty-six outstanding business leaders in France fifteen years ago—less than 2 percent of the sample—who received higher diplomas in military schools; table 5, only one. Military service in France—and, of course, for the Junker officers in Germany—catered to aristocratic rather than bourgeois or industrial values.

Technical instruction in commerce played little part in the formation of entrepreneurs in France as far as the record shows, apart from the banking families referred to. Business leaders do not come from schools of commerce, which provide instead the middle ranks. British and German mercantile education was usually sought through a year or years abroad in the counting house of a relative or business correspondent, along the lines set out in *Buddenbrooks*. The French were less ready to follow this practice. Graduates of the technical schools worked abroad for stated periods, as we have indicated, which perhaps accounts for the surprising statement in a history of the Ecole polytechnique that Polytechnicians emigrate readily—a statement supported by the odd example of a graduate who taught at the Harvard Business School.[95]

Nor is banking a profession acquired through learning, except perhaps in recent years. Over most of the period under consideration, access to it came through inherited wealth or apprenticeship. Beau de Loménie's major thesis is that virtually all positions of prominence in French politics, industry, and finance are occupied by the descendants of 200 families that established themselves in positions of power in 1789 or shortly thereafter and never let go. Evidently wide of the mark in industries such as automobiles, electric equipment, and much of chemistry, this observation applies better to iron and steel—with exceptions for Schneider, Benoist d'Azy, and Talabot—and best of all to banking. There were new entrants, but apart from the Rothschilds, these did not last long. The Saint-Simonian Péreires, educated at Centrale,[96] the speculators Mirès and Bontoux, engineers from Polytechnique and Ponts et chaussées, had moments of success, but ended up defeated. Successful bankers came from commerce, industry, engineering, or even *Lettres*,[97] but as a rule they descended from an old banking family, preferably Protestant and from Geneva.

In contemporary France, scientific and technical education does train for business, as tables 1-3 illustrate. Engineering dominates, and within engineering the Ecole polytechnique leads in public enterprise, Centrale in private. It will be recalled from Callot's data (see n. 15) that while a large number of the graduates of the Ecole polytechnique is in industry, a large majority, divided between civil functionaries including nationalized industry and the armed forces, is not. It is likely that the proportions of Polytechnicians entering government and private industry, as opposed to the army, have been rising from the first half of the nineteenth century to the middle of the twentieth, but figures to fix the point are lacking. The tables show only the position in the middle 1950s for industry—including nationalized industry —but not for government. The educational information is extracted from a wider study, which includes social and regional origins, size of family, and the like.

Table 1 is derived from biographical information in directories, mainly *Who's Who in France*, supplemented by surveys by *Entreprise*, *Bottin Mondain*, and *L'Annuaire Desfosses*. Information on education is 86.5 percent complete, so that 700 of the 800 recorded to be without diplomas can probably be said to have had no higher education. More than a quarter of those with diplomas had more than one, including 175 Polytechnicians with other scientific diplomas, 52 with nonscientific diplomas, 123 outside of the Ecole polytechnique with more than one scientific diploma, etc.[98] What is particularly striking, apart from the dominance of engineering, is the showing of Sciences Po, equal to the Ecole de droit and more than double Letters, Science, and the military schools.

Tables 2 and 3 furnish details of the educational training of top-level management in selected private and nationalized industries, respectively. "Not indicated" is not equivalent to those without higher degrees, which is not given. The figures again reflect the dominance of engineering, the preference of certain industries for particular mixes of training and institutions, whether because of the staple theory alluded to earlier or the alumni connections between firms and schools. The preference of nationalized industries for graduates of the Ecole polytechnique—or vice versa—is clearly shown, as is the much greater relative importance of Arts et métiers in private than in public industry. The rise of specialized engineering schools represents the culmination of a trend observed earlier. The schools of commerce are relatively unimportant in private industry and of no consequence in public.

Table 5, prepared by Fritz K. Ringer for a comparison of elites among leading industrial countries, is drawn from leading biographical dictionaries covering men born between 1810 and 1899. The business and technical elite form a small portion of the total—less than one-tenth. Thirty percent of them did not have university education, or their educational background is not known. Of those with university-level education, 75 percent went to either the Ecole polytechnique (39.6 percent) or other grandes écoles (36.1 percent). Another 11 percent were educated in science at the universities. For the so-called intellectual elite, the Ecole polytechnique was much less significant, whereas the other grandes écoles stand out, especially in arts and scholarship.

IV

An evaluation of the success of scientific and technical education in France in promoting French entrepreneurship is overdue, but one sociological point may be made first. In France, entrepreneurship typically had origins in banking, commerce, or artisanry and acquired scientific and technical capacities in later generations, whereas in Britain, firms were often started by men of scientific attainments whose sons moved away from science to letters, politics, and country living. The ranks of *maîtres de forge* who sent sons to Ecole polytechnique or the Ecole des mines include Wendel, Gargan, Janoyer, Reverschon, Thoyot, Dufaud, and others.[99] A Japy was usually at the Ecole polytechnique, a Peugeot heir at Centrale. The son of Panhard from Centrale moved up to the Ecole polytechnique. From Alsace, the Koechlins (textiles) and the Schlumbergers (textile machinery) went on to the Ecole polytechnique, although they did not always stay in the family line of endeavor; one Schlumberger moved into oil exploration equipment and another, later, into jewelry, and a Koechlin Polytechnician became a leading musician. The Ecole polytechnique produced doctors, musicians, painters, novelists, lawyers, men of holy orders, and diplomats as well as engineers,[100] probably representing those who had been launched by the *père de famille* on a technical and scientific career for which they were not suited.

The urge of the father to push his son into science and engineering in order to enable the former to improve his business is brought out in the long speech of M. Cardonnet, father of the hero Emile in George Sand's socialist novel, *Le péché de M. Antoine*. Emile had been sent to study science because his father arrived only by instinct at solutions to problems in geometry and mechanics useful in business. When Emile moved within the exact sciences to useless astronomy, his father forced him to switch to law. M. Cardonnet had sought to find a means to make his son useful. He had a fortune but was ignorant of law and at the mercy of perfidious counsel. Emile was to learn law, not to be a lawyer.[101]

In sharp contrast to this, of course, is the situation that obtained in Britain, where the sons of the founder tended to go to Oxford or Cambridge and study greats or modern greats for careers in politics, including the civil service, or the professions—if they did not retire to the country or the Riviera. The classic example is perhaps that of John Marshall of Leeds, in 1848 the leading flax spinner in the world, whose two sons coped feebly with his firm, and whose grandsons ruined it.[102] In Britain, professionalism in family firms diminished; in France it increased. A student of the Philosophical and Literary Society of Manchester, founded in 1761, observes that science in Britain was an avenue to social advancement for outsiders, and that in most cases it took the family away from science.[103] In France, as was noted earlier, the elite embraced science for those who had survived the Collèges royaux as being harmonious with elitism. "If I had intended my son for any branch of manufacture, I would not dream of sending him to the University," said T. H. Huxley to the Samuelson Select Committee of 1867.[104]

A hint of a still different pattern comes from Germany, where a French scholar notes that it was not the successful handworker who made it big but his son, who made the transition from powerful merchant to big entrepreneur, formed an *Aktiengesellschaft* ("joint-stock company"), and hired a technical man who remained in the second rank.[105] The scholar adds that there was no tension in the relations between the second-generation merchant-become-business-tycoon and his technical man. Desire for one's children to advance in the world is universal: in France it takes the form of providing them with a professional, preferably a scientific, education, which, at the same time, may enable the family concern to continue.

The weakness of the system lies in its elitism, in the arrogance of its graduates and their incapacity for personal relationships. The historical literature alludes to this somewhat. "But above all there remains at the head of the enterprise a man whose real qualities count for much, the director general in whom it is necessary to have technical competence, commercial sense, *aptitude for human contacts*" [italics added].[106] "Entrepreneurs did not go without risks in entrusting themselves to the *chef d'ateliers* [with his techniques]. This subjection accounts for the setback to Decazeville, while perfect technical knowledge, *accompanied by a policy of presence in the factory* [italics added], explains largely the successes of Wendel and Schneider."[107]

More direct evidence is available for the modern period. A non-American who changed his career from psychiatry to industrial consultation and spent a year in France with an American consulting company after having worked for four years in the United States with a similar company, has commented privately and anonymously on the "god-like" quality of the engineers produced by the grandes écoles. Survivors of a brutal competition that eliminates all aspirants with any weakness, and on the fast track to fame and power, they tend to be proud, obsessed with excellence, insensitive, often unable to relate effectively to others, and threatened by any questioning of their authority.[108] In a T-group experiment lasting two weeks and involving a large number of graduates of the Ecole polytechnique, this observer found that the behavior of the Messieurs "X" differed from that of similar German and English groups. The Frenchmen seemed at first to resent the authority of the psychologist group director, then to panic and be unable to function as a group when his leadership was withdrawn. The observer had the impression that the weakness of the French elite as a whole, not merely of the Polytechnicians, was that they had been taught to present their ideas as brilliant and final, rather than as initial statements in what was meant to be a give-and-take interaction in an open and egalitarian atmosphere. He thought that younger French business leaders who had had early outside contact with the Harvard, Chicago, or M.I.T. business schools had learned to open up and relax, and they were successful. The fundamental quality and talent are there, and the drive to achieve is strong, but the Frenchman needs exposure to other cultures, and to overcome his weakness in handling personal relations.

This insight led me to go back and contemplate those leaders of industry, many of the Messieurs "X," known to have traveled abroad. In steel, the list includes Benoist d'Azy, an engineer; Bessy (Loire); Boiguës; Cabrol ("X"); Dubost; Dufaud ("X"); Emile Martin ("X"), who devised the Martin process; Rambourg, who worked as a laborer in England and reported back on rolling and puddling; Schneider and Wendel ("X"),[109] On his trip to England in 1817, Dufaud had been impressed by cheapness even at the expense of quality, and later, at Fourchambault, he and Boiguës broke with technical traditions and habits of thought to emphasize large-scale production and cheapness rather than top quality in a factory that was tightly organized and effectively administered.[110] In metallurgy, Gouin, son of the banker and graduate of the Ecole polytechnique at the head of his class, resigned from the army to attend Ponts et chausées as an externe. He then went to England to complete his technical studies, working for several months in the factory of a locomotive manufacturer before returning to Paris to order locomotives for the Paris-Orléans railroad. A traction engineer for the Paris–Saint-Germain railroad from 1839 to 1845, he opened his own locomotive and structural iron factory in 1846.[111] Fourteen years later his locomotive shop was directed by an Englishman named Lloyd, which suggests that Gouin had maintained his capacity to imitate technology.[112]

Even earlier, there was Marc Seguin, a Jew and a social outsider (Gouin was an insider) but a member of the Academy of Sciences, an inventor, and a promoter of a steamboat company on the Rhône and the Saint-Etienne–Lyons railroad. He or a brother had been to England and had studied the Stockton-Darlington railroad. He was keenly interested in the development of the locomotive, for which he invented the tubular boiler, which Stephenson promptly adopted for use in Britain.[113] Five Seguin brothers in all were associated in the railroad promotion with Eduard Biot, an engineer, son-in-law of Becquey, the director general at Ponts et chaussées.[114] Seguin was a loner in French science, self-educated with the help of his great-uncle Montgolfier, the balloonist. He scorned the scientific elite who were "inflamed by mathematics, and suspicious of those who did not possess his branch of science. . . . Only one language had the privilege of being heard and imposing its oracles: the language of analysis, of differential and integral calculus, of analytical and celestial mechanics."[115]

Michel Chevalier, the Saint-Simonian economist and graduate of Ecole des mines, wrote more about general matters than questions of technical interest. He had traveled in the United States and written *Lettres sur l'Amérique du Nord.*[116]

A more modern example is furnished by Auguste Detoeuf, the president of Thomson-Houston, a firm founded by General Electric. It is not entirely clear how much of the foreword to the fictitious account by M. O.-L. Barenton, confiseur, can be transliterated into autobiography, but the main lines are evidently parallel. Barenton went to the Ecole polytechnique and into the artillery as a sub-lieutenant. He married, resigned, entered his father-in-law's firm, which manufactured corset springs (an early stage in the industrial career of the Peugeots, too), then tried and abandoned the export business. When corsets in cities were ruined by sport, which crossed the Channel from Britain, sales were shifted to the country. The market among peasant women was lost with World War I, and on returning from the army, Barenton went to America for a year. There he discovered ice cream. He invested the indemnity received from the damage to the corset factory, now his through inheritance, in a small ice cream factory—contrary to the advice of his friends, who claimed there was no market for it—and never looked back.[117] It seems clear that ice cream is a trope for electrical equipment and appliances and that the small factory was a subsidiary of General Electric. While the *Propos de O.-L. Barenton, confiseur,* can be read as aphoristic wit, at a more fundamental level it represents a critique of French entrepreneurship and its technical education by one who had been strongly affected by foreign business methods.[118]

In the long run, and once the point about interpersonal relations has been assimilated, French scientific and technical education will doubtless prove to be efficacious. Excessively deductive, Cartesian, geometric, mathematical, theoretical by nineteenth century standards, the system is coming into its own in a world of scientific sophistication, a world equipped with computers employed in linear programming, decision and information theory, game theory, and Bayesian statistical methods for making business decisions. Numerous business schools in the United States are reducing the inductive case method at a time when it is being introduced in France. Provided that they can acquire a little humanity, the products of French technical schools will bring to business tremendous power both in the field of technology and in that of administration. Financial skill is ubiquitous and has always been abundant in France. French business, although it may lag in commercial flair, should rapidly catch up as sophistication in this area increases.

There are some puzzles: why, for example, was Machine Bull unable to make the breakthrough from punch card to electronic computation on its own? Others failed, as well, such as General Electric and R.C.A. There may be mistakes in the trade-off between technological sophistication and practicality, as American engineers claim is the case with S.E.C.A.M. (French color television). Important dangers lie in wait: trying too much too fast, forcing science for science's sake, for *gloire*, so as to win seats at international scientific conferences, or a bigger share

TABLE 1
Distribution of a Sample of French Business Leaders, 1953–56, by Higher Diploma*

Institution	Number of Leaders	% of Leaders with Higher Diplomas	% of Total Leaders in Sample
Ecole polytechnique	456	21.4	15.5
Other engineering schools	640	30.1	21.7
Higher professional schools	86	4.1	2.9
Military schools	56	2.6	1.9
Science faculties	81	3.8	2.7
Letters	81	3.8	2.7
Law	188	8.8	6.4
Political science	190	8.9	6.4
Various studies (preparing for the liberal professions: medicine, architecture, etc.)	23	1.2	0.8
Not indicated	76	3.6	2.6
Total with diplomas	2,126	100	72.1
Total sample	2,947		100

SOURCE: Nicole Delefortrie-Soubeyroux, *Les dirigeants de l'industrie française* (Paris: Colin, 1961), p. 58.
*In the case of those with two or more diplomas (670 in all), only one diploma has been entered.

of Nobel prizes, instead of harnessing effort to the tasks at hand.[119] Nonetheless, French scientific and technical education are coming into their own. The staple theory of entrepreneurship suggests that the technological component of GNP has grown with time. I have not seen the Hudson Institute study, which predicts that France will grow faster

TABLE 2
Educational Background of High-Level Management of Some Enterprises in the Private Sector

Institution	One Oil Company	Ten Metallurgical Companies	One Electro-metallurgical Company	Two Associated Metallurgical Companies
Ecole polytechnique		30	(12)	(16)
Ecole centrale		34	(7)	(20)
Ecole des arts et métiers		68	(1)	(56)
Ecole des mines		28	(4)	(21)
Ecole suporieure d'electricité				
Technical electrical institutes		9	(7)	
Specialized engineering schools	2	14	(3)	(10)
Other engineering schools	1	14	(1)	(12)
Science faculties	3	20	(10)	(10)
Letters				
Law	4	11	(2)	(6)
Political science	2	6	(2)	(3)
Commercial schools	3	11	(1)	(14)
Textile schools				
Military schools		2		(2)
Foreign universities	4			
Various studies (preparing for the liberal professions: medicine, architecture, etc.)		4		(4)
Not indicated		68		
Total	19	319	(50)	(170)

SOURCE: Delefortrie-Soubeyroux, *Les dirigeants de l'industrie française*, pp. 142, 199,

than all the countries in Europe and North America and faster than most of those in the rest of the world; but if it relies on French technical capacity—and if the French overcome their weakness in human relations—theirs is a forecast from which it would be difficult to dissent.

One Automobile Company— Paris Region	Three Electrical Companies	Three Food Companies	Twenty-five Textile Companies	One Enterprise Engaged in Public International Service Assisting Navigation	One Large Department Store	Total
4	4		3	6		47
4	13	4	6	2	5	68
28	19	4	2			121
3						31
	7					7
	12					21
4	8		1	1		30
8	12	7	5			47
2	2	3	2	1	1	34
				2		2
3	5	1	2	9	5	40
2	4			7	3	24
2	4	5	6	2	19	52
			14			14
1	1	4		2		10
				9		13
	1				4	9
5			6		2	81
66	95	28	47	41	39	617

205, 208, 211, 221, 229, 253, 259, 263.

TABLE 3
Educational Background of High-Level Management of Twelve Nationalized Enterprises

Institution	Régie Renault	Construction Aéronautique	Charbon de France and Three Coal Basins	Gaz de France and Electricité de France	Compagnie Nationale du Rhône	S.N.C.F.	Air France	Compagnie Générale Trans-atlantique	Total
Ecole polytechnique	3	5	23	87	4	111	2	3	239
Ecole centrale	8	2	2	97		29	2		140
Ecole des arts et métiers	71	7		34		1	5	2	120
Ecole des mines			71						71
Ecole supérieure d'electricité				36		3			39
Ecole des ponts et chaussées						1			1
Ecole supérieure d'aéronautique		4					14		18
Ecole de pilotes							2		2
Specialized engineering schools	6		6	98		2		4	116
Other engineering schools	15	10	4	22			2	4	57
Science faculties	8	3	3	3		2	1	1	20
Letters	6		9	9		3	2	1 }	50
Law	3	3	6	1		1	7	9	18
Political Science	3	1					4	3	30
Commercial schools	6	2	7			1	8	7	10
Military schools	3	1					5	1	3
Various studies (preparing for the liberal professions: medicine, architecture, etc.)		1		1				1	
Not indicated			1	15		5	1		22
Total	129	39	132	403	4	159	52	36	956

SOURCE: Delefortrie-Soubeyroux, Les dirigeants de l'industrie française, p. 123.

TABLE 4

Student Enrollment in Higher Education by Faculties or Subjects, in France, Selected Years, 1913 to 1958, Selected Other Countries, 1913

Countries	All Numbers	Medicine	Law, Social Sciences	Social Sciences	Arts	Science, Technical	Other
France							
1913	38,000	21.7%	44.1%		16.8%	17.5%	
1924	48,000	23.1	35.4		19.0	22.6	
1930	66,000	24.5	29.5		25.5	20.5	
1932	78,000	32.3	29.6		18.7	19.4	
1951	142,000	26.1	27.8		26.2	19.9	
1958	226,000	18.2	16.5		27.7	35.1	
Other Countries			Law	Social Sciences			
Belgium	8,000	17.1%	13.4%	12.0%	36.8%	31.0%	
Germany	65,000	26.3	14.5	-21.2%	13.9	24.1	
Netherlands	5,000	35.1	18.5		6.8	29.8	
United States	206,000	14.7	11.2	1.9	28.1	14.3	8.0
Great Britain (1925-26)	40,800	21.3			50.9	18.0	15.4%

SOURCE: Joseph Ben-David, *Fundamental Research and the Universities. Some Comments on International Differences* (Paris Organization of Economic Cooperation and Development, 1968), pp. 40–41.

TABLE 5
Profession and Education of French Elites, ca. 1830–1930
(percentages by row, except as noted*)

	Educational Level Attained			Whole Sample	
Profession	Nonuniversity	University	Degree	Abs. Nos.	% by Column
1. Academics	2.6	18.0	79.4	383	16.2
2. Clergy	13.8	72.4	13.8	160	6.8
3. Arts, scholars	50.6	39.8	9.6	394	16.7
4. Publicists	54.3	24.8	20.9	153	6.5
1–4. Intellectual elite	28.8	34.9	36.3	1090	46.1
5. High officials	13.7	25.0	61.3	124	5.2
6. Military	15.8	1.1	83.0	442	18.7
7. Landowners	71.4	(2)	(0)	7	0.3
8. Politicians	50.9	9.7	39.4	175	7.4
9. Lawyers	(0)	(2)	98.0	100	4.2
10. Medical and related	(1)	7.3	92.0	150	6.3
11. Entrepreneurs	65.9	11.4	22.7	44	1.9
12. Executive employees	(2)	40.0	40.0	10	0.4
13. Technical professionals	13.2	23.7	63.1	152	6.4
11–13. Business-technical elite	24.8	21.8	53.4	206	8.7
14–17. Nonelite	60.6	21.1	18.3	71	3.0
18. Unknown	(1)	(0)	(0)	1	(1)
1–18. Total sample	25.0	21.5	53.5	2366	100

SOURCE: Fritz K. Ringer, "Elites and Education in Western Europe," unpublished paper, 1973.
*Figures in parentheses are (small) absolute numbers. Columns under "Whole Sample"

NOTES

1. Donald N. McCloskey and Lars G. Sanberg, "From Damnation to Redemption: Judgements on the Late Victorian Entrepreneur," *Explorations in Economic History* 9, no. 1 (Fall 1971): 89–108.

2. Guy Palmade, *Capitalisme et capitalistes français au XIXe siècle* (Paris: Colin, 1961), p. 242.

3. Ibid, p. 241.

4. Joseph Ben-David, *The Scientist's Role in Society: A Comparative Study* (Englewood Cliffs, N.J.: Prentice-Hall, 1971), p. 90.

5. Artz calls the founding "in some ways the most significant advance in the whole history of higher technical education in Europe" (Frederick B. Artz, *The Development of Technical Education in France, 1500–1850* [Cambridge, Mass.: M.I.T. Press; London: Society for the History of Technology, 1966], p. 151). In describing French scientific and technical institutions and accomplishments, however, Artz is somewhat prone to the use of superlatives (see, for example, pp. 136, 147, 160, 166, 170, 208, 217, 230, 232, 237, 248, 266).

Type of University-Level Education							
None, Unknown	Religious	Military	Polytechnical	Normal	Other Grandes Ecoles	University Humanities	Science
7.8	10.2	(1)	4.5	26.9	17.8	19.5	20.7
15.6	91.9	(0)	(0)	(1)	(3)	5.2	(0)
54.1	2.2	(1)	(2)	(3)	65.2	26.0	3.3
58.2	(3)	(1)	(1)	10.9	12.5	59.4	9.4
32.8	22.8	(3)	2.6	14.5	26.2	22.0	11.6
31.5	(1)	(3)	11.8	(0)	17.6	64.7	(1)
15.8	(0)	70.2	29.8	(0)	(0)	(0)	(0)
71.4	(0)	(0)	(0)	(0)	(1)	(1)	(0)
53.7	(0)	6.2	7.4	4.9	6.2	69.1	6.2
(2)	(0)	(0)	(1)	(0)	(1)	98.0	(0)
2.7	(0)	(1)	(2)	(0)	5.5	(2)	91.1
68.2	(0)	(1)	(3)	(0)	57.1	(2)	(0)
(3)	(0)	(0)	(3)	(0)	(1)	(2)	(1)
19.1	(0)	(1)	41.5	5.7	35.0	4.9	12.2
30.1	(0)	(2)	39.6	4.9	36.1	6.9	11.1
67.6	26.1	(0)	(0)	(0)	17.4	39.1	17.4
(0)	(0)	(0)	(0)	(0)	(0)	(0)	(0)
28.8	10.3	16.3	12.2	6.9	16.5	23.2	14.5

disregard subjects' educations. All percentages (by row) but those under "None, Unknown" in the section on types of university-level education are with respect to those in given professions whose type of university-level education is known.

6. Jean Sutter, R. Izac, and N. Toan, "L'évolution de la taille des polytechniciens, 1801-1954," *Population* (1958): 373-406.

7. Artz, *Technical Education*, p. 242.

8. École polytechnique, *Livre de centenaire, 1794-1894*, 3 vols. (Paris: Gauthier-Villas et Fils, 1895), 1:517-19.

9. Artz, *Technical Education*, p. 235. The few special nonclassical *collèges royaux* in secondary education from which one often applied to the grandes écoles were called by the opposition "pas Latin" or occasionally "*classes des épiciers*" (ibid., p. 195). In Germany technical institutes were sometimes referred to as "plumbers' academies" (Fritz K. Ringer, *The Decline of the German Mandarins: The German Academic Community, 1890-1933* [Cambridge: Harvard University Press, 1969], p. 482 n).

10. Le Baron Charles Dupin, *Forces productives et commerciales*, 2 vols. (Brussels: Jobard Frères, 1828), 2:320.

11. Artz, *Technical Education*, p. 243.

12. Auguste Detocuf, *Propos de O.-L. Barenton, confiseur, ancien élève de l'Ecole polytechnique* (Paris: Editions du Tambourinaire, 1958), p. 139.

13. Adeline Daumard, "Les élèves de l'Ecole polytechnique de 1815 à 1848," *Revue d'histoire moderne et contemporaine* 5 (1958): 227.

14. Ibid., p. 233; Jacques Boudet, ed., *Le monde des affaires en France de 1830 à nos jours* (Paris: Société d'Edition de Dictionnaires et Encyclopédies, 1952), p. 569.

15. Artz records (*Technical Education*, p. 239) that the graduates from 1795 to 1836 were not obliged to enter government service, although there was pressure to do so, and he records the following numbers of graduates and their destinations: 1700—artillery; 917—military engineering; 25—general staff; 108—geographical engineers; 19—state munitions manufacturing; 55—naval artillery; 118—naval engineers; 13—naval hydrographical engineers— 105—general navy; 196—Corps de mines; 118—Corps des ponts et chaussées. No number of total graduates is given, so one cannot calculate overall percentages. Nonetheless, these military and government careers represented a very sizeable majority. In 1836, only 9 of 120 graduates did not enter public service.

A century and a quarter later, three-fifths to two-thirds of the alumni are in public service and one-third in industry, according to Callot's rough figures (Jean-Pierre Callot, *Histoire de l'Ecole polytechnique: Ses légendes, ses traditions, sa gloire* [Paris: Les Presses Modernes, n.d. (1958?)], p. 288). Of 10,000 active alumni, there are 3,400 in industry, 2,900 civil functionaries, 2,270 military personnel, plus 60 international civil servants and 780 workers in nationalized industry. The proportions in private and public service may be affected by the fact that many in the Corps des mines, the Corps des ponts et chaussées, and the Génie maritime worked in industry on the basis of unlimited leaves or special missions (Ecole polytechnique, *Livre de Centenaire*, 3:557). See also tables 1–3.

16. Maurice Block, *Statistiques de la France, comparées avec les divers pays de l'Europe*, 2d ed. (Paris: Guillaumin et Cie, 1874), p. 259.

17. Commission de Recherche et de Publication des Documents relatif à la vie économique de la révolution. Vol. 9, *Fragments d'une enquête économique de Ministre Roland auprès des ingénieurs des Ponts et chaussées* (published by George Bourgin, Besançon: Imprimerie Jacques et Demontrand, 1942), pp. 2, 9.

18. Arthur L. Dunham, *The Industrial Revolution in France, 1815–1848* (New York: Exposition Press, 1955), p. 52.

19. Artz, *Technical Education*, p. 244.

20. Ibid., p. 146.

21. Block, *Statistiques de la France*, p. 259.

22. Dunham, *Industrial Revolution*, p. 253.

23. Paul M. Hohenberg, *Chemicals in Western Europe, 1850–1914* (Chicago: Rand, McNally, 1967), p. 68.

24. Artz, *Technical Education*, p. 217.

25. Michelina Vaughn, "The Grandes Ecoles," in *Governing Elites: Studies in Training and Selection*, ed. Rupert Wilkinson (New York: Oxford University Press, 1969), pp. 74–107.

26. Antoine Prost, *Histoire de l'enseignement en France, 1800–1967* (Paris: Collection "U," 1968), p. 302.

27. Artz, *Technical Education*, p. 115.

28. Dunham, *Industrial Revolution*, p. 186.

29. Ministère des affaires étrangères, *Documents diplomatiques: Exposé de la situation de l'Empire* (Paris: Imprimerie impériale, November 1863), p. 27.

30. Ibid., p. 94.

31. Prost, *Histoire de l'enseignement*, p. 303.

32. Block, *Statistiques de la France*, p. 262.

33. Prost, *Histoire de l'enseignement*, p. 303.

34. Ben-David, *Scientist's Role in Society*, chap. 6.

35. The *Exposé de la situation de l'Empire* for February 1865 (Ministère des affaires étrangères, *Documents diplomatiques*, 1865, p. 122) notes that in spite of all the prestige that attaches to the Ecole polytechnique, one sees candidates admitted to both competitions and in the first ranks who choose the Ecole normale. This assertion may protest too much. The same volume notes (p. 121) that the Ecole normale competition was dazzling with more than 300 candidates; that for 1866 notes 344 candidates for 35 places. Prost, however, observes that the *non-normaliens* who enter university teaching by the "back door" are generally of higher social origin than the *normaliens*, who are looking for security, standing, vacations, etc., and never dreamed of a different career, whereas the *non-normaliens* are often those who have suffered financial reverses (Prost, *Histoire de l'enseignement*, p. 378). For a contrary view, see Lawrence Wylie, Armand Begué, Louis Begué, *Les Français* (Englewood Cliffs, N.J.: Prentice-Hall, 1970), p. 243. They maintain that the *normaliens* can easily leave teaching and enter letters, statesmanship, and big industry; but see table 1.5.

36. Antoine Bouch, "Les Grandes Ecoles," in Boudet, *Monde des affaires*, pp. 572–73.

37. Pierre Lalumiere, *L'inspection des finances* (Paris: Presses universitaires de France, 1959), passim.

38. Bouch, "Les Grandes Ecoles," p. 573.

39. Fritz Redlich, "Academic Education for Business: Its Development and the Contribution of Ignaz Jastrow (1856–1937)," in *The Business History Review* 31, no. 1 (Spring 1971), reprinted in Fritz Redlich, *Steeped in Two Cultures: A Selection of Essays* (New York: Harper & Row, 1971) p. 233.

40. Prost, *Histoire de l'enseignement*, p. 304.

41. Charles K. Warner, "Comment," mimeographed, on R. E. Cameron, "The French Economy: Past, Present, and Future" (Paper delivered at the Meeting of the Society for French Historical Studies, March 1969), p. 22.

42. Wylie et al., *Les Français*, p. 245 n.

43. Ibid.

44. Bouch, "Les Grandes Ecoles," p. 571.

45. Stephen E. Cotgrove, *Technical Education and Social Change* (London: Allen & Unwin, 1958), p. 18.

46. William N. Parker, "National States and National Development: French and German Ore Mining in the late Nineteenth Century," in Hugh G. J. Aitken, *The State and Economic Growth* (New York: Social Science Research Council, 1959) pp. 201–12.

47. Palmade, *Capitalisme et capitalistes français*, p. 240.

48. M. B. Brodie, *Fayol on Administration* (London: Lyon, Grant, and Green, 1967), p. 40.

49. Dupin, *Forces productives et commerciales*, 2:32.

50. Henry E. Guérlac, "Science and French National Strength," in *Modern France: Problems of the Third and Fourth Republics*, ed. E. M. Earle (Princeton: Princeton University Press, 1951), p. 86.

51. Nicole Delefortrie-Soubeyroux, *Les dirigeants de l'industrie française* (Paris: Colin, 1961), p. 107.

52. Prost, *Histoire de l'enseignement*, p. 300.

53. George Ohnet, *Les batailles de la vie: Le maître de forges* (Paris: Paul Odendorf, 1880), p. 55.

54. Jacques Chardonne, *Les destinées sentimentales: Porcelain de Limoges* (Paris: Grasset, 1936), p. 77.

55. Detoeuf, *Propos de O.-L. Barenton*, p. 140.

56. E. Beau de Loménie, *Les responsabilités des dynasties bourgeoises*, vol. 3, *Sous la Troisième République: la guerre et l'immédiat après-guerre, 1914–1924* (Paris: DeNoël, 1963–64), p. 153.

57. Richard F. Kuisel, *Ernest Mercier, French Technocrat* (Berkeley: University of California Press, 1967), p. 46.

58. Palmade, *Capitalisme et capitalistes français*, p. 178.

59. Jean Vial, *L'industrialisation de sidérurgie française, 1814–1864* (Paris: Mouton, 1967), p. 129.

60. Joseph A. Schumpeter, *The Theory of Economic Development* (Cambridge: Harvard University Press, 1949).

61. Fritz Redlich, "Business Leadership: Diverse Origins and Variant Forms," in *Economic Development and Cultural Change* 6, no. 3 (April 1958), reprinted in Redlich, *Steeped in Two Cultures*, p. 96.

62. Ibid., 97.

63. Fritz Redlich, "Entrepreneurial Typology," in *Weltwirtschaftliches Archiv* 82, no. 1 (1959), reprinted in Redlich, *Steeped in Two Cultures*, p. 117.

64. Melvin H. Watkins, "A Staple Theory of Economic Growth," *The Canadian Journal of Economics and Political Science* 29, no. 2 (May 1963).

65. Heinz Wutzmer, "Die Herkunft der industrielle Bougeoisie Preussens in den vierziger Jahren des 19. Jahrhunderts," in Hans Mottek et al., *Studien zur Geschichte der industriellen Revolution in Deutschland* (Berlin: Akademie-Verlag, 1960), p. 159.

66. Friedrich Zunkel, *Der Reinisch-Westfalische Unternehmer, 1834–1879: Ein Beitrag zur Geschichte des deutschen Burgertums im 19. Jahrhundert* (Cologne: Westdeutscher Verlag, 1962), p. 66.

67. Wutzmer, "Die Herkunft der industrielle Bougeoisie Preussens," p. 25.

68. Zunkel, "Der Reinish-Westfalishe Unternehmer," pp. 28–30.

69. Eliane Mossé, *Problèmes de localisation dans l'industrie automobile*, mimeographed (Paris: Ecole pratique des hautes études, 6th section, Centre d'études économiques, July 1956), p. 19.

70. Boudet, *Monde des affaires*, p. 642.

71. Palmade, *Capitalisme et capitalistes français*, p. 236. Callot notes, however, that the Citroën company reflects peculiarly French characteristics in its poor production techniques and sales performance. It was brilliant in designing cars but performed "less happily on the financial level" (Callot, *Histoire de l'Ecole polytechnique*, pp. 270–71). The Michelin company, which took it over, was started by two brothers, André and Edouard, who began in two small metallic-scaffolding family factories before becoming fascinated with pneumatic bicycle tires and later automobile tires. It should be noted that Edouard Michelin was a student of painting in Paris at the Ecole des Beaux-Arts when his brother called him back to help out with the family business. The family tradition shifted to Centrale.

72. Guy Thuillier, *George Dufaud et les débuts du grand capitalisme dans la métallurgie, en Nivernais, au XIXe siècle* (Paris: S.E.V.P.E.N., 1959), quoted in Vial, *L'industrialisation*, p. 174.

73. Beau de Loménie, *Dynasties bourgeoises*, 3:67, 174.

74. A. E. Musson, "Introduction," in *Science, Technology, and Economic Growth in the Eighteenth Century*, ed. Musson (London: Methuen, 1972), pp. 3, 61.

75. Boudet, *Monde des affaires*, p. 675 ff.

76. Cyril Stanley Smith, "Art, Technology, and Science: Notes on their Historical Interaction," in *Technology and Culture* 2, no. 4 (October, 1970): p. 526.

77. Boudet, *Monde des affaires*, p. 178.

78. Jacob Schmookler, *Invention and Economic Growth* (Cambridge: Harvard University Press, 1966).

79. Peter Mathias, "Who Unbound Prometheus? Science and Technical Change, 1600–1800," in Musson, *Science, Technology, and Economic Growth*, p. 80.

80. Jesse R. Pitts, "Continuity and Change in Bourgeois France," in S. Hoffman et al., *In Search of France* (Cambridge: Harvard University Press, 1963), p. 241 ff.

81. Ibid., p. 81.

82. Palmade, *Capitalisme et capitalistes français*, pp. 237, 249. Pitts asserts that the aristocrat is typically not interested in applied-science aspects of production, in the problems of adding value to the goods or services produced, or in commercial selling (Pitts, "Continuity and Change," p. 241 ff). But Charles de Baudry d'Asson, an aristocratic friend of the comte de Chardonnet, provides a counterexample to this view by proving another of Pitts' contentions: that an aristocratic family that loses its money will work hard enough to restore what has been lost and then stop. Baudry d'Asson, the father, ruined himself "in prodigalities, more or less picturesque." The son, associated with a chemist, created a fortune in the Société de Viscose, a company based on the invention of Chardonnet. "The incursion into business had no consequence. The profits were reinvested into good properties. Today, Armand de Baudry, who made his studies in agronomy, is a deputy like his grandfather and father, but a rural exploitant like his father, not a businessman" (Boudet, *Monde des affaires*, p. 555). The marquis de Dion, associated in the early automobile enterprise with the simple mechanic, Bouton, is another exception to the rule about applied science and aristocrats.

83. Musson, "Introduction," p. 54.

84. John Weiss, conversation of January 1973.

85. Dunham, *Industrial Revolution*, pp. 293–96.

86. Jean Bouvier, *Le Crédit Lyonnais de 1863 à 1882* (Paris: S.E.V.P.E.N., 1961), p. 374.

87. Honoré de Balzac, *Lost Illusions* (New York: Fred Defau and Co., n.d. [French version appeared in 1837: my translation based on the 1844 edition]).

88. Boudet, *Monde des affaires*, p. 607.

89. Ecole polytechnique, *Livre de centenaire*, 3:52.

90. John P. McKay, *Pioneers for Profit: Foreign Entrepreneurship and Russian Industrialization, 1885–1913* (Chicago: University of Chicago Press, 1970).

91. Robert G. Albion, *The Rise of the Port of New York* (New York: Charles Scribner's Sons, 1939), p. 253.

92. Luigi de Rosa, *Iniziative e capitale straniero nell'industria metalmeccanica del Mezzogiorno, 1840–1904* (Naples: Giannini, Editori, 1968), chap. 9.

93. Jurgen Kocka, *Unternehmungsverwaltung und Angestelltenschaft am Beispiel Siemens, 1847–1914: Zum Verhältnis von Kapitalismus und Bürokratie in der deutschen Industrialisierung* (Stuttgart: Ernst Klett Verlag, 1969), pp. 15, 76.

94. Ecole polytechnique, *Livre de centenaire*, 3:560.

95. Callot, *Histoire de l'Ecole polytechnique*, p. 303.

96. Bouch, "Les Grandes Ecoles," p. 571.

97. The first part of the centennial celebration volume of the Société Générale was written by Jean Méary, a director of the bank, alumnus of the Ecole normale supérieure, agrégé in history and geography, and a member of the Inspection des finances. This must be the French equivalent of a triple first in greats.

98. Delefortrie-Soubeyroux, *Industrie française*, p. 59.

99. Vial, *L'industrialisation*, pp. 179, 396.

100. Callot, *Histoire de l'Ecole polytechnique*, pp. 298-99.

101. George Sand, *Le péché de M. Antoine*, 2 vols. (Paris: Michel Lévy Frères, 1857), 1: 152-54.

102. W. G. Rimmer, *Marshall of Leeds, Flaxspinners, 1788-1886* (Cambridge: At the University Press, 1960).

103. Arnold Thackray, "Natural Knowledge and Cultural Context: A Case Study in the Technical, Social and Cultural Backgrounds of Scientific Change in the Industrial Revolution," paper presented at a seminar at the Massachusetts Institute of Technology, 2 May 1973.

104. D. C. Coleman, "Gentlemen and Players," *Economic History Review*, 2d ser. 26, no. 1 (February 1973): 106. But compare: "Frederic Engel Dollfuss, born in 1818, was sent at the age of twelve to Paris. There he followed the course of the College Henry IV and dreamed of preparing for the Ecole polytechnique, but his parents, who were dubious of seeing him embrace a military career, dissuaded him from it and oriented him toward business" (quoted in Daumard, *Les élèves de l'Ecole polytechnique*, p. 229).

105. Pierre Aycoberry, "Probleme der Sozialschichtung in Köln im Zeitalter der Frühindustrialisierung" in W. Fischer, Hgbr., *Wirtschafts-und sozialgeschichtliche Probleme der frühen Industrialisierung* (Berlin: Colloquium Verlag, 1968), p. 518.

106. Palmade, *Capitalisme et capitalistes français*, p. 235.

107. Vial, *L'industrialisation*, p. 396. Decazeville, of course, suffered from exhaustion of its coal fields. So, too, did Commentry, although effective administration and scientific research by Fayol overcame this for a time. Brodie mentions that when the Academy of Science gave Fayol the Delesse prize in 1893, it paid tribute "to his powers of observation, his skill as an experimenter, his capacity to enlist the interest of his own engineers and workers in the investigation and his ability to secure the collaboration of distinguished scientists" (Brodie, *Fayol on Administration*, pp. 2-3).

108. These observations relate to Crozier's view that in French bureaucracy promotion is by objective examination rather than evaluation of performance by immediate superiors, because of the French need to avoid tense interpersonal relations, especially face-to-face confrontations (Michael Crozier, *The Bureaucratic Phenomenon* [Chicago: University of Chicago Press, 1964]).

109. Vial, *L'industrialisation*, p. 181.

110. Thuillier, *George Dufaud*, pp. ix, 41.

111. Ecole polytechnique, *Livre de centenaire*, 3:578.

112. de Rosa, *Iniziativa e capitale straniero*, p. 233.

113. Dunham, *Industrial Revolution*, p. 51.

114. James Challey, "Marc Seguin," *Dictionary of Scientific Biography*, forthcoming.

115. P. E. Marchal and Laurent Seguin, *Marc Seguin, 1786-1875: La naissance du premier chemin de fer français* (Lyon, 1957), pp. 130-31.

116. Dunham, *Industrial Revolution*, p. 58.

117. Detoeuf, *Propos de O.-L. Barenton*, p. 18 ff.

118. The emphasis is primarily on theory, but occasionally a note on human relations appears. Thus, the French industrialist has mediocre collaborators. That does not displease him; he detests eminent collaborators (Ibid., p. 69). Among international comparisons: "The Englishman is a practitioner, who has no theories"; "The German is a theorist who applies his theories"; "The Frenchman is a theorist who does not apply them"; "That is called with us having good sense" (ibid., 69). Cf. the remark of one Captain Hore, a British naval attaché in Paris, "The English have no system of naval education and the French have too much" (Artz, *Technical Education*, p. 265).

119. Robert Gilpin, *France in the Age of the Scientific State* (Princeton: Princeton University Press, 1968).

RELIGION AND ENTERPRISE:

THE CASE OF THE FRENCH TEXTILE INDUSTRY

BY DAVID LANDES

THE CASE STUDY that follows has two objectives: to throw light, first, on the character and performance of French entrepreneurship during the course of industrialization, and second, on the significance of religion for economic performance. A few words about each will suffice by way of introduction.

The significance of entrepreneurship for the timing and character of French economic development has long been a hotly debated topic. Roughly speaking, the lines have been drawn between those who believe that one can speak of group patterns of entrepreneurial behavior and that these patterns influence the nature of business decisions in the direction of greater or lesser effectiveness of performance, and those who believe that business behavior is on balance and in the long run rational, even optimal, and that the rate and course of growth can be entirely explained by conventional economic and material considerations. Specifically in the French context, the debate has been between two schools. The first feels that the relatively slower industrial development of France by comparison with Britain and, later, Germany from the mid-eigthteenth century to World War I can be attributed in significant part to the conservatism, caution, and limited horizons ("Malthusianism") of French entrepreneurs, reinforced by anticapital-

41

ist and anticompetitive attitudes on the part of the population as a whole and also by a value system that deprecated business by comparison with more honorific roles. The second school argues that value systems are symptoms rather than causes, that French business behavior has been as effective as conditions have allowed, that growth was more rapid than is commonly admitted, and that insofar as France lagged technologically, she did so because relative factor costs (scarcity of coal, high cost of capital) provided less incentive for adoption of the new industrial machinery. In particular, I have argued in other times and places that the pace and character of French entrepreneurship was set by family firms, owned and managed by blood relations, whose primary concerns were safety, continuity, and privacy. Not that there were no corporate units mobilizing the capital of strangers; there were, particularly in the capital-intensive branches of transport, metallurgy, mining, and heavy chemicals. But these entrepreneurs preferred the surplus profits of protected markets to price competition and were content to let the less efficient family enterprises lead the way; while this tacit entente was sanctioned by public opinion and sustained by commercial policy.

It is not my purpose in this essay to review this debate in detail. But the material that follows will add to the dossier some empirical evidence whose implications are worth considering.

The second issue, that of the significance of religion for economic performance, has given rise to even wider debate. The subject was first raised in scholarly fashion by Max Weber in his seminal (one of the rare instances where that word is deserved) essay, *The Protestant Ethic and the Spirit of Capitalism*. Since then a library has been published on the pros and cons: Did Protestantism, specifically in its Calvinist manifestations, generate an ethic, that is, a set of values governing daily life, that was conducive to effective business performance and, in so doing, lay the basis for the triumph of industrial capitalism? Again, this is not the place to review the debate in detail, but the present case study throws interesting light on the subject.

The essay that follows is a case study in successful French enterprise: the development of textile manufacture in the twin cities of Roubaix-Tourcoing during the course of the nineteenth century. The case is particularly relevant to the theses sketched above because the enterprises that constituted the *fabrique* and that were the vehicles of its growth were family firms of the classic variety, while the owners of these firms were, in the vast majority, practicing Catholics. The success

of the *fabrique* would seem, then, to constitute counterevidence to both
my own entrepreneurial thesis and the Weber model.

The specifically familial character will emerge in detail from the
discussion that follows, but a few words may be in order regarding the
Catholicity of the entrepreneurs. Under the best of circumstances it is
not easy to penetrate the hearts of men and judge their beliefs, and the
historian in particular must rely on such affirmations and external
signs as time has left him. By these indicia, there can hardly have been a
business group in France for whom Catholic observance and faith was
more important—in daily practice, in the schooling of their children,
in the *encadrement* and discipline of their work force, in the definition
and justification of their social and political ideology. Even more
significant, in an age when small families were the rule throughout
French society, when the hardest task of a good Catholic was to
conform to the laws of marriage and procreation, these manufacturers
had large families and reveled in their swarming children and grandchildren. And these, mind you, were not poor, ignorant workers who
spent their days toiling in the mill to return at night to sordid hovels
where conjugal intercourse was the only free distraction. They were
bourgeois, with substantial homes and fortunes, with ambitions for
their children and opportunities for leisure. Yet for years, the social
register proudly opened with a list of the larger families, beginning
with one or two with twenty-three or twenty-four children, another
perhaps with twenty-one, several with nineteen or twenty, and going
on to a dozen with fifteen or sixteen, a score with twelve and thirteen,
and columns of names with seven, eight, nine, or ten.[1] After four or five
generations, many a clan numbered its members in the hundreds and
even thousands, and the list of grieving relatives customarily given on
funeral cards had to be printed in booklet form—an abbreviation of the
family genealogy was unthinkable. Many of these children, needless to
say, went into holy orders; almost all of them were educated in
parochial schools, and the Church found here one of its most generous
recruiting grounds for both secular and lay clergy.

In short, these businessmen were good Catholics by any objective
criterion. Yet they were at the same time among the most prosperous
and progressive textile manufacturers in the country, so wrapped up in
their industry at the expense of other concerns that they became known
as the Americans of France. Even in competition with the Protestant
businessmen of Alsace, ideal examplars of Weberian capitalism, the
Northerners came to have the upper hand. Indeed, some of them have
been able to buy into and take over the old Calvinist firms, once

strongholds of dynastic wealth, but now given over to strange managers and stockholders.[2]

The success of Roubaix-Tourcoing is the more impressive because no special material advantages will account for it. To be sure, the region as a whole has an old manufacturing tradition, going back to Roman times. The names of Tournai, Ghent, and Bruges testify to the age-old eminence of Flanders and Picardy in the production of textiles for wide markets, and one town, Arras, has entered the language as a noun along with such other eponymous fabrics as muslin, calico, and denim. In French Flanders, the primary center from the seventeenth century onward was Lille, the administrative capital and military strongpoint. Roubaix and Tourcoing were villages, some twenty kilometers away. Tourcoing at least was on the main road to Courtrai, but Roubaix was a dead end. In a world of primitive transport, this made for higher costs and social isolation; by way of compensation, the cost of living, and hence the cost of labor, was lower than in the big city nearby.

This was the great advantage of the countryside in the prefactory era: an abundant supply of cheap labor. Flanders has always been far more fertile in people than in crops, and for centuries the burgeoning villages of the countryside found in home manufacture an indispensable source of additional income. In the eighteenth century, a period of rapid increase of population after the destructive wars of the late seventeenth century, the spread of rural industry was especially rapid, in spite of all efforts of Lille and other urban centers to halt the process. In 1771, Roubaix and its surrounding villages employed or supported 40,500 in textile production, of whom 30,000 were spinners as far south as Artois. In 1786, the population of Roubaix was probably about 12,000[3]—higher than it was to be again for a generation; Tourcoing was even larger, with perhaps 15,000 inhabitants in 1750.[4] Roubaix and Tourcoing still gave the impression of overgrown villages, but they were industrial centers nonetheless.

The individual textile enterprise was, of course, small—a place to store raw materials, receive finished work, and stock goods pending sale. The work itself was done outside, in the cottages of the spinners and weavers or in shops specializing in dyeing and finishing. The "staff" of the enterprise consisted of husband and wife, helped occasionally by factors who distributed the raw fiber, collected the yarn, and gave it out again to weavers. More often than not, it was the master who did everything, even serving as his own traveling salesman. The techniques of production were simple and slow to change. Wool and cotton were spun on the big and little wheels, and as late as 1789 only a few small jennies had made their appearance; a decade later the mule was still almost unknown. The cottage weaver used the traditional handloom, sometimes but not always assisted by the fly shuttle. The worker was generally owner of his tools and equipment. As a result, the merchant-manufacturer was spared costly outlays for fixed capital and could transfer much of the risk of production to the worker: if business was bad, he could simply desist from buying cloth. These were arrangements that made for easy entry and considerable resiliency in the face of commercial fluctuations.

Even so, the Revolution dealt the textile industry, along with the rest of the French economy, a severe blow.[5] Around 1800, the population of Roubaix was down to about 9,000; that of Tourcoing, to about 12,000. Then, with respite from civil war and with changes of regime, trade picked up. Dieudonné, prefect of the Nord, describing a visit to Roubaix around 1802, wrote of "the repeated strokes of the weaver 'beating' his cloth, the murmur of his wheels, and the click-clack of his shuttle, [which] gave the travelers who entered the commune the idea of a unique and immense manufacture."[6] These were the years that saw the establishment of the first cotton spinning mills, housing jennies and mules and driven by hand and animal power. None of these was large, a fact that may well have saved them when the hothouse enterprises of the empire were smitten in the great crisis of 1810-12.[7] When peace returned in 1815 and France could once again put up tariff barriers against the import of cheap British goods, the manufacturers of Roubaix-Tourcoing could mobilize small but solid fortunes for investment in industry, whereas the more mechanized giants of the boom had been driven into bankruptcy.[8]

Yet one would have hardly predicted a great future for towns so poorly endowed by nature for the kind of large-scale production implied by the new machine technology. As the cost of plant and equipment rose, along with the scale of production, such factors as transport, raw materials (which, in cotton manufacture, was a function primarily of the cost of shipment), and capital became more important, and labor less. Roubaix and Tourcoing were, as already noted, poorly situated to receive cotton; indeed, the Nord as a whole was at a disadvantage in this regard by comparison with the older and larger cotton *fabrique* of Normandy, which lay directly up the Seine from the port of Le Havre. (The other major center of manufacture—in and around Mulhouse in Alsace—was even more isolated, but had other advantages to compensate.)

The transportation factor was to become even more important once steam power was adopted. The industry of the Nord, unlike that of Normandy or the Vosges, could make no use of water power; the land was as flat as a table. But the steam engine requires coal, and coal is a bulk commodity that cost in those days a fortune to move—unless, that is, it could be shipped by water. There is coal near Roubaix, and already in the eighteenth century, the plain of Flanders and Picardy was laced with a network of canals. None of these, however, went to or by Roubaix or Tourcoing—not until the 1840s, that is, when these cities already constituted one of France's major centers of manufacturing. The canal, in other words, came to the *fabrique*, not the *fabrique* to the canal.

Despite this, Roubaix and Tourcoing were able to get cheaper coal than, say, Mulhouse, or even Rouen, which could import by sea from Britain. Claude Fohlen attributes the rapid expansion of the *fabrique* from the late 1840s to the discovery and exploitation in that decade of major deposits in the Pas-de-Calais, which was destined to become the most important field in France. (These new mines were more than just a source of fuel; they were for a number of manufacturers a most profitable investment and a source of income that was used to finance expansion in textiles.)

Yet coal clearly could not make that much difference, for it represented only a small portion of the cost of the final product—1 to 3 percent in cotton spinning in the 1860s. If we allow regional cost differentials of as much as 100 percent (a ratio of one to two), we are still talking of advantages of only a point or two.[9] In fact, the margin was usually much smaller, and coal was not a decisive locational factor, as evidenced by the readiness of one entrepreneur in Normandy, for example, to operate two plants, one of them buying coal at 20 francs per ton, the other at 30.[10] Whatever advantage Roubaix and the Nord in general enjoyed in this sphere, moreover, was eroded over time as customs duties were reduced, sea freights fell, and the Northern coal mines, in an effort to regain old and win new customers, worked out a discriminatory rate structure that favored distant buyers.[11]

This modest advantage in coal was partially negated by a shortage (surprising for soggy Flanders) of that most important and most easily overlooked of industrial raw materials: water. It is impossible to produce cloth without water, which is used for washing the raw fiber (especially in the case of wool), for fulling the cloth (again wool), for bleaching and dyeing. For decades, the inadequate local supply was to be a problem: under the empire, industry was deprived of water two to three months a year;[12] later on there was sometimes not even enough to fill the boilers of the steam engines.[13] Not until the discovery of a deep layer of water in the 1830s was the difficulty eased, and then only for a time. In the end, the inhabitants had to lay pipes and bring water in from a distance; the link to the Lys was completed in 1861.[14]

Under the circumstances, it is not surprising that these cities, for all the rapidity of their industrial expansion, were slow to adopt the steam engine, and then only in small sizes. In 1834 the cities' mills were using fifty-four engines that averaged only nine horsepower each, and in 1838, eleven out of thirty-nine cotton mills in Roubaix were still running on horse gins.[15] These were hard years for the cotton industry of Roubaix, which saw the number of machine spindles decline from 255,000 in 1818 to 170,000 in 1833, and to 116,000 in 1840.[16] Over the same period the *fabrique* of Tourcoing marked time with some 60,000 to 70,000 spindles. Only the rapid growth of wool manufacture, where fuel represented a smaller part of the total cost, saved the two cities from a serious decline. Roubaix particularly took up the more costly fiber with great success: the first mill was founded in 1831; by 1838, thirty-one factories were driving 105,000 spindles with engines totaling 405 horsepower. Tourcoing, long a center of trading in raw and combed wool, saw the volume of combings handled rise from 267 tons in 1830 to 5,800 in 1838.[17]

From about 1850, cotton picked up again, and the two branches grew side by side. This versatility, which may seem routine at first consideration, was in fact an uncommon virtue: wool and cotton are very different fibers, calling for different treatment, and they are ordinarily handled by separate manufacturing centers each with its own experience and traditions. How much of the credit goes to enterprise, how much to labor, is impossible to say. But the Nord was almost the "compleat" textile *fabrique*: when cotton faltered again in the 1860s owing to the American Civil War, Lille switched over to linen, and Roubaix-Tourcoing shifted over to wool.

Then, during the last decades of the century, it was cotton's turn to flourish. The loss of Alsace, with its modern and highly competitive cotton *fabrique* in and around Mulhouse, was a windfall to the other French centers, and the Nord won its share and more of the new business: from 1881 to 1909, the number of cotton spindles in the arrondissement of Lille rose 155 percent, from 864,000 to 2.2 million. By comparison, wool continued to grow, but more slowly than before, 18 percent from 1881 to 1911 as against 258 percent from 1856 to 1881.[18]

Combining the growth in both cotton and wool with concomitant gains in complementary branches, the nineteenth century was, on balance, a time of remarkable success for Roubaix-Tourcoing. This success entailed and depended on a rapid increase in population; Roubaix in particular came to serve as a symbol of the mushroom industrial city—a world of chimneys, stone pavements, long factory walls, drab and often deadly slum housing. Only at the turn of the century, with both wool and cotton output and employment leveling off, were there serious warnings that the secular boom was over. But we shall turn to that question later on.

This rapid growth of population offers a clue to what was unquestionably a significant factor in Roubaix's industrial success: an unusually elastic supply of labor. In the long run, there was the remarkable fertility of the Flemish population, whose birth rate stood far above the national average; but this may well have been nothing more than a response to employment opportunity, that is, a dependent variable. More pertinent was the availability of a large reserve of labor across the border, just a few kilometers away, in Belgium. Belgian Flanders in the eighteenth and early nineteenth centuries offers a classic example of overpopulation and impoverishment under conditions of receding Malthusian limits. As in Ireland, the cultivation of the potato made it possible to support more and more people on smaller and smaller holdings. The introduction of cottage industry, particularly the spinning of flax, enabled many Flemings to eke out a meager income from the soil, but from the 1820s on, hand-spun linen was threatened by machine-spun yarn, and the efforts of the Belgian government to sustain the dying trade only protracted the misery of the spinners. Then, in 1845, the potato crop failed, and Flanders was caught in the grip of a famine that sent thousands begging from door to door and had the authorities burying the victims at night for fear of terrifying the living.[19]

Flanders, in other words, like Ireland and Switzerland, was a generator of labor for more enterprising areas. From the beginning, the textile manufacturers of Roubaix were able to draw on an abundant supply of cheap, sometimes desperate, always docile labor, which offered the inestimable advantage of being disposable. It was one thing to put French workers out on the street: they could make trouble, and in a country with a habit of revolution, unemployment was a matter of national concern. But Belgians could be shipped back across the border at little or no political cost. And if French labor got difficult, the Belgians were always ready to serve as scabs. It was as close as anyone could come to an ideal Marxist schema of capitalist exploitation.[20]

Yet it would be wrong in my opinion to treat this elastic supply of labor as a causative determinant of the growth of the textile manufacture in Roubaix and its neighborhood. For one thing, cheap as Flemish workers were, they were better paid than the German or Swiss peasants who streamed into the mills of Mulhouse. We have no standardized regional wage data for the nineteenth century, but such figures as are available from tariff inquiries and industrial censuses show that textile wages were highest in Normandy, next highest in the Nord, and lowest in Alsace. In addition, the employment of Belgian labor was more a response to growth than a precondition thereof. It was less important in the first half of the century than it was to be later, when manufacturers deliberately built their mills right on the border and instituted private bus services to supplement vastly improved means of public transportation. At the same time, employers had increasing recourse to the low-cost labor of women and children—inversely to what was happening in most advanced industrial centers.[21] As a result of this shift, the wages of adult males remained the same or fell slightly over long periods, even in times of inflation. This was undoubtedly a competitive advantage, although it was paid for in lower productivity and a reluctance to mechanize that exceeded in the long run the bounds of optimality. We shall return to this point later.

Location, raw materials, labor—if none of these will account for the success of Roubaix, there remain the employers and the quality of their performance as entrepreneurs. This is from every standpoint the most difficult aspect of the problem. Entrepreneurship is a loose concept to begin with and one that lends itself to circular reasoning: how does one distinguish here between cause and effect? Wages can be quantified; coal prices, compared. Management is an imponderable.

What is more, our sources are disappointingly meager. What we would like to have is a good collection of business and private papers, covering a representative sample of firms over time, to be compared with similar evidence on entrepreneurs in other centers. Instead, we have only scraps of material; the manufacturing firms of the nineteenth century were extremely lax in this regard, and most of what was not deliberately destroyed has been lost in wars and occupations. Of what is left, only a small part has ever been opened to outsiders; as we shall see, the houses and society of the North are notoriously *fermées*.

The analysis that follows is based, then, on a small fraction of the ideally relevant evidence. I have been able to examine a few private archives—but only a few—through the courtesy of enlightened and hospitable gentlemen. There are also several works published for private circulation that contain informative letters and documents of the period. In particular, the volumes of Gaston Motte, industrialist and historian, provide an invaluable insight into the life and milieu of one of the leading families in Roubaix; indeed, they constitute one of the most revealing studies of a business dynasty for any region of France.[22] Moreover, if one is willing to include, for purposes of studying the social attitudes and psychology of the region, materials on the related and very similar milieu of Lille, the documentation increases substantially; there are even some collections of family papers from the period before 1815 on deposit in the public library there. Finally, there are precious details and much understanding to be gleaned from both official and semiofficial archives and a great variety of printed sources—genealogies, business histories, memoirs, newspapers, inquiries, and scholarly monographs.[23] When all is said and done, however, we have a meager catch *qui nous laisse sur notre faim.*

This thinness of the evidential base necessarily limits the confidence one can attach to the argument that follows; so much rests, as we shall see, on the experience of one or two families. I submit, nevertheless, that the analysis proposed is plausible and correct—first, because the families in question served as role models to other, less prominent members of the community of employers; and second, because such evidence as touches on other persons and related aspects of the problem is concordant. The pieces fit together.

The textile manufacturers of Roubaix-Tourcoing were, with rare exception, family entrepreneurs. The firm was an extension of the household, an extension that was usually juridically separate but that was identified so closely with it socially and operationally that it was sometimes hard to say where the one ended and the other began. This was particularly true of the early days of the industry, when business and family occupied the same quarters and drew their cash from the same box, while the *patron* and his wife moved from apartment to shop and back again as from one task to another—and not as from one world to another.

At present, dear friend, I get up at 7 o'clock [wrote one wife to her husband, who was away on business]. I often breakfast while giving the breast to one [of the children] and feeding [*appatelant*: a word normally used of mother birds feeding their young] the two others. I then go to the office to get my notes in order, bring the books up to date, etc. . . . After that, I accept no. 2's [a type of calico]; I number what there is, or I give it for dyeing; I mark; I do, in short, whatever has to be done. When I have more time, as today for example, I employ part of my morning in writing to you. At 12:30 I have dinner; after dinner I pay all the *fabricants* of the no. 2's I bought in the morning. After that I check on the dye work or number striped "callemandes." Sometimes I go to the shipping brokers. . . .[24]

This woman was only one in a long lineage. Gaston Motte cites on his subject the Florentine historian Francesco Guicciardini: "The women [of this country] are sober and very active and attentive, concerning themselves not only with domestic matters, which the men have little care for, but also buying and selling merchandise—and this, with such skill, intelligence, and diligence that in several places their husbands leave them in charge of everything."[25]

This active role of the wife and mother in the management of the enterprise—Mme Virnot-Barrois wrote some letters while giving the breast to the baby—was, of course, indicative in itself of the familial character of the business. The Roubaisiens and Tourquenois of today never cease to marvel at the energy and talent of their great-grandmothers—of women like this widow Lefebvre-Ducatteau, whose firm, employing almost five hundred workers, was highly praised by the jury of the industrial exposition of 1844 for its maternalistic character: "To the virtues of an excellent product, Mme Lefebvre joins that of not having any unemployment, of never firing a worker for lack of a market; and, aided by her children, she does not need for management of her business and of the details of production either foremen or designers. It is an industrial enterprise all the better cared for in that it is a family enterprise, and that nothing important is done except by the owners themselves."[26]

With the growth of large factories and the entry of children and grandchildren into firms that began as one-man, or more often, man-and-wife, enterprises, the physical separation of plant and household became marked, although for decades the mills were built in and around the houses of the proprietors—in adjacent wings, on the other side of the courtyard, in the back orchard. The social identification, moreover, remained: the firm was at once the material support of the family and the basis of its status; the reputation, honor, and strength of the one were the reputation, honor, and strength of the other.

Family and firm existed for each other. When the Abbé Brédart, curé of Dinant, learned that his nephew Motte-Brédart of Roubaix was expecting a child, he wrote to congratulate him: "I see it is a good augury for your cotton business, which requires a lot of activity."[27] And when the same Motte-Brédart, after twenty years of successful enterprise, decided to retire, his wife (who had managed the mill while he handled the selling) refused to allow him to liquidate. She herself would continue to run the woolen mill in collaboration with the oldest son: a family with three children had a duty to pass on to them an instrument of production.

This tight bond between family and firm had important implications for economic behavior; I have had occasion to discuss these in other contexts. Suffice it to note here that a family firm of this kind places great stress on independence and privacy, and avoids credit because of its incompatibility with these primary values. He who borrows must open his books and explain his behavior; the *fabricant* of the Nord therefore never borrowed unless compelled to—and the very character of credit as a matter of last resort, as a sign of serious weakness that might affect a firm's position vis-à-vis all manner of suppliers, customers, and other connections, reinforced the abhorrence of it.

To be sure, recourse to short-term commercial credit was unavoidable; if Roubaix-Tourcoing wanted to sell, it had to take paper, and if it wanted to realize its paper, it had to endorse it and discount on its signature.

Yet there is a world of difference between short- and long-term credit, and it is particularly the latter that threatens injury to the status and dignity of the family firm. This the *fabricants* resisted for generations, and only the destruction caused by World War I and the inflation that accompanied it weaned them from ingrained prejudices and taught them to borrow from strangers. In the nineteenth century the taboo was intact, and only exceptionally do we find derogations, carefully concealed in the account books of private bankers. If the manufacturer of Roubaix-Tourcoing needed money, he preferred to ask the help of some friend or relation, perhaps admitting the lender as a partner in the firm. Such arrangements were rare and often temporary; the exclusively familial unit was the norm to which business organization constantly tended to move. In the meantime, however, the *fabricants* allowed the firm to secure resources without accepting the formal stigmata of the debtor. "The guarantees that I can offer," wrote one industrialist, proudly refusing a government loan that called for a mortgage as security (mortgages have to be recorded and cannot be kept confidential), "are the firm signature of D. Wilbaux-Florin, which engages four brothers who possess in partnership a considerable establishment free of debt or lien."

If the firm was to grow without recourse to credit, it had to accumulate its own resources; and everything was bent to this end. Business was conducted as parsimoniously as possible, with meagerly furnished offices, a minimum of clerical help, and the smallest possible expenditure for travel and similar "nonproductive" but indispensable activities. In the larger firms, the partners drew as little as possible from the year-to-year profits for their own use; indeed, many if not most firms explicitly limited such withdrawals by contract so as to enforce a process of self-financed growth. In an age when long-run demand was growing steadily and the pecuniary advantage of the new equipment over traditional hand methods of the earliest machines was spectacularly large, a carefully run enterprise in which master and mistress, aided by children still in their teens, did not spare or count their own labor could accumulate capital with extraordinary rapidity.

All of this, of course, depended on the observation of the strictest economy in both private and business life, and the establishment of thrift—if not parsimony—as a virtue in both spheres reinforced it in each and facilitated its incorporation as an integral part of the entrepreneurial personality. To be sure, with the passage of time and the acquisition of wealth, this pristine modesty gave way somewhat to new tastes and desires; we shall have occasion to look at this process in greater detail later on. Yet even in the latter years of the century, the luxuries of the wealthy Roubaisien or Tourquennois were of the moderate variety: vacations at nearby watering places, riding horses, a country house where the whole family could relax and play. The home of the bourgeois was almost never lavish; it was what the French call *cossu*—solid, substantial, comfortable. The large domain, the social "season," the pursuit of *élégance* were unknown; the family remained the center of leisure as of work, and the biggest expenses were food and shelter for the rapidly increasing clan.

Thrift, of course, was only one aspect of the *fabricant*'s personality. Of equal if not greater importance was his attitude toward work: he was thrifty of time as well as money. This is not to say that, like the "ideal" Calvinist, he felt that all distraction was sinful and that every waking moment need be productively employed; in particular, the pleasures and relaxation of family life had their own virtues and made valid claims upon him. But he believed in a long, hard working day, beginning at dawn before the workers reported to the mill and going on long after dark, checking and supervising, processing one day's work and getting ready the next, lending a hand if need be on repairs or in emergencies. He was above all a production man, and this was very much like the industrialists of Alsace, who liked to contrast themselves favorably in this regard with the manufacturers of Normandy—speculators and merchants at heart. Unlike the Alsatian, however, who early began to send his children to technical schools, the Northerner long continued to learn his techniques in the mill, *en mettant la main à la pâte*.

This fundamental belief in the virtue of work has as its corollary an unshakable confidence in the efficacy of work. If many a Northern balance sheet noted the year's profits with a formal expression of thanks to God, the underlying assumption remained that God helps those who help themselves. The tenacity of the Roubaisien or Tourquennois in the face of the disappointments and reverses that are inherent in enterprise was one of his strongest assets. One of the most impressive examples is that of the Motte-Bossut firm. In 1843-44 the founder, Louis-François-Joseph Motte-Bossut, built the largest spinning mill in Roubaix, a five-story plant containing 18,000 spindles, all self-acting, that so impressed contemporaries that they called it the *filature monstre*. A year later, in July 1845, it burned down, with losses estimated at over a million francs, covered by only 872,000 francs of insurance. For the first twenty-four hours, Motte-Bossut was prepared to throw in the sponge; to an uncle who came to present the condolences of some of his relatives, he vented his anguish: *"Un avenir brisé, mon oncle, un avenir brisé!"* The next day plans were made to rebuild.

Ten months later production resumed and by 1847 the new mill was fully equipped with 44,000 spindles of the latest design; by 1853, the number had increased to 55,000; a decade later, there were 70,000, to which must be added over 20,000 in a second plant, built on new "fireproof" lines in 1863–64. The design was put to a test in 1866, when the two top floors were consumed; the rest of the building was saved by its incombustibility. There was no insurance; in spite of the special construction, the companies had been unwilling to set a lower rate and Motte-Bossut had refused to pay the regular premiums.

A month later, this unhappy history of disasters reached its climax in a gigantic blaze that swallowed the older mill. The loss, estimated at 1.8 millions, was covered by only 1.2 millions in insurance. According to family tradition, the ashes were still warm when Motte-Bossut sent off a telegram to England ordering new machines. His silent partners were not made of the same stuff. They asked to be bought out, and Motte-Bossut abandoned the entire indemnity to that end.

These, to be sure, were only the most spectacular moments in a life that was something of a living monument to the image of the "compleat *fabricant*." Again and again Motte-Bossut gave evidence of perseverance and boldness that contrasts sharply with the cautiousness of most French enterprises. When the market for yarn slackened, he built a weaving mill to absorb a good part of his own production; when the market for cloth failed, he built a larger warehouse to hold his stock against better times; and when, in the 1880s, falling prices and foreign competition discouraged his sons, he took the occasion to give them a fight talk:

> I showed you a few days ago that even at four francs and counting everything below its real price, velvet was bringing in nothing, even less than nothing. This role of contractor [*façonnier*] without the unforeseen, without elasticity, is doomed to mediocre results. Is that a reason to be discouraged? I foresaw this negative balance sheet when, a week ago, I wrote you that in spite of our bad fortune, we had notwithstanding to persevere. When we have a brand name—and you will make one—when you have continuous warps,

when it is recognized that your quality does not vary, you will reap in this field also.[28]

Or take Motte-Bossut's brother Alfred, who made a career of setting skilled technicians up in business and marrying his capital and connections to their know-how, thereby generating a whole series of new entrepreneurial dynasties. In 1882 he was ill for a time, deprived for some months of the pleasures of work: "I can tell you," he wrote his friend Gillet in Lyons, "that it is a veritable punishment to have to give up the occupations one loves. Each of us in one way or another has his cross to bear." He had indeed plenty to be concerned with, at a most difficult time:

> Don't I have a large combing mill to launch? My mission is to create establishments that bring in only a little more than 6 percent, interest and amortization included. Even in today's conditions, I think it wise to place one's own capital in industry. You have a return equal to that of the highest-yielding securities. You have, in addition, the possibility of prosperous years. Lastly you have—an invaluable benefit—the obligation to work every day, on penalty of seeing everything collapse if you neglect the supervision of your plants.[29]

In short, work was a sort of panacea. Consider the letter that Motte-Bossut writes to his eldest son, who was apparently very short and somewhat sensitive about it. The father affectionately calls him "*Léon poucet*": "Do like me, my boy; after all, I got used to it; habituation made me forget nature's avarice toward me. . . . Let us return to our blind refrain: work, work, work some more. The smaller one is, the more one must work, and you may be sure that that is what I do. It is better to be small and educated than big and ignorant."[30]

Labor omnia vincit—even an inferiority complex.

The significance of this stress on work is better understood when one examines the problem encountered in preparing the child of one of these business families for the role of entrepreneur. For the process of socialization was complicated by a serious contradiction: on the one hand, there was the family with its tradition of prosperity and growth and its corresponding demands on the individual; on the other hand, there was the family with its provision for the individual, the position it created, the resources it made available, the support it guaranteed in time of need. The industrial dynasty of Roubaix-Tourcoing considered it an obligation to place each of its children. Both daughters and sons received marriage portions to enable them (or their husbands) to go on in life as members of the entrepreneurial community. There was no question of finding a job or making a place: with the growth of the firm, there was an increasing need for specialized executive help, and there was always the possibility of acquiring or building a new plant for the new adult to direct. The saying was, *"Pour se marier, il faut une cheminée qui fume."*

Under the circumstances, the ethic of work assumed special importance as the antidote to the complacency implicit in success. Consider once again the Motte family. The founder of the firm, Louis-François-Joseph Motte-Bossut, grew up in a moderately well-to-do family that had not yet begun the rapid, cumulative ascent characteristic of the nineteenth-century business dynasty. His father retired after securing a comfortable income; it was the mother who carried on a part of the enterprise and trained the children to be industrialists. There was as yet no problem of spoiling the children: the family lived modestly; its reputation was not what it was later to become; the children, although aided by an initial capital, clearly would have to build their own careers.

What is more, mother Motte-Brédart made sure that her children had no real sense of the family's means. "My mother," her second son Alfred was to write later,

was an extraordinary woman, in that, married to the most peaceful and gentle of men, a man with the strongest antipathy to industry, she was compelled by circumstances to take over the management of the enterprise and the spinning mill. At the same time, she took care of the education of her children, and it is fair to say that she inspired all of us with a love of knowledge and a taste for work. She ran her firm with care, and although fortune often turned its back on her, my mother, by dint of good management, succeeded in leaving us a handsome patrimony. We knew nothing of her resources, and knowing that on several occasions our parents had lost a good deal of money, we never dreamed that my mother could leave us what she did.[31]

As the French proverb has it: *"Bénéfices connus, enfants perdus."*

Louis-Francois-Joseph Motte-Bossut was sent off to a Catholic boarding school at the age of thirteen. Discipline was strict, and the children were allowed home only twice a year, at Easter and during the summer vacation. In the case of Motte (as the oldest son, he was always known solely by his patronymic—even to his wife—a custom well calculated to instill a sense of family continuity and obligation to tradition), this isolation from loved ones and home was the more painful because neither father nor mother came to visit; the boy was being trained to be a man. At one point, the lad broke down and wrote home that he was ill. His mother arrived and found him in good health. "Well?" she asked. "I thought I was sick. . . ." "You thought too soon." And she turned and walked out.[32]

Mme Motte-Brédart was a businesswoman and had no time for nonsense. In April 1832, she wrote her son, who had just turned fifteen, a note, "donnée en notre bureau," entitled: "Recommendations to Motte." The first recommendation was: "Assiduous work, accompanied by much application to repay his parents for the sacrifices they have made in order to educate him and for the pleasures they have sought to provide him during his stay."[33]

At the age of eighteen, Motte returned home. One of his first jobs was to liquidate the stocks of his father's old business, to which end he was sent to Paris, where sales were slow—1838 was a bad year. We have another letter from his mother on this occasion. The themes are tenacity ("Come, my friend, courage, the times are not very agreeable, but we must win out"); thrift ("If you were to perceive that your presence in Paris was not doing any good, you would return at once"); and work ("It is unfortunate that the Carnival should take place while you are in Paris. . . . Use your time to run from morning till night, do not lose a minute.")[34]

For Motte himself, however, the problem was somewhat different than it had been for his mother. In training his children, who could look forward to places in one of the most important textile firms in France, he felt it advisable to stress not only the virtue of work for its own sake but also the uncertainties of life. Thus he wrote Léon in 1855:

> You are interested in business, you ask me if everything is going as I would like; I would be wrong to complain about the present situation, but it is impossible—know this for the future—that everything should work like a dream. Industry is a life of continuous struggle. Your neighbor does better than you: you have to do better than he; this "better" is the fruit of work, often of stubborn work; it is a task of every day, in which one seeks, by means of imagination, by means of effort, to surpass one's neighbor; therefore, work, work, always work.[35]

This theme of the survival of the fittest recurs on other occasions. In 1856, disturbed by some school reports that Léon was not serious enough in his work—the word *serieux* has connotations for the French bourgeoisie that go far beyond those of our word *serious*—he wrote:

> I want you, Léon, to be less childish and not to play any more while working. One obtains nothing, one becomes nothing if one does not study with perseverance and tenacity; and he who is light, flighty, inattentive, of dubious assiduity in his young age, runs a strong risk of being the same in his business and his conduct as an adult. Now, you know that we are living in an age when men have value only by themselves, and when intelligent and courageous clerks are every day taking the places of their masters when these last, by their lack of energy and their levity, are obliged to descend from the rank that seemed forever assured to them.[36]

Such severe words were suited to the occasion; Motte hauled his children up short when their more frivolous side got the best of them. On other occasions, however, when their work pleased and reassured him, he could be deliciously indulgent. Thus, in 1857, he wrote his boys in boarding school:

I am delighted that you recognize by your assiduity (which your success gives me the measure of) the sacrifices of all kinds that we impose on ourselves for you. . . . Continue, my good friends, and we shall again make some fine trips another year. We shall go to Germany, to Saxon Switzerland; we shall go to Holland and see its polders and canals, and if, later on, Europe is not enough for us, we shall go and make a small tour of the United States, visit the virgin forests, bathe in the waters of the Mississipi [*sic*], etc., etc. Oh! how many things there are to do, how many plans to carry out, how many castles in Spain whose tricks are not yet cooked! In short, if you behave yourselves well until the end of the year, you know, my friends, that I will know how to recompense you. The past will answer for the future.[37]

It should be noted that the gay—by Roubaisien standards, frivolous—tone of this letter was not the momentary product of a prosperous economic conjuncture. On the contrary, business was bad and raw cotton was down 30 percent, while the Motte firm was too well stocked at the old price. The point is that the education of his children was too important to Motte and too well thought out to be affected by the winds of circumstance. At the same time, of course, he did not lose the opportunity to point up the lesson of adversity: "My conclusion is the following: it is that many people have become impoverished this year, and that this state of affairs has ruined numerous families. . . . It's not the end of everybody, but it's the commercial end of many a body. . . . Prepare yourselves to see misery and remember that man earns his bread by the sweat of his brow. Every day, we recognize more and more the truth of these harsh words of the Creator to his creatures."

The letter closed with an affectionate touch to make the bitter sweet: "Until the day when you'll be harnessed to the plow and sweating like lovable little oxen ("*petits amours de boeufs*"), have a good time, work hard, take care of yourselves, and remember your loved ones."

Needless to say, no two of the bourgeois families of Roubaix-Tourcoing brought up their children identically; different material circumstances and personalities meant different methods and points of emphasis. Even within a single family, as we have seen, changes in status and wealth over two generations gave rise to a new educational tone.

Yet underneath all the variety, certain uniformities of the process of socialization may be discerned, uniformities implicit in the homogeneity of the values of the community and the stability of its institutional structure. Thus, in every case, the primary vehicle of education was the family, which included for this purpose collateral descendants of a common ancestor, who was generally still alive or who had, while living, established durable kinship bonds among his descendants.

The historical pattern was usually the following: in the first half of the nineteenth century—though sometimes before and occasionally after—a textile manufacturer would, by the act of creating an independent household and a new firm, begin a dynasty. Sometimes the patriarch was an immigrant to Roubaix or Tourcoing from one of the surrounding villages or towns, in which case the autonomy of his line was established from the beginning. Sometimes, on the other hand, he was a member of a local clan, and for a time his own household was identified with a larger kinship group. But in most cases, the creation of an enterprise in a period of rapid industrial development and change tended to mark a new departure. In view of the congruency of family and firm, the founder of the latter tended to become the patriarch of a new branch, tied by cousinly bonds to collateral branches, but a relatively autonomous kinship unit withal. With the passage of generations, of course, the sheer problem of numbers compelled further fission, usually of both business and kinship structures. Thus the Motte family, a coherent unit composed of grandfather and grandmother Motte-Brédart, children, grandchildren, and—for a while after the deaths of the founders—even great-grandchildren, gave rise by the end of the century to the branches of Motte-Bossut, Motte-Desurmont, and Motte-Grimonprez.

Within this large family group, much of the educational process was the work of the nuclear family: father, mother, and minor children. The role of the mother seems to have been particularly important, partly because of the father's preoccupation with business, partly because the mother was herself sufficiently immersed in business matters to imbue the children with a sense of direction and a feeling for industry and trade that no general discipline could have provided. In short, professional training began in the cradle, and the minds of the children of the *cotonniers* and *lainiers* were turned to manufacture even amid the classical texts of their Catholic *pensions*. Witness Alfred Motte, a brother of Motte-Bossut, whose letters from the Collège Stanislas are filled with concern for the operation of his elder's new mill. And Alfred, it might be noted, was destined to be a notary. The only legal document he ever drew up was the contract of his own partnership as a dyer.

In this process of education, the efforts of the nuclear family were seconded and, indeed, reinforced by the influence of the larger kinship group. For one thing, the extended family was the bearer of its own values: it was the embodiment of the name and reputation of the clan; it was a living expression of continuity and status. In addition, it depersonalized and objectified to some degree the training inculcated within the nuclear household. In this larger world of uncles and aunts, nephews and nieces, cousins who were at once dear friends and friendly rivals—in their own minds and, even more, in the minds of their elders—the socialization of the child was no longer a haphazard thing left to the vagaries of the mother's love or a father's indulgence, but a defined, semistandardized process whose results were under constant scrutiny. The situation was one that lent itself readily to comparison and emulation, with the reputations of the parents involved as much as those of the children.

The key institution here was the regular (usually weekly, but often more frequent) family dinner. Presiding at this occasion was the prerogative of the wife of the head of the clan—*bonne maman* or *grand'maman*—and attendance was *de rigueur* for all linear descendants, plus occasional collaterals and special friends. Thus Alfred Motte, writing to his good friend Charles Gillet, dyer of Lyons, shortly after the death of his mother, Mme Motte-Brédart: "Up to the very last month, she always received us, all of us, children, grandchildren, Sundays, holidays, and Thursdays, at the great family table. And if the food was unpretentious [*"bourgeoise"*] and the drink moderate, the charm of these family reunions was so penetrating that we have resolved to continue them in turn. We cannot deprive ourselves of this cement of solidarity which constitutes the strength of our city."[38]

Motte's pride in "this cement of solidarity" and "the strength of our city" was neither exceptional nor feigned. The bourgeois of the Nord was very conscious of the special strength and character of his institutions; he understood perfectly well what the system was and why. A descendant of one of the oldest dynasties cites the following testament of his great-grandmother:

I exhort you, my very dear children, with all the tenderness of my heart, to bend all your efforts that the peace and unity that prevail among you not be troubled ever. Know, if necessary, how to make even a small sacrifice rather than disturb the good harmony that has always reigned in the family. A united family is such a good thing that it gives almost a foretaste of the happiness of heaven, because personal happiness is doubled while pain is softened when they are shared among one's own. So if it should happen that one of you should fall on unfortunate times, I beg of you with all my love as a mother, that each of you come to his aid. Consult among yourselves on the most suitable means, the most advantageous means of pulling him out of difficulty, either by getting him honorable employment or even by monetary help. . . . In order that intimacy and confidence may continue to prevail among you, my children, you must see each other often. Look at those families that are most united here: they get together often. Well, I ask that once a month (when you will have lost both of us) each in his turn give a dinner at which no more than three courses will be served. Each of you must make it a duty to attend, because it is at meetings like that, that the heart opens up, that you exchange your little confidences, that you succeed in maintaining that tenderness and fraternal friendship that makes the happiness of families. Don't think, though, that it's enough to see one another once a month. No. I hope that each week, and each in turn, you will make it a rule to meet for coffee, or for the evening perhaps, and in all cases simply, without expense, simply for the pleasure of seeing one another.[39]

The document is a fascinating testimony to mother love, family solidarity, and the values of a quieter, less mobile age. All of these things leap to the eye and heart, as it were. Still, there are two somewhat less obvious aspects of this maternal injunction that are worth attending to. The first is the reference to "the families that are most united here." For all the completeness of the family group, the industrial bourgeoisie of the Nord had this sense of membership in a larger community: just as people observed and modeled themselves on one another within the family circle, so the families observed and took their examples from one another. (The Mottes, I have argued, were an important role model for many others.) Secondly, nothing testifies to the astuteness of this old mother as well as her prohibition against competition: no meal to exceed three courses; simple coffees and soirées, without expense. She knew that fortune would smile on her children unequally, that some would be richer than others, and she was not going to have them remind one other of these differences by conspicuous hospitality.

These regular gatherings of the clan, then, were both instrument and symptom of family solidarity. At least as important from our point of view, however, was their latent educational function—that of controlling and reinforcing the values instilled by the nuclear family. These meetings were an occasion for mutual inspection, where the elders in particular had a chance to observe and pass judgment on the young. Here cousins could be compared and shaped to group standards of comportment and attitude; here prospective spouses were brought for general scrutiny; here the influence of parents was reinforced or corrected by that of relatives, above all, that of grandparents. It was the family dinner, in other words, that gave effect to the moral ascendancy of the ancestors and thereby insured the transmission of values, not simply from one generation to another, but across the generations.

The third pillar of the edifice was the school system. French education—and this was even truer in the nineteenth century than now—was a machine to inculcate the habit of serious and highly competitive effort. Everything was so arranged as to extract unremitting labor from the pupils, who had to copy long passages from their texts in a neat, tiny hand and memorize gobs of material, some of it eloquent and poetic, some of it the driest of operational rules that in other systems would be learned in the doing. All of this, moreover, was done in the context of an unceasing struggle for place. Every month saw the headmaster or headmistress come in and read the results to the class, starting with the poorest student (get the bad news over first) and moving triumphantly to the best. Every year saw its major examinations, carefully averaged grades, published standings, palms and prizes for achievement. Moreover, all of this was intended as preparation for those crual tests that determine in large measure the lifetime career of the student: the entrance examination for the lycée or other liberal secondary school, the first baccalaureate, the second baccalureate, the competitions for admission to the grandes écoles.

French parents have always watched the schoolwork of their children closely, first, to be sure that the children achieve at least the minimum requirements for advancement to the status of an educated person, and second, to encourage them to obtain the highest possible standing in their classes. In a society like that of Roubaix-Tourcoing, the second reason was if anything more important than the first—not because parents wanted their children to be scholars (Heaven forfend!) but because achievement in school was a measure of a child's seriousness, diligence, and competitiveness—in short, a foretaste of his virtues as a man.

To this recipe, the Catholic boarding schools that were a must for the sons of the bourgeoisie of Roubaix (the daughters as often as not went to local Catholic day schools and lived at home) added a few special ingredients: spartan hardship, severe discipline, the fifth commandment, and the daily practice of prayer and piety. Here is one memoir of the *collège* at Saint-Omer in the early nineteenth century:

The education in this *collège* was profoundly Christian. Unknown then the excessive attention and the delicate regime of our modern institutions, which are obliged to condescend to the demands of all too human tenderness of the parents of our day. The students were treated there with a quite military severity; one could have thought himself in Sparta, so much did the training resemble that given in antiquity to the young Spartans.

In this establishment, fireplaces were unheard of. The classrooms were never heated, and when, in the depth of winter, the cold became unbearable, the children were taken out to the courtyard several times a day and gained back the lost heat by stamping their feet and slapping their arms.[40]

By the end of the century, then, the good old days were over. (They always are.) Parental affection had intruded its ugly head. In the meantime, the men who made the Industrial Revolution at Roubaix-Tourcoing were trained up in schools like these. They came out with a tender appreciation of the warmth, literal and figurative, of the family home; also with a certain impatience for the weaknesses of those of lesser fortitude. This meant workers especially, whose improvidence (they never seemed to put enough aside for a rainy day) and general lack of bourgeois virtues strained the understanding and sympathy of their employers. But they could also be hard on their own children.

The result of this combination of large families, extensive intermarriage, common economic interest, constant emulation, and uniform education was the development of a remarkably homogeneous, highly conformist, mutually sustaining cousinhood—the extended family writ large. All it took was one, at most two, generations for even the newcomers (and there were entrepreneurial recruits coming in from the surrounding countryside throughout the century) to be related to everyone else.

Membership in this patriciate entailed, as in all groups, certain privileges and responsibilities. It was assumed, for example, that promising young men could count on the help of relatives, first, and and then of friends, and conversely, that those who could afford to help others would do so. The correspondence of Motte-Bossut and his brother Alfred Motte is sprinkled with references to launching and rescue operations of this kind. Thus, in June 1871, Alfred sent a young M. Wallaërt to Lyons to see his friend Gillet about the possibility of setting up in business there: "I come across a young *père de famille* who assures me that he wants, by *assiduous work* [italics in text], to rebuild his position. Can I tell Wallaërt that he will have to do without my aid (assuming, of course, that allowing for the difficulties of an enterprise, the enterprise is basically good)? No, absolutely *no*. That is why I told Wallaërt that if, by a trip to Lyons, he could discover a field of work, I would assist him in establishing himself."[41]

If group solidarity and the ties of friendship imposed an obligation to help when possible, how much stronger were the ties within the

immediate family! Louis Motte-Bossut joined with his brother Alfred
and his sister Adélè Dazin-Motte in a persistent but repeatedly disappointed effort to set their brother Etienne on the path to wealth.
Etienne tried his hand at weaving, spinning, sugar refining, then
spinning again. Nothing seemed to work out well, and when he had
run out his string to the tune of almost a million francs (say, two
million 1975 dollars), it was time to assist Etienne's children. In 1874
Alfred wrote to his friend Gillet a disenchanted but determined letter
on the subject: "You will understand that this situation vis-à-vis·the
children of my brother (who are double nephews, if I may call them
that) imposes large obligations on me. With the help of God, I shall
fufill my duty; but I will not hide from you that it is painful to lose
one's time and trouble to repair the follies of others. The honor of our
name could be at stake; we will not permit it to be injured."[42]

Yet it would be a mistake to see these open-ended, diffuse family
obligations as unlimited. The bourgeois of Roubaix-Tourcoing, like
their counterparts elsewhere in France, had a well-honed sense of
pecuniary merit and just deserts. French civil law, with its careful
provision for the more or less equal division of the patrimony among
all the children, encouraged careful reckoning of shares and outlays. "I
say *your money*," wrote Motte-Bossut to his son Léon, when his
honeymoon expenses exceeded his father's gift for the purpose, "because you've now spent what I granted, and the surplus will be debited
to your account."[43] Nor was this procedure confined to personal
luxuries and extravagance with a view to discipline: it was not uncommon to calculate as closely as possible the amounts expended on
each child's education, for example, and debit accordingly his share in
the eventual estate.

Money matters were too serious to leave simply to affection. Cousins
and brothers felt no hesitation in raising these issues or insisting on the
strictest application of their rights. Thus Motte-Bossut, who wrote his
mother to reemphasize his offer of a moderate sum for her old mill,
owned at the time by his brothers and sisters, whom he reproached for
what he felt were their unwarranted demands: "Now that I've said
everything, I await the decision of my brothers and sisters; if this
building remains unoccupied, no one will be able to blame me. But if
you were to find a tenant or another buyer than myself, I would be
happy. I would be happy not to take it over and to carry out my project
on the other side of the canal."[44] Similarly, when it was time to
withdraw from Alfred's firm, Motte-Bossut found himself in disagree-
ment with his brother regarding the evaluation of the plant. They

argued tenaciously, but this in no way diminished their reciprocal affection and esteem—as the family papers bear out.

Nowhere was this pecuniary rationality more important than in making places for children and other relatives in the family enterprise. Here not only the patrimony but the reputation and status of the family were at stake, so that while almost every son (and son-in-law) of the *patronat* was expected to be a businessman for whom a place was to be made if it was not already available, care was taken to keep incompetents away from posts of responsibility and to prevent them from dilapidating the family fortune. The great-grandfather of Eugène Mathon called his daughter to him on his deathbed and told her: "Your husband is not cut out for business; at the first inventory in deficit, you're to liquidate the firm." And so it was.

Similarly, Alfred Motte, generous in establishing his own sons and known for his readiness to set a talented, ambitious artisan up in business if the affair promised well, was careful not to allow his obligations to his son-in-law to exceed the sum transferred at the time of marriage in the form of dowry. When the same Eugène Mathon, who had taken Motte's daughter Louise to wife, approached him for "advice" on his (Mathon's) plan to build a factory, Motte silently took a scrap of paper and wrote: "It costs a lot of money to become an industrialist." "I have nothing to add," he told his son-in-law.

The overriding importance of family continuity was nowhere so apparent as in the periodic crises called death, which often necessitated a division of the property and could, in the usual circumstances, precipitate the liquidation of the firm (or firms). Paradoxically, a death was generally an occasion for a reaffirmation of family unity. At such times the estate was so arranged as to distribute only those parts that had no relevance to the status and wealth of the family as a group. The business itself was simply reorganized, and special interests (in executive positions, policies, etc.) were subordinated to those of the group as a whole.

The Motte family, for example, suffered the loss of three of the sons of Motte-Bossut in the space of three years—Louis in 1901, Léon in 1903, and Georges in 1904. Suddenly, that whole generation was gone except for the youngest son, Edouard, then in his late 40s, who found himself at the head of a multiple business and a young team of third-generation relatives. The firm was thereupon reorganized. Each branch of the family contributed its part of the plant and received in return shares in a joint-stock partnership known as Motte-Bossut Fils. The division of each branch's shares was left to its members to work out. A board of directors was set up to govern the enterprise, with Edouard as chairman, and the contract of organization provided that the board should always include a member or representative of each of the branches. As before, the responsibilities were generally assigned by branch—one looking after cotton spinning, another wool, still another velvet. But all were collectively responsible to one another, and no department or mill was maintained for sentimental reasons.[45]

In short, the very adversities of life were turned to advantage.

We have, then, in Roubaix-Tourcoing a close-knit, single-minded entrepreneurial community, much of whose success can be understood in terms of the virtues it so assiduously cultivated: seriousness, work, careful management, and mutual support. It was not the only such community in France; one can cite, for example, the comparable *patronat* of Mulhouse, also clearly delineated and identified, much intermarried, and given to mutual support. But the *cotonniers* of Alsace were Protestants rather than Catholic, and Calvinists at that. They could have stepped out of the pages of Max Weber, so filled were they with their election and the high seriousness of their role as producers and employers. On balance, they were more open to technical change than the *gens du Nord*; they were also more consciously liberal and paternalistic, more articulate in their formulation of their obligations to society and progress. Nothing in France matches the public spirit and pursuit of technical and moral improvement of the Société Industrielle de Mulhouse. One might be inclined, then, to explain the spectacular success of the Alsation *fabrique* in Weberian terms; indeed, it has been done.[46] How to account, though, for the parallel achievement of Roubaix-Tourcoing? Also in religious terms?

My first inclination in trying to solve the problem was to try to do just that, that is, find something in the Catholicism of Roubaix-Tourcoing that would resemble the Protestant ethic of Weber. It was just possible, for example, that an examination of the local theological environment would disclose a strong current of Jansenist thought (admittedly long since condemned as heretical but, like most heresies, always lurking to seduce the willing believer), which is generally seen as that version of Catholicism closest in spirit and moral implications to Calvinism. Further investigation, however, quickly excluded this solution. For one thing, although Jansenism had made some inroads in the Lille area in the seventeenth century, it had, like Protestantism earlier, been quickly extirpated, Also, such writings as we have of French Jansenist businessmen bear little resemblance to those of our Northern industrialists. The values and comportment are the same, more or less, but the motivation, anxieties, and justification are decidedly different.

Take, for example, the comments of a Jansenist merchant of Lyons to his nephew and godson at Marseilles, chiding him for his dejection in the face of a trade crisis:

> I see in what a state of discouragement circumstances have driven you. Take care that it not be a temptation all the more subtle, in that detachment [from worldly goods] is enjoined upon us. Remember that Adam was condemned to earn his living by the sweat of his brow. That means that a man who is in business must make use of all his energy and all his prudence to gain the most he can, first, because of the example he sets for his children, and then, in order not to fall into a miserable state [*état fâcheux*]. Detachment makes itself known afterward by the use one makes of his wealth. Our condition is so wretched that we are caught between two extremes, equally dangerous: ambition and quietism.[47]

The activist note—the stress on energy and maximum gain—and the desire to set an example remind us here of the Roubaisien's reiterated injunctions to respond vigorously to misfortune and his equally tender concern for his children. But the tone is drastically different. Nothing like this doctrinally justified ethic of work and gain can be found in the papers of our northern manufacturers; the danger of wealth never seems to have troubled them; the goal of "detachment" would have made no sense to them. They took material ambition for granted, saw wealth as a legitimate reward of effort, and looked upon life and business as a ceaseless struggle in which only the best use of their full talents and resources would allow them to hold their own.

Even further was the Roubaisien from the position of the Weberian Calvinist, with his sense of election confirmed by virtue and success. Do you want to hear the archetypical Calvinist businessman as he survived into the nineteenth century? Go to the mountains of the Jura, where hard-working Swiss peasants learned to make fine watches in their idle hours and developed a cult of work and quality. Listen to Jules-Samuel Jéquier, who notes in his journal that as an apprentice, he often found his master demanding and arbitrary; why couldn't he too go off to the mountains with his friends once in a while? "I even remember having passed some moments of despair, but I recognized later how lucky I was to go through such a school and how good it is for man to bear the yoke from early age. God had a great task in reserve for me and He was preparing me for it. And indeed, what would this large family have become if I had not been accustomed to continued and constant work?"[48] Elsewhere Jules-Samuel notes that his future wife, herself an only child, had worked for two years as governess in a family with ten children. This he interpreted as another example of divine intervention, by way of preparing her for her great task as the future mother of fourteen.[49]

Again we have nothing like this in the Nord. On the contrary, life for the devout Catholic was full of traps and reverses; there was time for play as well as work, and the task was to combine the two in reasonable and virtuous proportions; God was not necessarily on your side, and you had to earn his favor and grace.

In short, if religion was a prime mover of northern entrepreneurship, it was a version that was significantly different from those usually associated with achievement-oriented business behavior. And indeed, when I posed the question to business people in Roubaix-Tourcoing, I found that most of them had great difficulty understanding what I was driving at. Religion and enterprise? Well, their faith did teach them of their duty to their fellow men, especially their employees, and of their general obligation to contribute to charity. But an impetus to work and moneymaking? No, not really—.

In the end, after much searching and correspondence, I reluctantly came up with a verdict that in Scottish law they call Not Proven. In the conclusion to a preliminary version of this essay I put it this way: In sum, we do not know; we can only say that, such as it was, the ideology of the textile *patronat* was a powerful force in channeling and motivating energetic, dedicated business performance; that once established, it seems to have been perfectly able to sustain itself without religious sanctification; and that it had a logic of its own that hastened the evolution of the pattern of entrepreneurial behavior, accelerating in effect the rate of industrial growth.

It was a letter of Gaston Motte, grandson of "Motte," that gave me the clue. In despair at my failure to elicit the sort of answer I was looking for by confronting Roubaisiens with the Weber thesis, I sent him a rough draft of the essay and asked once again for his comments on a possible link between religion and enterprise. He replied: "What follows is my own opinion. It was never my intention to try and prove that the Catholic religion is the animating principle at the source of industrial development in Roubaix-Tourcoing. . . . The determining principle, I think, is to be found in the spirit of enterprise of the old Roubaisien (Turquennois) and in his ardent desire to free himself from an "inferiority complex" in regard to the advantages—let's say, rather, privileges—enjoyed by the Big City (Lille), to whose prosperity he knew he contributed."[50]

I read and reread this letter, which produced in me what James Joyce calls an epiphany and what cartoonists like to represent by a glowing light bulb near the head of the character who has just had an idea. That is, all the evidence suddenly began to fall in place. What we have, if Gaston Motte's analysis is correct, is an emulative community seeking to affirm its place and dignity in the face of an advantaged rival. Success in business becomes a mode of self-assertion; and religion, rather than a prime mover, is itself a symptom of this drive.

This is the behavior of a minority under the pressure and implicit humiliation of discrimination. But why should the industrialists of Roubaix-Tourcoing, French for generations, at least as Catholic as the vast majority of their compatriots, French-speaking, white-skinned—why should they behave like a minority? Protestants are a minority in France, and in the nineteenth century they conducted themselves as one—even more than at present. The Jews are a minority even now. But Catholics? The first time I suggested this thesis to an audience of Roubaisiens, I could fairly feel their rejection. By the time I had finished the explanation, however, they came up to tell me that the argument made sense; who would have thought it?

The sense of separateness and inferiority of Roubaix-Tourcoing went back to the Ancien Régime, when Lille had been favored by all manner of exclusive privileges of manufacture, which it did its best to preserve in the face of repeated violations by the producers of the *plat pays*. Again and again the crown acceded to the demands of the master clothiers and *échevins* of Lille and reaffirmed their monopolies; the very reiteration of this confirmation is evidence of its nullity. The weavers of the country villages had lower costs than the guild masters of Lille; they also were freer to innovate; indeed, product innovation was the best way to evade monopolies explicitly linked to specified fabrics. In medieval Flanders, when the weavers of the urban centers were faced with similar competition, they marched out into the country-side and broke every wheel and loom they found; as a result they effectively killed these rural centers of industry; they also sounded the death knell of their own guild-fettered *fabriques*. The weavers of Lille would undoubtedly have done the same had they been able to. But in a centralized monarchy, in a city that was the principal military garrison on the northern frontier, they were not so free to take matters into their own hands. The one time official representatives went off to Roubaix with seizure in mind, they were stoned by the populace and forced to take shelter overnight and flee the next day. The Roubaisien could be nasty where his livelihood was concerned.[51]

These pretensions and privileges were eventually abolished: in 1762 the government belatedly recognized the fact of rural manufacture by authorizing it. But it took fifteen years to register this edict in Flanders, and the people of Roubaix nursed their resentment.

Their sense of separateness was maintained by the social and cultural gap between a village grown large and the big town. After the Revolution, as before, Lille remained the administrative (*préfecture, ponts-et-chaussées, mines, service du Trésor*) and military center of the region. The university was shared with Douai, the Church with Cambrai, and although Douai was the seat of the court of appeals, Lille had and needed the largest judicial apparatus in the area. Lille was also a major seat of industry, with important textile (cotton and linen), chemical, and engineering sectors. The result was a city of great social diversity, with a numerous and varied professional class alongside the business bourgeoisie, and a correspondingly varied assortment of styles of life.

By comparison, Roubaix was a one-industry, multicompany town. The vast majority of the inhabitants worked or depended on workers in the mills. There were a few indispensable shopkeepers, doctors, notaries—the hired help, who almost never mixed with the good society of the employer class. Life was simple in the sense that it was uncomplicated by the tensions and temptations of alternative ways of life. The workers had little time for anything besides the job, food, and sleep. They found their diversions in the cabarets (cheap bars), which multiplied like vermin (one for every twenty-two families in the 1870s), and in the frequent weekend *kermesses*, which became accessible for some miles round by excursion train from the fifties on. When you live in a *courée*, in a two- or three-room up-and-down with the floor space of a parking slot, or in an all-male workers' barracks, you want to get out as much as possible.

The *patronat* lived in a world of their own with the family hearth at its center. To begin with, the house was a pleasant, roomy, warm place, usually located close to the office. (As we have seen, this was especially true during the early years of an enterprise.) It was filled with children at play, happy noises, affection. It is easy, of course, to romanticize, but the correspondence of the Motte family gives evidence of considerably more harmony, more mutual respect combined with love, and a more successful reconciliation of work and play than we are accustomed to in our day.

Outside the home there was a void. Members of the employer class did not go to cabarets or *kermesses*. There were no clubs, no teen-age amusement or recreational facilities, none of the other refuges charac-

teristic of highly developed urban society. When the *filateurs* of
Roubaix and their families wanted to get away from home, they went
to visit relatives in the surrounding countryside; with time and wealth
they bought themselves suburban residences, with lawns and orchards
and room to ride horses, and all the children and grandchildren came
to visit. Only in the last third of the century was there a proliferation of
various *cercles* and *sociétés* where serious men could talk about their
business interests, politics, and religious questions. These made possible, no doubt, a certain dilution of the intensity of the hearth-centered
life style; but they were intended and served as reinforcements of the
employer ethos, "consciousness-raising" devices for coping with a
changing world.

This cult of family and home (I use the word "cult" advisedly) was
lauded by the Roubaisiens as a special local virtue and a sign of divine
grace. By comparison, the urban world outside was a sink of iniquity
and temptation—too much diversion, too much amusement, too many
strange and subversive ideas. Lille was bad enough; Paris, "*c'est le
tombeau.*" They sent their children forth on their first business trips
with all manner of warning against the seductions of the big city;
remember Mme Motte-Brédart's injunction to her son Motte: "It is
unfortunate that the Carnival should take place while you are in Paris
. . . use your time to run from morning till night; do not lose a
minute."

They need hardly have bothered: so well was the Roubaisien
antiurban value internalized that in that time, at least, the children
could hardly wait to get home again. Their parents were sometimes
worse: some of them went to Lille no more than once or twice a year;
their workers traveled more than they did. Those who had to go to
Paris on business returned home as fast as they could; at least this is
what they said and wanted to believe. When Motte-Bossut went on
vacation-convalescent trips to the Riviera in his latter years, he was
counting the days till his return from the moment he unpacked his
bags.

Here as in so much else, these values and preferences were conscious
and explicit: simplicity was an ideology at Roubaix. Here is Motte's
reaction to a letter from his wife, who was enjoying a short visit to
Brussels with their little daughter Célina:

I received your good letter Friday and read in it with pleasure of the success
of my daughter Célina. But I am beginning to fear that our young lady is
becoming too worldly. She already cries to be taken to the theater—at seven
years of age. What will she do then at seventeen? Flower garden, summer
casino, zoo, botanical garden, concerts, plays, ballets, vaudevilles—to know

everything at the age of seven, what an advanced education! To have frequented the finest society of Paris and Brussels, to have made a splash in these two capitals, what a success! But will she still know how to make her life in our humble village? Will she still know how to accept our modest ways? Our so simple family life, the monotony of a dining-room conversation? I am beginning to fear that she won't. She'll want to ride horses, run to swimming school, shine at the concert, make an impression at all the balls. Well . . . count on it, my little girl! Make the most of it while you can, because once back in Roubaix, we'll give you your balls, your concerts, your baths. You'll get up, you'll put on your short skirt, your clogs; you'll be off to the class to learn your grammar and arithmetic; you'll hear the mad music that your little brother Edmond makes; in the evening, you'll darn my socks (because I use up a lot of them); you'll eat a dish of beaten milk, then you'll go to bed. What a contrast, eh? And yet, you'll try to be happy. That's why it's time you came back so that you will still know how to find pleasure in the peace of our home.[52]

(Poor man! He need not have worried. Two years later, little Célina, "the best of all our children," along with her younger sister Mathilde ["*comme elle est mignonne, comme elle est gentille!*"], was swept away by typhoid fever. Motte consoled himself with prayer: "God, who made her too perfect to stay on earth, has called her back to him . . . He has taken from us a child who gave us only joy and whom we were perhaps too proud of. . .").[53]

All of this gave the Roubaisien a sense of superiority to his neighbors in Lille. He worked harder, prayed better, lived better. Social contacts were minimal, and marriage with Lillois was discouraged; you could lose a daughter that way.

Even so, there was also a nagging feeling of inferiority. The Lillois, after all, were more sophisticated, more fashionable, more knowing. They saw the Roubaisiens and Tourquennois as country bumpkins grown rich and found their airs of virtue and *sancta simplicitas* tiresome. And indeed, the Roubaisien cultivation of their work-and-purity ethic was in large part a defence mechanism—an instrument of self-reassurance and self-assertion. The pattern is a familiar one: one finds similar responses among all identifiable minority groups confronted with socially prestigious modes of behavior and threatened with the dissolution that comes with assimilation—from the "wall" that rabbinical tradition has built to separate Jews from gentiles to contemporary Black Nationalism and the "Black is beautiful" campaign.

As in all such situations, the evolution of a counterethic takes time: as a response to outside pressures and temptations, it is almost instinctive at first but assumes definition with the practice of contact; and its lineaments are the sharper as contact increases and the threat of assimilation grows. So with Roubaix: Motte's mother did not have to give much thought to her behavior; she did what came naturally. But Motte was very conscious of his problems, of their larger significance, and of the moral implications of his decisions. He thought about what he did and defined it in universal terms. In effect, he formulated an ideology and played the role model.

The result of this heightened self-consciousness was an increasing pressure to conform. This is the kind of thing it is not easy to get evidence of, but such records as we have testify to the exceptional solidarity of Roubaix and its intensification over time. Three potentially divisive, critical issues illustrate the process:

1. *Child labor.* In 1841 the French parliament, after some years of agitation and debate, finally passed a law for the protection of children working in factories. The law set minimum ages and maximum hours and provided for a corps of voluntary inspectors to check plants and enjoin compliance. The law met with opposition in many industrial centers, for obvious reasons; and nowhere was enforcement more difficult than in the Nord, where the small family firms saw state protection for workers not only as an inadmissible interference with private contract and enterprise but also as an immoral violation of the relationship between father and children.

But there are degrees of harshness. As difficult as the Northerners were, the most difficult were the Roubaisiens. To begin with, it proved impossible to get any member of the *patronat*, active or retired, to serve as inspector, for no one was willing or dared to intrude in this way on the privacy of friends and relations. By dint of hard searching among the professions and trades and with a mixture of eloquence and temptation, the prefect finally succeeded in constituting a commission: a doctor of medicine, a pharmacist, and three *rentiers*, two of them former manufacturers. Four months later, there were only three left—not really a quorum. Still, at Roubaix one had to make do. From Paris came angry, prodding reminders: the Nord was setting a bad example to other departments; enough time had been lost.[54] So the commissioners proceeded very gingerly, confining themselves at first to friendly conversation and observations. As Motte's uncle Bossut put it—he was mayor of Roubaix—"the commissioners hope that gently, bit by bit, everyone will satisfy the law. These gentlemen know the area and seem to understand their mission perfectly: to lead people to conform to the law without exercising too much rigor—because after all, what the worker needs most is bread!"[55]

In the end, however, the task of the inspectors proved impossible. There was violations everywhere, and violators were in no mood to heed these gentle hints. Community sentiment hardened, and the inspectors found that they were putting their personal situations in danger. They offered their resignations *en masse*, pointing out that further pressure on the manufacturers would only cost the children their jobs; besides, working conditions were good, and where they were bad, as in the preparing rooms, where temperatures ran from 18 to 25 degrees centigrade and the air was filled with noxious fluff and "miasmatic" odors, there was simply no way to do without children. And anyway, these conditions "are not so injurious to the children's health." They were healthier than children employed in cottage weaving, which was not subject to factory inspection. The prefect's efforts to dissuade the inspectors were unsuccessful. They were only too glad to be rid of the task.[56]

Six years later, Roubaix was still holding out; it was impossible to put a commission together. This was the only such holdout in the Nord; as far as I know, the only such in all of France. In desperation the secretary of the prefect called for a paid inspector. This took the onus off members of the Roubaix community; and once a few of the manufacturers fell into line, they became enthusiastic supporters of enforcement on the others. By August of 1852, some ten years after passage, the law finally came to Roubaix.[57]

2. *Tariff.* French textile manufacturers were resolutely protectionist, even prohibitionist. The only exceptions were those branches producing in large measure for export and unafraid of foreign competition—the silk trade of Lyons, fine cotton printing in Alsace. Some of the makers of fine woolens, worsted, and mixed fabrics in the Nord were in a similar position, but they never broke the solidarity of the protectionist front.

This solidarity showed at its strongest in the 1860s, when the imperial government moved to institute a regime of freer trade and concluded to this effect a series of commercial treaties with the major European powers. The first and most important of these was the so-called Cobden-Chevalier treaty of 1860, which was drafted on the basis of private, semisecret negotiations and was presented to the French business community more or less as a *fait accompli*. The famous tariff inquiry of that year, which gave us perhaps our most voluminous single official source on the structure of French industry in the nineteenth century, was conducted after the fact to determine at what level the new, lower duties should be set.

The industrialists of the Nord were incensed at the whole procedure, and once again the Roubaisiens were most persistent in their resentment and most solidary in their subsequent refusal to cooperate with the government; when, almost a decade later, the authorities tried to get manufacturers to testify at a new tariff inquiry, the Roubaisiens replied with indignant reminders of the highhandedness of 1860. Efforts to persuade individuals to violate the general interdiction foundered on their perfectly reasonable apprehension that they would be made to suffer both commercially and socially. One letter from a good friend of the prefect (they used *"tu,"* the familiar form, with each other) regarding the prefect's success in enlisting the cooperation of the man's nephew, a cotton spinner named Eugène Crépy, gives some sense of what was at stake. The letter notes that Crépy is young, just starting on his career as an industrialist, and related by blood and marriage to many other manufacturers of the area. "That would be enough already to impose silence on a young beginner who has his career to make and who, rightly enough, fears lest he sow the seeds of hatred and hostility that would undoubtedly go beyond his role simply as an industrialist. I had enough trouble myself ten years ago to blame my son-in-law for his reserve; he knows how to keep his counsel."[58] In other words, Crépy is probably going to have to pull out, and I'd be grateful if you let him off the hook.

Crépy was from Lille; and while we have nothing comparable for a representative of the *fabrique* of Roubaix, we should not infer therefrom that the *patronat* there would have been any less severe in punishing deviation. Quite the contrary. Consider the interesting case of Louis Eeckman, textile broker of Roubaix and member of the Chambre consultative de commerce of the city from 1849. Eeckman, as a merchant, made the mistake of dreaming dreams about the cultivation of export markets; the agitation of the industrialists for high protection was in his opinion a mistake. As a result, he lost business and resigned from the chambre in 1869. There was no room for heretics at Roubaix.[59]

This brings us to our third area of conformist pressure:

3. *Religion.* Roubaix was not always so fervently Catholic as at the end of the nineteenth century. In the eighteenth century, what later generations were pejoratively to call Voltairean ideas penetrated the consciousness of the local bourgeoisie and gave rise to a local version of *le rouge et le noir*—skeptics and *bien-pensants*. This split survived to the middle of the nineteenth century. There were already families of extreme devotion, but this was much less common than it was to become. Lambert-Dansette theorizes that the new, rising industrial dynasties had less time for prayer and repentance than the older, established families, many of them gently losing out in business or retired and living on rents and annuities (*rentes*). He cites the "Souve-

nirs" of Toulemonde-Dazin, who, together with his young wife, made it a rule in 1860 to attend mass daily, a practice they maintained for the rest of their lives. "We followed," he writes, "the good example of M. et Mme Toulemonde de Mollet, even though attendance at weekday mass was much less customary [*dans les usages chrétiens*] in 1860 than today."

What had happened? Two things: first, the revolution of 1848 had thrown a fright into the *patronat* that it was never to forget (in the case of Roubaix this was compounded by the almost unprecedented experience of major strikes the following year); second, the community sought to define its position and institutionalize a set of values that would have normative force. As the years passed, freethinkers and other religious dissidents found themselves cut off from the most precious personal and social connections: dinner invitations to the right homes; good friends and potential spouses for their youngsters; membership in the clubs that counted. More and more of the cultural, political, and even business life of the *patronat* came to be explicitly tied to the Catholic church and church-connected organizations; the *cercles catholiques* for the workers from 1872 (with employer participation); the Association des patrons chrétiens, founded 1878; the retreats of Notre-Dame de Hautmont, from 1880.

The rise of a legitimate labor movement (the right of workers to form unions was not accorded by law until 1884) further stimulated the "devotionalization" of enterprise. The employers were scandalized at the prospect of class conflict in the form of an adversary relationship between workers' organizations and employers. It was not only that work and wage disputes could be costly; the *patrons* were at least as troubled by the implicit breach of the father-child relationship. (The typical response of a Roubaix employer to a strike was that it was fomented by outside agitators.) It was no coincidence, then, that the passage of the new labor legislation should have been followed in Roubaix by the inauguration of a series of *syndicats mixtes*—"unions" comprising both workers and employers—and that these should have been deeply imbued with Catholic ideals of social harmony, the priority of the spiritual over the material, and the obligations of charity.

Along with this development went an increasing intrusion of religion into the work situation itself. The motivation here emerges clearly from an earlier report on the subject from a linen manufacturer of Marquette (a village north of Lille) to the prefect of the Nord: "We think we have succeeded up to now in protecting the working population of our establishment from the pernicious doctrines that for some years now have wreaked so much havoc in that class of society; and we are bending all our efforts to instill in them a dignified comportment and to maintain them in the Faith, which is so necessary to support life's trials, whatever may be our position in the world."[60] Already in the first half of the century there were pious employers who converted their shops on occasion into chapels. One son of a *fabricant*, addressing the Société de Saint-Joseph in 1842, remembered singing the litanies of the Virgin with the workers of his father's mill, followed by a *De Profundis* for those workers who had died during the year.[61] But this was just a harbinger of things to come: the cult of Notre-Dame de l'Usine, the recitation of prayers before work, annual retreats for women workers, omnipresent statues of the Virgin in offices and shops, use of nuns as moral supervisors in the women's workrooms, gifts to children on communion, classes on catechism for the children, time off for services, and so on. In this kind of plant, a freethinking worker stood out like a bad apple and risked being cast aside as a bad apple. Small wonder that one of the grievances expressed by witnesses from Roubaix before the parliamentary inquiry into labor conditions of 1904 was the tyranny of religion in the mill.[62]

The growing preoccupation with the Church and religion from the 1870s reflected not only the fear of subversion from below but hostility to the anticlericalism of the new republican regime. Most of the manufacturers of the Nord were profoundly conservative, to the point of supporting the monarchist forces in the early years of the Third Republic. One of the rare exceptions was Alfred Motte, brother of Motte—rare in the sense of both his liberalism and his economic ability to sustain his political independence. In 1877 he made a brief allusion to the penalties of deviancy in a letter to Gillet: "I wish you could know the danger incurred, in a small city, by a manufacturer [*façonnier*] rash enough to oppose head-on the opinions of the ruling class. These people have no notion of their political obligations. They will not concede that it is possible to oppose them with the sole aim of serving our country. By the very fact of not espousing their likes and dislikes, their prejudices, even their errors, you cost yourself their co-operation."[63]

For all the tenacity of the local *patronat*—in spite of ingenious efforts to gerrymander the electoral districts and smother the irreligious urban vote with the voices of right-thinking country folk—they were forced to yield one position after another to the rising tide of democracy. First they lost their pocket seats in the national parliament; then their control of local government. Before the century was out the first socialist mayors were sitting in the city halls of the Nord.[64]

This is not the place to follow this passionate and protracted struggle between the vested patriciate and the proletarian adversary it had created. Suffice it to point out that the notables chose to fight the battle on the issue of church and state and turn it into a nineteenth-century version of the millennial struggle, going back to Creation, between the powers of light and darkness. They fought the establishment of public schools, especially for girls. When the Jesuits were expelled, the *patronat* founded a program of retreats, moved into their quarters, and tried to maintain their influence under another guise. These and similar initiatives were resented by the authorities, who saw them as an evasion of the law and as schools for reaction. The *cercles catholiques* were suppressed in 1889. The retreats and the Catholic Ecole de Haut-Mont were closed down in 1901. There ensued more than a decade of litigation, wound up in 1914 by the expulsion of the clerical personnel and confiscation of the property. Then came the war, and the church-state struggle lost much of its immediacy. In 1918 the school bought the property back and resumed its program of saving the souls of those members of the elite who were "desirous of leaving for a few days the affairs of this world to concern themselves in solitude with the great business of eternal salvation."[65] In sum, everything concurred to give the *patron* of Roubaix the sense that he was a beleaguered fighter in the army of virtue; that he was indeed the member of a victimized minority; and that his way of life was not simply a by-product of his values but a declaration and sign of faith—in effect, an end in itself.

The trouble with ideologies is that they take on a life and force of their own. The *patronat* of Roubaix could not expect that religion harnessed to the cause of class harmony and hierarchy would always follow familiar congenial paths. They should not have expected the clergy of the dour, damp northern factory town, with its ghastly *courées*, atrocious infant mortality rates, and militant socialist propaganda, to echo indefinitely the soothing remonstrances of the Bishop of Nîmes: "And you, good workers, . . . learn to understand the intelligent and Christian generosity of your chiefs, or rather, of your fathers. While giving you work, they also want to give you principles. They are not satisfied simply with providing you with the bread of this world; they want to help you with the conquest of heaven. May this kindness find you [one word illegible] and grateful."[66]

The primary aim of the Church and its lay coadjutors was to reopen the dialogue with the lost sheep; the purpose of the devotionalist employers was to enclose and domesticate their workers and shield them from dangerous ideas. With time a potentially sharp conflict developed between the Association catholique des patrons du Nord and the Oeuvres des cercles. The latter saw the coexistence of wealth and misery as evidence of the great breach made by liberalism and the Smithian economy in the happy equilibrium that purportedly had once prevailed between employer and employed. They deduced therefrom, under the influence of Alfred de Mun, La Tour du Pin, and Léon Harmel, that only a reorganization of the economy under corporatist lines and the acceptance by employers of a new set of social responsibilities would set things aright. The employers in turn saw any corporatist control as an infringement of their freedom of enterprise, a threat to employment, and a vehicle for eventual state intervention. The conflict focused on the usefulness of the syndicat mixte: the Church came to be convinced that there were legitimate interests of the workers that could not be handled within mixed unions and began to sponsor "independent" or "free" unions; eventually the Bishop of Lille formally asked the *patronat* to abandon the *syndicat mixte* and learn to live with workers who were no longer their children.

This was after the war, and the *syndicats mixtes* were already moribund. The mills had been devastated. Inflation had replaced a century of monetary stability. The challenge of socialism had been sharpened and transformed by the triumph of the Bolsheviks in Russia; and the *patronat* had to learn a new way of life and work in a new world. It was a world in which the family spirit and moral militancy that we have analyzed here had lost some of its virtue and potency. This is a subject that takes us beyond the confines of the present essay, but let me review briefly some of the changes and their consequences for the structure of entrepreneurship:

1. The last quarter of the nineteenth century saw the demand for textiles level off with the population. This was especially true for French firms, long accustomed to selling behind the shelter of tariff walls and hence confined by necessity and habit to the home market. Meanwhile, advances in technique increased substantially the cost of new equipment and the scale of efficient operation. The small family firm of Roubaix, which had been well suited to respond to the whims and fluctuations of the much fragmented but growing market of the mid-nineteenth century, now found itself confronted by a technology it could not afford. Its habit of short runs, special orders, wide variety, and product innovation still gave it a certain suppleness; but it was beaten in the market for the best-selling staples.

The family enterprise had real advantages in time of contraction. It owed little or nothing and so did not have to support the burden of continuing overhead outlays. By employment of family members, the white collar payroll could be kept to a minimum; if times were hard, the partners pulled in their belts. Bigger and better equipped enterprises might sink under the weight of their financial commitments; the small *boîte familiale* would hang on. This tenacity in adversity, however, had one serious disadvantage: it was often linked to a nonrational attachment to the patrimonial enterprise and a reluctance to face up to change and reality. The assumption was that toughness, persistence, and work were enough; plug away, and the balance sheets will take care of themselves. As a result, the enterprise could slide into a series of ever worsening losses that would in the end swallow the patrimony. Already in the 1870s Alfred Motte commented on the paralysis of initiative in the face of adversity, on an unconscious avoidance of bad news, on "ostrich entrepreneurship"; writing to Gillet about his own insistence on up-to-the-minute balance sheets, he noted with disappointment and even disgust:

> At least we, we know every month, how we're getting on. If the results are disastrous, they are followed or preceded by others that are better. But when you don't keep track of your business, so to speak, on a day-to-day basis, you sometimes end in catastrophe. . . . What bowls me over, is the apathy of these people who are just rushing to their ruin. You'd think they were hypnotized and nailed to the spot; their lethargy is almost physical; their attitude is that of fatalists who expect heaven to restore their prosperity. I don't know what I would do if I were in that kind of situation; it seems to me, though, that I couldn't sleep. . . .[67]

The solution to growing competitive pressures lay in mergers and conversions to joint stock, but this came hard to Roubaix. Instead, there was a kind of regression to the responses and attitudes of an earlier era. Every effort was made to compress labor costs, primarily by maintaining a working week that was as long as possible and by replacing adult males with women and children. In contrast to the pattern that prevailed in other advanced industrial centers, the women and children spinning cotton in the Nord went from 26 percent in 1845 to 59 percent in 1896; in weaving the percentage rose from 52 to 65 percent over the same period. At the same time, there was increased reliance on cheap, docile Belgian workers—in spite of their instability and allegedly lower level of skill.[68] Meanwhile, the industrialist turned to the government for favor and support, denounced all programs of social insurance that added to his tax or wage bill, and espoused the extreme protectionism of his forefathers.

In short, the *patronat* tried to preserve its place and profits by regression to underdevelopment. In the short run, it made good sense.

In the long run, it encouraged technical obsolescence and set the stage for a winnowing the more painful for its postponement. Worse yet, it was the workers who paid most of the bill. The following analysis by German technicians puts the matter very well; they speak of

the tendency of French industrialists to keep using existing installations so long as they do not give rise to losses. As the installations are old and have usually been handed down from one generation to the next, all revenue net of the cost of raw materials, wages, etc. . . . is pure profit. Interest on initial capital and amortization of the plant are no longer relevant in most cases. These establishments, though they may take on the form of corporations, are owned by a few members of the same family. Whereas in Germany, this financial situation would encourage firms to go on improving their equipment . . . the French, with the mentality of *rentiers*, cling fearfully to installations that yield them the same income for years, preserving them like precious family mementos. These conceptions and these habits, which are changing only very slowly, have been in every respect a serious obstacle to technical progress.[69]

2. Malthusian population pressures within the *patronat* inevitably burst the protective shell of a closed society. Whether one tries Fibonacci sequences or geometric progressions, there is simply no way in which job creation can keep up with the kind of birth rate practised among the bourgeoisie of Roubaix-Tourcoing. When Motte's daughter Marie died in 1940, she left behind 1,388 nephews and nieces, grand-nephews and -nieces, great-grandnephews and -nieces, great-great-grandnephews and -nieces, and great-great-great-nephews and -nieces. It was all well and good to say, *"Pas de mariage sans cheminée qui fume,"* but where could anyone put that many chimneys and find a market for their products? The more enterprising Roubaisiens moved out to other pastures—to the United States, where there is a veritable colony of them in the Pawtucket area; to French North Africa; to nontextile holdings (in the late nineteenth century, brewing was a special favorite). An increasing number of children went into the Church—not so much a sign of greater piety as of increased progeny. Even so, there began an inevitable drain of talent to nonbusiness occupations and to other cities. This was the path that the great Protestant dynasties of Mulhouse had already followed two and three generations earlier. How're ya gonna keep 'em down on the farm. . . ?

The *courées* have now all but disappeared; the Belgians have been replaced by North Africans; the mills continue to produce, but most of the family enterprises of the past have merged into joint-stock companies and linked up with textile interests in other parts of the country. The social register no longer proudly prints its honor roll of prolific families, partly because there are many fewer of them, but more particularly because it is no longer the sort of thing people brag about. The old mansions on the wide boulevard that goes out of Roubaix toward Lille have long since been subdivided and rented to proletarians. Roubaix itself has increasingly merged into the larger Lille conurbation, and easy transport has broken down much of the sense of local identity.

This is the story of most minorities in an open, highly assimilative society. They have to fight to preserve their separateness, and after a while, the fight does not seem to be worth the effort. In the crucible of French society, the distinctive bourgeoisie of Roubaix-Tourcoing held out longer than most. Some of them are still holding out, cultivating the memories and values of yesterday in an unpleasant, changing world. The difference between them and their ancestors, however, is that the great-grandparents and grandparents were in the forefront of economic growth and developed an ethic to suit their drive and enterprise. What we have today is more the sociology of nostalgia.

NOTES

1. *Les grandes familles de Roubaix-Tourcoing et environs* (Lille: La Croix du Nord, 1936–); Bibliothèque Nationale (hereafter cited as B.N., followed by the carton number), Lc^{35}. 34.

2. To avoid complications, I shall treat Roubaix-Tourcoing in this essay as a single unit characterized by the same social structure and values. In point of fact, Roubaix-Tourcoing began as separate villages, and it was only as a result of industrial expansion that the two agglomerations spread and merged in the course of the nineteenth century (see the maps in Raoul Blachard, *La Flandre* [Paris, 1906], pp. 442–43). There were subtle differences in style and character between the two communities, and the analysis that follows is probably more applicable to Roubaix than to its neighbor. Blanchard writes, at ibid.: "There exists a Roubaisien spirit and a Tourquennois spirit, each as far from the other as possible. Roubaix is bold, enterprising; the Roubaisien willingly calls himself an American; like the Anglo-Saxon, he devotes himself with as much ardor to recreation as to business, and he cultivates sports more than his counterpart in any other French city. The Tourquennois . . . is as thoughtful and as punctual as his neighbor is lively and impetuous [*"primesautier"*]." The reader will note, however, that these are not necessarily differences in values, but in personality and manner.

3. Blanchard, *La Flandre*, pp. 375, 394. The figure given on p. 394 differs somewhat from that on p. 375. The source is Théodore Leuridan, *Histoire communale de Roubaix*, 5: 88.

4. Blanchard, *La Flandre*, p. 441. On the decline in population after 1789, see ibid., p. 400.

5. See François Crouzet, "Les conséquences économiques de la Révolution: à propos d'un inédit de Sir Francis d'Ivernois," *Annales historiques de la Révolution française* 34 (1962): 182–217.

6. Dieudonné, *Statistique du département du Nord*, 3 vols. (Douai, 1804), 2: 322.

7. At the time, the largest cotton-spinning enterprise in the Nord was Gautier-Dagoty at Douai, with 9,000 spindles, integrated with weaving and printing. In 1808 there were about a million spindles in the country as a whole, of which 450,000 were in Normandy and 132,000 in the Nord (45,000 in 1806; 200,000 in 1810). Louis Bergeron, *L'épisode napoléonien: aspects intérieurs, 1799–1815* (Paris: Seuil, 1972), p. 201.

8. On these crises, Odette Viennet, *Napoléon et l'industrie française* (Paris, 1947); Alexandre Chabert, *Essai sur les mouvements des revenues et de l'activité économique en France de 1789 à 1820* (Paris, [1949]), esp. bk. 6, chap. 3.

9. The share of fuel in total costs varied with the kind of equipment employed and the fineness of the product. The data given by manufacturers at the tariff inquiry of 1860 do not permit an accurate breakdown; still the overall proportions are a rough guide. Cf. *inter alia* France, Ministère de l'Agriculture, du Commerce, et des Travaux Publics, Conseil Supérieur du Commerce, de l'Agriculture et de l'Industrie, *Enquête: Traité de commerce avec l'Angleterre*, 8 vols. (Paris, 1860), 4: *Coton*, pp. 232, 242, 359; 3: *Laine*, pp. 409, 537, 618. Another measure: even when one compares Britain and France, where coal prices were in a ratio of 1 to 3, 4, or even 6, one finds that the difference in fuel costs accounted for only a modest fraction of the total cost. Thus, a delegation of cotton spinners from Lille, where coal cost about 3.5 times as much as in Britain, estimated that the difference in fuel costs represented only 5.75 percent of the product and only 12 percent of the overall margin between the two industries (ibid., 4: 207). In weaving, where the French were still relying heavily on cottage labor in the 1850s and 1860s fuel was even less of a factor.

10. This is not to say that coal made no difference. It was no accident that the plant buying coal at 20 francs was the newer one (ibid., 4: 55, 57 [testimony of Octave Fauquet]).

11. François Crouzet, "Le charbon anglais en France au xixᵉ siècle," and Marcel Gillet, "L'âge du charbon et l'essor du bassin houiller du Nord et du Pas-de-Calais (xixᵉ siècle–debut du xxᵉ siècle)," in *Charbon et sciences humaines: Actes du colloque organisé par la Faculté des Lettres de Lille en mai 1963*, ed. Louis Trénard (Paris: Mouton, 1966), pp. 25–52, 173–206; Marcel Gillet, *Le bassin houiller du Nord et du Pas-de-Calais de 1815 à 1914: études économiques et sociales* (Université de Lille-III, 1972) pp. 401–42. This photo-offset version has since been republished in printed form as *Les charbonnages du Nord de la France au xixᵉ siècle* (Paris: Mouton, 1973). The corresponding pages are 241 ff.

12. Roubaix, Archives Municipales, F IIᵈ 1, letter of A. Renaux, 10 October 1814.

13. Charles Dupin, *Forces productives et commerciales de la France*, 2 vols. (Paris, 1827), 1: 234–35.

14. On 13 August 1854, in the middle of the dry season, Louis Motte-Bossut, perhaps the leading cotton spinner in Roubaix, wrote his wife who was away on vacation: ". . . If I have the good fortune to have enough water in the canal to work without stopping, I'll do everything I can to spend a week at Blankenberghe with you. What a time I'd have playing the do-nothing!"([Gaston Motte, ed.], *Motte-Bossut: une époque —1817–1883—lettres de famille* [privately printed: n.p., n.d.], p. 42).

15. France, Ministère du Commerce, *Enquête relative à diverses prohibitions*, 3 vols. (Paris, 1835), 3: 189, testimony of Mimeral; Maurice Lévy-Leboyer, *Les banques européennes et l'industrialisation internationale dans la première moitié du xixᵉ siècle* (Paris: P.U.F., 1964), p. 164.

16. Lévy-Leboyer, *Les banques européennes*, p. 165.

17. Ibid., p. 167.

18. These figures are derived from Paul Spagnoli, "The Arrondissement of Lille in the Nineteenth Century: A Study of Demographic Change" (Ph.D. Diss., Harvard University, 1974), chap. 2, table 9.5

19. The classic source is G. Jacquemyns, *Histoire de la crise économique des Flandres (1845–1850)* (Brussels, 1929). On nighttime burial, see p. 345.

20. On the place of Belgian workers in the textile industry of Roubaix-Tourcoing, see Pierre Reboul, "Les troubles sociaux à Roubaix en juillet 1819," *Revue du Nord* 36 (1954); Firmin Lentacker, "Les ouvriers belges dans le département du Nord au milieu du xixe siècle," ibid., 38 (1956): 5–15; Centre d'études de Lille, "Aspects industriels de la crise: le département du Nord," in *Aspects de la crise et la dépression de l'économie française au milieu du xixe siècle, 1846–1851*, ed. C.-E. Labrousse [Société d'Histoire de la Révolution de 1848, "Bibliothèque de la Révolution de 1848," vol. 19] (La Roche-sur-Yon, 1956), pp. 101–7; Georges Franchomme, "L'évolution démographique et économique de Roubaix dans le dernier tiers du xixe siècle," *Revue du Nord* 51 (1969): 201–47.

21. Alain Hennebicque, "A propos de la conjoncture économique dans l'arrondissement de Lille au début du xxe siècle," *Revue du Nord* 50 (1968): 85.

22. I owe special thanks to Gaston Motte, a gentleman and scholar if ever there was one. It was he who first introduced me to the psychology of Roubaix and the Roubaisiens; he who made it possible for me to penetrate what would have otherwise remained a closed and somewhat inscrutable society. My interviews with other representatives of the *grandes familles* were all made possible by his friendship and encouragement, and the readiness of others to help me was tacit testimony to their universal esteem and affection for M. Motte. A wonderful man: gentle, courtly, always neat and proper and yet warm and relaxed; I shall never forget the twinkle in his eyes and his ready smile.

23. The most important of these monographs is the voluminous study by Jean Lambert-Dansette, *Origines et évolution d'une bourgeoisie: quelques familles du patronat textile de Lille-Armentières (1789–1914)* (Lille, 1954), which, though it deals with Lille and Armentières, contains considerable material relating to Roubaix-Tourcoing. In addition to such data as were presented in this book and a number of articles, Mr. Lambert-Dansette has been good enough to make available to me his manuscript notes on Roubaix-Tourcoing, and these have helped to fill in the story. I should like to take this occasion to thank him for his generous assistance and encouragement.

24. The husband's trip, which took him all around France and to Italy gathering orders, kept him on the road over four months, during which time his wife was in sole charge of the business. See Henry L. Dubly, *Le caducée et le carquois: correspondance du Sieur Barrois et de sa femme, 1790* (Lille, 1926), pp. 227–28 (letter of 19 September 1790).

25. Gaston Motte, *Motte-Bossut: un homme, une famille, une firme, 1843–1943* (Tourcoing: privately printed, 1944), p. 19.

26. Jules Burat, ed., *Rapport du jury central sur les produits de l'industrie française à l'Exposition de 1845*, 2 vols. (Paris, 1845), 1: 176.

27. [Gaston Motte, ed.,] *Lettres de famille*, p. 8 (letter of 10 December 1816).

28. Ibid., p. 185 (letter of 4 November 1882).

29. *Lettres de famille* (letter of 15 September 1880).

30. Ibid., p. 52 (letter of 25 November 1855).

31. *Lettres de famille* (17 February 1871, letter to Charles Gillet).

32. Ibid., p. 9.

33. Ibid., p. 10.

34. Ibid., pp. 11–13 (letter of 22 February 1838). The mother was all business, but the father added a postscript that, for all its exhortations to enterprise, made some allowance for spare time: "I want not to be disappointed in my expectations. Therefore visit lots of

friends, even more religious services, few or no shows, and every day a prayer in one or another church." Both parents, it should be noted, addressed their son as *vous*.

35. Ibid., pp. 49–50 (letter of 22 October 1855).

36. Ibid., p. 56 (letter of 11 February 1856).

37. Ibid., p. 77 (letter of 27 November 1857).

38. *Motte-Bossut: un homme, une famille, une firme*, p. 80.

39. Cited in a letter from Pierre Bayart, an attorney of Lille, 18 June 1858.

40. Abbé Huard, *Edouard Lefort* (Paris, 1893), pp. 8–9.

41. *Lettres de famille* (letter of 12 June 1871). Cf. also the cases of Alfred Delesalle, Alfred Dazin, and Aimé Delfosse-Motte, respectively friend, nephew, and brother-in-law of Motte-Bossut (ibid., pp. 127, 152, 155).

42. Ibid., p. 133. Motte-Bossut had joined earlier with his brother-in-law Louis Wattinne-Bossut (the husband of his younger sister Pauline) in financing the first industrial steps of Alfred.

43. Ibid., p. 125 (letter of 10 May 1872).

44. Ibid., p. 104 (letter of 16 February 1866).

45. *Motte-Bossut: un homme, une famille, une firme*, pp. 119–33.

46. Henri Laufenburger and Pierre Pflimlin, *L'industrie à Mulhouse* [H Laufenburger, *Cours d'économie alsacienne*, vol. 2] (Paris, 1932).

47. Louis Bergasse, *A la mémoire de Dominique Bergasse, négociant lyonnais, victime de la Révolution (1749–1793)* (Marseilles, 1943), p. 10.

48. François Jéquier, *Une entreprise horlogère du Val-de-Travers: Fleurier Watch Co. SA* (Neuchâtel, 1972), p. 49.

49. Ibid., p. 50, n. 29.

50. *Lettres de famille* (letter of 31 January 1958).

51. The best source is A. de Saint-Léger, "La rivalité industrielle entre la ville de Lille et le plat-pays, et l'arrêt du Conseil de 1762 relatif au droit de fabriquer dans les campagnes," *Annales de l' Est et du Nord*, 2d ser., 2 (1906): 367–404, 481–500; see especially pp. 369, 380–81, 486, 494.

52. *Lettres de famille*, p. 44 (letter of 24 September 1854).

53. Ibid., p. 60 (letter of 12 July 1856, Motte-Bossut to his sons). Mathilde, who seemed to be doing well, died about a week later.

54. Archives Nationales., F^{12}-4712, letters of 5 December 1842, 6 July 1843, 11 November 1843, 29 March 1843, and 20 February 1844.

55. Archives Départementales, Nord, M-613/5, letter to the prefect, 28 February 1844.

56. Archives Nationales, F^{12}-4712, undated letter of resignation from the Sub-Commission of Inspection for Roubaix to the president of the Commission for the Nord; same to same, 28 October 1844.

57. Ibid., letter to the Secretary-General-Delegate of the prefect of the Nord to the minister of agriculture, 10 October 1850; extracts of register of deliberations of the *Conseil Général du Nord*, 1 September 1851 and 27 August 1852.

58. Archives Départementales, Nord, M-572/4, letter of Adolphe Poullier [Poulliez?], undated. See also, in the same *carton*, letters of Motte-Bossut, 8 December 1869; Charles Jongler, 7 December 1869; and Scalabre-Delcour, 10 December 1869.

59. Ibid., M-555/7 and M-572/3.

60. Ibid., M-605/4, letter of 1873. I owe this reference to Jean Lambert-Dansette.

61. Huard, *Edouard Lefort*, p. 22.

62. France, Chambre des Députés, *Session de 1904, No. 1922. Annexe au procès-verbal de la 2e, séance du 12 juillet 1904*. Even the explusion of the congregations does not seem to have halted the practice. Thus one witness: "The day the decree hit

their congregation, they [the nuns, *congréganistes*] removed their robes and their hoods and put on blouses and hats like the others; but they stayed in the shop, in the same place, watching over the same women workers, asking them if they go to mass and if their children go to the sisters' school. The majority of the women workers at Motte-Bossu [*sic*] belong to the *syndicat mixte*, because they are obliged to" (testimony of M. Vanwaerrebeke, p. 172). The evidence makes it clear that the greatest pressure was felt by the women and children, partly because the French were resigned to male indifference in matters of religion, partly because the woman and children were more easily intimidated.

63. *Lettres de famille* (letter of 22 November 1877). Alfred Motte had presumably been "on the wrong side" in the parliamentary crisis of 16 May 1877. The use here of the word "*façonnier*" is significant: these were specialists producing yarn or finishing cloth for other industrialists rather than working solely for their own integrated enterprises —hence, they were particularly susceptible to economic reprisals.

64. See especially Jacques Ameye, *La politique à Tourcoing sous la Troisième République* (Lille, 1963), pp. 13–108.

65. Notes of Lambert-Dansette.

66. Ibid. No source given.

67. *Lettres de famille* (letter of 26 December 1877).

68. Hennebicque, "A propos de la conjoncture économique," pp. 85–86.

69. This comes from the German report on industry in occupied France (1914), as cited in ibid., p. 86. The passage refers to the machine-building industry but would be equally applicable to textiles.

INNOVATION AND BUSINESS STRATEGIES IN NINETEENTH- AND TWENTIETH-CENTURY FRANCE

BY MAURICE LEVY-LEBOYER

FOR SOME TIME it has been customary in France to criticize business leaders and underrate their achievements. At first this may seem odd, since the performance of the French economy has rested on the ability of entrepreneurs to keep concerns going in competitive markets and at best to promote mechanical and organizational innovations whenever possible. But economic progress is often a source of mixed feelings. In the early stages of industrialization, the *notables* —*rentiers*, landed proprietors, members of declining trades and industries—were bound to lose prestige and power. Consciously or not, many people tended to look upon technological change as socially wrong and upon profit as the outcome of financial speculations or abusive exploitation of the workers, who had been enticed away from the land. To this group of critics, large and vocal in the post-Napoleonic era and again in the 1880s, should be added all the people in the middle and lower classes who suffered unemployment or capital losses during the economic depression, since many individual firms were unable to maintain a steady economic growth or to redress the system through which incomes and wealth were distributed. Doubts were raised in progressive circles about the efficiency of the market mechanism: in the early 1900s and even more in the 1930s, it was widely held that a minority of families could manipulate the market for their own advantage, slow down technical progress, and even fail to exploit the potential of innovations. Thus, economic change was interpreted as benefiting the few at the expense of the many.

These negative and conflicting views, which assume that the flow of inventions depends somewhat arbitrarily on the good will of individual entrepreneurs, are in no way peculiar to any single industrial country. But in France, partly because of the massive retardation that followed the two world wars and partly because of the rigidities inherent in French society, what might have been a guarded and skeptical attitude towards business in general gave way to active opposition. No doubt feelings of frustration help to explain this attitude and limit its validity. But at least two of the arguments that gave weight to this thesis of poor French industrial performance should be given here.

The first argument is qualitative and refers to management procedures. Although corporations were catching up with family enterprises in the early twentieth century,[1] it is well known that French business organizations remained somewhat ill adapted. They were highly structured, led by authoritarian managers who demanded from their collaborators strict discipline but no initiative. They denied themselves both the security of any sort of cooperation with their competitors and also the facilities of outside credit—perhaps because they were afraid of losing control and, with it, the possibility of handing down the firm to a successor of their choice. Firms remained less efficient than they could have been, the staff being unable, it was argued, to make urgent and simultaneous decisions, to absorb technical change when the pace quickened, to expand operations, to reach a level where size automatically leads to economies of scale, etc. Many pictures of French businessmen have been drawn along these lines. One, by Auguste Detoeuf, writing in 1938, is a classic. It purports to describe the career of one Oscar Barenton, an imaginary Polytechnician of a class in the early 1890s, who had first worked in a family firm engaged in light engineering and reached fame in the interwar period as the founder of a multinational trust, starting in the ice-cream trade, the C.G.C.G. (Compagnie générale de la crème glacée). This industrial empire was, in fact, doomed to failure because the chairman had simply transferred the ideas and the outmoded methods of the typical family entrepreneur to his new position:

The French industrialist [i.e., O.-L. Barenton] works extremely hard. Since he pays his collaborators poorly, they are mediocre. But he does not mind. He hates eminent collaborators. Therefore he is obliged to do their work and does not have time to do his own. He is peerless in a middle-sized enterprise where the eye of the master can see everything, but mediocre in a big firm where one should trust others. He does not get along with anyone, except sometimes with his old clients, because he serves them conscientiously. But he is as isolated in dealing with his competitors as he is with his staff. He never takes chances. He hates the thought of borrowing from a bank, and considers himself dishonored if any drafts of his are in circulation.

The French industrialist lives for the present, with no thought of the past. He asks nothing of the future. For him, the future is that very bright day when he will retire and hand over his business to one of his sons. If the truth be known, he will die in harness because his sons are not up to the task and because he will never believe that anyone else, no matter who he is, can do as well as he does.[2]

The second argument in support of the thesis that French industrial performance was "sluggish" has a factual basis. It calls attention to the size, unusual among industrial nations, of French business units. In 1962, France had about 500,000 établissements and 5,275,000 people working in the industrial sector; that is, an average of 10.6 employees per unit. Such a figure is not exactly comparable with those recorded earlier for French shops (which excluded one-man firms and the smaller shops); these were 16.7 in 1840–44 and 14.0 in 1861–65. It amounts to only half of the average registered in present-day industrial countries of northern Europe and one-fifth of the average in the United States. Clearly, such a statistic is no basis for generalization: French établissements include, without distinction, all manufacturing sites enumerated by commune; they must not be confused with industrial establishments as they are listed in other countries or with French industrial firms. These terms do not refer to the same bookkeeping entities.[3] Yet it is correct to view them as the indirect sign of very decentralized industrial structures—contrasting sharply with the administrative bureaucracy. And they have remained essentially unchanged: according to the censuses of the working population, since 1850 the number of patrons (heads of establishments or self-employers) has remained stable, in the neighborhood of 1.5 million for a salaried labor force of 4 to 5 million. This means that the ratio of employer to employee must have been approximately 1 to 2.5 until about 1880, and only slightly higher than 1 to 4 (for men) in the early 1920s.

Obviously, if these two points have any foundation, one could argue that outmoded management went along with outmoded structures and made the French economy less adaptable to the modern world. Since the managers had the responsibility for making investments and adopting more productive methods, they should be held responsible for the results and called to account.

However, it should be stated clearly that this view, though current in Detoeuf's day, is no longer justifiable forty years later.

First of all, there is a strong temptation to equate economic stagnation with poor management and, conversely, to give an enterprise credit for such success as it may encounter. So, now that quantification has enabled us to go beyond the narrow framework of business cycles—the only measuring device available to the observer or the historian in the depression of the 1930s—it is clear that the overall performance of the French economy has been satisfactory. Except for one difficult period when the volume of output per head increased by only 0.6 percent, that is, from 1860-64 to 1890-94, the annual rate of growth has been steadily rising: from 1.3 percent in the period 1820-65, to 1.6 percent in 1895-1928, and to 1.9 percent in 1929-63. This fact alone calls for a revision of certain prejudices about managerial practices.

In addition, the small size of the average French *établissement*, which is taken to represent a business unit, is still considered a statistical proof that managers sacrificed business expansion to family security. And the argument seems plausible. There are strong reasons to believe that smaller firms are at a disadvantage. They are unable to benefit (or they benefit less) from economies of scale, as can be seen by comparing values added per man in firms of various sizes (table 7[1]). Small firms seem reluctant to invest, probably because of the disproportionate burden of amortization when the volume of sales is limited. And since they deprive themselves of external financing, they are quite

TABLE 6
Employers and Salaried Employees in France, 1851-1921, Selected Years
(in thousands)

	Industry, Transportation, Commerce (men only)						Industry Only (men and women)			
	1851	1866	1881	1896	1906	1921	1866	1896	1906	1921
Employers	1670	1730	1665	1535	1790	1485	1450	1350	1760	1425
Employees	2110	2495	2715	3820	4000	5210	2275	2915	3010	3945
Total number of workers	3780	4225	4380	5355	5790	6695	3725	4265	4770	5370
Average number of workers per firm	2.26	2.44	2.63	3.51	3.20	4.50	2.57	3.16	2.71	3.77

SOURCE: F. Simiand, *Le salaire, l'évolution sociale, et la monnaie* (Paris, 1932), 3:54. The averages per firm have been calculated without distinguishing between employers who worked alone and those who had salaried employees.

TABLE 7 (1)
Labor Force and Capitalization of French Industrial Firms, 1962–66

Size of Firm by Number of Employees	% of Total Labor Force	Value Added per Employee (in millions F)	Annual Investment per Employee (in thousands F)	Fixed Capital/ Sales Ratio[a]	Cash Ratio[b]	Financial Ratio[c]
Fewer than 20	24.7	13.0	1.06	0.28	1.45	1.78
20 to 99	21.5	17.7	2.16	0.32	1.27	1.63
100 to 499	27.0	19.2	2.60	0.47	1.55	1.57
500 to 999	9.5	20.8	3.35	0.68	1.90	1.44
1000 and over	17.3	28.6	5.43	1.10	1.97	1.25
Total	100.0	—	—	—	—	—

SOURCE: A. Babeau, "La croissance et le financement des petites entreprises industrielles," in *La capacité de concurrence de l'industrie française* (Dijon, 1970). For the annual rates of growth in sales and profits, see M. Didier, *Croissance et dimension des entreprises*, INSEE, E (1), 1967, p. 125.

[a]The fixed capital/sales ratio relates gross fixed capital to 1962 sales.

[b]The cash ratio is the product of cash assets (ready and available cash and inventory, minus short-term debts) divided by the monthly sales.

[c]The financial ratio represents the share of fixed capital financed by permanent resources (capital and reserves).

vulnerable to short-term fluctuations: self-financing and interfirm credit are the first to be affected by recessions.

Yet one should not make too much of this type of reasoning. Size is not always the relevant criterion for efficiency: in many instances the constraint of indivisible equipment does not hold, investments being made by discrete units; there are branches (the garment industry, as opposed to steel mills) where economies of scale are minimal; markets, especially in the luxury and sporting goods trades, may be quite narrow, so that they require limited series and therefore limited units of production. Moreover, it seems likely that the use of labor, which so far has not been entirely supplanted, is optimal in smaller firms where efficiency and motivation can be stimulated. Finally, recent statistical studies in France have shown that rates of growth in terms of sales and output per firm are at a maximum in medium-sized firms, probably because these are in a better position to absorb technical innovations and specialize in risky novelties, while large firms make decisions rather slowly, according to formalized institutional procedures, and are tempted to seek security through diversification. This latter fact, incidentally, might explain why their level of profit is higher (table 7[2]). In short, one could argue that medium-sized firms, so widespread in France, actually sacrifice profit and family security to growth. This is contrary to the accepted view.

TABLE 7 (2)
Sales and Annual Growth of French Industrial Firms, 1962-66

Sales per Firm (in millions F)	Average Annual Rate of Growth	
	As % of Sales	As % of Gross Profits
0 to 9.9	6.5	5.6
10 to 49.9	8.5	4.8
50 to 99.9	10.5	6.7
100 to 499.9	7.8	6.1
500 and over	6.6	10.8
Total	7.4	7.7

SOURCE: See source for table 7 (1).

A third reason for finding Detoeuf's view unacceptable today is the modern view of management. Management remains central in all discussions because people used to regard it as an independent variable. They had the impression that, irrespective of technical change and market conditions, there was *one best way* to organize business, allocate work and assign responsibilities, minimize conflicts, stimulate collective and individual motivations and incentives, etc. But research in the psychology of organizations has suggested that management (as well as size) is somehow determined by environmental circumstances. Two types of management stand out. One is based on a vertical hierarchy, with an independent manager and a responsive personnel—a structure Henri Fayol described at the turn of the century. It was the result of a stable environment where the process of production could be rigidly divided once and for all, leaving the staff free to deal with current problems of finance and marketing. The other type is a loose organization, meant for bilateral consultations, where work is fragmented and kept flexible and where the management is accessible and the personnel independent because priority is given to product differentiation or, better, to research and development of technical innovations.[4] In this respect, the small number of levels in the hierarchy and the vertical command that Detoeuf derided when describing Barenton's activities were probably not the result of his family leanings but of the static technology the C.G.C.G. used and the limited market it supplied.

Step by step, when reviewing opinions and research findings, one is led to believe that preconceived ideas have been accumulated against business managers ever since the days of Balzac and Zola but that the realities of French business life are not, as yet, well covered by the historical literature. There is a discrepancy between the apparent immobility of business structures and the overall development of the industry; between the geographic dispersion of the workers, the multitude of small shops as they are registered in French statistics, and the actual size of the production units at different points of time; between the weight attributed to family considerations—which did have their true importance in the past, when money markets were poorly organized—and the decisive impact of technology and market constraints on present-day managerial practices. Too often, the gaps in our knowledge have been filled by ideas circulated in novels and in the press: people were trying to find out what was wrong with French business organizations and personnel. But the procedure should be turned around. If it is agreed that there is no set rule for management, no ideal size for business units, and more specifically, that the performance of many firms has been quite satisfactory—the sustained growth of the French economy is a datum to be reckoned with—it becomes necessary to look anew at the record of French businesses, to reevaluate their success, and to specify the ways by which they expanded, absorbed technological change, and adapted to the environment in which they operated. This calls for an investigation of business enterprises from the points of view of (1) their personnel or labor force, (2) their managers, (3) their objectives, and (4) the types of strategies they adopted.

SMALL BUSINESS

Cost factors are often neglected when dealing with French manufacturers' attitudes. And yet, as industry supplied mainly labor-intensive products, one should mention at the outset the rising cost of labor among changes that shaped nineteenth-century production and business policies. It is a fact that, due to the growth of incomes and the diversification of economic activities in the agriculture sector, such reserves of underemployed labor as existed until the 1830s had become exhausted. After a long period of stagnation, nominal wages doubled between 1840 and 1880, and they continued to rise because of improvements in productivity and unionization. Moreover, since technical progress originated in a few large cities and spread unevenly through the country, wage disparities between urbanized regions and the countryside remained high. Compared to the average found in southern, central, and western France, net per capita income in 1864 (and 1954) was twice as high in Paris and its surrounding area and stood at some 20 percent higher in the industrialized regions of northern and eastern France.[5] Ways had therefore to be devised to protect industry against these changes. This effort led, at an early date, to experiments in the field of personnel management and eventually contributed to the development of small-scale enterprise.

Employers had to choose one of two policies. They could move activities away from Paris and other cities, where labor was demanding, to cheaper areas or sections of the country. Many businesses were indeed decentralized for this reason, mostly in the 1760–1840 period, and relocated in the countryside; in 1848, some 1.2 million industrial workers lived in the rural districts, 85 percent of these in the processing stages of work. Again in 1880–1900, when female labor came to be more widely used in industry, the number of home workers rose, to more than 1.5 million in 1896 and close to 1 million in 1936.[6] Yet, as work and plant relocation became less efficient with the passage of time, manufacturers sought to remain competitive while keeping to the same lines, by developing new machinery, revamping their organizations, and above all by professionalizing their personnel. Paternalism, that is, a practice in which the work force is trained and protected by its managers, was to some extent forced upon the employers by the very conditions of the labor market and became a permanent feature of management-labor relations.

Paternalism had been a set rule in artisanal industries, which depended on the transmission of crafts through apprenticeship and which always required close contacts between masters and workers. But it remained necessary in the new industries, for the mobilization of a large number of hands and the discipline of factory work posed two problems: (1) creating a stable labor force, although life in the countryside had accustomed people to irregular patterns of work, seasonal absenteeism, and a very high annual turnover; and (2) training workers for specific tasks, because certain skills in mule spinning, puddling, hewing, etc., were rare and sometimes lacking in the initial stages of industrialization. It should also be noted that while technical innovations eventually made it possible to substitute unskilled for semiskilled workers by training them on the job in a few weeks, they never completely eliminated the need for highly skilled personnel: 30 percent of the labor force in the first printing works; 25 percent in the cotton mills around 1840; about the same ratio in the coal mines of the 1860s, and so on.[7]

Accordingly, from the early decades of the nineteenth century, restrictive measures were adopted. Skilled workers were hired under long-term, automatically renewable contracts. Working conditions were made subject to internal regulations, were registered with the public authorities, and provided for penalties in case of violation or absence. And the instability of the labor force was somewhat restrained by legal devices, work books (1803), identity cards (1811), etc. At the same time, however—and these measures were to prove the most effective—manufacturers sought to create a kind of company loyalty by establishing and subsidizing general or technical schools and by offering services such as medical dispensaries, cooperative stores, and low-cost housing. From the very beginning some firms, irrespective of their size, created emergency funds in which fines as well as sums withheld from salaries were kept in order to provide for indemnities in case of accident, for pension schemes, sick benefits, and help for widows and orphans.[8]

Until about 1840, this policy was confined to the textile mills and the clock and machine shops in Alsace and Franche-Comté—and to this day these regions show the highest concentration of students in technical schools—as well as to a number of iron works and coal mines in isolated places; by 1883, about 90 percent of the 124,000 French miners were affiliated to such emergency funds. But as industry spread throughout the country and as larger sums were collected—more and more frequently from both employers and employees—social services provided by manufacturers were found in more and more places, from the northern textile mills to the paper and silk plants of the Dauphiné to the sugar refineries of Marseille. The most comprehensive schemes were in such large enterprises as Anzin, Saint-Gobain, or Le Creusot (whose work force after 1860 reached some 12 to 15,000 hands), which had fairly large sums to manage. At Le Creusot, where schools were opened in 1837, the social budget amounted to 200,000 F per year in 1869 (23 percent for the purpose of education) and reached 2 million F in 1900.[9]

While one might not claim, as one historian does, that "in the midst of the surrounding countryside French industrial plants appeared [in mid-nineteenth century] as centers of intellectual life,"[10] some facts suggest that manufacturers' policy did have a positive effect. In the 1870s, for example, before primary education had become compulsory and free, the literacy rate reached 93 percent in the capital and in the industrialized regions around Paris and in eastern France, compared to an average of only 78 percent in the agricultural areas and 86 percent in the intermediary regions of the North-West and the Rhône-Alps, where rural migrants had just begun to settle.[11] However, the rise in the cost of labor, equipment, and raw materials and the increase in taxes eventually put an end to these paternalistic policies. Employers had to limit their wage costs by specializing the workers, mechanizing and rationalizing operations, and by substituting paid child labor for adult labor. This led to a growing disregard for apprenticeship contracts: those in Paris dropped from 19,730 to 16,900 between 1860 and 1872, while the total work force kept rising from 390,000 to some 470,000.[12] Furthermore, technical progress made it necessary—so it was argued by the trade associations as early as 1863-64—to give workers a general training before teaching them specific skills, which were bound to become obsolete.

Thus, after the 1860s, the links between schools and factories were somewhat loosened because of changes in labor costs and educational curriculum. Nonetheless, the results achieved up to that point should not be neglected. Nor should it be forgotten that as a substitute for what had been done in the past by individual firms, manufacturers' organizations, together with the local authorities, founded and operated in the main industrial cities a large number of schools in order to train managerial personnel and lower-level staff for the traditional industries, and at a later date to diffuse efficiently modern technical innovations. At the beginning of the twentieth century, aside from the practical instruction still given on the job for people at work and the extra-credit courses available in the public schools (some 1,500 offered these in 1902), there were perhaps 35,000 students in technical institutions—42 percent of them in the private and municipal schools, according to a sample analysis published in 1906 at the behest of the Conseil Supérieur du Travail—and an average number of 64,200 in the 1935-39 period.

In short, the morale and well-being of the workers have been of concern to certain groups of employers. And it is only fair for historians to describe paternalistic policies as the result of religious and social attitudes. But the technical and educational aspects of paternalism have also had their importance, for they no doubt contributed, albeit not exclusively, to the establishment of norms and attitudes in the work force that had a true impact on business development.

In the absence of statistical studies on levels of education and on work motivation at various points in time, it would be risky to attempt a judgment about collective behavior. Still, given the artisanal tradition, the emphasis given to technical training, the widespread availability of general education,[13] and also the fact that 65 percent of the population in 1880 (and still 49 percent in 1931) lived in rural districts—so that large numbers of city dwellers had kept ties to the land and agrarian values—it seems evident that many workers must have had not only technical skills (the wage range was narrower in France than in other industrial countries at the end of the nineteenth century)[14] but also a genuine desire for autonomy and self-realization through work, which are the driving forces of small businesses. Proofs after the event are difficult to produce. Yet one could mention the feelings of frustration, despite material improvement, which have been an important factor in the strike movements of the late nineteenth century, the rapid and fairly constant absorption of new technologies, and the fact that every innovation was propagated through a proliferation of small shops.[15]

This unusual tendency toward dispersion can be explained, first, on the demand side, by the initial isolation, both social and geographic, of the consumers (patterns may have been regionally different) and by the time lag in terms of innovation that kept transportation technology behind that of production. New techniques spread over the country and remained unconcentrated. There were some 165 printing works in 1806 and still 90 in 1852; about 700 cotton-spinning mills in 1860 and more than 400 (with a similar capacity of 5 to 6 million spindles) in 1880; 2,380 electric power plants and distribution companies by 1914 and still 1,200 in 1931.[16] The use of beet roots in the sugar industry, to add another example, raised the number of inland mills from 60 to 540 in the 1830s; the differential in freight rates (by land and by sea) had theretofore confined refineries to the ports and limited their number to 70. Transportation costs, consumer habits and probably the high proportion of rural clients contributed to the continued partition of markets. In the automobile industry, three-fourths of the factories in 1914 were located in provincial towns close to the countryside, which absorbed 45 percent of the output. Panhard and Levassor had primarily sought the market of country physicians, and after the war, the first customer to purchase a Citroën car, on 1 June 1919, was a cattle-dealer from Beaulieu-sur-Dordogne. Business had to adjust to a decentralized market.

On the supply side, the skills and flexibility that labor had acquired, thanks to a sometimes very advanced division of industrial work, must also be taken into account. The conversion of the engineering industries of eastern France, during the phase of overcapacity experienced in 1880–1900, has been explained by the possibility of "turning to specialists who would supply cast-iron and aluminum parts, castings and bearings for electrical motors, motor and cylinder blocks, transformer vats, sheet metal chassis for automobiles, aluminum or steel oil-pumps, etc."[17] The new automobile firms were manufacturers in name only, since they ordered most or all of the necessary parts from outside and simply assembled them on a chassis, leaving the finishing to an independent body-shop. Many other cases could be listed, shifts from one to another line being facilitated by experience acquired on the job and, quite often in the later part of the century, in a school. It should be recalled here that the leading technicians after the war years in the

Renault, Citroën, and Peugeot plants had been trained in the 1890s, Louis Renault at the Ecole Diderot, Jules Salomon at the Ecole supérieure de commerce et d'industrie at Bordeaux, and Philippe Girardet at the Institut d'électricité of Grenoble.[18] In this respect the success of the 1900–1930 period can be taken as a result of the employers' earlier interest in technical education.

In the second phase, when the problem was no longer that of introducing but of actually exploiting new techniques, when firms had to find an optimum size according to potential levels of demand and also to factor costs, dispersion remained a permanent feature of the industry. Indeed, while many innovations made it possible to substitute capital for labor and to set up large factories, they also led to a multiplication of service jobs and of small production units. During the first industrialization period, many industries increased their output by relocating in the countryside. In upper Normandy, for instance, the cotton industry gave employment to a stable number of factory workers (24,000 and 26,000 in 1829 and 1847), while outdoor personnel in the weaving and finishing branches grew from 70,000 to 125,000; the ratio between modern and traditional employment thus changed from 1:3 to 1:5. And this was not peculiar to one region, since out of a total number of 4,000 firms in the French cotton industry around 1860 (compared to 700 in Normandy), there may have been 2,900 in the weaving trade.[19] Again, in the post-1890 industrialization period, quasi-artisanal shops experienced a renewal of activity because the wider availability of energy at home boosted work in the weaving and the cloth trades and also to such branches of the industry as tools and precision instrument making. Furthermore, the installation, repair, and maintenance of durable goods created jobs halfway between industry and services. Partly as a result, 70 percent of the employers in 1906 (and 61 percent in 1926) still had no employees at all. This of course tends to distort statistics, for the average firm is arrived at by relating the whole work force to the total number of employers. It should be added that if the industrial *établissements* declined in the countryside after 1860 (quite sharply in the 1880s), urban artisans adapted better to the interwar depression: units of less than ten workers employed 58 percent of the industrial personnel in 1906, 41 percent in 1926, but still 39 percent ten years later, and about a fourth after the war; periods of strain helped them to survive.

Economic fluctuations had another paradoxical result in the case of medium and large concerns. Expansion periods made it possible to increase both productive capacities and the number of firms, since any influx of orders could be filled (partially and at enhanced cost) by the creation of independent units or by subcontracting some of the extra orders. The study of the 496 manufacturing concerns that operated at Saint-Denis during the second half of the century seems conclusive: there was a large increase in the total number of firms in periods of sustained growth—203 foundings and 15 closings have been noted for 1850-74—and a relative stability, that is, 106 foundings and 73 closings, in the next recession (fig. 1). And one finds the same process in the automobile industry: statistics show a total number of 30 assemblers in 1900, 57 in 1910 (after the crisis of 1907), and at least 155 firms in the prosperous period just before the war—perhaps as many as 210, if one uses the figures provided by the trade association; thereafter, they dropped to 85, only to rise again to 117 in 1920, and 156 in 1924, as sales and firms grew side by side. And though depressions had the opposite effect, it should be pointed out that the departments of very large firms

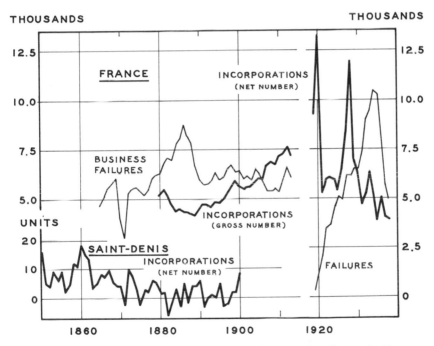

FIGURE 1. Number of Business Incorporations and Failures in France, 1850-1939

SOURCE: *Annuaire statistique de la France* 52 (1946), pp. 68–70; J. F. Nicol, *l'industrialisation de la commune de Saint-Denis dans la seconde moitié du XIXe siècle* (Nanterre: University of Paris-X) 1972).
NOTE: Business incorporations have been presented in net numbers, i.e., after deducting firms that were closed or dissolved during that period, for Saint-Denis from 1850 to 1900 and for France after 1919.

were sometimes split off as a protective measure—such cases have been noted, for example, in the Alsatian textile industry (1820–40) and in the steel industry of central France (1880–1900). Similarly, medium-sized firms survived the 1932 crisis by the expedient of converting, for instance, from watches to meters, or else by taking up intermediary productions left to them by better situated companies; in 1936 Renault stopped making carburators, radiators, etc., and distributed its orders among subcontractors. In short, phases of prosperity brought a great surge of firms, while depressions may not have had a commensurable effect in reducing their number.

In this perspective, even if we leave out of the picture the less than marginal shops, it seems that French business structure presents at least two original features. One is the continued existence of small firms inherited from earlier centuries (table 8, cols. [1], [2], and [3]). They are decentralized by their very nature, but more so in France than elsewhere, no doubt because French industry was able to supply more labor-intensive products than industries in other countries; in these older fields, shops of fewer than 100 workers still occupy in France some 60 percent of the labor force (col. [4]), compared with 51 percent in Germany and 38 percent in the United States.

The other feature is the "de-concentration" of large enterprises in periods of expansion. This seems to be warranted even today in the newest industries, where one would expect fairly large units of production: in the automobile, engineering, and shipbuilding sectors, the percentage of the labor force working in the fewer-than-100-worker plants is again 27 percent in France (col. [12]), compared with 15 percent and 16 percent in the other two countries. In other words, large establishments are about the same size everywhere because technology is similar from branch to branch and dictates the optimum level of production per plant—in France in 1962 we find an average of 2,310 employees per plant of more than 1,000 workers; in the other western countries, 2,435. But France stands apart since the share of the total labor force employed by small and medium-sized firms is of unusual importance, for reasons having to do with skills and social norms, interfirm relations, product range, etc. Consequently, we have here a dual structure that is apt to mask the very existence (and significance) of big business.

BUSINESS LEADERSHIP

Even though nineteenth-century techniques were such that business firms grew through discrete investments with small capital

TABLE 8
Structure of Industrial Establishments in France, 1962

Industries[a]	Group 1				Group 2				Group 3				Total (13)
	Food (1)	Metals (2)	Textiles (3)	Subtotal (4)	Mining (5)	Chemical (6)	Paper (7)	Subtotal (8)	Machine (9)	Auto (10)	Steel (11)	Subtotal (12)	
% of total labor force	10.4	11.6	29.9	51.9	4.0	9.0	2.4	15.4	17.1	5.2	5.8	28.1	100.0
% of total no. of plants	18.8	18.7	42.0	79.5	2.6	3.0	0.6	6.2	6.3	5.0	1.0	12.3	100.0
Median no. employees per plant	28	69	78	—	120	260	160	—	518	4,000	2,100	—	144
Average no. employees:													
all plants	6	7	7	7	16	31	39	26	36	52	234	47	11
plants with 50 employees and over	155	180	151	—	204	251	181	—	269	714	232	—	215
plants with 1,000 employees and over	1,301	1,556	1,477	—	1,667	2,107	1,348	—	1,982	4,025	2,919	—	2,311
% of total labor force in plants of:													
1,000 and over	1	4	5	4	9	20	5	15	26	66	67	42	17
500–999	7	8	7	7	13	16	13	15	12	10	11	11	10
100–499	24	26	30	28	32	30	45	33	31	12	16	24	27
10–99	28	34	32	31	30	24	31	27	25	8	5	18	27
1–9	40	28	26	29	16	9	6	10	6	4	1	5	19
Total	100	100	100	100	100	100	100	100	100	100	100	100	100

SOURCE: J. P. Nioche and M. Didier, *Deux études sur la dimension des entreprises industrielles*, INSEE, E (1), 1969.
[a] The industries have been grouped together in order to facilitate the reading of the table. Reference at (1) is to agricultural and food industries; at (2), to the manufacture of metal goods, including precision instruments; at (3), to the textile, leather, wood, and printing industries; at (6), to chemicals, glass, rubber, and plastics; at (9), to the construction of electric and nonelectric machines and also to ship-building; and at (11), to the production and refining of ferrous and nonferrous metals.

coefficients in plants offering limited economies of scale, and though competition in an open market system with almost no barrier to entry afforded opportunities for turnover of leadership, it is well known that French business leaders formed a rather closed group. This was partly due to the consolidation of inequalities that came about in the early part of the century, when the twenty-years' depression that followed the sale of national properties and the end of war slowed down new investments in real estate. Moreover, since industry is one avenue for upward social mobility, the smallness of the entrepreneurial class was also due to the business failures of the first two generations of manufacturers. Those engaged in industry during the prerevolutionary era were ruined in the 1790s by inflation, shortages of raw materials, and the regression of incomes and of demand. As for those who temporarily benefited from the .artificial isolation of the country during the Napoleonic wars, they were faced with a too-drastic debasement of inventories and with British competition in the decade after 1810. To be sure, new leaders did appear in France. But by comparison with other countries, fewer among them were workers rising through the ranks and more were merchant-manufacturers, partly because many among them had been able to hedge against financial insecurity by sending their capital abroad, which enabled them subsequently to gain control of the market. Besides, the weight of the financial sector remained preponderant for a long time to come. The board of the Bank of France, which may be used to represent the employer elite, has long been dominated by merchants and merchant-bankers: this group still retained 47 percent of the seats in 1840–60 and 36 percent in 1860–80, while new men coming from industry at large reached 35 percent of the votes only in 1880–1900, and 43 percent as late as 1900–1920. With the passage of time industrialists gained status, but only after the 1860s.

Hence, for a long time, upward social mobility among industrialists remained uncommon. Plants requiring a higher than average capital coefficient, i.e., ironworks, spinning mills, and even sugar refineries, were often set up by merchants' associations; this was the case in Alsace from the early part of the century, in the outlying ports in the second quarter, in northern France after 1840. In all the industrial regions very large concerns—big from the start, led by industrial dynasties—existed side by side with a mass of smaller firms, whose drive and whose shortcomings have already been delineated. So far, only the cotton industry of Normandy did not fit into this pattern. In 1847, with 34 percent of the national productive capacity, 300 spinning mills, and an average of 4,400 spindles per plant (compared with 15,000 in Alsace), it

appeared to be an open milieu run mostly by successful clerks and
foremen who had moved upward. But research has shown this situation in Normandy to be a statistical anomaly based on an analysis of
averages. In fact, the variance of plant sizes was very high in the region,
and there was a host of derelict shops, about a hundred in the 1820s,
which had no power-machinery and which were only marginally used
alongside of a small group of large plants that were managed by two
sets of manufacturers. The members of some ten Protestant families
from Bolbec had entered the cotton-printing trade in the 1750s,
working at times with artisans from Switzerland or South Germany.
The descendants of general merchants and bankers from Rouen and
adjoining cities had done the same, the bankers having either financed
the mills that were built in the 1780s by English mechanics or started
their own upon their return home after the French Revolution.
Together, these two groups dominated the field as long as the problem
of financing inventories remained central to the industry; in the 1840s,
to take one case, the ten largest firms among them employed 60.4
percent of the labor force working in the regional printing works. They
strengthened their hold when the use of power looms, self-acting
mules, and coal made the textile sector more capital-intensive and
consequently more concentrated. In 1806, the ten top firms, with a total
of 80,000 spindles, owned 26.8 percent of the spinning equipment;
but in 1868, they had 560,000 spindles and some 6,000 power looms,
i.e., 29.1 percent and 35.2 percent respectively of the regional capacities.[20]

The other feature of business life at that time was inertia. Families
very seldom lost control of a firm they had founded. At Saint-Denis in
the second half of the century only 134 out of the 496 firms already
mentioned came under a new trade name; that is, 27 percent of the total
number, probably 12 percent per generation (or 15 percent if we
include firms that went into bankruptcy). Changes in ranking were
also infrequent. The big firms, once established, remained in the lead
and, from a social point of view, in the same hands. They had easier
access to external financing, a more efficient commercial network, and
wider margins, and by reinvesting profits they did adapt to the more
widespread use of coal and the wider (internal) markets that opened up
in the 1840–60 period. The three leaders in printing, to refer to
Normandy again, were on the average 70 years old in 1855, and the four
leading spinners in the Lillebonne district around 1900 had been in
business for 85 years. Similar examples could easily be duplicated in
other regions and branches, since older firms have always had the
advantage of an early start and have been protected by lesser firms that

sprang up in the later phase of an upswing and were the first to fold under the impact of a recession. At Nantes, to cite an example from the sugar industry, the eighteen partners of the three leading firms, which supplied about a third of the regional market between 1815 and 1863, remained in business on the average for 14.8 years each (27.5 years, if we exclude the younger men in the sample who had just started their careers in the early 1860s); while their competitors, numbering seventy-one in the same period, had an average of only 7 or 8 years of professional experience at the head of a firm.[21] Social stability favored business elites, while rapid turnover paradoxically plagued the lower end of the social scale.

But even though the nonegalitarian structure of the industrial society—its viscosity—is rightly deprecated, it must also be stated that the lack of upward and downward mobility was general throughout nineteenth-century Europe. And it is difficult to see how things could have been different. Some innovations enabled a few technicians to enter the elite groups, but their promotion could hardly have modified the distribution of wealth and power. In 1840–60, for instance, a second wave of innovations partially renewed leadership in the cotton sector. But apart from the fact that the branch as a whole remained a minor one (cotton contributed then only 3.15 percent to the value added by industry), the plants of 70,000 to 100,000 spindles that were set up (either by going concerns or by newcomers with credit opened by machine builders) amounted to but a small fraction of total output: 2.25 percent regionally for the three foremost Norman spinning mills in 1859, 4.45 percent for the three Alsatian leaders in 1869, and so on. Besides, most of the new industrialists (people like A. Pouyer-Quertier in the 1840s, or E. Vaucher in the 1860s) themselves came from privileged backgrounds. The important step upward we expect to find in social mobility no doubt takes more than two generations to accomplish. Even today, although technology is progressing rapidly and although society seems more open, 41.2 percent of French business managers are still sons of industrial leaders, 15.3 percent are sons of high officials in the public and private sectors, and 14.5 percent belong to professional families.[22]

Once social immobility is taken as a constant feature of the past century, and its problem set aside, two questions still remain: (1) to what extent did the system, unfair as it was, produce efficient managers? and (2) how did the system generate a new set of leaders after 1860–80, when science-based technology had become a key to economic success? One way to answer these points is to examine anew norms and patterns of higher technical education. Today, taking the 1953 sample already quoted, 17.9 percent of business managers are graduates of the Ecole polytechnique, 25.1 percent of other engineering schools, while 50.4 percent have completed graduate studies in other fields. Second, in the past, French manufacturing circles have always had a very high regard for education, since traditionally it was looked upon as one of the possible means of catching up with the most advanced foreign competitors. So, without going from one extreme to the other, one could argue that the very concept of "industrial dynasties" and their apparent immobility is apt to give rise to misrepresentation. Company names, of course, often remained unchanged. But within the same firms (or families), skills may have changed through more advanced training. And with the passage of generations, a new type of manager may have taken different responsibilities and, eventually, control of the firm.

In the early industrialization period, training remained informal even in so progressive a region as eastern France. Before 1840, business leaders there went through a simple (commercial) apprenticeship in the country or abroad, just as their predecessors had done; only a few among them (N. Koechlin, E. Dollfus, E. Schneider, etc.) had already attended the Conservatoire des arts et métiers, the only school then in existence. But in the next generation, after the founding in 1829 of the Ecole centrale des arts et manufactures (a private institution taken over by the government in 1857), some thirty Alsatians, two-thirds coming from prominent business families, graduated before 1860—and their sons came after them, since in the later part of the century one-fourth of the student body had fathers who had gone through the schools. Other regions followed the same pattern of family continuity, specifically the two most advanced centers, Paris (the capital providing some 38 percent of the students) and the Nord (17 percent), because of the high cost of preparing for and attending these schools (80 percent of the graduates came from well-to-do families) and because of the absence of a true selection procedure until 1866 and the emphasis put on applied sciences (abstract sciences took no more than 15 percent of the time schedule, compared with 37 percent at Polytechnique). Furthermore, former students of the school had 70 percent control over the board of the Société des ingénieurs civils de France from its inception in 1848, and as early as 1862 they established an employment bureau which assisted their classmates in their careers. During the 1829–85 period, they placed 40 percent in the industrial sector, 27 percent in the railroads, 9 percent in building and public works, 16 percent as consulting engineers, and 4 percent as professors. More than 5,000 engineers were trained during those years. And it may be assumed that the school answered the two-fold purpose of promoting the diffusion of advanced technologies among progressive firms and, after the 1860s, of bringing new talent into the business community.

But technical education did not remain the privilege of a favored minority. After a period of slow enrollment, due either to a marked preference for scientific studies (in the 1880s), and/or to a relative decline in the salaries of managerial personnel, the total number of students in the four main engineering schools (including the Ecole centrale) reached an average of 303 per year from 1895 through 1904 and 351 in the next ten-year period, from an average of 226 in the years 1865–94.[23] At the same time, increased attention was given to problems of objectives and methods. It was then believed that French industry was deficient in high-level technicians comparable to those leading German and American concerns or those who would be trained in the new scientific institutions opening in London and Brussels. Various personalities, especially the members of the Société pour le développement de l'enseignement supérieur, led a campaign to instill a new morale among industrial managers and to enlarge their social base. They were eager to give precedence to application over invention, to technical proficiency over administrative and financial expertise. So they wanted the *grandes écoles* to teach comprehensive, even encyclopedic, courses based on mathematics, which would enable graduates to assimilate on their own, once at work in the field, techniques needed in a specific industrial branch.[24] Such a program, which had to be absorbed in a minimum of time (then for reasons of military preparedness), made it necessary to select a high-level, homogeneous student body, able to follow an intensive course of study. This may explain why the pattern of recruitment changed during those years. The share of the provincial students increased at Polytechnique after 1900 from 69.1 percent to 77.9 percent. So did the weight of the least favored social classes: they made up 38.8 percent in 1872; 35.6 percent in 1886, at a time when the Army and research careers attracted the best among the graduates; but as early as 1900, they reached 45 percent of the class, and 54 percent in 1925 (compared with an average of 24.4 percent at the Ecole centrale in 1920–25). Similar ratios could be found in the specialized schools: 45.3 percent and 54.4 percent, before and after the war, at the Ecole des mines; 40.8 percent and 43.1 percent, at the Ponts et chaussées, etc.[25]

Obviously, the engineering schools were opening the way to social promotion and possibly to a new type of industrial leadership (table 9). But the professional integration of engineers remained an important issue, for at least two reasons. First, from their foundation between 1747 and 1794, Polytechnique and the various schools of applied sciences had had to train military personnel, scientists interested in research and teaching, and state engineers in charge of the supervision of important sectors of economic activity: the transportation network, the mines and iron works, new industrial equipment, etc. With such authority at their command, at least until the 1860s, these men had come to control (and often to retard) business initiative. It could therefore hardly be expected that their attitude would predispose them to working in industry; no more than eighty Polytechnicians, 1.9 percent of the total number in the first half of the century, resigned their commissions upon graduation to accept a position in a business firm. Second, there had always been a gap between overly abstract studies and the routine of daily life, between frequently excessive aspirations and the career opportunities that firms were able to offer; a firm's scope of operations was usually too small to warrant the cost of a fully trained technician. In the Loire basin, to choose an example from the coal industry, it was not until 1826 that the management of a firm was given to a former member of the royal engineering corps and not until 1844 that a merger between companies making up 85 percent of the regional output made it possible to rationalize production under a team of Polytechnicians. As a matter of fact, it is this feeling of uselessness and frustration that explains the frequent uprisings among students of the engineering schools in the early part of the century, the vogue of Saint-Simonian ideas, and Clapeyron's offer in 1833 to open schools for applied industrial and commercial sciences, which would have bridged the gap between the Ecole polytechnique and concrete professional activities.[26]

Temporarily, in the 1840–80 period, the ceiling placed on the number of admissions—except for military emergencies (fig. 2)—helped to reestablish an equilibrium between supply and demand. The building of the railroads also attracted outstanding engineers, such as Clapeyron, Didion, P. Talabot, and A. Jullien, and when problems of efficiency and profitability were raised, people like Audibert, Jacquemin, and Surell. Moreover, the increasing scale of investment, together with the growth of the work force in industrial plants, the use of complex technologies, and the handling of large inventories, came to justify a more frequent resort to state engineers in steel mills, shipyards, machine works, and the like. Altogether, some 575 Polytechnicians held positions in the private sector at the end of the 1870s.

But in those early days technicians with a more industrial bent obviously did play a less conspicuous, though more effective role, even in the public utilities sector, since the great construction companies (Seguin, Flachat, G. Eiffel) and the leading railroad, the Compagnie

TABLE 9

Social Origin of Students in the Principal French Engineering Schools, 1800–1932 (by percentage)

Category	C.N.A.M. 1800-1813	Arts et Métiers 1815-40	Arts et Métiers 1860-75	Centrale 1830-1900	Centrale 1900-1925
High-income groups					
Rentiers, landowners	0.9	14.9	12.5	31.8	24.9
Industrialists, wholesalers	5.9	11.5	7.1	34.6	27.8
Professionals	7.4	6.9	3.2	12.7	25.2
Subtotal	14.2	33.3	28.9	79.1	77.9
Low-income groups					
Low-level employees	14.3	25.4	17.1	10.9	13.9
Artisans, shopkeepers	60.2	23.4	26.8	5.4	5.2
Small farmers	11.3	17.9	27.2	4.6	3.0
Subtotal	85.8	66.7	71.1	20.9	22.1
Total	100.0	100.0	100.0	100.0	100.0

SOURCES: M. Bouillé, *Enseignement technique et idéologie au XIXe siècle* (1972); C. Mercié, *Les Polytechniciens, 1870-1930. Recrutement et activités* (1972); F Gautier, *Les ingénieurs du Génie maritime de 1810 à 1930* (1973); C. Baucher and A. Moore, *La formation et le recrutement des ingénieurs civils des Mines, 1817-1939* (1973); G. Champarou and C. Lhomer, *Les ingénieurs de l'Ecole centrale* (1973); G. Langlet, *Les*

du Nord, liked to recruit their staff at the Ecole centrale. The same remained true during the 1880–1900 economic slowdown. The conversion of the heavy industries, for example, was the work of graduates of that school (Jordan, A. Dreux), and of lesser institutions, who had made their way as technicians (H. Fayol at Commentry-Fourchambault) or as sales managers (C. Cavalier at Pont-à-Mousson) and who eventually gained control of the Comité des Forges in 1905–6 over the traditional ironmasters. Experimentation with new techniques was mostly carried out at that time by the same group of engineers in sectors as different as the glass, aluminum, and electrical industries; the first successful automobile factory was set up by R. Panhard and E. Levassor, both graduates of the Ecole centrale (class of 1864), as were the Mors brothers, R. Peugeot, the pioneers of aviation, etc.[27] A sample analysis for the years 1885–1925 shows that graduates from that school had left the traditional industries, such as textiles (which attracted a mere 2.6 percent of their total number), the railroads (11.1 percent) and metallurgy (10.2 percent) and had moved into engineering (14.7 percent), chemicals (10.4 percent), electricity (7.6 percent), etc. But either because of the declining influence after 1866–67 of the technical services in the public administration or because of the rearmament program, the role of graduates from Polytechnique still remained quite modest in the economy.

Polytechnique			Génie Maritime	Mines		Ponts et Chaussées	
1800-1870	1870-1900	1925	1865-95	1890-1914	1920-25	1883-1914	1914-32
30.1	19.1	2.3	10.1	9.8	3.7	10.7	4.2
13.8	16.2	15.8	14.5	14.3	10.1	17.4	15.5
32.0	26.4	27.3	50.8	41.7	45.4	31.1	37.2
75.9	61.7	45.4	75.4	65.8	69.2	59.2	56.9
18.1	20.6	28.1	17.4	22.7	28.6	22.4	31.3
4.2	12.0	19.7	5.8	9.3	6.7	5.6	6.2
1.8	5.7	6.8	1.4	2.2	5.5	12.8	5.6
24.1	38.3	54.6	24.6	34.2	40.8	40.8	43.1
100.0	100.0	100.0	100.0	100.0	100.0	100.0	100.0

ingénieurs des Ponts et chaussées, 1880-1930 (1974). All of these studies are theses presented to the Faculty of Letters at the University of Paris-X at Nanterre.
NOTE: All these institutions, except the three *Ecoles des arts de métiers*, are located in Paris, including C.N.A.M. (*Conservatoire national des arts et métiers*).

After the turn of the century, however, Polytechnicians did take an active part in the building up of new industries. The constitution of a staff of technical officers within the Army, as stipulated by the law of 15 April 1873, was practically accomplished by the end of the 1890s. Thus, resignations from public service upon graduation, which earlier had mainly involved the privileged (57 percent among them were sons of businessmen) and specific groups of state engineers, became more frequent, even at a later period in professional life: 42.9 percent of the class of 1872 left public service either upon graduation or later; scarcely 20 percent of that of 1888, at a time when it was the fashion to aspire to a military career; and the ratio reached 37.3 percent for the class of 1900 (many were killed in the war) and 78.8 percent for the class of 1918–19. In addition, the recovery of such sectors as transportation, building, and energy and the development of the basic industries favored some sort of migration into the private sector: in 1877, some 200 Polytechnicians held positions in the transport and heavy industries, and their numbers rose to 565 in 1905, and to more than 1,100 in 1930. Before the war, engineers of the Corps des mines were leading some of the main corporations (E. Vicaire, Th. Laurent, J. Aubrun, etc.). Finally, the use of advanced technology provided the graduates of Polytechnique with activities in keeping with the scientific tradition of their school. In the past, about two-fifths of those entering a private career had acted as

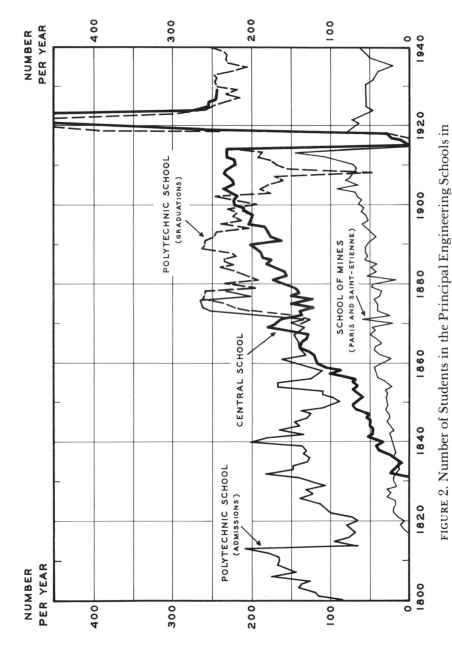

FIGURE 2. Number of Students in the Principal Engineering Schools in France, 1800–1940

SOURCE: See source for table 9.

consulting experts; 225 in 1877, and 515 in 1905. But in 1877, 28 Polytechnicians also had some responsibilities in a firm using a new technology (electricity, engineering, chemicals), and their number rose to 143 in 1905, and as high as 435 in 1930.[28] In the meantime, with the demobilization that followed the war, out of an average of 7,000 Polytechnicians in active service, the share of those in a public service (including the Army) fell from 85.1 percent to 49.7 percent. This means that the number of those who moved over to the private sector increased from 1,620 to 3,330.

On the whole, although very large firms, sometimes led until the 1880–1900 period by the same industrial families, had been in control of a substantial share of the market, it would be deceptive to portray French employers as making up a closed and immobile cast. The diversification of industries and the widening market constantly promoted the rise of newcomers, who had either specific technical skills or some expert knowledge of trade. It is their presence, together with a high respect for education, that explains why established families made it a rule that the competence of their members be brought up to date in every new generation. Moreover, from the 1890s on, transfers of state engineers became common, because the supervisory function formerly assigned to them lost some of its importance and because administrative careers were saturated. After the war, between 1919 and 1924, 1,394 Polytechnicians leaving school went into the private sector—almost 5,000 engineers in all, if we add the graduates of the other (higher) schools. In addition, resignations among civil servants rose sharply: in 1930, the ratio between Polytechnicians over forty who left public service and those who remained in the Army or the administration was five to one; in 1905, it had been only two to one. This shift in employment, coupled with a more democratic recruitment, must have contributed to a renewal of management personnel and, in turn, to a restructuring of the organizational staff in business.

ATTITUDES AND OBJECTIVES
OF MANAGEMENT

The dual structure that has been examined here regarding the size of business units and the social origin of leading personnel very probably extended to objectives and methods of management. Small and medium-sized firms, limited as they were when it came to external financing but quite efficient in their use of labor, were obliged to adapt to market variations since their influence on price and demand was almost nil; at best, they could work for technical achievement or greater product differentiation in order to meet customers' requirements. Big firms, on the other hand, which had committed themselves to sizable investments, must have made it a rule to amortize equipment through mass production, to keep the market regularly supplied, and to stabilize long-term profits. Generally speaking, big firms may have been expected to be more successful, because technical progress, the growing availability of energy, a more rational use of inventories in the production and distribution process, and better personnel management made it possible for them to standardize products and, by capital intensification, free manpower for more productive uses. Actually, this trend is borne out by the statistics. Between 1906 and 1931, wage earners in the industrial sector (one-man firms excluded) rose from 3 to 4.5 million, or from 15 percent to 23 percent of the active population. As to the personnel working in factories of more than 500 workers, it rose during the same years from 750,000 to 1,440,000.[29] *Grande industrie*, almost nonexistent in the past century, had become a reality within less than thirty years, despite a major war waged on French territory.

But, although a step forward had thus been taken, it must also be stated that the industrialization process remained incomplete. At the lower end of the scale of size of business units, as mentioned earlier, the artisanal labor force, working in isolation or in very small shops, first experienced a sharp drop, from 63 percent to 41 percent of the active industrial population; it remained stable thereafter, during the 1930s and 1940s (table 10[a]). At the higher end of the scale concentration did not proceed as might have been expected. With minor exceptions, the distribution of the work force among industrial "establishments" with more than 20 wage earners hardly changed at all (table 10[b]). And the larger units, those with more than 500 wage earners, did not attract any more personnel than the others; for some forty years, they kept a more or less fixed average of 2,345 workers per unit. Of course, various explanations have been offered. In particular, saving on financial costs and the exploitation of labor in violation of social and fiscal legislation are said to have contributed to the survival of the smaller production units in the artificial conditions that prevailed after 1932. Yet, in a profit-maximizing economy, it is difficult to account for the fact that the larger firms, with their obvious competitive advantages—diversification, economies of scale, and so on—were not able to increase further their control over production factors. The nonsubstitution, or at least the very partial substitution, of big business for small concerns appears as one of the paradoxes of twentieth-century French history. As such, it certainly calls for an explanation.

TABLE 10
Distribution of the Labor Force among Industrial Establishments in France, 1906–62 (by percentage)

Number of Wage-Earners per Establishment	All Industrial Establishments* (a)					Large Industrial Establishments* (b)			
	0	1–4	5–20	21 and over	Total	21–100	101–500	501 and over	Total
1906	27	26	10	37	100	32	35	33	100
1926	14	21	12	53	100	31	32	37	100
1931	12	16	13	59	100	30	33	37	100
1936	17	16	12	55	100	30	33	37	100
1954	6	13	11	70	100	30	34	36	100
1962	5	11	9	75	100	30	35	35	100

SOURCE: M. Didier and E. Malinvaud, "La concentration de l'industrie s'est-elle accentuée depuis le début du siècle?" Economie et statistique, no. 2 (1969), p. 3 ff.

*Table 10(a) lists the labor force in all industrial establishments. The first column represents either one-man establishments or those who are "self-employed," usually artisans and not wage-earners or employees. Table 10(b) lists only those establishments of 21 or more wage-earners. By French standards these can be called "large establishments." [The word "establishment" (établissement) has been retained for reasons discussed in the text (see p. 89) and n. 3; "business unit" is the closest approximation.—Trans.]

To explain this slow evolution, the choice is among three hypotheses.

1. As observed at various points, differential costs, such as freight or credit, lost some of their importance after the 1860s with the unification of markets and with cheaper transportation, so that in every branch of activity, irrespective of the country concerned, the size of productive unit tended to be somewhat predetermined by the technology used, and concentration was determined by the relative importance of the different branches. In 1931, if we take as a criterion of concentration by branch the share of the labor force in plants of one hundred workers and more, we would find that only six branches had more than 90 percent of their work force so employed (mines, steel, cotton, and worsted spinning mills, shipyards, and railroad works); ten had more than 70 percent in the same category (rubber, paper, electrical machinery, etc.). But they could not loom large in the total, since they represented only 8.34 percent and 6.46 percent of the active industrial population. No doubt progress had been made: between 1906 and 1931, these sixteen branches increased their share from 10.64 percent to 13.62 percent, while some thirty-two traditional industries, having more than half of their personnel in shops of less than twenty workers, fell from 53.1 percent to 39.0 percent. But in a calculation of weighted averages, the influence of those sectors, operating by small production units, is bound to prevail. Coefficients being based on value added or labor employed, the inherited structures in an old industrial country like France will mask any trend toward concentration. Or to put it differently, it may well be that technology was progressing correctly and that the impression of immobility is partly fictitious.

2. The same reasoning can be reversed, however, since the weight of the older sectors should be less significant in this calculation than that of the newer branches, whether they were fairly concentrated (steel, petroleum, chemicals) or very concentrated (automobiles, synthetic fibers, lubricants, or aluminum). If these activities had had a strong development, they would have modified the overall weighting of the various sectors. In the automobile industry, the three major firms accounted for some 29 percent of total production in 1913 and 56 percent in 1925; they really dominated the market with 75 percent of the sales only in 1936, when the depression forced competitors out of business. In this period the total number of firms fell from 150 to 38. It was thus the reduction in demand rather than a policy of expansion that contributed to strengthening the position of the leaders. This suggests that the new generations may have missed opportunities during the years of prosperity, made mistakes, or more simply, not been dynamic enough.

3. An analysis of the gross financial assets of the companies listed on the Paris stock exchange leads to similar conclusions. Between 1912 and 1936 the larger firms seem to have lost some of their relative importance: the share in total assets of the four leading companies was reduced from 9.7 percent to 9.1 percent between these two dates; that of the first fifty, from 52.5 percent to 42.0 percent. Of course, this financial deconcentration is partly artificial. It reflects the growing number of firms trading their stock in the market; this is clearly the case with the older sectors, since the number of companies rose more sharply in this group than in others (table 11). But again the countermovement of concentration, which seems characteristic of the new sectors, was lacking in vigor. The reason generally offered is that interest groups tried to prevent mergers, total or partial, among business firms because they did not want to jeopardize the high and artificial profits their control of the market gave them. From this perspective, the lack of concentration within industries was apparently the result of a consciously Malthusian strategy, that is, "voluntary restraint," even among the large firms.

The present state of research probably does not permit us to decide among these hypotheses. There is too great a gap between abstract and general theses and what we know about isolated individuals and specific companies. Yet, setting aside the first hypothesis, since structural imbalance can best be accounted for by variables other than entrepreneurship, we are left with the usual two criticisms of manag-

TABLE 11

Concentration of Active Gross Assets of Firms Listed on the Paris Stock Exchange, 1912 and 1936

Industry	All Firms (number)		Assets of All Firms (in thousands F)		Assets of One Leading Firm (%)[a]		Assets of the Four Leading Firms (%)[a]	
	1912	1936	1912	1936	1912	1936	1912	1936
Food	43	127	4,199	6,209	17.9	6.4	43.4	19.6
Wood, leather	22	88	2,484	6,265	20.7	16.6	53.1	37.7
Textiles	18	59	2,192	4,403	19.5	12.5	59.1	37.1
Mines, metalurgy	84	134	16,561	15,843	7.3	9.4	25.1	25.2
Energy	25	63	9,694	12,900	17.8	10.7	51.6	32.2
Building, glass	18	64	2,992	4,668	45.4	30.7	81.8	44.9
Paper products	19	32	1,753	1,776	22.5	27.9	53.6	65.8
Chemical	33	82	3,436	7,382	15.7	15.6	36.3	40.8
Metal processing	68	145	15,718	13,103	8.6	8.3	18.7	25.3
Other	118	181	29,255	20,455	–	–	–	–
Total	448	975	88,284	93,006	3.4	2.9	9.7	9.1

SOURCE: Jacques Houssiaux, Le pouvoir des monopoles. Essai sur les structures industrielles du capitalisme contemporaine (Paris, 1958), pp. 292, 298–308.
[a]% of total assets for each industry.

ers: lack of foresight or drive, and unfair practices. On a priori grounds it seems likely that technicians with a more modest background than in the past and engineers recruited by means of an academic curriculum, men who were often interested chiefly in the scientific side of their profession or who came from rigid public services, would not be prepared to play the role of innovator in remodeling norms and methods and in restructuring the economy, however necessary these tasks were in the 1900–1930 period. Were French managers indeed ready to accept new methods for the organization of plants, establish large production units, and improve industrial productivity? Are there signs of significant change in their attitudes and behavior?

At first sight, it would seem that any widening in the recruitment of managerial personnel should have favored innovation. In fact, when problems of achieving efficiency in large, technically complex factories arose, F. W. Taylor's methods were received with approval. This was probably because experiments with maximizing returns of labor costs had been conducted since the 1880s, especially in the railroads, and also because Taylor's time-and-motion studies, payment by results, and production and quality controls corroborated studies made by French engineers or answered their queries. H. Le Chatelier published in 1907 a translation of Taylor's paper "Shop Organization," which had been circulated for four years, and in 1912 he published Taylor's *Principles of Scientific Management*, then only one year old. A total of twenty thousand copies, one-third before the war, were sold in France during the next twelve years. Again in 1915, when the workers complained that they were overworked and did not receive their fair share of the increase in productivity, the ideas of H. L. Gantt, urging better management-labor cooperation and a more satisfactory wage scale, were summarized and commented upon with equal interest.

However, the initial results were not rewarding. Before the war, scientific management had been introduced at the shipyards of Penhoët, at the Arbel plants in Douai, and in the automobile industry at Reims, Lyon, and Billancourt. Louis Renault, for instance, set up a department for time-and-motion studies as early as 1908; in 1909–12 he sent three engineers on a study tour in the United States and went himself to Philadelphia and Detroit in 1911 to consult with Taylor and Ford. But labor hostility and the 1912 strikes restricted the scope of the technique. No doubt it could be used to increase productivity among unskilled workers; but in France 95 percent of the work force at the Renault plants in 1906, 71 percent in 1914, and 65 percent at Peugeot in 1920 still consisted of skilled personnel whose wages were more strictly defined, if not reduced, under Taylor's system. Eventually the war, the entrance into factories of 350,000 untrained women, and the support of Albert Thomas, then minister of armaments, brought about some product standardization and a more efficient division of operations. Scientific management, in fact, became widespread only in the interwar years. The use of assembly lines made it possible to reduce the number of skilled workers—to less than 46 percent at Citroën as early as 1925.[30] And later, social legislation, the forty-hour law in particular, brought about a shift of personnel into the nationalized and semipublic sector, promising greater job security. A good many of the supervisors and the most competent workers left private industry, thus hastening both the decline of skills and the adoption of Taylor's system.[31] But if scientific management had depended solely on employers' initiative, it would have become a reality much earlier.

During the postwar years the main concern was no longer the rational use of labor and its level of skill but rather the structure of industry. This interest was stimulated, first, by the knowledge of and admiration for American achievements, by the recovery in capital investment that had taken place at the turn of the century (fig. 3), and by the building of production units whose efficiency was predicated, more than in the past, upon size. Technical change had made it possible to set up equipment of unheard-of capacity—power plants conceived on a regional scale, integrated steel mills with an output of 500,000 tons (150 to 200,000 tons per plant had been taken as a prewar limit), and so on. The use of machine tools, more widespread since 1907, and the desire to handle inventories more efficiently had confirmed the idea that there were levels below which a plant or an industry remained unprofitable. For instance, in 1929 a national stock of 100,000 automobiles and a yearly demand of 20,000 to 25,000, according to André Citroën, was unprofitable. As early as 1921 it was also realized in the chemical and electrical industries that the financial burden of research could only be borne by companies that controlled a major share of the market. Similarly, the wartime economy, improvised under Louis Loucher's guidance by a team of engineers who had taken charge of the armament programs in 1916–17, opened the way to new schemes and ideas. Some manufacturers and public administrators felt it would be possible to organize a peacetime economy around a few large corporations. They would be able to raise large capital funds on cheaper terms, improve their profit margin by negotiating their prices, and more easily finance the costs of purchasing, setting up sales agencies, and paying financial and administrative staffs. Citroën, for instance, who had operated a shell factory and was studying new lines

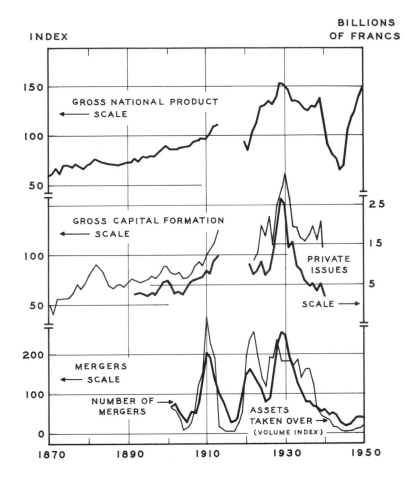

INDEX

BILLIONS OF FRANCS

FIGURE 3. Indices of Economic Growth, Investments, and Mergers between Companies in France, 1870–1950

SOURCE: The volume index of the G.N.P. and that of gross capital formation for the period after 1914 are those given by the *Annuaire statistique de la France* 72 (1966) and by J. J. Carré, P. Dubois, and E. Malinvaud, *La croissance française: Un essai d' analyse économique casuale de l'après-guerre* (Paris, 1972); they have been carried beyond 1938 with data taken from R. Froment and P. Gavarnier, "Le revenu national français," in *La France économique de 1939 à 1946* (Paris, 1948), pp. 105–30. The data concerning the issues of stocks and bonds (in current francs) by private companies have been taken, for the years 1892–1914, from the *Annuaire statistique* (1966), p. 532, and for the years 1921–38, from M. Malissen, *L'autofinancement des sociétés en France et aux Etas-Unis* (Paris, 1953); prewar amounts were multiplied by five in order to make up for the devaluation of the franc. Finally, the number of mergers and the compensations for assets taken over (in 1914 francs) were first calculated in the form of indices and then changed into a three-year moving average by removing the trend factor; these figures are based on Houssiaux, *Le pouvoir des monopoles*, table 8, p. 340.

of production, in 1918 proposed the creation of specialized firms under the control of a Ministry of Industry, in the manufacturing either of automobiles (assuming one type of car per firm and a maximum of five or six trademarks) or of interchangeable parts to be sold to the automobile manufacturers.

Whatever the origin of the ideas—a better understanding of recent technical change or an awareness of the potential role of the government—it is obvious that the institutions, i.e., the organization of the production system and that of the market, had become a common concern. The publications of the Redressement français, an employers' association with Polytechnician leanings that held meetings in Paris in 1927, and the speeches and writings of many manufacturers and journalists in the 1920s abundantly confirm this point. There was at the time a general agreement in the new generation of managers as to the need for a three-fold reform. First, competition was considered outmoded and inefficient; it should be replaced by cartels or, better, by mergers between firms that would enhance the scope of operations, reduce prices, and shorten terms of delivery. Cooperation with the state, incidentally, was welcomed because its patronage or financial assistance could help new business firms acquire an international dimension sooner. In March 1931 the state was to subscribe 31 percent of the capital of the Compagnie française des pétroles, an oil company that had been founded only seven years before, in conjunction with ninety firms, by E. Mercier, the leader of the Redressement français. Second, the consumer had to be reeducated and a special effort made to explain to the public at large the usefulness of mass production in terms of quality and prices. It is "a legend to believe that products made in limited quantities can be more carefully polished and are therefore better handled," wrote André Citroën in May 1929. Ten years earlier, he commented, he had started production making 100 cars per day at 6,950 F each (this was half the prewar average price, even though the currency had depreciated); since then, output had been raised to 300 and would soon reach 500; the firm was even preparing to produce 1,000 cars a day in the not-too-distant future.[32] Third, as a corollary to concentration and as a basis for increased production, the need for a larger market had also been acknowledged. To turn the worker into the principal customer of industry—the French interpretation of "Fordism"—was explicitly accepted, and with it, a policy of high wages, social benefits, and consequently, increased productivity. "Mass production necessitates an active consumption—an increasingly active consumption—which can only be obtained by a reduction of prices and the improvement of the quality of products. It is this which creates between producers and consumers a positive community of interest that would automatically prevent the producer from abusing the practical absence of effective competition."[33]

THE PROBLEM
OF MALTHUSIANISM

Even though French leaders had become aware of the impact of new technologies and of industrial concentration upon market organization and firm management, a gap between principles and concrete policies was still possible. First, because of their technical bias and their former experience in public service, some managers may have paid insufficient attention to the market potentials. Those who failed to set up sales organizations at an early date were likely to find themselves unable to nurture demand and increase output and hence were unable keep up with technical change. The automobile industry, for instance, at one time the most progressive (by international standards), lost ground, specifically in the export trade: sales fell almost continuously between 1925 and 1935, from 65,000 to 19,000 cars per year, i.e., from 36 percent to 12 percent of annual production. Consequently, by the 1930s French builders, alone among western builders, were unable to bring cheap utility cars onto the market.[34] Excess capacity slowed down innovations. Second, financial policies may have been too conservative. Firms were apt to save on their investment programs. Or, mergers being a partial substitute for investments, they may have adopted informal market sharing, cartels, or joint ventures, instead of pooling resources more extensively. Assets taken over through mergers, when calculated as a percentage of the assets of absorbing companies, show a declining trend: from an annual average of 35.8 percent in 1900–1919 to 17.1 percent in 1920–39 (table 12). This is due partly to the greater number and smaller size of the companies listed on the stock exchange in the 1920s. But it is also due partly to the fact that consolidations of assets between firms of equal size were more frequent before than after the war: the external growth of business (through mergers) was discontinued, with companies preserving their identity and some of their financial autonomy. Consequently, they were prevented from expanding capacity and sales at the expense of weaker competitors. Prices remained higher than they might have been, and assuming a demand elasticity higher than unity, market potentials were not fully utilized. Undercapacity plagued industry. Thus, whether we approach the problem from the commercial or the financial angle, we are led to believe that management procedures were detrimental in the long run. So, independently of their

TABLE 12
Yearly Averages of French Mergers, 1900–1939

Year	Number of Mergers[a]	Total Assets[b] of Companies Absorbed (in millions F)		Total Assets[b] of Absorbing Companies (in millions F)		Combined Total Assets (in millions F)		Ratio[c] (%)
		Current F	1914 F	Current F	1914 F	Current F	1914 F	
	(1)	(2)	(3)	(4)	(5)	(6)	(7)	(8)
1900–1904	1.6	1.2	1.5	8.7	10.9	9.9	12.4	13.8
1905–9	3.0	7.6	8.8	16.3	18.9	23.9	27.7	44.1
1910–14	9.6	24.9	27.8	61.6	63.6	86.5	91.4	43.7
1915–19	3.4	6.9	3.3	27.0	12.7	33.9	16.0	25.9
1920–24	19.0	100.3	26.9	299.3	80.3	399.6	107.2	33.5
1925–29	29.4	132.0	23.3	811.4	143.3	943.4	166.6	16.3
1930–34	44.2	207.4	42.5	1,115.2	228.6	1,322.6	271.1	18.6
1935–39	27.0	197.5	35.9	1,510.8	274.3	1,708.3	310.2	13.1
1900–1939 (yearly average)	17.2	84.7	21.2	481.3	104.1	566.0	125.3	20.4

SOURCE: Houssiaux, *Le pouvoir des monopoles*, table 8, p. 340.

[a]The sample is based on the firms listed on the Paris stock exchange and cannot be considered as perfectly representative, since the total number of companies listed changed after World War I (col. 1). Furthermore, assets are not consolidated; parent companies and their subsidiaries are tabulated and entered in the calculations as independent entities. Lastly, major firms, which had a large percentage of the market and were nationalized, have been excluded from this table.

[b]Total assets of the companies absorbed and those of absorbing companies are presented here in millions of francs. Columns 2, 4, and 6 list the evaluation at current francs at the time of the merger, and columns 3, 5, and 7 list the evaluation in 1914 francs.

[c]The ratio (col. 8) between absorbed assets and those of the absorbing companies is arrived at by dividing col. 3 by col. 5. The decline in this ratio is a sign of a fall in external growth.

norms and attitudes, we should reexamine business leaders' behavior, this time with reference to the appropriateness of their methods.

At first glance, the arguments about a lack of commercial drive among manufacturers do not seem warranted. Sales promotion has always been imperative in a country with a stagnant population, where industry has long been considered a mere adjunct to trade. Without giving undue importance to the fact, it should be recalled that in the early nineteenth century, manufacturers who took up new methods of production marketed their products themselves through a network of warehouses; those at Mulhouse had as many as forty such agencies, and after 1840 they also used the service of traveling salesmen. In the 1880–1900 depression chain stores enabled companies to combine retail sales and manufacturing, especially in consumer durables.[35] Also, market sharing, which is presented as customary, was very seldom utilized. In the forward sectors, those most sensitive to variations of demand (and to the cost of labor and supplies), it was the custom to liquidate inventories and to adjust production seasonally. Moreover, credit and other facilities provided to new entrants made strict adherence to any agreement rather dubious: the sugar cartel of the 1880s only had the effect of decentralizing industry for the benefit of those who had not joined; the agreements made in the textile sector in 1899 and 1902 lasted only a few weeks; and in the 1930s attempts by the administration and the trade associations to organize production in a number of processing industries failed almost completely. In the backward sectors, of course, we do find rigid cartels with production quotas and/or a central marketing board. But they were fewer in France than in many other countries, and they were frequently used to develop outlets for new industries, such as those producing aluminum and other products of electrometallurgy, as well as for more traditional ones. It is often forgotten that the first Lorraine steel cartels were set up because local ironmasters, cut off in 1871 from their processing centers and hampered by the late-nineteenth-century depression, established, in 1876, the Comptoir de Longwy to open up a market for Thomas steel and to overcome prejudices against the local Lorraine ore and, in 1896, the Comptoir des poutrelles to promote the use of steel girders, despite the slow urbanization movement. The purpose of these and other specialized agencies was to stimulate sales and innovations and not to allocate a reduced output among participants.[36]

Still, it might be objected that the automobile industry was successful only when it was based on the technical expertise of French manufacturers supplying costly products to an exclusive clientele and that it became stagnant in the 1930s as soon as competition made it a necessity to promote sales and adapt to a depressed market. But even here the argument does not seem valid. Initially, production called for skilled labor (wages amounted to one-fourth of the final cost) rather than financial resources; at the Renault plants in 1916, the capital-output ratio (on the basis of 21 million francs for plant and fixed equipment, and 58 million francs in sales) was less than 0.4. And financing did not present serious problems, thanks to partial payment of orders eighteen months before delivery, and thanks to profits which reached an average of 40 percent of the annual turnover at Renault in 1899–1913, and 40–47 percent at Panhard in the early 1900s. In fact, the success of an individual firm was directly related to its selling ability. Louis Renault's success is explained by the use of commercial methods borrowed from the textile trade, in which his elder brother had been trained. Sales at the factory were discontinued in 1903, when his brother joined the firm, and a network of agencies set up; there were 125 in 1914, and 1,285 in 1929, including respectively 31 and 120 distributors abroad. André Citroën, for his part, adopted American methods after the war, including exclusive dealerships, after-sale services, installment credit plans (for 10 percent of the sales as early as 1929), and overseas assembly plants. All these experiments, of course, were adopted by competitors as well.

Diversification had always been designed to meet customers' requirements: taxis were built after 1905 (a third of the prewar London cabs were French-made); cheaper and lighter cars (after Delahaye) by 1907; military trucks and aircraft during the war, etc. Neglect of such a policy in the 1930s would thus seem contradictory. But sales promotion was a costly venture. Out of roughly 157 million francs invested by Renault in the 1930s, 45 percent was reserved for sales agencies—75 percent, if finance companies, real estate and garage, trucking, etc., are included. Besides, credit had to be extended during the depression, when the second-hand car had come to account for two-thirds of the sales, compared with one-half in 1930. These outlays no doubt tied up funds. They compelled the leading firms not to launch cheap utility cars in 1935, even though the models were ready; such a step would have led to an unacceptable depreciation of inventories and a heavy blow to car dealers.[37] As a result, the depression was not overcome. Industry operated at 76 percent of its 1929 capacity. But this state of overcapacity must be attributed to an earlier excess in commercial policies rather than to some technical bias or indifference to market conditions.

We are then left to explain economic stagnation and assess entrepreneurial strategies with the criticism related to "Malthusian" profit-taking. The abnormally low rate of investment (and the consequent

high cost of French products), in the interwar years has been attributed
to deliberate choice. Managers are accused of having shunned total
amalgamations or mergers between firms of equal size in favor of loose
combinations or joint interest ventures, which preserved autonomy
among associates and reinforced their position of power by "creating
diffuse networks of financial and personal relationships." And they are
supposed to have conducted an overly hesitant absorption policy,
although takeovers of secondary firms would have made it possible to
functionalize staff organizations and improve technical efficiency—and more generally, economic productivity, which is to a certain
extent a function of size.[38] But whatever its attractiveness, such a thesis
is not precise enough to be tested statistically. All that can be contemplated here is (1) a comparison of nineteenth-century and twentieth-
century policies, to see whether (horizontal) mergers were a regular
procedure, constantly enforced and discarded only in recent years, i.e.,
in the 1920s; and (2) a concrete examination of partial amalgamations
in order to discover their objectives.

As a matter of expediency, amalgamations were resorted to in the
past century whenever a shortage of capital hampered expansion,
particularly in the heavy industries, since they required "lumpy" and
discontinuous investments. This was the case in the 1840-60 period,
when railroad construction accelerated. A number of coal mines,
unable to carry out new works in isolation, consolidated into the
Compagnie des Mines de la Loire (1840-45), a big concern that
supplied one-fourth of the national output during the next nine years.
In the nearby districts, which had been a center of charcoal metalworks,
a small number of modern plants, based on coke smelting, were built at
the same time by large associations of ironmasters and mine operators.
These plants operated with some efficiency; three of the companies
organized through mergers in 1845-53, Chatillon-Commentry, Terre-
noire, and Marine, were to dominate the market in the 1860s, accounting for one-fifth of French metal manufacture. And in the early 1880s,
at a time of heavy investments and technical change, large companies
(by French standards) were set up by way of amalgamation in the
cement and soda industries and also in metallurgy—the first eastern
steel mills, using the Thomas patent, were erected at Joeuf and
Longwy in Lorraine. They were equally successful, since these Lorraine corporations in 1913 accounted for 21.8 percent of the pig iron
and 33.8 percent of the steel produced in France. In each case, concentration was hastened by mergers.[39]

Yet between these two stages, policies had already undergone an
evolution. The first agreements, those made before 1860, had been

concluded by companies situated in the same line of production, quite
often having complementary resources. Total integration was then a
logical step to take. But, to keep to the smelting-iron case, the
experiments with the Bessemer technique in 1858–62, the lower cost of
transportation, and the decline of iron ore production in central France
compelled ironmasters either to build new plants, to finance mining
operations in the Mediterranean area (and eventually to set up metal
works along the sea shore), or else to move forward and take up metal
processing or machine-tool building. At the end of the 1860–80 period,
companies were thus engaged in too many different activities to retain
identical interests and resources. Accordingly, partial mergers became
more frequent. They made it possible to develop the mines and metal
works in Lorraine and to start the construction of the two greatest steel
works of the prewar era: Caen, financed by a Franco-German syndicate,
and Pont-à-Vendin, a joint venture of Commentry-Fourchambault and
the Lens coal company in northeastern France.[40] Diversification of
activities, together with the massive cost of investments, had made it
necessary for manufacturers to modify their amalgamation policies.

The two species of association have persisted into the twentieth
century, particularly in the immediate postwar years, when demand
was heavy and rising prices and increased taxation curtailed business
financial means. Complete integration between firms having similar
activities was then found especially in the public utilities sector and in
various modern industries, provincial companies often being absorbed
and sometimes manned with new industrial staffs appointed from
Paris. This was the case in the aluminum sector, as Pechiney increased
its share of the market from 30 percent in 1912, to 90 percent, once the
company had absorbed two rival groups, in 1916 and 1921. And Ugine
became the leader in electrometallurgy after combining six companies
in 1915–23. More examples could be found in sectors as diverse as the
food industry (the Motte group accounting for 61 percent of oleomar-
garine production after it had merged in 1928–33 with six competitors)
or in synthetic fibers.

But partial consolidations were to prevail over total mergers. Given
rapid technological change, old established firms with large industrial
plants had to adopt new techniques as they came into the market
and/or convert existing facilities to bring out new products. In the
chemical industries, the great soda works, using Leblanc's method, lost
62 percent of the market in 1873–86 when the Solvay patent was
introduced. So they had to develop substitutes such as sulphuric acid
and superphosphates (Saint-Gobain, in 1914, supplied respectively 60
percent and 45 percent of these products) and synthetic dyes (Kuhl-

mann's share of this market rose from 60 percent to 90 percent in 1923, when it took over a subsidiary). Diversification had become the rule. Conversely, in the newer sectors, such as the electrical industries, firms using techniques that could be put to a number of applications found it necessary to develop separate departments, which they eventually turned over to a branch firm. This was done voluntarily when a firm wished to specialize and give up some of its activities, involuntarily when it was overextended; the Grammont group, for instance, a typical family firm from Lyon, thus had to be dismantled in 1928. Hence the appearance of companies with a quasi-monopoly of certain light electrical appliances, such as the Compagnie des lampes, founded in 1921 by pooling together the identical departments of Thomson-Houston, C.G.E., and Philips. Other companies dominated a market less adaptable to mass production: Alsthom, for instance, was set up in 1928 by combining the heavy generating equipment sections of an Alsatian firm and that of Thomson-Houston (at that time directed by Auguste Detoeuf), while the Matériel S. W. resulted in 1929 from the restructuring of the Schneider, Westinghouse, and Grammont companies.[41]

It was this diversification and the consequent interlocking of interests between parent firms and various entities—departments, branch establishments, subsidiaries—that gave observers the impression that the economy had become dominated by financial groups having the power to retard technical change. Of course, the 1920s was undeniably a period of financial and industrial concentration. A few great industrial corporations had become financial institutions acting as holding companies, and in some sectors, such as the coal industry, engineering, and public utilities, those firms having surplus funds set up investment banks to manage their portfolio.[42] At the same time, the gap between big and small business, regarding scale of operations and often profitability, had probably widened. But, contrary to the idea that the great organizations of the period had deliberately opted for a Malthusian policy, there are no indications that it was in their power either to narrow the productivity lead that size may have given to the large firms or to further the integration of the various branches of industrial activity. There are at least three reasons for this.

1. Amalgamation policies were not the result of autonomous decisions taken independently by entrepreneurs. Statistically, mergers have been resorted to whenever, productive capacities being fully utilized, manufacturers were eager to serve the market without waiting for new investments to mature. The number of mergers, as recorded in the stock exchange listing, is closely related to the volume index of capital

formation and also to the value of new stock issues, probably because high prices and sales in the market made it possible to sell new securities to the public. As can be seen in figure 3.3, the three series follow a parallel course: they peak in 1878–83, at the end of the 1890s, again in 1909–11. They culminate in 1926–29: sixty-five mergers were concluded in 1929 compared with an annual average of twenty-five in the interwar period. It was during that year that the (French) Shell Oil Company, the Lyonnaise des eaux et de l' électricité, and Rhône-Poulenc were founded.[43] In short, amalgamations were used as a partial substitute for investment to save time in periods of high activity.

But the same process worked when the depression set in. After 1932, with the tapering off of demand, entrepreneurs postponed new commitments, especially in the backward sectors, since long-term production processes made it difficult to assess their effect further down the line. And as a consequence, amalgamations were discontinued, except in such industries as steel pipes, telephone equipment, petroleum, etc. The decline in business amalgamations can therefore be explained, not by any desire to hamper the economy, but more simply, by a realistic appreciation of the risks involved in a period of acute difficulties.

2. When the analysis is carried out over a long time span, one finds that there were very few growth potentials that big business failed to exploit. Actually, after 1860 and for about half a century, French market demand remained rather weak as a consequence of the demographic stagnation, the immobility and low productivity of the rural labor force, and the slow urbanization process. Moreover, periods of expansion, when investment and amalgamations were rewarding, were few. The long swing, which in most industrial countries culminated in 1873, was postponed in France for nine years as a result of the Franco-Prussian war; and the post-1882 recession to a large extent canceled out the effect of the next international cycle, that of the 1890s. Thus it was only from 1905 on that the French economy experienced a period of rapid growth, with the qualification that World War I prevented its effects from being felt until 1926–29 (fig.3). Economic initiatives thus met with a whole set of unfavorable circumstances that slowed the process of changing the relative balance between big and small business.

3. Perhaps it should be added that the government did not always support economic concentration. First, in order to preserve some social balance, measures were taken to prevent department stores from competing with small business and also to subsidize and protect, through fiscal and other devices, sectors that had been weakened by

technological innovations. Second, because the administration had the desire to avoid regional discrimination, it spread railroads and public utilities evenly through the various regions, whatever their economic future, and it fought against possible monopolies. In the mining sector it prohibited mergers (1852), dismembered the Compagnie des Mines de la Loire (1854), divided the newly opened coal basin of the Pas-de-Calais among some twenty concession-holders, and favored the smaller operators by agreeing to the formation in 1901 of a sales cartel, the Comptoir de Douai, which worked against concentration; the three major mining companies, which had supplied 55 percent of the regional coal output in 1865-69, contributed only 42 percent in 1890-94 and 36 percent in 1908-12.[44]

Step by step we are led to a revision of the problem. Structural change, which many of the experts of the interwar period believed was the best way to increase productivity and reduce the gap between French industry and her competitors abroad, was not hampered by the attitudes and strategy of French management in the years 1900 to 1930. Of the three hypotheses offered here to explain the so-called imbalance between small and big business—external factors, mistaken or poor managerial decisions, and "Malthusian strategies," i.e., the refusal of entrepreneurs to increase the scale of operations—the first hypothesis, external factors, seems most persuasive, at least in the present state of research. It is my contention that entrepreneurial ability was only one factor among many that conditioned French economic growth and that such talent was not lacking.

It might be misleading to end this short essay in a negative fashion by simply exonerating business leaders of the 1900–1930 period from responsibility for the mistakes they allegedly made. In assessing their performance our aim has not been to pass value judgments on individuals or to appraise the importance of entrepreneurial talents or Malthusian practices. Rather, it has been to collect those few data that can be quantified on the size distribution of business units over time and to seek an explanation for their high variance or, to put it differently, for the dual structure that has been a constant characteristic of the French economy.

Actually, the very simple assumptions made at the outset seem fully warranted. As might be expected, the rise of complex technologies and the broadening of markets, especially after the 1890s, have had two results. In the modern sectors it has meant the development of big concerns that were able to supply large quantities of standardized products and that aimed at diversifying production or controlling a significant fraction of the market. Yet a decentralized system of small and middle-sized firms was maintained, specializing in unit products where style or design was crucial or where rapid technological progress made standardization impracticable. Obviously such a structure can be found in every industrial country because the flow of goods through assembly lines raises technical and financial problems that are best solved when productions stages are vertically integrated, when markets are stabilized by advertising, and so on. At the same time, the development of new products in a limited time span requires technical expertise from the labor force and a high degree of participation, and hence, small-scale production units, where contracts are close between managerial staff and personnel. In this respect France does not deserve to be treated as a special case, the only qualifications being that factor costs and socioeducational values in France have traditionally favored small-scale enterprise and that World War I and the wave of mergers in the 1920s contributed to an abrupt and unexpected concentration of business in a few key sectors. As a result, this dualism has appeared to be more extreme in France than in other countries. And it seems all the more unjustified since the same economic structures and the same social inequalities have persisted since the early nineteenth century. Nevertheless, this immobility does not mean that there has been no change in personnel or in the attitudes of high-level managers.

As we have seen, large firms in the past century often combined production and distribution. They were already under certain constraints as to the geographic dispersion of plants and sales agencies and the allocation of inventories and finance. But their conception of the "long-run" was somewhat different from that of the present generation of managers, and so were the attitudes and training of their staffs. Much of the profit a firm could make was dependent upon the short-run decisions the various partners had to make about the maximum price the market could bear, the range of opportunity costs that determined wages, and so on. Traditional norms and experience were the decisive elements then. This may explain why entrepreneurs came from a narrowly circumscribed milieu, parental and religious, and were satisfied initially with simple commercial training. Today, on the other hand, the smooth functioning of large modern plants at full or nearly full capacity in order to reduce overhead costs has made long-term planning about production schedules and markets a condition of survival. The radical changes that have been observed at the turn of the century in advanced technical education and, as a consequence, in the recruitment of the managerial class was an important step forward, not only for economic growth but also for social mobility.

In the nineteenth century and even after, industrial production was very flexible, fixed capital was relatively small, piecework occupied a high proportion of the labor force (some textile firms in the early nineteenth century employed as many as 2,500 or 3,000 cottage workers), and the distribution of dividends among partners was eliminated or at least delayed. The main goal in business was financial autonomy, so that entrepreneurs might be ready to take advantage of a run of good seasons and, conversely, be protected in case of recession. Business management often amounted to no more than the adminstration of a bank account or a family budget. Today this is no longer the case. Once across the threshold of size, once profit is regarded as dependent upon price stability and a minimum volume of sales, and once time-and-motion studies and amortization rates have become critical factors calling for new goals and more formal staff-line arrangements—then more managers will be forced to face entirely new financial, technical, and human challenges, even in the so-called family firms of the twentieth century. By 1936 Peugeot counted 15,000 stockholders and 15,000 workers. This alone made the process of decision-making more complex and called for a new organizational structure. At the Renault plant in the same year there were no less than 29,550 workers and employees, but also some 2,475 administrative officers and 95 directors.[45] Enterprises such as these had already broken with the habits and objectives of those of the past century.

Near the end of the nineteenth century both groups of business leaders were faced with a long-term depression. In the 1880s rural industry collapsed. Managerial pessimism must have been deep and genuine, judging by the favorable response of business leaders to the ideas of J. Méline, a representative of the eastern textile districts. Claiming that "industrial consumption had an irreversible tendency to decline," Méline advocated the need for protecting the market against foreign competition, closing the cities to rural migrants, and dissuading the children of the "elites" from pursuing "industrial careers."[46] But the attitude of twentieth-century business leaders has been entirely different. Even though industry faced real difficulties in the 1930s, everyone remained confident about the future, expressing their faith in applied sciences ("there is nothing wrong with technical progress," commented the chairman of Kulhmann in 1933), their will "to lower costs in order to bring prices in line with consumer purchasing power," and their determination to refuse any help from the government lest it lead to a permanent condition of subsidized overproduction, as had occurred in the sugar industry in the 1884–1902 period. A government proposal in 1935 to form a cartel in the automobile industry was refused by the leading manufacturers on the grounds that it might save the weakest firms, "without modern equipment and research departments," although the leading firms lent their own capital to the small firms to enable them to merge and make the market more competitive.[47]

If these fundamental economic and social changes are taken into account, the traditional questions that have been raised about the "irrationality" of the French entrepreneur, his alleged refusal to increase the scale of his operations, will lose much of their validity. There is a paradox only to the extent that commentators insist on considering the nineteenth-century textile family firm as representative of the modern corporation in the growth sectors, and Méline as the authentic spokesman of the manufacturers of the 1930s. One can understand why historians would take such a position, for in a study of the continuities underlying change it is often useful, as a working hypothesis, to assimilate the present to the past. But August Detoeuf had no excuse for confusing the two genres. And the question can still be raised: Why did he claim, in the quotation above, that the French entrepreneur was no better when acting as the chairman of a large corporation than he was at running a small family firm? Perhaps this was an ironical way of drawing attention to his own achievement as the founder of the leading company in the electrical industry.[48] Or was it an admission that his generation had failed? In any case, the persistent efforts of many entrepreneurs to enlarge production units and discard a narrowly competitive notion of business, to rationalize industry by sectors and subordinate individual firms to trade associations, to exploit new technical innovations and find a better definition of the roles of management and labor in business organizations—all these approaches were already popular in the 1920s and early 1930s and are proof of the French entrepreneur's commitment to dynamic, modern industrial development. Moreover, no specific demands were made of the public sector. "In an organized economy," wrote Detoeuf in 1936, "governmental intervention will be reduced to a minimum." Yet in a country where small firms remained so numerous, one may question whether industrialization could have developed fully unless the government became involved in the economy by stimulating growth and concentration and by making certain that the social costs of the shift from small to large firms were equitably distributed.[49]

NOTES

1. Family businesses under company names were still more numerous in 1939 than joint-stock companies (sociétés anonymes): in that year, there were 151,044 of the former

and 43,080 of the latter. But the family businesses had smaller assets. Furthermore, their number had stopped growing: in the period 1800–1890, an average of 1,464 family enterprises had been founded per year (deducting those that were closed or liquidated); in 1900–1919 the figure was 2,057, and in 1928–1938 it had dropped to 1,223. The number of stock companies, on the other hand, increased annually by 343, 638, and 1,330 during these three periods. In terms of percentage of the total number of these companies founded, this represents a rise from 14.5 percent to 17.2 percent and to 21.0 percent, compared to 61.7 percent, 55.6 percent and 19.3 percent for family-type enterprises. See P. Combe, *Niveau de vie et progrès technique en France depuis 1860* (Paris, 1953), p. 342.

2. Auguste Detoeuf, *Les propos de O.-L. Barenton, confiseur, ancien élève de l'Ecole polytechnique* (Paris, 1952), p. 67–68.

3. J. P. Nioche and M. Didier, *Deux études sur la dimension des entreprises industrielles*, INSEE, E (1), 1967, p. 23. The difference is partly a matter of vocabulary. The French *"établissement"* is not, in fact, a financial unit as defined, for example, by autonomous bookkeeping, but rather "the totality of persons working together in a specific place under the direction of one or more representatives of the same firm." A man assisted by his wife who works without an employee is considered as an *établissement*; see table 10, translator's note.

4. P. R. Lawrence and J. W. Lorsch, *Organization and Environment* (Boston, 1967), pp. 189–98; Alfred D. Chandler, *Strategy and Structure: Chapters in the History of the Industrial Enterprise* (Cambridge, Mass., 1962).

5. N. Delefortrie and J. Morice, *Les revenus départementaux en 1864 et 1954* (Paris, 1959), tables 30 and 51, pp. 196–98 and 208–10.

6. F. Charpenel and A. Magot, *L'industrie rurale en France d'après l'enquête de 1848 sur le travail agricole et industriel* (Nanterre: University of Paris-X, 1970); M. Guilbert and V. Isambert-Jamati, *Travail féminin et travail à domicile* (Paris, 1956).

7. P. Caspard, *Recherches sur la main-d'oeuvre industrielle aux débuts de machinisme: Les ouvriers de la fabrique neuve de Cortaillod, 1754–1819* (Paris: University of Paris-I, 1969); R. Trempé, *Les mineurs de Carmaux, 1848–1914* (Paris, 1971), pp. 147–54.

8. M. Lévy-Leboyer, *Les banques européennes et l'industrialisation internationale dans la première moitié du XIXe siècle* (Paris, 1965), p. 171–72; G. Monin, *Les entreprises Peugeot dans la première moitié du XIXe siècle* (Paris: University of Paris-I, 1970), pp. 48–50, 81–82, 114–17.

9. E. Levasseur, *Questions ouvrières et industrielles en France sous la Troisième République* (Paris, 1907), p. 805.

10. G. Duveau, *La vie ouvrière en France sous le Second Empire* (Paris, 1946), p. 442.

11. *Annuaire statistique de la France* (1878), p. 310.

12. M. Jonot, *L'apprentissage à Paris, 1860–1880* (Nanterre: University of Paris-X, 1972); Y. Legoux, *Du campagnon au technicien* (Paris, 1972); C. R. Day, "Education, Technology and Social Change in France: The Cluny School, 1866–1899," *French Historical Studies*, Spring 1974, pp. 427–44.

13. C. de Lasteyrie, *L'enseignement primaire et élémentaire à Paris en 1867–1877* (Nanterre: University of Paris-X. 1972).

14. At the end of the nineteenth century the wages of unskilled workers in France amounted to 66 percent of those of skilled workers, compared to 57 percent in England, 47 percent in the United States, and 36 percent in Germany; see E. H. Phelps-Brown and M. H. Brown, *A Century of Pay* (London, 1968).

15. L. Karpik, "Urbanisation et satisfaction au travail," *Sociologie du travail* 8, no. 4 (1966): 179–204; and "Expectations and Satisfaction in Work," *Human Relations* 21, no. 4 (1968): 327–51.

16. J. Tchernoff, *Les ententes économiques et financières* (Paris, 1933), p. 144.

17. M. Laferrère, *Lyon, ville industrielle* (Paris,1960), p. 106.

18. Ph. Girardet, *Ceux que j'ai connus* (Paris, 1952); S. Reiner, *La tragédie d'André Citroën* (Paris, 1954); M. Flageolet-Lardenois, "Une firme pionnière: Panhard et Levassor jusqu'en 1918," *Le mouvement social* 81 (1972): 27–50; P. Fridenson, *Histoire des usines Renault: I. Naissance de la grande entreprise, 1898–1939* (Paris, 1972).

19. C. Fohlen, *L'industrie textile au temps du Second Empire* (Paris, 1957); Lévy-Leboyer *Les banques européennes*, p. 70; H. Suzuki, *L'evolution de l'industrie cotonnière dans la région rouennaise au XIXe siècle* (Paris, 1969).

20. Suzuki, *L'industrie cotonnière*, part 2.

21. Information received from J. Fierain.

22. N. Delefortrie-Soubeyroux, *Les dirigeants de l'industrie française* (Paris, 1961).

23. Not counting the graduates who pursued careers in the army, the average annual number of engineers graduated from the Ecole polytechnique, the Ecole centrale, the Ecole des mines and the Génie maritime were the following:

1850–54	108	1870–74	197	1890–94	251	1910–14	351
1855–59	137	1875–79	216	1895–99	292	1918–19	364
1860–64	173	1880–84	246	1900–04	314	1920–24	953
1865–69	198	1885–89	249	1905–09	306	1925–29	—

24. H. Le Chatelier, "Du rôle de la science dans l'industrie," *La technique moderne 10* (1909); H. Le Chatelier, "Quelques reflexions sur l'enseignement technique supérieur," *Revue internationale de l'enseignement* (1909), and *L'enseignement technique supérieur: Ses buts et ses méthodes* (1911).

25. Following C. Mercié, *Les Polytechniciens, 1870–1930: Recrutement et activités* (Nanterre: University of Paris-X, 1972), and C. Baucher and A. Moore, *La formation et le recrutement des ingénieurs civils des Mines* (Nanterre: University of Paris-X, 1973). The lower income categories comprise employees in the private and public sectors, low-level civil servants and petty officials, artisans and shopkeepers, and school teachers.

26. G. Lamé and E. Clapeyron, *Plan d'écoles générales et spéciales pour l'agriculture, l'industrie manufacturière, le commerce et l'administration* (Paris, 1833). For the Saint-Simonian engineer, see particularly G. Thuiller, *Témoins de l'administration* (Paris, 1967), pp. 180–81, and more generally, P. Guillaume, "Notes sur les ingénieurs des charbonnages de la Loire au XIXe siècle," in *Charbon et Sciences Humaines: Actes du Colloque organisé par la Faculté des Lettres de l'Université de Lille en Mai, 1963* (Paris, 1966), p. 221.

27. *Ecole centrale des arts et manufactures: livre du centenaire* (Paris, 1929); J.-P. Callot, *Histoire de l'Ecole polytechnique* (Paris, 1949); Jacques Boudet, ed., *Le monde des affaires en France de 1830 à nos jours* (Paris, 1952); F. Caron, *La compagnie du chemin de fer du Nord, 1846–1937: Histoire de l'exploitation d'un grand réseau* (Paris, 1973); M. Rust, *Business and Politics in the Third Republic: The Comité des Forges and the French Steel Industry, 1896–1914* (Ph.D. diss., Princeton University, 1974); C. Kent "Camille Cavallier and Pont-à-Mousson: An Industrialist of the Third Republic" (Ph.D. diss., Oxford University, 1973).

28. Mercié, *Les Polytechniciens*, p. 39 ff.

29. M. Aucuy, "Les structures industrielles," in Ch. Rist and G. Pirou, *De la France d'avant-guerre à la France d'aujourd'hui* (Paris, 1939), pp. 153–57.

30. Nusbaumer, review of H. L. Gantt, "Work, Wages, and Profit," in *Revue de la Metallurgie* 12 (1915); V. Cambon, *Le taylorisme* (Paris, 1917); G. Bricard, *L'organisation scientifique de travail* (Paris, 1926); M. Daclin, *La crise des années 1930 à Besançon*

(Besançon, 1965); C. S. Maier, "Between Taylorism and Technocracy: European Ideologies and the Vision of Productivity in the 1920s," *Journal of Contemporary History* 2 (1970): 27-61; J. M. Laux, "Travail et travailleurs de l'industrie automobile jusqu'en 1914," *Le mouvement social* 81 (1972): 22-26.

31. P. Lévy, *L'origine des agents de la Régie autonome des Transports parisiens,* (Nanterre: University of Paris-X, 1971). In Franche-Comté the recession of the 1930s brought about a reverse migration of skilled workers into the factories; J. P. Ollier, *Seloncourt: Evolution d'une commune du Pays de Montbéliard* (Paris, 1968); B. Dezert, *La croissance industrielle et urbaine de la porte d'Alsace* (Paris, 1969).

32. André Citroën, "L'avenir de la construction automobile," *Revue politique et parlementaire,* 10 May 1929, p. 232 ff.

33. E. Mercier, "Les conséquences sociales de la rationalisation en France," *Cahiers du Redressement français* 1, no. 10 (1927): 20, cited by F. R. Ruisel, *Ernest Mercier, French Technocrat* (Berkeley and Los Angeles, 1967), p. 53, and, by the same author, "Technocrats and Public Economic Policy: From the Third to the Fourth Republic," *Journal of European Economic History* 2, no. 1 (1973): 53-100. Cf. also H. De Peyerimhoff, "Le programme patronal," *Revue des vivants,* 2 (1928), and "Les formules d'organisation économique," *Revue des deux mondes,* 15 March 1929. See also A. Detoeuf, *Observations sur l'Amérique* (Paris, 1926), and *La réorganisation industrielle* (1927), and the comments of M. Blain, *Un aspect des idées patronales de l'entre-deux guerres: A. Detoeuf et les "Nouveaux Cahiers"* (Nanterre: University of Paris-X, 1973).

34. M. Schwartz, "L'industrie automobile: rapport au Conseil national économique (July 1936)," *Journal Officiel,* 27 August 1936; Fridenson, *Les usines Renault,* p. 263 ff.

35. Various examples taken from such sectors as leather goods, small arms, and sewing machines, etc., are presented in P. Passama, *L'intégration du travail: Formes nouvelles de la concentration industrielle* (Paris, 1910). But a textile company like Saint-Frères, which processed 35 percent of the French jute, also owned plantations, weaving plants, and sixty-seven sales outlets.

36. A. Aftalion, "Les cartels de la région du Nord de la France, 1899-1907," *Revue économique internationale* 5 (1908): 107-65; O. de Magondeaux, *Les ententes industrielles obligatoires et le corporatisme en France* (Paris, 1937); E. Dussauge, *L'état et les ententes industrielles* (Paris, 1937); J. M. Jeanneney, *Forces et faiblesses de la France* (Paris, 1956).

37. For these problems, cf. Fridenson, *Les usines Renault.*

38. The danger inherent in concentration, i.e., the fact that a monopolist may secure excess profit by restricting output and keeping prices artificially high, did not unduly concern French writers. What they did fear was the lack of concentration, the fact that a given market might continue to be shared by two groups of companies, since disparity in size, and hence in productivity, might enable the larger ones to dominate a given branch of industry and, by fixing prices at a high level, keep in activity minor firms, thus procuring for themselves an artifical rent. The dual structure of business thus would make it unnecessary for them to lower prices in order to increase their sales. Hence the distinction made by Jacques Houssiaux *(Le pouvoir des monopoles: Essai sur les structures industrielles du capitalisme contemporaine* [Paris, 1958], pp. 2-3, 209) between the economic power of big business, which would be measured by some index of concentration, and its power of *strategic* action: "from leadership to mutual interdependence, from competition to tacit collusion."

39. Comité des Forges, *La sidérurgie française, 1864-1914;* C. Precheur, *La Lorraine sidérurgique* (Paris, 1959); B. Gille, *La sidérurgie française au XIXe siècle* (Paris, 1968), pp. 189, 234; P. Guillaume, *La compagnie des Mines de la Loire, 1846-54* (Paris,

1966); M. Gillet, *Les charbonnages du Nord de la France au XIXe siècle* (Paris, 1973), p. 174-79.

40. In addition, cf. *La société de Commentry-Fourchambault et Decazeville, 1854-1954;* (Paris, 1955); Tchernoff, *Les ententes;* J. Wolff, "Decazeville: expansion et déclin d'un pôle de croissances" *Revue économique,* 1972, pp. 753-85.

41. Charles Wilson, *The History of Unilever* (London, 1954), 2: 266; P. Baud, *L'industrie chimique en France* (Paris, 1932), pp. 104, 253; Cie de Saint-Gobain, *Livre du bicentenaire, 1665-1965;* C. J. Gignoux, *Histoire d'une entreprise française* (Paris, 1955), p. 113; M. Laferrère, *Lyon, ville industrielle* (Paris, 1960), pp. 318-22; H. Morsel, *Les industries électro-techniques dans les Alpes françaises du Nord de 1860 à 1921,* in C.N.R.S., *L'industrialisation de l'Europe au XIXe siècle* (Paris, 1970); Houssiaux, *Le pouvoir des monopoles.*

42. In 1931, Saint-Gobain held shares in some 120 companies, this portfolio being entered in the accounts for 570 million francs (compared with 225 million francs capital); Kulhmann and Pechiney together held 450 million francs capital and 450 million francs in shares; the Compagnie Générale d'électricité, with 130 million francs capital, held a portfolio of 365 million francs; Tchernoff, *Les ententes,* pp. 108-9; A. de la Bouillerie, *La société des forges et des ateliers du Creusot* (Paris, 1957).

43. The correlation coefficient between the merger index and that of capital formation is only in the order of 0.25 because in the immediate post-war years numerous mergers took place while investments were still lagging. This was the case in such new industries as the automobile: André Citroën took over some assets left by Clement Bayard and Mors, while Peugeot absorbed those of Dedion-Bouton. In the petroleum industry oil companies started off in many cases by combining local firms; the Anglo-Iranian Company, for instance, when it opened in France in 1921 already had 13.6 percent of the market. Besides, war indemnities were often pooled by a large number of firms in order to rebuild one single and modern plant facility in a particular industry. Finally, sequestered German properties were sold to groups of companies that associated for the purpose.

44. A. Aftalion, "Le cartel des mines de charbon du Nord et du Pas de Calais," *Revue économique internationale* (1911): 254 ff; M. Giller, *Les charbonnages du Nord.*

45. M. Jordan, *Quelques remarques sur un example d'économie dans une société anonyme (Peugeot)* (Montbéliard, 1936); Fridenson, *Les usines Renault,* pp. 325-26. For a general discussion, cf. J. K. Dent, "Organizational Correlates of the Goals of Business Management," *Personal Psychology* 12 (Autumn 1959): 365-93; G. P. Dyas, "The Strategy and Structure of French Industrial Enterprise" (Ph.D. diss., Harvard University, 1972); Bruce Scott, "The Industrial State: Old Myths and New Realities," *Harvard Business Review* 51, no.2 (1973): 133-48.

46. J. Méline, *Le retour à la terre et la surproduction industrielle* (Paris, 1905). The same theme was echoed later by J. Huet, G. Duhamel, and others.

47. R. Berr, "Les techniques chimiques devant la crise," *La science appliquée au service de la nation* (Paris, 1950).

48. Auguste Detoeuf's disenchantment is commented upon in M. Blain, *Auguste Detoeuf,* p. 41, and is based on *Les nouveaux cahiers* 14 (1937): 3.

49. For a comparison with Great Britain, see Leslie Hannah, "Managerial Innovation and the Rise of the Large-Scale Company in Interwar Britain," *Economic History Review* 27, no. 2 (1974): 252-70.

ENTREPRENEURIAL PATRONAGE
IN NINETEENTH-CENTURY FRANCE
BY ALBERT BOIME

THE PATRONAGE of the entrepreneur and the influence of the entrepreneurial mentality on nineteenth-century French art are the main themes of this essay. If anything in this study is new to students of either entrepreneurial or art history, it is likely to consist less in the facts about either area than in their interconnection. I shall try first to characterize different kinds of entrepreneurs and their collections; second, to show how entrepreneurial activity affects art beyond the realm of patronage; and third, to indicate how the entrepreneurial mentality and artistic occupations dovetail in the period under study. Insofar as the two areas of activity have been understood as antithetic, both have been to a large extent misconceived, and their common relationship to the general cultural background neglected.

To Max and Dorothy.

A project of this complexity requires the aid of a large community of scholars, and I am particularly grateful for assistance to Jean d'Albis, Peter Bermingham, Jerome Boime, Janet Brown, Carroll Coates, Robert Forster, Jacques Foucart, Francis Haskell, William Hauptman, Robert Herbert, Janine Herzberg, Lawrence McGinniss, Joseph Moody, Ellen Oppler, D. Stephen Pepper, Theodore Reff, John Rewald, Rodolphe Walter, and Gabriel Weisberg. I am also grateful to Chris Focht for his photographic expertise. But my greatest debt is to Irene Falkenstein and Madeleine Fidell-Beaufort, who generously checked references and dug up research materials: I am happy to record my warm thanks to both of them.

137

The term *entrepreneurial mentality* is used not only to refer to entrepreneurs as such but to characterize a whole range of group experiences involving broad segments of French society. By linking this outlook with art, my discussion goes beyond the confines of the classic patron-artist relationship to include artists who themselves acted as entrepreneurs and entrepreneurs who created works of art. I also understand new aesthetic directions to be an outgrowth of this mentality, as entrepreneurs provided an environment of workers and mechanisms, bridges and chimneys, railroads and steamships, for innovative artists who required new subject matter "to be of their times."

THE COLLECTORS

Two difficulties, at opposite extremes, confront the student of the entrepreneur-patron: the want of documentation on the private lives of entrepreneurs and the pervasive impact of entrepreneurs on the epoch under consideration. Too little information on the one hand and too wide a territory for investigation on the other impede the forming of tough generalizations. Consider for a moment that young Eugène Carrière earned his livelihood by doing letterheads, advertising vignettes, and signboards for entrepreneurs—commonplace commissions in the modern period far too vast to examine in the present context. Entrepreneurs affected every area of social and economic life, and an exhaustive investigation of their influence would have to include the areas of packaging and labeling, greeting cards, menus, invitations, and a galaxy of items in the commercial and applied arts. Making no pretense to such an inquiry, I have restricted this study to the "major" forms of entrepreneurial patronage as opposed to the "minor" ones—recognizing, of course, the relative nature of these terms especially when taken in a quantitative sense.

This study also singles out business magnates rather than shopkeepers, a limitation arising from the vagaries of the literature. The small businessman crops up often enough in biographies of the artists, but generally as a shadowy figure in the first chapter who aids the young artist and then conveniently vanishes. But the local tavern owner, greengrocer, and baker evidently made signal contributions to artists' careers, since, unable to afford old masters or popular contemporaries, they protected the living rather the dead, the unknown rather than the official favorite. They commissioned decorations and portraits, and occasionally even helped subsidize tuition at an art school. The neighborhood art dealer or shopkeeper very often exchanged his goods for a canvas, thereby attaching both economic and qualitative importance to an artist's work. The careers of Millet, Magaud, De Coninck, van Gogh, Monet, and Pissarro would have been significantly different had they not been supported by their local merchants.

Given these considerations, the following conclusions may safely be set forth: (1) the collecting of art was an urgent need for most entrepreneur-patrons; (2) entrepreneurs who amassed important collections were business leaders in their respective areas and helped set contemporary taste; (3) entrepreneurs who hired artists to design their industrial products likewise innovated in their field, and in cases where this practice was joined to a taste for collecting, entrepreneurs revolutionized their industries; and (4) the relationship of an entrepreneur's politicial and economic ideals to the character of his collection and patronage was highly variable. The consistency of Jean Dollfus, the director of the textile factory Dollfus Mieg, and Eugène Schneider, the awesome manager of the ironworks at Le Creusot, is exceptional: the former inherited his father's liberal politics and paternal attitude toward employees and supported the Impressionist vanguard, whereas the latter was an imperious personality who used state troops to subdue recalcitrant workers and rigorously collected faultless specimens of seventeenth-century Dutch painting.[1] More typical was the zealous eclecticism of Isaac and Emile Péreire, railway magnates and founders of the Crédit Mobilier, who overcrowded their jointly-owned mansion with old and contemporary masters, conservatives, and independents.

The period is dominated by eclectic tastes that militate against an analysis of the collections as expressions of individual temperaments. Only in the last quarter of the century do a number of vital entrepreneurs emerge who reveal in their collecting habits independence or individuality. Buying large portions of their collections in the boom years following the Franco-Prussian War, their taste also reflects a preoccupation with native French painters who depicted a changing, dynamic world. Indeed, a parallel exists between the hedonistic character of Impressionist outdoor scenes and the frenetic speculation of the 1870s and early 1880s. Similarly, the anarchic tendencies of late nineteenth-century art are echoed by the attitudes of these individualistic-minded patrons. The same collectors are also more generous to the state than were earlier pioneers, sometimes leaving whole collections to the city of Paris or to France. They were motivated both by jealous regard for their collections and by a superpatriotism based variously on guilt feelings, a sense of cultural inferiority, and ethnic self-consciousness. As in the case of Thomy-Thiéry the sugar refiner and Isaac de Camondo the banker, a defensive chauvinism lay behind their patronage and generosity to the state.[2] Perhaps this is also a reflection of the stagnant economy in the late years of the century, and of the isolationist attitude reflected in the inward-turning spirit of the Symbolists.

The earlier collectors, who began accumulating in the July Monarchy and the boom years of the 1850s, were more inclusive in their taste and more possessive about their collections. These were generally sold off at auction following the death of the owner—a fate that tormented the enlightened critics of the period.[3] This group of collectors, however, bought mainly for their private enjoyment and for the sake of being surrounded by the work of artists whose achievements paralleled their own business successes.

Insofar as patronage is a form of financial support, the method of dispensing it remains fairly stable; nevertheless, certain changes in the classic relationship between patron and beneficiary distinguish the nineteenth century from earlier epochs. For one thing, the entrepreneur-patron of the later period is the parvenu who springs from the undistinguished mass of mankind and stands in a different relationship to the artist from that of the old ruling classes. If he is called a *mécène*, in honor of Maecenas, the archtypal princely patron, this is often done with tongue-in-cheek irony. Both entrepreneur-patron and artist come from the same social background, and this identity of social and psychological dispositions essentially annuls any semblance to classic forms of patronage, where the artist was employed as a personal servant or otherwise dependent on an aristocratic class.[4]

Another difference in the nineteenth century is the blurring of the categories of collector and patron, which in prior epochs had been sharply distinguished. Formerly, the collector had bought the work of the past and had required some sort of broker to help him, while the patron had strictly protected living artists; it was not common to find the two loves residing in the same person. In the nineteenth century, the patron in this traditional sense became far less important, since he was replaced by the collector of both old and new paintings. The two enthusiasms became fused, a change facilitated by the annual official exhibitions known as the Salons and by the emergence of dealers, as well as by the eclectic proclivities of the period.[5] Then, too, by combining both types in his own person, the entrepreneur discovered another way to outshine the aristocratic models he had tried to emulate when he gained his fortune.

Among the various schools represented in the collections of entrepreneurs around mid-century, two stand out significantly from the rest: seventeenth-century Dutch and eighteenth-century French painting.[6] The major private collections enumerated in the *Paris Guide* of 1867—the majority of them formed by such entrepreneurs as James de

Rothschild, Casimir Périer *fils*, Achille Seillière, François Delessert, Eugène Schneider, and the brothers Péreire—conspicuously reflect this tendency.[7]

Among those in the first rank would be Schneider's remarkable collection of Dutch paintings which, unlike the others mentioned, was relatively small, consisting of fifty-five examples and a supplementary cabinet of drawings.[8] Highly possessive, the owner of the ironworks at le Creusot did not encourage visitors, and he kept the key to the drawing cabinet on his person at all times. Most of his paintings were of exceptional quality and included such splendid works as Rembrandt's early portrait of the pastor *Johannes Elison*, presently in the Boston Museum of Fine Arts. Contemporary critics did not fail to notice the relationship between the meticulous character of the collection and the owner's temperament: indeed, the severity of Elison's gaze is matched only by Schneider's in the portrait by Delaroche.[9] Each picture in Schneider's collection underwent a scrupulous examination for blemishes and restorations, since Schneider refused to purchase a work with the slightest imperfection.[10]

Seillière assembled an outstanding collection of Rembrandts; the Péreires, Delessert, Rothschild, Pourtalès-Gorgier, and the duc de Morny all achieved spectacular success in gathering representative Dutch pictures. Yet it should not be mistakenly assumed that this emphasis on the Dutch betokened a conservative attitude. Not surprisingly, the interest in Dutch genre and the growth of nineteenth-century French landscape painting developed simultaneously. Along with the English tradition also inspired by the art of the Lowlands, the seventeenth-century Dutch provided the primary precedent for French landscape and genre painting of the nineteenth century and contributed to a revival of the Dutch cult on the market.[11] The Barbizon group, the realists, and the Impressionists were informed by Dutch paintings, perhaps the most consistent external influence on the art of nineteenth-century France. Most of these artists copied and, like the entrepreneurs, even collected examples of Dutch work. The receptivity to the art of the Lowlands made France seem like a mecca to such Dutch expatriates as van Gogh, Jongkind, and Meyer de Haan. Animal painters like Brascassat, Decamps, Rosa Bonheur, Jacque, Troyon, van Marcke, and Philippe Rousseau modeled themselves after Cuyp and Potter, while Meissonier and Bonvin attest to the influence of Ter Borch, Metsu, and de Hooch. Even Gérôme—an academic history painter—disclosed a love of the Dutch in his small, finely painted pictures, and he did a work entitled *Rembrandt Etching*, notable for its striking pattern of lights and darks. It is no coincidence that the banker

François Delessert and the duc de Morny, an adventurous entrepreneur in the sugar-beet industry, joined to their Dutch collections a number of Meissoniers.[12]

Courbet, Manet, Pissarro, and Monet, all of whom visited the Lowlands, never entirely abandoned the formative Dutch influence. The literature of the period also consecrates the sanctity of the Dutch: Thoré-Bürger, who wrote the chapter on the private collections in the *Paris Guide*, published a two-volume work on Dutch museums during the years 1858–60 and continued to publicize Dutch painting in subsequent years.[13] A close friend of the naturalists, he had chosen Holland for his place of exile in the aftermath of the 1848 revolution. In 1868 Taine began a series of lectures at the Ecole des Beaux-Arts on the art of the Lowlands, a series he published the following year, and in the same period Emile Montégut published an extensive account of his voyage to this region and his impressions of Dutch art in the *Revue des deux mondes*.[14] Finally, Fromentin published *les Maîtres d'autrefois* in 1876—the year of the Schneider sale—which included a separate discussion of the Dutch influence on contemporary French painting.[15] He called special attention to the contribution of Jacob van Ruysdael, who was well represented in Paris collections.

One Paris collection was that of Emile and Isaac Péreire, two of the most daring French entrepreneurs of the period.[16] The Péreires pioneered in railway transport and innovated in the realm of investment banking and credit procedures. In 1835 Emile obtained the charter for the first common carrier railway in France and two years later confounded his critics by successfully achieving the run between Paris and Saint-Germain. The line became an immediate financial and psychological success and inaugurated the large-scale railroad development that took place in the subsequent period.[17] During the Second Empire the Péreires founded the Crédit Mobilier to help provide capital and credit for rapid industrialization.[18]

The Péreires shared an extravagant mansion on the Faubourg Saint-Honoré, Emile occupying the upper floors, and Isaac the lower. Between them they owned hundreds of works ranging from the Italian primitives to contemporary artists of all stamps. Concentrating their wealth more upon their home and personal comforts than on public display, the Péreires were somewhat overwhelmed by their own surrounding luxury. Leading guests quickly through the salons where the gilt coruscated under enormous gas-chandeliers, one of the Péreires would murmur in modest deprecation: "Il y a trop d'or ici," and take them to a gallery of pictures, where he would add: "Voilà mon véritable trésor."[19] Evidently, the collection vindicated the lavish decoration that appeared vulgar and pretentious.

But it was all quite respectable to one of their earlier biographers, who wrote that the Hôtel Péreire was not the residence of a parvenu but the "palais d'un prince," and he could even forgive the Péreires' "Jewishness" for their high level of taste.[20] In his estimation the Péreires satisfied the model of the grand bourgeois collector who had achieved as much enterprise in his taste as in his business affairs.

Thoré-Bürger, who carefully studied the collection, proclaimed it one of the finest in Paris.[21] He naturally preferred the Dutch examples, which included Ruysdael, Hals, Cuyp, Hobbema, Ter Borch, De Hooch, Dou, and Adriaen Van de Velde. The critic responded especially to two works, Rembrandt's portrait of Jan C. Sylvius (now in Cologne), which he felt was the best work by the master of Paris, and Vermeer's *Geographer* (now in Frankfurt). Thoré-Bürger literally opened up Vermeer studies with his pioneer article in the *Gazette des Beaux-Arts* of 1866, an early attempt to sort out the master's works. Undoubtedly, the *Geographer* contributed to his interest in this area.[22]

When describing the great collections in Paris, Thoré-Bürger—a passionate devotee of Dutch art—noticed that he was referring so often to Dutch works that he felt called upon to apologize parenthetically: "Ce n'est pas ma faute si, dans toutes les collections, les hollandais priment tout." Generally given exclusive credit for the revival of interest in Dutch painting, Thoré-Bürger here situates himself in proper perspective: the entrepreneur-amateur, by his purchases and patronage, shaped the taste for Dutch realism and contributed as much to this revival as the leftist and revolutionary critics of the period. Stanley Meltzoff, in his classic article on the revival of the Le Nains, claimed that the promoters of most of the nineteenth-century revivals were at odds with society and convention, emphasizing that it was not the Bank of France but the revolutionaries and counterrevolutionaries who initiated the new taste.[23] In fact, it was precisely bankers like Seillière and Pourtalès, owners of precious Le Nains, Rembrandts, and Hals, and the Rothschilds, with their Dutch cult, who could be counted among the pace setters and who bore eloquent witness to the changing fashion.[24]

Marx said that the ruling ideas of any age are the ideas of the ruling class, and this seems to hold true in the case of the art world in mid-nineteenth-century France. Recounting a visit to the duc de Morny in 1847, Delacroix rhapsodized about the sugar refiner's marvellous collection of Dutch paintings, which "[l]'ont paru le comble de l'art, parce qu'il y est caché tout à fait." A change in taste requires the presence of concrete objects exposed to view, and in this sense Barbizon realism reflected the predisposition of the entrepreneurial class. The historian Léon de Laborde bitterly denounced profit-seeking collectors who systematically collected Dutch and Flemish pictures, as well as their French, Belgian, and English imitators, and concluded: "Ce que gagnent chaque année en valeur et ce que se vendront plus tard sont les tableaux hollandais et flamands, les Decamps, Meissonier, Rousseau, et autres oeuvres modernes que s'arrachent les connaisseurs. . . . Telle est la direction que nos nouveaux Mécènes donnent à l'art et à l'école."[25] In retrospect, it now appears that rather than flaunt middle-class ideals, the so-called antiacademic trend rationalized the taste of the *haute bourgeoisie.*

Just as the ruling classes created the conditions for a "revival," so the successive derivations from the new taste—realists, naturalists, and Impressionists, whom we subsume under the rubric of the "avant-garde"—also attained salvation in the arms of later entrepreneurs who began to emancipate themselves from their aristocratic model and search for exotic styles to complement their budding individuality.

Not that the Dutch-picture cult was novel: it had enjoyed a vogue in the previous century and had never really gone out of fashion; but the early nineteenth-century entrepreneurs modeled themselves after the eighteenth-century aristocracy and adopted their status symbols. The later, more dynamic derivations coincide with a gradual displacement of the aristocratic model (and this includes the assimilation and modification of eighteenth-century art) and the self-assertive ideals of the later entrepreneurs. These demanded distinctive trappings to define their nonconformity, and the result was an anarchy of stylistic developments that has continued to the present day. This does not imply that the taste of the ruling classes is still not the generative factor: on the contrary, the taste for ever-increasing exoticism is the concomitant of status in the modern world.

Coincidental with the taste for the avant-garde was a greater sense of responsibility to the state: while the reasons for donating a collection to the public domain may be multifarious, one obvious factor is the attachment in perpetuity of the donor's name to the collection. The association of the donor's name with the work reflects the jealousy of personal taste. Thus, the original work of the Impressionists and the Post-Impressionists was a function of the needs not only of the artists but of their patrons as well.

Like the revival of the Dutch cult, the mania expressed for the *dix-huitième* by the enrepreneur-patrons reflects a general reawakening to the taste that had been driven underground by the revolutionary and Napoleonic epochs.[26] This occurs already in the romantic epoch but becomes à la mode during the Second Empire. The Goncourts' writing, the revival of the commedia dell'arte, and the court taste created an atmosphere conducive to working in this mode. Renoir, who admitted that he had been brought up "on the eighteenth-century French masters," reflected characteristics of Fragonard and Boucher in his mature work.[27] The Péreires, like most of their peers, owned several eighteenth-century paintings, including examples by Boucher, Fragonard, Greuze, Lancret, and Pater.

Still another important section of the Péreire collection—and in this it was unique—was the first-rate Spanish works, including examples attributed to Velázquez, Murillo, Cano, Ribera, Zurbarán, El Greco, and Goya. Many of the Spanish pictures had come full circle, since they had been in the collections of Maréchal Soult and Louis-Philippe prior to the 1848 revolution, and the Péreires bought them on the English market in the early 1850s.[28] Delacroix, who was attracted by one of the works when it was shown in the window of a restorer, anticipates the subsequent obsession of the French with the Spanish school.[29] It played a major role in the evolution of realism and Impressionism, and although the ground had been prepared in the July Monarchy, the Péreires exhibited more than a fashionable interest in the Spanish painters.

The Péreires also patronized their contemporaries, not only by direct purchase of completed works but through original commissions as well. They had in their collection paintings by Delacroix, Ingres, Rousseau, Diaz, Meissonier, Delaroche, Decamps, Chassériau, Tissot, Gérôme, and Ary Scheffer. They owned such major works by Delacroix as the *Marino Faliero*, *Combat de giaour et du pacha*, *Christ endormi dans la barque*, and a version of the *Medea*; and by Ingres, the *Odalisque à l'esclave*, a major compositional drawing for the *St. Symphorian*, the Valpinçon *Bather*, and a replica of the *Oedipus*.[30] Delaroche's portrait of Emile stood out like a beacon amid the cluttered Victorian setting and was perhaps the gem of the collection (figs. 4 and 5). The artist was a close friend of the family, and Emile helped organize the painter's posthumous retrospective at the Ecole des Beaux-Arts in 1857.[31]

The Péreires commissioned young artists in the 1850s to decorate their sumptuous mansion. In 1857, Bouguereau painted allegorical personifications of the seasons and the zodiac for two of the salons, while the following year Jalabert, a pupil of Delaroche, followed this pattern for the bedroom and used allegorical figures of Sleep, Meditation, and Study to provide appropriate atmosphere.[32] These commissions had a popular success and significantly advanced the careers of the young artists. Although revealing a conservative disposition, the decorations from the Péreires' private sanctuary probably attest less to an academic taste than to the limited institutional channels of communication with the wider community of artists.[33] In general, the brothers display a need for Faustian universality rather than partisan exclusiveness. By their inclusive outlook and patronage they exemplified the new breed of entrepreneur-patron.

Adolphe Thibaudeau was another railroad magnate who blended organizational and administrative capabilities with a distinctly creative sensibility. He helped establish the railway from Paris to Rouen and Le Havre, and shorter routes in Normandy and Brittany, sat on the boards of the Chemin de fer de Rouen and the Compagnie des chemins de fer de l'ouest, and speculated in a number of other industrial enterprises. In addition to his business activities, he found time to write newspaper articles and amass an outstanding art collection, whose drawings were spectacular. Preoccupied with what lay behind the appearance of things, he wrote a probing preface to Charles Blanc's *Trésor de la curiosité*, analyzing the taste and motivations of the contemporary art collector. Blanc himself attested to Thibaudeau's fascination for draw-

FIGURE 4. Interior of Emile Péreire's mansion on the Faubourg Saint-Honoré

FIGURE 5. Paul Delaroche, *Portrait of Emile Péreire*, 1855. Present whereabouts unknown.

ings as the revelation of the intimate thought of the artist: "C'est ici, me disait-il, la confidence des maitres, leur intimité. Il me semble qu'ils sont là, dans leur atelier, près de nous, essayant la forme de leurs pensées, ébauchant leur génie, et que nous les regardons faire, d'un ocil indiscret, par-dessus l'épaule."[34] This conviction Thibaudeau shared with Schneider, who also assembled a major drawing collection, reflecting the growing preoccupation with sketches and sketch techniques on the part of avant-garde artists and critics who advocated a spontaneous approach to artistic production.[35]

Art collections were maintained by the powerful bankers and financiers of the period, including the Delesserts, the Mallets, Perrégaux, Laffitte, the Rothschilds, the Hottinguers, the Foulds, Seillière, Casimir-Périer, and Pourtalès-Gorgier. The majority of these were Protestant or Jewish, and their initial quest for art objects was rooted in the self-conscious need for respectability and elegance along the lines of the landed aristocracy.[36] The continuity of the family enterprise, however, enabled the later generations to convert the original quest into an insatiable passion for works of art. The Delesserts were compulsive collectors: old man Benjamin accumulated plant species and shells, as well as paintings; his brother François owned a spectacular cabinet of 236 paintings (fig. 6),[37] while François's son, also named

Benjamin, added to the family acquisitions a vast repertoire of prints and engravings. Indeed, in the 1850s this last Benjamin wrote a biography of the Bolognese engraver Marcantonio Raimondi, almost one hundred and fifty of whose engravings he had collected.[38] It would be interesting to speculate on the extent to which Delessert popularized Raimondi, because a few years later Manet used a Raimondi engraving of a lost Raphael as the basis of his *Déjeuner sur l'herbe*.[39]

Pourtalès-Gorgier compiled a monumental collection of everything imaginable, and his combined catalogues number over a thousand items.[40] Bronzes, ivories, faïences, enamels, Greek and Roman antiquities, marbles, terra cottas, armor, and an extraordinary selection of tableaux filled his mansion on the rue Tronchet (fig. 7). The painting collection was exceptional for its Italian examples, which included Antonello da Messina's haunting *Condottiere*, a Giovanni Bellini, and a Bronzino. Pourtalès also owned such extraordinary works as Hals' *Laughing Cavalier* (now in the Wallace Collection), Le Nain's *Intérieur d'une tabagie*, and the notorious *Orlando muerto*, then attributed to Velázquez.[41] The debt of Manet and Gérôme to the *Orlando muerto* is well known, and it is highly probable that they had direct access to

FIGURE 6. Interior of the gallery of François Dellesért

FIGURE 7. Interior of the gallery of Pourtalès-Gorgier

this picture.[42] Although Pourtalès did not make his collection readily available to the public, critics, artists, and other private visitors were permitted to view it. Gérôme sought out the banker's set of gladiator armor to ensure that his painting *Pollice verso* would possess archaeological verisimilitude. Like other private collectors, entrepreneurs provided an alternative to the museums for study, since the public institutions had large gaps and responded more slowly to changing tastes.

Since old Meyer Amschel began with his coin collection, five generations of Rothschilds have distinguished themselves as patrons of the arts. The Rothschilds have been perennial supporters of individual artists, museums, and government art schools.[43] Insatiable collectors, they have demonstrated an innate need to envelop themselves in opulent surroundings. Rothschild collections have embraced—and still do embrace—every conceivable kind of art object: furniture, tapestries, manuscripts, enamels, ivories, porcelains, bronzes, glass, jewels, gold and silver objects, and paintings of all periods. Indeed, five generations of art historians and cataloguers could not keep pace with the art treasures accumulated by the various members of the Rothschild family.[44]

Until relatively recent times, the Rothschilds were also the most conservative of collectors, venturing openly into the modern field only around 1920.[45] James concentrated his interests primarily in the seventeenth-century Dutch and Rococo periods, and also in medieval and Renaissance antiquities. There were very few contemporaries represented, and they were limited to isolated examples of Scheffer and Flandrin and to interior decorations for his mansions on the rue Laffitte and the country châteaux at Ferrières and Boulogne. His most impressive commission was the portrait of his wife, Betty, by Ingres, which brilliantly captures the luxurious character of the Rothschild surroundings.[46] The country home was built in 1857 by Paxton, the English architect who designed the Crystal Palace. Decorated in Baroque splendor according to the orders of Baron James, its centerpiece was a ceiling by Tiepolo.

The Rothschilds have scrupulously separated their collecting habits from the taint of speculation; unlike other entrepreneurs, they did not permit entire collections to reach the market. As each generation of the Rothschilds has passed on, some of the finest pieces in the family's possession have gone to enrich museums, while the remainder has been divided up among the children. Baron James, the founder of the Parisian branch, and his eldest sons, Edmond and Gustave, reflect the possessive tendency common to the entrepreneur-patron prior to 1870, except that they preferred to keep their collections in the family, rather than disperse them after their deaths. But James's daughter, the Baronne Nathaniel de Rothschild, his youngest son, Alphonse, and the grandchildren followed the general pattern in the period after the Franco-Prussian War, generously donating whole collections to public institutions.[47]

As the century progressed, it became increasingly fashionable to offer the state or a town a package deal on the condition that the donor's name be displayed in the institutional setting. Sometimes the setting itself was provided ready-made when an entire mansion and its contents were donated. Bruyas, the banker-*mécène* from Montpellier, supplied the Musée Fabre in that town with its core, the "Cabinet Bruyas," and served as its curator as well.[48] A devoted patron of Courbet and an amateur painter himself, he was immortalized in the former's celebrated picture, *Bonjour, Monsieur Courbet* (Paris, Louvre), whose theme exemplifies the nineteenth-century democratization of the relationship between patron and protégé.

Isaac de Camondo, who descended from an important Jewish banking family, left his indelible mark on the national collections with an extraordinary bequest to the Louvre in 1908.[49] In addition to furniture and *objets d'art*, he presented the museum with more than 135 paintings and drawings of the modern school and with 450 Japanese prints. A fervent collector from an early age, he began with Renaissance objects and eighteenth-century furniture before systematically pursuing Far Eastern and avant-garde art. Camondo became a member of a group of Japanophiles that met regularly at the gallery of Samuel Bing, and he began building the vast holdings of Japanese prints, porcelains, and sculptures that eventually entered the Louvre.[50]

As in the case of the Dutch and Rococo revivals, the rediscovery of Japanese art after mid-century provided a stimulus to contemporary artists. By 1875 the influence of Japan on the applied arts was already far more extensive than the chinoiserie of the eighteenth century had ever been. The Japanese colorprint had a fresh and invigorating effect on the art of Manet, Degas, Monet, van Gogh, and Toulouse-Lautrec. Here again entrepreneurs were responsible for a fashion that mesmerized French artists: curio and antique dealers, ceramic, metal work, and textile manufacturers—even proprietors of tea warehouses, candy shops, and department stores established channels through which creative minds made contact with Japanese art. The popular vogue for *japonisme* coincided with the use of Japanese motifs in "high" art, and in some cases decorative designers were in advance of painters in their penetrating assimilation of such motifs.[51]

Significantly, Camondo began buying from the painters who responded to Japanese art. He formed a fabulous collection of works by Degas, Monet, Manet, Sisley, van Gogh, and Toulouse-Lautrec. Among his prize pictures were Manet's *Fifre* and *Au piano*, four of Monet's Rouen series, Cézanne's *Maison du pendu*, Sisley's *Inondation à Port Marly*, Degas' *L'absinthe*, *Femme à la potiche*, and many others of equal importance. Camondo represented the new breed of astute entrepreneur-*mécène* who had unfailing confidence in the new school and saw in it the means by which he could personally belong to the avant-garde.[52] One obvious reason for the growing emphasis on originality and innovative styles was the growth of public collections. Art was no longer the province of the privileged classes, and the entrepreneur diverged from the path of the national museums, which were old-master conscious, to seek his objects among the avant-garde painters. Camondo revealed equal agility in his business and artistic affairs: his bank helped sustain the stock market in the aftermath of the crash of the Union Générale in 1882.[53] He was also an artist in his own right, composing musical pieces in his spare time, one of which—*Le clown*—was performed at the Opéra-Comique in 1910. Fénéon recounted that Camondo harbored a secret dream to transcribe paintings into music.[54]

Two other entrepreneur-collectors, Henri Cernuschi and Emile Guimet, shared Camondo's interest in the art of the Far East and belonged to Bing's cenacle.[55] Cernushi, a naturalized Frenchman from Milan, founded the Banque de Paris and played an active role in promoting the liberal movement. Together with his friend Duret, the critic who befriended Manet, he traveled to the Far East in 1871–72, there acquiring the nucleus of his great collection, including the nearly five-meter-high bronze buddha of Meguro.[56] Guimet, an industrialist who owned a powder mill and manufactured synthetic ultramarine, was a devoted patron of music and the arts.[57] He was himself a competent composer and writer. But like Cernuschi, his first love comprised the Chinese, Japanese, and Indian antiquities he accumulated over the years from pilgrimages to Asia and steady visits to Bing. Both men presented their collections to the state, and today the Musées Guimet and Cernuschi are chief resources for the study of Asian art.

As a class of entrepreneurs, the department store magnates were usually enthusiastic, if conservative, art patrons. A department store is itself a kind of lively museum for spectators, and just as these pioneers delighted in surrounding themselves with sundry objects at work, so they enjoyed a home environment filled with a variety of art objects. The founders of La Samaritaine, Ernest Cognacq and Louise Jay, like Nélie Jacquemart and Edouard André, attached their names in hyphenated perpetuity to fabulous collections of eighteenth-century art.[58] In 1872 Cognacq, who had a modest business, married Louise Jay, the head saleswoman at Au Bon Marché, whose savings enabled them to purchase the adjoining shops. They called the new complex La Samaritaine after a sculptural relief of the Samaritan woman at Jacob's well on the front of an old waterworks built alongside the Pont Neuf.

It is probably not fortuitous that they named their firm after a work of art, since almost simultaneously with the inauguration of the new enterprise they began collecting art objects. Some pieces were earmarked for the decoration of the store, some were destined for their adjoining picture gallery, and some for their apartments. Initially, they bought Impressionist paintings, but they eventually sold them, save for a few precious examples by Monet, Boudin, and Degas. They preferred to concentrate on the eighteenth century, a period not only more suitable to their taste but perhaps more assuring as well. The rococo opulence of La Samaritaine de Luxe found an equivalent expression in the sumptuousness of their dwelling. Rarely socializing and preferring isolation during off-hours, Ernest and Louise adorned the two poles of their existence—work and home—with the elegance of Louis XV.

Alfred Chauchard, the founder of the Galeries du Louvre, formed an exceptional collection of the Barbizon landscape painters, which he donated to the Louvre.[59] A former shop assistant, Chauchard acquired from the Péreires—who became his backers—the lease of a corner in the building then being built near the Palais Royal, where in 1855 he established the Galeries du Louvre. He treated customers royally, offering up salons, lounges, and buffets, holding regular sales, and distributing redeemable coupons—selling principles much in vogue today, but then novel. Chauchard began collecting only after retirement in the 1880s, when the prices of the Barbizon school were already inflated. Vollard reports that Chauchard cared little for the avant-garde, and the record shows that he preferred Meissonier (he owned 26 of his works) to Monet.[60] When he began collecting, however, he did so with great passion, even to the point of outbidding American millionaires to acquire Millet's famous *Angelus*. His late start, and the haste in which he gathered his pictures prompted even his grateful recipients at the Louvre to question his motives.[61] The evidence intimated that Chauchard's bequest reflected a yearning to be remembered more as a princely patron than a "Novelty King." Nevertheless, he assured the Louvre of a high-level selection of Barbizon masters, including Millet, Dupré, Corot, Troyon, Diaz, and Daubigny.

Aristide Boucicault, who in 1852 launched Au Bon Marché, the first modern department store, and George Dufayel, the founder of the great ready-to-wear-goods store on the rue de Clignancourt, were even more restricted in their taste. Boucicaut's collection was most significant for its dazzling precious stones and jewelry; except for portraits of himself and his wife by Bouguereau, his pictures were for the most part examples of watered-down realism and Barbizon painting.[62] Dufayel constructed a sumptuous palace on the Champs-Elysées, where he accumulated antique marbles, bronzes, faïences, sculptures, and erotic nude statuary. He commissioned Edouard Detaille, the academic military painter, to decorate some of the ceilings.[63] Bader, the director of the Galeries Lafayette, lived well into the twentieth century, and his taste gradually shifted from the Barbizon School to the Impressionists. He owned works by Degas, Guillaumin, Renoir, and Pissarro, but his most adventurous purchases were six paintings by Soutine, whom he got to know personally.[64]

One exception to the generally conservative outlook of the department store chiefs was Ernest Hoschedé, an energetic entrepreneur who unflaggingly engaged in one enterprise after another. Durand-Ruel remembered him as a financier, while Gimpel noted that he owned a restaurant.[65] In the decade of the 1870s he was involved in at least three department stores: Hoschedé, Tissier, Bourely, et Compagnie; Hoschedé, Blémont, et Compagnie on the rue Sentier; and Au Gagne petit on the avenue de l'Opéra.[66] Although he went through several fortunes, he seemed always to have a steady fund of capital to risk. Versatile and dynamic, he created in 1880 a periodical that made use of costly color illustrations, *L'art de la mode,* but this had only an ephemeral existence. In the year of his death, he tried again to create an art periodical with a special art column reserved for himself.[67]

Hoschedé has the honor of being one of the earliest and strongest champions of the Impressionists. Already in 1874, before the Impressionists had their first group exhibition, Hoschedé had accumulated a sufficient number of their works to hold a sale.[68] Indeed, he bought paintings from the young artists as long as he had cash, but when one of his schemes failed, he sold them—much to the artists' chagrin—to pay off debts and finance a new undertaking. In 1878 he was forced to auction a remarkable collection of 117 tableaux—including 5 Manets, 12 Monets, 13 Sisleys and 9 Pissarros—at such ridiculously low prices that Pissarro moaned, "La vente Hoschedé m'a tué."[69]

All this occurred in the decade of the 70s, so there was very little chance for speculative gain: Hoschedé bought and sold paintings according to his financial situation. In fact, he was a genuine *mécène,* inviting artists regularly to his country estate in Montgeron and occasionally giving them an original commission.[70] Totally immersed in the art world, he culminated his career as a professional art critic. He dedicated his review of the 1882 Salon to Manet and Charles Cros and struggled for the recognition of young independent artists.[71] One of his own daughters became a painter, and his last published article was a

sympathetic review of the young generation of female artists emerging
in France at the end of the century.[72] In Hoschedé's case, there seems to
be a direct relationship between his bold entrepreneurial ventures and
his active support of avant-garde and independent artists. His numerous enterprises attest to a total immersion in the contemporary world,
and his restless, driving energy can be compared to the expressive
character of Impressionist painting.

Henri Rouart's involvement with the Impressionists is somewhat
similar: a trained engineer and industrialist who pioneered in the use
of refrigeration, he totally identified with the Impressionist movement.[73] When Rouart was not running his large metallurgical establishment or conceiving of new entrepreneurial ventures, he painted and
sought out the work of contemporary artists. Through his friendship
with Degas, he became involved in the group shows of the Impressionists: not only did he help defray their expenses but he took advantage of
the opportunity to exhibit his own work.[74] Alexandre emphasized the
link between Rouart's innovations in industry and his "discovery" of
fresh talent. Rouart owned an astonishing repertoire comprising such
works as Degas' *Dancers at the Bar*, now at the Metropolitan, Manet's
Music Lesson, and a general selection from Gauguin, Monet, Renoir,
Cézanne, Toulouse-Lautrec, Morisot.

Another group of fascinating entrepreneurs are those whose industry related intimately to the fine arts. They were patrons in a double
sense: they employed artists in their business and also formed important collections. Jean Dollfus, director of the large textile center in
Alsace, Dollfus Mieg et Compagnie, inherited a long artistic tradition:
one of the founding ancestors of the firm was a painter who made the
designs for its first cotton fabrics.[75] Dollfus himself studied painting
under the popular Alsacian master, Faller, an ex-pupil of Delacroix
and Delaroche who became Dollfus' advisor when Dollfus joined the
family firm. Dollfus carried over his aesthetic interests into his work,
applying himself to the improvement of his printed fabrics through
greater harmony of colors and fresh designs. To this end he employed a
number of industrial artists, who made his fabrics among the most
sought after in France.[76]

Dollfus also consecrated a major part of his activity to amassing
tableaux and art objects. In addition to his tapestries and Far Eastern
antiquities, he assembled an impressive collection of fifteenth-century
primitives and seventeenth century Dutch painters (figs. 8 and 9). After
the Franco-Prussian War, Dollfus moved to Paris, where he began
buying Barbizon masters and the Impressionists. He gravitated espe-

FIGURE 8. Interior of Jean Dollfus's mansion on the Champs-Elysées

cially toward Renoir, whom he met socially, ultimately earning a reputation for his small but choice representation of that artist, and also of Boudin, Sisley, and Pissarro.[77]

Charles Haviland, the owner of the famous porcelain factory at Limoges, inherited the firm from his father David, an American who became a naturalized French Citizen.[78] David planned from the outset to export his porcelains to the United States and, placing great emphasis on decoration, maintained an atelier of 100 apprentice painters and 4 art instructors. The Maison Haviland continued to expand this program, and out of a total of 500 employees in the 1860s, 165 were painters. David's enormous success stimulated the porcelain industry in Limoges and also induced his fifteen competitors to export to the United States. The French government, in appreciation of Haviland's contribution to its economy, awarded David a silver medal at the World's Fair of 1855.

FIGURE 9. Interior of Jean Dollfus's mansion on the Champs-Elysées

After the Franco-Prussian War, Charles and his brother decided to overhaul their styles, and for this purpose they hired the services of Bracquemond, a leading Parisian etcher who belonged to the Impressionist circle and who was then art director of the porcelain manufacture at Sèvres.[79] Very open to contemporary ideas, he had exhibited with the Impressionists in their first group show. Haviland appointed him director of an atelier at Paris, where he could be free to invent new designs and decors. Bracquemond was an ideal choice since he played an important role in promulgating the Japanese style in French industrial art. Under his supervision the Parisian atelier became a veritable laboratory for contemporary design: in anticipation of Art Nouveau, he developed a flat, linear style in the Japanese mode, which was colored with the broad touches of Impressionism. Bracquemond employed the well-known sculptor Dalou for the three-dimensional motifs. Through his contact with Haviland, Bracquemond was also able to help launch Gauguin as a ceramicist by putting him in touch with Ernest Chaplet, whom Haviland had set up with a small pottery shop to experiment with new stoneware techniques.[80]

Charles's contact with Bracquemond sparked the entrepreneur's involvement in the art milieu of Bing, Burty, and Goncourt. Thereafter, Charles formed a collection of Japanese art with passionate enthusiasm and devotion; his immense accumulation required more than fifteen catalogues, published during the years 1922–27. At the same time he began his collection of objets d'art, he became a friend of the Impressionists, collecting paintings by Degas, Jongkind, Manet, and Cassatt, and also sculptures by Rodin and Barye.[81] As in the cases of others we have discussed, Charles Haviland's innovative entrepreneurship finds its complement in the enthusiasm for the creations of painters and sculptors.

The great fashion designers like Jacques Doucet, Paul Poiret, and Jeanne Lanvin provide another example of entrepreneurial involvement in the arts combined with active encouragement of fine artists. Not unexpectedly, creators of contemporary fashion styles reveal a taste for all things modern. That Doucet was for many years an eighteenth-century enthusiast, is explained partly by Goncourt's influence on his early taste and partly by the fact that this suited his immature ideal of worldly elegance.[82] But in 1912 he astonished the international art world by selling his enormous collection of eighteenth-century paintings and compiling, during the subsequent decade, an equally impressive modern collection.[83] In addition to the Impressionists, Doucet purchased Douanier Rousseaus, van Goghs, Bonnards, van Dongens,

Matisses, and Picassos. From Picasso he purchased a picture generally acknowledged to be the key work in the evolution of twentieth-century art, *Les demoiselles d'Avignon*. Doucet's new development was complemented by a change in his life style: he sold his elegant mansion on the rue Spontini and moved into an ultramodern apartment. Obsessed now with modernity, he constantly renewed his collection by selling off parts of it and then buying more contemporary works by the same artists or by supporting fresh talent.[84]

Meanwhile, Doucet had been spending a major part of his time building a vast library of art books and original documents concerning artists, and this he donated to the Université de Paris, which housed it in an institution now known to all students of art history as the Bibliothèque de l'art et de l'archéologie, or in its shortened version, the Bibliothèque Doucet.[85] No wonder that a tearful Gimpel, the famous art dealer who worshipped Doucet, could write after the latter's death: "Ce couturier fut le grand Seigneur de notre époque, le Médicis de nos temps rétrécis."[86]

A fashion king for over twenty years, Paul Poiret also painted and plunged enthusiastically into the contemporary art world.[87] He modeled himself after his culture hero, Doucet, who had bought Poiret's first fashion drawings. Poiret actively promoted exhibitions of young artists and derived deep pleasure from bringing them before the public with a splash of publicity. Like a talent scout, he was in and out of independent ateliers and those of the Ecole des Beaux-Arts, seeking gifted artists to sponsor. A close friend of many of the original Fauves and their followers, he purchased the work of Vlaminck, Matisse, Derain, Dufy, Marquet, Rouault, Utrillo, and Dunoyer de Segonzac.[88] But his favorite artist was Dufy, whom he commissioned to sculpt wood-block designs for an exclusive line of Poiret's dresses. The success of this project inspired Poiret's competitors to take up the idea for their fabrics.

Poiret encouraged the commercialization of modern art, adapting it to fashion and cultural style. He wished to bridge the gap between art and industry and between art and the masses. He hoped to realize this in part by providing young girls from the working classes with art instruction. In 1912 he founded the Ecole d'art décoratif Martine and took over the responsibility of instruction himself, although Dufy and others participated in the project. Poiret's method was quite novel for the period: he made students work from the live model without supervision, and although he guided them on field trips he encouraged them to paint freely. He intended to stimulate their imagination by structuring the environment but at the same time deliberately avoided overt influence. According to his own testimony, the school achieved outstanding results.[89]

Jeanne Lanvin (1867–1946) was the most successful female artisan in France. Incredibly energetic, she supervised a top team of designers and revolutionized the fashion industry. As an active collector she worshiped the Impressionists and Fauves.[90] She commissioned her portrait from Vuillard—one of his most effective creations in this genre. Lanvin owned outstanding works by Degas, Sisley, and Renoir, but rather than treat the paintings as valuable objects, she studied them for ideas. Totally identifying herself with the artist, she once answered in response to the question, "How do you get your ideas?": "Si vous demandez à un peintre comment peignez vous? il serait fort embarrassé, il est possible qu'il vous dise simplement, 'mais avec des pinceaux, de la couleur, une toile, l'inspiration et cette force qui est en moi et qui m'oblige à m'exprimer.' Je vous dirai donc également que je crée avec des ciseaux, des étoffes, mon imagination et aussi mon inspiration."[91] Thus the innovative entrepreneur and patron discovered a kinship between his activity and that of the group committed professionally to full-time creative pursuit.

THE BOOK
PUBLISHERS

French entrepreneurialism in book publishing is rarely discussed in economic literature, but in 1867 the jury reports of the World's Fair cited the publishing trade as an example of "la grande industrie."[92] As much as transport and banking, the book industry responded to the democratization of society and invented new approaches consonant with the times. One distinct change from the previous century is the dramatic increase of books without bindings: a wider reading public called for cheaper reading materials, and these unbound books are interesting as forerunners of the "livre de poche." New developments in reproducing illustrations altered the appearance of books and opened mass markets to artistic production. Most publishers who actively engaged artists were remarkably forward-looking and made brilliant contributions to the taste for modernity.

Traditionally, the Left Bank is the center of the commercial activity stimulated by the production and sale of books. It also happens to be the center of student and bohemian activity: the book trade was thus guaranteed a steady flow of business and an army of writers and artists to tap at will. Publishers of illustrated books functioned as *mécènes* in three ways: they provided artists with bread-and-butter money, helped develop young talents by giving them a more modest format to start with than the grandiose Salons, and finally, offered the possibility of greater publicity and exposure than that of the dealer or the Salon. Illustration could also become a full-time occupation, but it had the advantage of allowing a measure of freedom akin to contemporary freelance opportunities.

While the transition from the engraved to the lithographic illustration is generally celebrated as a shift from the neoclassic to the romantic ascendance, it also reflects the publishers' need for a cheaper mode of reproduction to meet the demands of an expanding market.[93] Baron Taylor and Charles Nodier are the individuals who did most to promote the dissemination of the new technique in France.[94] The chief artistic enterprises accomplished under Taylor's direction were eight monumental travel publications, primarily describing regions he himself had visited and sketched. Of these, the most impressive was *Voyages pittoresques et romantiques dans l'ancienne France.* This consisted of twenty-four folio tomes containing over three thousand plates in vivid lithography. To accomplish this herculean project Taylor enlisted the services of the best scholars and artists of the period, and their production constitutes not merely a treasure for bibliophiles, but also a remarkable collection of lithographic landscapes. The emphasis on topographical views and the description of regional scenes in this work contributed significantly to the taste for landscape painting in nineteenth-century France.[95]

Taylor and Nodier, whom Taylor selected to do the text, admired the arts of the Middle Ages, and many of the illustrations glorify French medieval monuments. Here the lithographic technique was made to order: just as it gracefully rendered natural scenery, so it characterized the "picturesque" monuments in a haunting manner. A roster of the artists involved would make any publisher envious: this included Géricault, Bonington, Isabey, Dauzats, Gigoux, Viollet-le-Duc, Charlet, Vernet, Ingres, and Delacroix. Even Daguerre, an ex-associate of Taylor, contributed in a style prophetic of his early daguerreotypes.[96] Taylor's achievement stimulated Delacroix to make his famous series of lithographs for Goethe's *Faust,* which one critic labeled "le cri de guerre du romantisme." It also signaled the creation of a new periodical, *L'artiste,* founded in 1831 by Arsène Houssaye as an outlet for the views of the new school and the work of artists excluded from the Salons. *L'artiste* is a major source of topical imagery from the romantic period and its aftermath.

Wood engraving also enjoyed a revival at this time, facilitating the production of inexpensive books for a popular audience. Since wood engraving is a form of relief like the printing process itself, it was discovered that an engraved vignette could be combined with the typographic characters and passed with them simultaneously under the press. The old forms of engraving required a double operation, one for the text and another for the illustration, so that the new method offered greater rapidity and economy, as well as greater consistency in the appearance of the ink. Not only did this encourage publishers to use more artwork, as exemplified by the early careers of Gigoux, Daubigny, Meissonier, and later Doré, but it provided the basis of yet another market for the artists, the illustrated magazine.[97] The *Magasin pittoresque* appeared in 1833, and inspired numerous imitations: *l'illustration*, founded in 1843 by Paulin, followed later by the *Monde illustré*, and *Tour du monde* (1860).[98] These periodicals hired legions of artists to make drawings, which were then transferred onto wood by special engravers. Together, they performed the same function as the tabloid photographer of today.

Léon Curmer was perhaps the outstanding producer of wood-engraved books during the July Monarchy.[99] A disciple of Saint-Simon, he dreamed of cheap, handsomely illustrated editions of famous works for the masses.He believed that his mission was to provide an outlet for young rebels and that it was necessary to participate "au mouvement du courant social et des idées de son temps."[100] His remarkable *Les français peints par eux-mêmes* of 1840 fulfills these demands, since it not only embraces the writing and the illustrations of the most advanced minds of the day but also provides a cross section of contemporary French society as represented by characteristic social types. His concern for the artist is shown by his unique practice of listing in his publications the names of all artists who collaborated on his project together with the titles of the individual vignettes they designed.

Furthermore, Curmer did not stint on production costs, especially when it came to the artists. His budgets reveal that the allocation for artists was higher than for writers, constituting a significant proportion of the overall cost.[101] One-eighth of his entire budget for *Français peints par eux-mêmes* went to the artists, and another eighth went to the engravers, representing together one-fourth of the total for art. This is why people like Meissonier and Français—artists whose careers were launched by Curmer's publications—were delighted to work for him. Artists also appreciated the high quality of Curmer's work, as exemplified by his famous *Paul et Virginie* edition of 1838, perhaps the most beautifully illustrated book of the nineteenth century.

Pierre-Jules Hetzel was another daring publisher of this period, and he shared many of Curmer's ideals.[102] Like Curmer, he appreciated the need to reach a wide audience but wished to emhasize his artwork even more as a means of upgrading the public taste. He provided job opportunities for numerous artists throughout his career, which culminated with a major illustrated magazine, *Magasin d'éducation et de récréation* in 1864. From 1840 to 1842 Hetzel published *Scènes de la vie privée publique des animaux,* a work inspired by Curmer's *Français peints par eux-mêmes,* but which showed a notable difference: whereas Curmer used the illustrations as adjuncts to the text, Hetzel made the text an adjunct to the illustrations. He thus gave great play to Grandville,whose 323 vignettes and drawings placed him in the forefront of France's caricaturists.[103] Later in the same decade, Hetzel published the works of Gavarni, while for his magnum opus, *Diable à Paris* (1845-46), Hetzel employed the most important writers of the period and commissioned over a thousand drawings. A breezy look at modern Paris, the work epitomizes Hetzel's headlong plunge into contemporary life through channels provided him by creative minds.

Georges Charpentier, whose father innovated the original book format "in 18," which became known as *format Charpentier,* carried forward this enterprising spirit in his own publications. While noted primarily for his publications of the realist authors Daudet and Zola, Charpentier also experimented with novel techniques of reproduction, and he received favorable comment for his display in the World's Fair of 1878. His edition of *Promenants japonaises,* with its extraordinary color reproductions of Régamey's landscapes, was singled out for admiration, along with Alphonse de Neuville's illustrations for Quatrelles' *A coups de fusil.* De Neuville's charcoal illustrations represented a pioneering application of this medium in book illustration. After recording the striking impression the illustrations made on him, a critic declared that the work would remain "une des pages les plus originales dans l'histoire de notre librairie illustrée."[104]

Rewald observed that Charpentier was one of the earliest and most faithful supporters of the Impressionists. His collection, which was put on the market after his death, contained pictures by Renoir, Degas, Pissarro, Sisley, Cézanne, and Puvis de Chavannes.[105] We know also that his wife kept up a Salon in which she tried to launch fresh talents, perhaps her most successful attempt being Renoir. Renoir painted a remarkable portrait of Mme. Charpentier and her family, which now hangs in the Metropolitan Museum in New York.[106] The patronage of the Charpentiers reflects the attitude of older publishers who were responsive to a changing, contemporary world.

The dealer Ambroise Vollard published some of the most original illustrated books of the modern period.[107] He too shared the concerns of his predecessors for pushing new talent and providing opportunities for them to experiment. From 1900 until his death in 1939, he devoted his wealth, energy, and limitless enthusiasm to the production of exquisitely illustrated books. Not deeply read, his interest was first and foremost the artists and their illustrations. The author's work was always secondary, and Vollard rarely interfered with the artist's interpretation. He commissioned Bonnard to do lithographic illustrations for Verlaine's *Parallèlement*, and the artist audaciously scattered his arabesques over the margins.

Vollard later commissioned Rodin, Dufy, Rouault, Picasso, and Chagall to illustrate his books. Picasso's illustrations for Balzac's novel *Chef d'oeuvre inconnu* date from a late period but provided the artist with an opportunity to sum up the lessons of his experiments by returning to the representational form and improvising on it in his several styles. Since Vollard allowed wide scope for experimentation, his commissions generally resulted in succinct expressions of the artist's symbolic repertoire. This is true of Rouault's brilliant etchings for the *Cirque de l'étoile filante* and Suarès's *Passion*, and Chagall's great illustrations for the Old Testament, which he incidentally executed with a variety of instruments, reminiscent of his treatment of the stained glass windows for the Hadassah Medical Center in Jerusalem.

We have referred to the way in which wood-engraved periodicals contributed to the art market, but mention should also be made of the general growth of the newspaper industry and its influence on artistic taste.[108] Emile de Girardin, the forceful newspaper entrepreneur, founded the pioneering journal *La presse* in 1836, at a time when romantic painting had gained in stature and there was a need for skilled critics to interpret new currents for the public. The *Presse* was the first newspaper to use paid ads, and revenues from this source enabled Girardin to undersell his competitors. The great French press coincides with the advent of advertising, and so does art criticism for the masses. Girardin wanted a nonpolitical journal stressing cultural events, and his choice of Gautier, who had something nice to say about every one, was certainly inspired.[109]

Villemessant's *Figaro*, founded in 1848, had the same goal: designed to entertain the reader, it made use of a concise style, regular interviews of celebrities, special issues devoted to outstanding events, and a large beaux-arts section. Here the public was exposed to the breezy reviews of Albert Wolff as compared with the long-winded harangues of Delécluze in the *Journal des debats*. Later, Villemessant, to offset competition from a daily (*Figaro* was then a weekly), launched *L'événement*, which had only a modest success. But it is remembered here because it provided the occasion for one of Emile Zola's first assignments as a

free-lance writer, the review of the Salon of 1866.[110] In a series of
outspoken articles, Zola attacked the official artists, defined his concept
of realism, and hailed Manet as the true artist. The first articles aroused
such public indignation that Zola's contract was canceled before he
could complete the series. But more significantly, his extreme independent position and wider access to the public portends the emergence of the new system of art patronage brought about by the
conjunction of the critic's choice and a dealer just crazy enough to take
him up on it.

THE DEALER AS
ENTREPRENEUR

Art dealers stand apart from all other nineteenth- and twentieth-century entrepreneurs in their enormous impact on the artist and
on his livelihood.[111] Above all, the dealer definitively severed the direct
link between artist and patron in the classic sense. Since he mediated
between these two parties, both had to negotiate with him and thus
assume an attitude not unlike that of the dealer himself. This is even
more true in the collector's case, since he was forced sooner or later into
a position of both selling and buying. But Picasso's wily manipulation
of his dealers attests to a similarity of dispositions on this level as well.
From the moment a work of art is consummated in the artist's studio it
becomes a marketable object and must be treated in part as a commodity. Artist, art dealer, and patron share a common set of assumptions
about the work-as-commodity, independent of their peculiar aesthetic
appraisals of the object.

Dealers have expanded the art market, raised the value of individual
artists and works, and most important of all, they have made the
greatest progress in introducing aspirants or unknowns. The pioneer
dealers, moreover, galvanize their artists and help launch new movements. Champfleury named a new school after the color merchant and
dealer Desforges, who in the mid-1840s exhibited a relatively unknown
group of painters sharing several formal characteristics.[112] The art
dealer is generally an art lover, often accumulating his own solid
collection of favorites.[113] The fictional model of this type is Balzac's
character Elie Magus, the avid merchant who shops compulsively for a
bargain and houses his personal collection in Renaissance sumptuousness while he sleeps in squalorous conditions. In *Pierre Grassou* and
La rabouilleuse, Magus is the penurious miser, but in *Cousin Pons* he
evolves into an obsessed collector who is prepared to sacrifice all for a
beautiful painting. He transcends his habitual miserliness at the sight
of a masterpiece.[114] Either way, however, the central point about Magus

is his adoration of the work of art. A second issue, which we shall take up again in another context, is that Magus is Jewish. While Toussenel and Drumont were forever haranguing the great Jewish financiers, the artists seized as their special target of anti-Semitism the art dealer, who, even when a gentile, could be affected by the spirit of "juiverie."[115]

In *L'oeuvre*, Zola gives us two antithetic types of dealer: Père Malgras and Naudet. The first is adept at convincing hapless artists that he cannot really pay them more than the pittance he offers; he contents himself with modest profits, however, and like Magus, genuinely loves pictures. The other is a slick operator who has few scruples and introduces all kinds of gimmicks to promote the sale of his pictures. While Zola based these characters on living people, it would be an arduous task to find a dealer who conformed to these outlines in reality.[116] Zola's protagonists are caricatures: while dealers like Petit, Brame, and Durand-Ruel indulged in aggressive promotion techniques, they had a genuine regard for the painters and pictures they distributed. If Durand-Ruel preferred the Impressionists, Petit genuinely loved Meissonier, and later Le Sidaner and Besnard.[117]

Zola's notes inform us that Malgras is based primarily on Père Martin, a dealer who also sold art supplies on the rue Laffitte before the Franco-Prussian War. His shop was indeed a veritable cenacle for the young Impressionists and their circle.[118] But he dealt also with wealthy clients such as Rouart and Count Doria, and sold the works of the Barbizon School when their star was rising. Somewhat akin to Martin, Julian Tanguy, known as Père Tanguy, combined the retailing of art supplies with the sale of pictures. A colorful personality, Tanguy does resemble, in some respects, a Balzacian character.[119] The Impressionists and Post-Impressionists held reunions at his shop on 14, rue Clauzel. Often, he would take a canvas in exchange for art supplies, and he managed to collect a number of Cézannes and van Goghs. Tanguy, a self-styled revolutionary, identified with these radical innovators and delighted in displaying their works in his shop window, where they never failed to check the passers-by.

Instances of the combination shop abound in the nineteenth and even the early twentieth century: Dubourg made frames; Portier sold paints; Père Soulier (all these "pères" seem to have been less sympathetic than the sobriquet suggests) sold bedding across from the Cirque Medrano and during the years 1904–09 hung on his bed cases pictures by Metzinger, Lemaire, Dufy, Picasso, and the Douanier Rousseau.[120] Haro was a protean personality whose career spans the nineteenth century: color fabricant, restorer, art supplier, dealer, expert, and author of a popular book, *Histoire des procédés et des matières colorantes employés dans les beaux-arts*, he played Friday to the adventurers of the art world. Haro worked closely with Delacroix and accumulated in his notable private collection twenty of the master's pictures, including the *Sardanapalus*. He also owned Courbet's *L'atelier* and a host of other works by such masters as Daubigny, Bastien-Lepage, Sisley, and Jongkind. In addition, he had an outstanding Dutch collection, and his expertise in this area made him the ideal consultant for entrepreneur-collectors like Schneider.[121]

These amalgamated concerns recall that the combination shop-gallery is the forerunner of the modern commercial gallery. Almost without exception, the largest dealers emerged from a partial retail outlet, gradually shifting emphasis from items like stationery and art supplies to the sale of paintings and art objects. Sometimes, the retail end of the business was carried on as a means of promoting the picture sales, as in the cases of Goupil et Compagnie and Cadart. Goupil—later Boussod and Valadon—was founded by Adolphe Goupil in 1827.[122] Initially an artist, Adolphe found it more rewarding to publish carefully executed engravings after the work of others. He established an international reputation for the high quality of his reproductions after such masters as Vernet, Delaroche, Meissonier, and his son-in-law Gérôme. He and his son Albert created the famous helio-gravure process, which reproduced pictures with a remarkable fidelity. Meanwhile, they began buying the originals of the works reproduced, and after circulating the reproduction sold the originals and, very often, special replicas made by the artist. They recognized the power of reproductions to popularize paintings, and exploiting this discovery, they sold the originals for high prices and ordered replicas by the painters for the growing international market.[123] Goupil opened branches in New York, The Hague, Vienna, London, Brussels, and Berlin and mounted major exhibitions of international art works.[124]

While Albert left an important collection to the Louvre,[125] Goupil is perhaps best remembered today for its links with the van Gogh family: Vincent's uncle supervised The Hague division, and Vincent himself worked at several of its branches. His brother Theo became manager of the gallery on the boulevard Montmartre and for a time changed it partially into a showcase for the work of Impressionist and Post-Impressionist painters. Goupil's role in van Gogh's decision to become a painter should not be underestimated: it not only surrounded most of Vincent's young life with an environment of contemporary art, but its sumptuous publications furnished the illustrated material upon which van Gogh based his early style.[126]

Cadart, an editor and publisher of prints, owned a shop at 79, rue Richelieu, which became the center of the Société des acquafortistes in the early 1860s.[127] The society, supported by leading art critics, made a unique contribution to the revival of etching during that period. The aim of the organization was to gather in one group a large number of artists who would participate in the publishing of an annual album, including five etchings distributed monthly to every member. Cadart brought to the attention of the public the old and new printmakers and helped coordinate the society, gathering about him the artists, ama-teurs, and critics committed to reviving the art. Influential critics like Baudelaire, Gautier, Thoré-Bürger, and Burty reviewed the annual folios, always identifying Cadart as the mainspring of the etching revival.

Cadart had a phenomenal success. He branched out, and his shops and varied publications disseminated numerous collections of etchings, including the prints of young Manet and Whistler. Like the book publishers, Cadart assisted young painters and etchers by publishing their prints. But eventually he entered into the purchasing and sale of paintings, although he never ceased to publish and sell prints. Cadart was among the first French dealers to tap the American market: in 1866 he traveled to New York with an enormous cargo of paintings, including examples by Courbet, Corot, Daubigny, Jongkind, and Ribot. At the same time, he brought with him materials needed to establish "etching clubs" in New York, Boston, and Philadelphia. He hoped that this would stimulate interest in French artists and lead to an international organization with his Parisian House as its headquarters.

He opened a well-attended exhibition of French paintings, water-colors and etchings at 625 Broadway, New York, but did not have the commercial success he expected, and the following year in Boston he was compelled to sell most of the works he had brought over from France. Nevertheless, as a result of his initiative, Americans were able to view numerous etchings and paintings by Boudin, Daubigny, Diaz, Dupré, Decamps, Troyon, Jacque, Ziem, and others, and in this way Cadart laid the groundwork for Durand-Ruel's successful venture in the United States nearly two decades later.

No entrepreneur affected the development of nineteenth-century French art more directly than Paul Durand-Ruel.[128] His father, Jean Durand-Ruel sold stationery and art supplies, and dealt in pictures as a sideline. He inclined toward marginal painters, those not always in official favor and who worked in a nonacademic mode. Jean thus speculated on talent and assumed the risk of supporting unknowns. But he was preeminently conservative in his approach, treating paintings like dry goods and satisfying himself with a small turnover of profit.

When Paul took over, he wanted to specialize in artists with strong temperaments or those exhibiting a marked group affinity. He innovated the concept of mass purchases, buying entire collections or the contents of an artist's studio. But for this he needed large capital and experienced judgment, and he often overreached himself during his early years as director. He bought Manet's work and also that of Puvis de Chavannes when both were more or less held up to public derision. He early supported Degas, Monet, Pissarro, Sisley, and Renoir, but constant pressures from clients and the press forced him to relinquish support for their work in the 1870s. His early attempts to organize exhibitions of their work most often ended in failure.

It was not until 1880 that Durand-Ruel began to make progress. The director of the Union Générale, Feder, second in command only to Bontoux, placed large amounts at his disposal thanks to which he was able to support his favorite painters again. He now bought regularly from Monet, Pissarro, Renoir, Degas, and Sisley and systematically boosted the prices of their works in sales. He could do this partly because by 1880 they had ceased being jokes in the public mind and were getting favorable comment from some sectors of the press. Both Durand-Ruel and the Impressionists, however, profited from the general economic boom of the period, then suffered along with everyone else after the crash in 1882. The Union Générale itself sums up this development in microcosm: a corporate investment bank, it went from success to triumph in a dizzy upward spiral and down to disaster even more suddenly. At the beginning of 1882 its shares stood at 3,000 francs, but on 19 January, one of its filials, the Banque de Lyon et de Loire, suddenly closed its doors, and in less than two weeks the shares fell by more than 2,000 francs. On 2 February it stopped payments itself, and shortly thereafter Bontoux, Feder, and other of their associates were arrested. The crash of the Union Générale triggered one of the worst financial crises in France, and the depression that followed was one of the longest in its history.[129]

The financial collapse of the Union Générale dealt another severe blow to Durand-Ruel. He had to pay back all the money advanced to him by Feder and had to sublet his flat and galleries to make ends meet. He was forced to stop buying the work of the Impressionists on a regular basis, and the next four or five years were very difficult for the art dealers and his artists. In 1884 he was in debt for over 1,000,000 gold francs, and it was only in 1886, when he organized an exhibition of the Impressionists for an American show, that he begin to see daylight. Eventually, he opened a gallery in New York, and Americans, who heretofore had bought his school-of-1830 pictures, now began purchasing the Impressionists. The United States proved to be his salvation, enabling him to recoup on the home front. The Impressionists, now beginning to enjoy international fame, showed with him on a fairly regular basis, and their names became indissolubly linked with his ever after.

Without Durand-Ruel's constant encouragement and aid, the Impressionists might never have overcome the hostility of the public. The social position of Durand-Ruel is thus ambiguous: he functioned as both businessman and patron. His speculative venture was inseparable from his benevolent support of artists not in favor with the public, and his entrepreneurial risks embraced not only the profit motive but a genuine desire to identify himself with the innovative activity of those whose future he guaranteed.[130] In this he resembled the collector-patron of the Renaissance, promoting the collaboration of creative minds and delighting in being surrounded by the products of their genius. That he could vindicate his faith by saying, "I told you so," was a bonus, but not his primary motivation. An entrepreneur bringing off a project is like an artist bringing off a sketch, and in this sense, radical artists find their complement in the dealer who gambles on them.

By the time Ambroise Vollard (1867–1939) arrived on the scene, the mythology of the ultimate triumph of a persecuted avant-garde had been well established.[131] This was expressed in a later comment by the dealer Gimpel, when viewing a contemporary show at the Metropolitan Museum: "A l'ouverture de cette exposition des gens riaient; je ne permets à personne de rire devant quelque tentative que ce soit. Je ne ris pas, j'ai trop peur que l'avenir s'avise de rire de moi."[132] But Vollard's abiding faith in such artists as Cézanne and Rouault astounded his peers, who recognized that this was no mean effort when he first began his campaign in their favor. He differed radically from his predecessors in the way he exploited antagonism and ridicule. Instead of courting approval he enjoyed flouting the public and the critics. Rather than hush up insulting epithets he published them widely, and people got in the habit of going to his gallery to be shocked—in his eyes, the best kind of publicity. It was of course a measure of Vollard's understanding of the nature of "avant-garde" art that gave him the kind of confidence he had; he could afford to sit back and wait, recalling the same effect the Impressionists created.

As we have seen, Vollard's art dealing eventually became a means to another end, the publication of fine prints, handsomely illustrated books, and issues of bronzes. In this sense, he seems to have reversed the older order of priorities, where the art dealer's sidelines were an aid in the sale of pictures. But Vollard's activities were part of a consistent outlook: the commitment to undiscovered talent and to the undisclosed potential of a proven talent. He ventured into bronze editions after discovering young Aristide Maillol's terra-cotta statuettes. Always on the watch for new or unknown artists whose work promised a profitable investment, he purchased a few pieces and had them cast into bronze. The sale of the small figures provided Maillol with a modest existence, and the sculptor could remark at the time: "C'est grace à Vollard que j'ai pu vivre."[133]

Discounting the profit motive, Vollard's activities suggest an attempt to understand the nature of the creative process. Either by encouraging nascent talent or by bringing out hidden qualities of a mature artist, Vollard involved himself in the artist's mental life. This is emphatically reflected in his writing on Cézanne, Renoir, and Degas. Treated informally in the interview style, Vollard's biographies tried to disclose the problems of contemporary artists and achieve something close to a primary document on their life and thought.[134]

Daniel-Henry Kahnweiler follows in the tradition of his two heroes, Durand-Ruel and Vollard, from whose experiences he greatly profited.[135] Kahnweiler's most fascinating characteristic is his identification with contemporary artists. When he first contemplated a career as an art dealer, he immediately ruled out buying the works of Cézanne, an artist then actively promoted by Vollard: "Il me semblait que cela était une époque passé, pour moi tout au moins, et que mon rôle à moi était de batailler pour ceux de mon age. J'ai connu et défendu ceux de mon âge."[136] Kahnweiler wrote that he did not want to be the kind of dealer who pandered to the taste of his customers, but instead preferred to give exposure to someone unknown, to expand the horizon of the public and make a way for the artist. Undoubtedly, this was a projection of his feelings about himself and his isolated relationship to the art world early in the present century.

Kahnweiler, like Vollard, originally contemplated another career; in his case, it was music. He decided that conducting was best suited to his talent, for it would allow him to function as an intermediary between the composer and the musicians. He used this an an analogy to explain his notion of a good art dealer, who according to Kahnweiler, mediates between the artist and the public. He believed that great painters make great art dealers: "Il y a eu Durand-Ruel pour les impressionnistes, il y a eu Vollard pour tous ceux qui ont suivi: Cézanne, Gauguin, ensuite les Nabis et bein d'autres peintres puisque Vollard, malgré tout, a été le premier à montrer des choses de Picasso."[137] Kahnweiler's promotion first of Braque, then of Picasso and the entire Cubist circle, was an act of artistic faith and self-confidence. As in the case of Durand-Ruel and the Impressionists, the Cubists required Kahnweiler's faith for the group coherence it needed to survive. This kind of faith transcends the mere marketplace; it springs from a firm belief in one's creative judgment.

Two other dealers, Spitzer and Bing, contemporaries of Durand-Ruel and young Vollard, are discussed separately because they dealt primarily in the applied arts. Baron Spitzer seems to have fallen into utter obscurity, but in the last quarter of the century he possessed the largest collection of *objets d'art* ever accumulated by a private individual in Paris.[138] When Spitzer arrived in Paris from Vienna in 1852, the applied arts were in an extraordinary state of fermentation as the result of England's Great Exhibition in 1851. He decided to specialize in industrial art from the earlier periods, recognizing that at that moment enlightened Frenchmen were exploring the positive aspects of the relationship between the fine and decorative arts.[139] Eventually, he assembled a prodigious collection of over 4,000 objects, including tapestries, ivories, enamels, faïences, furniture, marbles, bronzes, and glass—mainly from the medieval and Renaissance past—which required nearly a dozen specialists to analyze it.[140]

Spitzer enjoyed a phenomenal business success and became very public-minded; he organized a virtual *collection raisonné* of industrial art in his mansion on 33, rue de Villejuste, and for over twelve years (1878-90) the Musée Spitzer was a mecca for the general public, for artists, and for European aristocrats. It was compared to the South Kensington School and Museum and likened, on the basis of its educational impact on the artists and the public, to a musée des arts décoratifs. The popularity of Spitzer's museum coincided with the emergence of the Art Nouveau taste, and it is surprising to find it overlooked in the literature devoted to the subject.

This brings us to Samuel Bing, who, as an organizer and critic, became the central figure of the Art Nouveau movement.[141] His ideas and leadership in Paris from 1895 until his death in 1905 significantly contributed to the development of the modern movement in all phases of the visual arts. A native of Germany, Bing was originally employed in the ceramic industry, an interest he never abandoned, not even when he went into business for himself. In 1871 he moved to Paris, where he became a naturalized citizen and opened a shop for the sale of objects imported from the Far East. As a dealer in oriental art, Bing first came to the attention of the art world at the Paris Exhibition of 1878, where he exhibited Japanese porcelains, ceramics, and prints. The discovery of Japanese prints by English and French painters in the 1850s is well known; by 1878 it was possible to state that "on pourrait écrire un mémoire solennel sous ce titre: *De l'influence des arts du Japan sur l'art et l'industrie de la France.*"[142] Bing was then the most important dealer in Japanese art in Paris; among his clients were Cernushi, Camondo, Goncourt, Burty, Haviland, Gérôme, and the young Dutch painter van Gogh, a frequent visitor to Bing's gallery who was ultimately granted privileged access to its storerooms and even functioned as Bing's traveling salesman for a time.[143]

In May 1888 Bing launched a monthly periodical entitled *Artistic Japan*—"an illustrated journal of arts and industries"—issued in English, French, and German. The periodical was addressed primarily to those interested in industrial arts, including manufacturers, artisans, book illustrators, architects, decorators, manufacturers of wall papers, painters, weavers, potters, bronze workers, and goldsmiths. Thus Bing's far-ranging interests stemmed essentially from his passion for Japanese art and were expressed in his increasing emphasis on decorative design. At the request of the government, Bing visited the United States in 1893 to investigate its level of development in the various arts. He came back a changed man and converted his shop from a gallery of oriental art to a Salon de l'Art Nouveau—an outlet for new ideas.[144]

From this gallery on 22, rue de Provence, would emanate the Art Nouveau movement in France, which revolutionized aesthetic decor at the end of the century. It was his fervent wish that the decorative arts, linking man to his home and man to his environment, would dissolve what he felt to be a fictional barrier between arts and industry and restore the primitive harmony that existed between man and art. As part of his new commitment, he championed young craftsmen and designers and exhibited in his gallery examples of their tapestries, glass, ceramics, and furniture. Among the artist-craftsmen he supported were George de Feure, Eugene Colonna, Paul Pierre Jouve, and Emile Gallé.

Bing helped legitimize the movement through his negotiations with leading museums. As in the case of other dealers we have investigated, his profit motive was not pure: it was balanced by a genuine desire to see the new art preserved and housed amidst the fine works of the past. One of the largest depositories of Art Nouveau ceramics—the Musée des arts décoratifs—was built up in part by Bing through sales and the bequest of his family. His patronage is therefore of a two-fold nature: first, he supported young designers in their pursuit of fresh ideas; and second, he made certain through his promotions and negotiations that the works were appreciated. Bing's preoccupation with the interrelationship of the arts thus fulfilled one of the utopian ideals of the century.[145]

THE ENTREPRENEUR
AND THE INDUSTRIAL ART

The union of art and industry was an idea in ferment since the July Monarchy, but it was not the outraged artist who first tried to reform the ugly products of machines. Although artists answered to the call for remedial action, in point of priority, the entrepreneur has the better claim. French industrialists were hard hit by English competition; the World's Fairs emphasized the need to improve the quality of industrial commodities, and these exhibitions spurred French entrepreneurs to harass the government with pleas for action. This harassment ultimately forced widespread pedagogic reform in official beaux-arts institutions.[146] As early as the 1830s, however, when French industry began to assume its modern form, the aesthetic character and improvement of goods preoccupied enlightened manufacturers who stimulated artists to campaign for them. The combined efforts of the entrepreneurs and artists established an atmosphere highly conducive to the development of the fine arts and their application to industry. These two segments of the community generated reforms in artistic pedagogy that ultimately brought an end to academic elitism.

A group of art teachers emerged, calling for the popularization of art instruction and the dissemination of art instruction among the proletariat. Individuals like Dupuis, Mme Cavé, Roulliet, Etex, Gélibert, and Lecoq de Boisbaudran wanted to introduce art instruction to the working classes, not only for their general enlightenment but also to improve the quality of French industrial design.[147] They argued the necessity for reuniting art and industry to enrich the individual worker through self-fulfillment and to bridge the gap between art and the masses. Not surprisingly, these reformers generated active government support despite their advanced—and sometimes radical—ideas.[148]

The French grew increasingly apprehensive over England's export industry as the English began implementing programs to raise the aesthetic level of their mass-produced goods.[149] Responding to the challenge of Great Britain, which had founded the Government School of Design for industrial artists in 1837 and opened branch schools a few years later, Louis-Philippe's administration broadened the base of its own industrial art schools—the Ecole de dessin in particular—and encouraged artists and pedagogues to invent new methods for teaching art to the masses.[150] This essentially called for the simplification and abbreviation of conventional approaches, which in turn fostered criticism of the Académie des beaux-arts's painstaking and laborious procedures. Many of these pioneer reformers were followers of the Saint-Simonist tradition and believed that for the worker to cultivate a taste for the industrial and fine arts he had to be emancipated from the yoke of repression—in the artistic as well as the political and labor domains. They emphasized a more spontaneous and intuitive approach to release the creative energies of the proletariat.

Those Frenchmen who contributed most to develop the spirit of enterprise among artists and entrepreneurs were the Saint-Simonists.[151] Saint-Simon himself had made a fortune in speculative risks but spent most of it acquiring an education and trying to fashion a philosophical and social system that would regenerate mankind. He was one of the first thinkers to appreciate fully the significance of modern science for industrial technology and to foresee the possibility that machines would someday eliminate human drudgery. Saint-Simon never completed his philosophical synthesis, and his followers, who developed and proclaimed his doctrines, failed in their attempt to convert society to the system as a whole.

Nevertheless, many of the young men from the Ecole polytechnique and from banking and commercial circles who belonged to the group —among them Michel Chevalier, Prosper Enfantin, Paulin Talabot, Emile and Isaac Péreire—subsequently carved out distinguished careers as captains of industry and finance. They pioneered in the application of science to technology and were primarily responsible for developing techniques of investment banking and of managing the large-scale industries they had created under the July Monarchy and the Second Empire. They established banks, railways, public utilities, and mining and metallurgical enterprises throughout France and Europe.

Not fortuitously, the doctrine of Saint-Simon assigned an important place to the fine arts.[152] While it may be interpreted to show that the artist and his work were destined to function as an arm of the government, the doctrine nevertheless recognized the artist as a primal force in society. "L'art pour l'art" was indeed condemned, but Saint-Simonism proclaimed that good art was socially inspired and guided —that it described reality and stirred the masses to action. It thus enlisted the sympathies of those who would participate in the realist and naturalist movements of the subsequent years. At a time when many believed that art had fallen into an irreversible state of decline, the Saint-Simonists offered a vigorous challenge to artists, placing their activity on an equal level with that of science and industry.

Saint-Simon's organization posited an industrial parliament consisting of three chambers: invention, examination, and execution. The first chamber comprised artists and engineers who would plan annual programs of public works and festivals; the second, the scientists who would analyze these projects and administer the educational program; the third, the captains of industry who would administer the budget and carry out the projects. The artists were further considered vital to the program by helping to form opinions propitious to the system. It is no wonder then, that along with the future entrepreneurs, Saint-Simon's group attracted a number of artists, including the Scheffer brothers, Raymond Bonheur, and a host of others who never officially enrolled in the sect.[153] Indeed, the literature reveals that there was hardly a single musician, artist, or man of letters unmoved by the philosophy of Saint-Simon. This preoccupation may also explain the enthusiasm of Saint-Simon's most successful disciples for the fine arts: Michel Chevalier, Paulin Talabot, and Emile and Isaac Péreire.[154]

There is still another area in which enlightened entrepreneurs regenerated the fine arts, and that is through their interest in general educational reform. In 1794, pressed by urgent demands for both military and civil engineers, the Convention established the Ecole des travaux publics, renamed the following year the Ecole polytechnique.[155] The Convention also decreed the establishment of the Conservatoire des arts et métiers—a combination technical school and museum of technology that placed applied science on the same level as theoretical science. Popular lectures on applied science and industry, held free and requiring no entrance exams, were widely attended by Frenchmen of all classes. Among its students were Joseph Jacquard, the future inventor of the silk loom, Eugène Schneider, future manager of the metallurgical works at Le Creusot, and Emile Dollfus, a leader of the Alsacian textile industry.[156] Recognizing its importance for the development of French industry, James de Rothschild ardently supported this institution.

In addition to the Ecole polytechnique and the Conservatoire des arts et métiers, the Ecole centrale des arts et manufactures was founded to advance the application of science to technology.[157] In 1828–29, a group of enlightened citizens, including a number of entrepreneurs who felt that the supply of trained engineers for private industry was too small, established this institution under private auspices. Its first board of trustees comprised scientists, educators, engineers, industrialists, and bankers. The Ecole centrale's curriculum resembled that of the Polytechnique except that it stressed applied courses and practical demonstration at the expense of pure mathematics.

Significantly, these schools of applied science, in line with specialized art schools like the Ecole de dessin, all provided industrial drawing instruction as an integral part of the curriculum (figs. 10 and 11).[158] The Conservatoire des arts et métiers had a school effective enough to

FIGURE 10. Evening drawing instruction at the Ecole polytechnique, ca. 1852–53

FIGURE 11. Drawing instruction at the Conservatoire des arts et métiers, ca. 1852–53

attract both potential industrial and fine artists: Couture, Gavarni, and Etex studied there and went on to concentrate in the fine arts.[159] The Ecole polytechnique devoted a major section of its program to drawing, and hired the services of such outstanding artists as Mérimée (Léonor, Prosper's father), Charlet, and Cogniet. [160] While the Ecole centrale did not have a separate drawing program, it provided regular drawing instruction, which it made one of the foundations of its program.[161] In this way all potential entrepreneurs and engineers received a large dose of art instruction, and not simply of the drafting sort. These programs had much in common with that of the Ecole de dessin, whose formative goal was "d'instruire des ouvriers artistes, des fabricans, des entrepreneurs, en un mot des praticiens."[162] Some years later, one of the instructors of the Ecole de dessin declared that the application of art to industry should get the widest publicity: "Alors les capacités artistiques qui se consacreront à l'industrie seront connues non seulement des entrepreneurs de travaux et fabricants, mais aussi du gouvernement et du public; l'honneur qui leur en reviendra, créera entre eux une émulation profitable à l'art, au goût générale et j'ajouterai même au commerce du pays."[163]

Thus, the institutions of applied sciences provided, along with the specialized centers, springboards for the spreading of aesthetic ideas among future entrepreneurs. On the one hand, potential entrepreneurs absorbed a taste for art, which they expressed avocationally through personal collections, and on the other hand, entrepreneurs were induced to put more aesthetic value on machine-made products. Artists were hired by industries of all kinds, including the textile and silk centers, silver and gold manufacturers, costumers, wall paper fabricants, furniture makers—every field that required industrial design. Entrepreneurs, especially those stirred to action by Saint-Simon, encouraged artists directly by hiring them for their firms or indirectly by providing a market for their talent. As already noted, Haviland hired several apprentices to train in his own shop, and this activity may also be considered a form of entrepreneurial patronage.

The art-in-industry movement comes to a head in the Paris World's Fairs, where France, following England's precedent, tried to exhibit its twin prowess in the fine and applied arts. The great art displays were meant to serve as complements to the industrial displays and to demonstrate that superiority in one area necessarily entails superiority in the other. Encouraged by the government, the artists provided models for industrial designers and insured a certain degree of harmony between the sections.[164] The special Art-Union edition devoted to the 1867 Paris Exhibition attributed the supremacy of the French to artists and artisans rather than to manufacturers and entrepreneurs, since it felt that French training for artists and designers was the finest in the world.[165]

But it was the entrepreneur who demonstrated how the fine arts could be applied to manufactured goods and who showed the mutual advantages to be derived from such collaboration. Firms like Christofle et Compagnie, which fabricated works in silver, bronze, and gold, contracted full-time sculptors like Madroux, Michau, Mercié, and Carrier-Belleuse, who in turn employed his apprentices Delaplanche, Rodin, and Falguière.[166] Businessmen tried to encourage artistic education by setting up special training programs or by organizing exhibitions. In 1863 a group of entrepreneurs founded the Union centrale des Beaux-Arts appliqués à l'industrie, an organization that Charles Blanc heralded as the regeneration of fine arts in France. Inspired primarily by Guichard, an architectural designer and interior decorator, the Union opened an applied arts museum along the lines of the one in South Kensington, containing collections of ancient and contemporary objects exemplifying the unity of arts and crafts. The Union also sponsored special exhibitions of the decorative arts, established a library, held courses for the working classes, and organized public lectures and competitions, all in the interest of promoting the applied arts. The consultative committee included well-known painters, sculptors, and critics, including Barye, Aimé Millet, Burty, Louvrier de Lajolais, and Mantz. An effective association of entrepreneurs and artists, the Union showed how the two groups could amalgamate their ideals and pool their respective talents.[167]

It is in this context that we can appreciate the attitude of Renoir, who, although he shifted from porcelain decoration to the fine arts, emphasized throughout his career the need for a close relationship between art and industry.[168] As we have seen in the case of Haviland, the porcelain industry offered numerous opportunities to painters, and not surprisingly we find that artists either began their careers as decorators (Cabat, Dupré, Diaz) or in their mature years created designs for well-known manufacturers (Ziégler, van Marcke, Bracquemond). Gaugin's decision to make ceramic sculpture for extra income grew out of a rich historical tradition as well as the contemporary mania for the applied arts.

In 1883 Gaugin's interest in the crafts led him to suggest a revival of tapestry weaving, and he personally executed several tapestry designs. This recalls the importance of the French textile industry for artists, not only in providing jobs but also for its active support of regional art schools, where artist-craftsmen were recruited. Flandrin started in the silk industry at Lyon and later trained at that city's Ecole des Beaux-Arts, which maintained links to the applied arts. Matisse studied at an industrial art school in Saint-Quentin as well as the Ecole des arts décoratifs, and his involvement in tapestry design and other areas of the decorative arts can be traced to this early training. Dufy and Picasso also executed designs for tapestries when they already enjoyed world-wide fame.

The important bronze industry in France relied heavily on artists for its decorative casting and enameling. Barbedienne, the owner of a famous foundry, employed large numbers of artists, and according to one critic of the period; one had to "enter the sculptor's studio, and there find the first geniuses of the age busy modeling forms of beauty and grace, to be afterwards copied in plaster, and ultimately cast into bronze. The expenditure on such models, where—as is the case with M. Barbedienne's enterprise—the foremost artists of France are put under requisition to furnish original designs, is necessarily enormous; and this fact alone is sufficient to keep up the high price of artistic bronzes."[169]

After the procelain and bronze manufacturers, wallpaper (*papiers peints*) and fan production were perhaps the most critical industries that hired artists. Like the other firms mentioned, they depended on well known artists to produce models or designs or even to work directly on the product. Charles Müller's monumental painting *La jeunesse* was adopted for wallpaper, while certain of Thomas Couture's works were taken up by the House of Desfossés, the foremost wallpaper manufacturer in France.[170] The fan industry employed the talents of artists like Gavarni, Diaz, Lami, Cicéri, Hamon, Isabey, Philippe Rousseau, Roqueplan, Baron, Français, Corot, Couture, and later, Pissarro, for its production. Two of the most renowned fan producers, Duvelleroy and Alexandre, worked closely with contemporary painters to create a special category of fan labeled "éventail d'art," as distinct from "éventail d'exportation."[171]

Many industries retained gifted artists on the payroll to serve as aesthetic consultants. Bracquemond and Chaplet advised Haviland, Carrier-Belleuse worked for Christofle and the ceramic industry, Dubois for Barbedienne, Dumont for various wallpaper concerns, Choiselat for furniture manufacturers requiring sculpted forms, Steinheil for Champigneulle, a stained-glass producer.[172] Entrepreneurs thus worked in intimate association with artists to produce the impressive displays at the World's Fairs.[173]

So close were the interests of the two groups that it was not uncommon to find individuals like the bronze manufacturer Paillard, the jeweler and goldsmith Froment-Meurice, the ceramicist Deck, the furniture designer Beurdeley *fils*, who were artist, fabricant, and merchant all rolled into one—"a combination," wrote an English critic reviewing the Paris Exhibition of 1867, "unknown in England, though common in France."[174] The democratization of society encouraged cheaper means of production and a diffusion of arts in industry, and the artist, no longer sustained by an aristocracy, evolved out of necessity into the entrepreneur-craftsman who sought his patronage among the people. He had little fear of debasing himself: the innate French contempt for mass production and the growing distaste for eclecticism brought the artisan and the artist into a working harmony that culminated at the end of the century in a rejuvenation of the material environment.

ENTREPRENEURIAL ECOLOGY

If it is feasible to speak of an "entrepreneurial psychology" it is also appropriate to speak of an "entrepreneurial ecology," although in this day and age these may sound like mutually incompatible terms. But the entrepreneur, insofar as his activities transform the physical nature of the environment and thus the conditions of experience, creates what I call the *entrepreneurial ecology*. The term as I use it expresses the changing character of the contemporary world through material signs of modernity. Not only do entrepreneurs furnish conspicuous evidence of change, they are the first to call attention to it by their life-style. They were among the first tourists, the first owners of bathrooms; they flew the first balloons, drove the first automobiles, and now engage in activities associated with the term *jet set*.

The entrepreneur need not extend his personal patronage to affect creation; he alters the conditions of aesthetic expression simply by going about his business. I am here not only considering the inevitable impact on the economic facts of life but the way in which businessmen restructure the material world. Just as the pervasive presence of electronics and synthetic materials forces present-day artists to shift their frame of reference, so in the nineteenth century those wishing to depict the contemporary world were affected by entrepreneurial innovation. Daumier, the realist, built a poignant theme around the third-class railway, and some years later even a pretentious painter like Couture could suggest the locomotive as a fit theme for noble painting.[175] Monet painted his famous Gare Saint-Lazare series on the very spot where Emile Péreire directed his workmen in the building of the first successful railway line.[176] Pissarro and Manet delighted in the painting of steamship and railroad events, and indeed, it may be generally stated that the Impressionists celebrated the achievements of the entrepreneurs of the Second Empire. The Impressionists and their followers set in motion twentieth-century movements like Cubism, Orphism, and Futurism, which in several ways faithfully attempted to record the changes wrought by businessmen.

As early as 1840, the painter Bonhommé, sick of conventional genre and landscape subjects, discovered in the factory an image of modern life, and his series on this theme appealed to his contemporaries.[177] A critic wrote about his depiction of the Fourchambault iron and steel company: "M. Bonhommé a pensé, avec raison, que les forges de Fourchambault offraient au peintre un sujet curieux et intéressant. Il s'y rencontre des beautés particulières, et pour ainsi dire inconnues en peinture. Rien ne peut être plus original que l'aspect d'une usine avec son mouvement, ses accessoires, sa foule laborieuse."[178]

Bracquemond, whom we encountered earlier, sought inspiration for his designs in shops and department stores catering to the vogue for Far Eastern art; he once informed Goncourt of the precious shipment of oriental rugs that Boucicault obtained for Au Bon Marché.[179] Here we may note as well how Art Nouveau artists, in collaboration with entrepreneurs, created a self-fulfilling aesthetic by transforming the interior and exterior worlds.

And what of the activities of French entrepreneurs in colonial possessions? The entrepreneurs in North Africa opened this route to countless French artists including Marilhat, Decamps, Delacroix, Fromentin, and Gérôme, who, looking for fresh environments, made pilgrimages to this area for sensations of light and color appropriate to their sensibilities.[180] The Compagnie française de Tahiti and the Société de l'Océanie, organized to establish commerce between France and Oceania, created the mechanism that permitted Gauguin to throw off the fetters of his bourgeois culture and indulge his desire for the life of a "noble savage."[181]

Still another aspect of entrepreneurial ecology and its influence on nineteenth-century painting revealed itself in the establishment of fashionable tourist resorts. After 1830 tourist facilities expanded rapidly, including hotels for vacationers and huge casinos to provide entertainment and places for reunion. Trouville became an important center of tourism, attracting an English as well as a French clientele. It drew artists like a magnet, and the numerous landscapists who searched for motifs there helped generate more tourism. Boudin's vivacious seaside views capture the vacationers of the Second Empire in the same way that Guys's views capture the atmosphere of a more urban setting. The success of Trouville encouraged entrepreneurs like Morny to invest in Deauville, and before long the two resorts were competing for the tourist crowd. Entretat and Dieppe, also in the north, were other favorite spas of artists and tourists, while in the south, Antibes, Biarritz, and Nice attracted a large contingent of artists. These fashionable resorts offered man-made and natural images of modernity situated in a liberating atmosphere of casual play and comportment appropriate to the developing aesthetic taste.[182]

The growth of advertising—*la publicité*—depended on the development of the book and newspaper industries, but it is mentioned here for its pervasive impact on the visual world. As soon as the function of advertising changed from information to persuasion, entrepreneurs opened a new mass market for artists: *l'affiche*. The modern illustrated poster has its roots in Paris, where it was devised by entrepreneurs in the service of entrepreneurs. When Jules Chéret opened a printing plant at Paris in 1866 he became the world's first full-time poster artist.[183] Using multiple printing techniques derived from book illustration and images drawn from popular folk symbols, Chéret created a medium that ultimately exercised an enormous influence on contemporary culture. His arresting posters literally covered outdoor Paris for decades and have become synonymous with the Belle Epoque. Chéret's graphic shorthand and brilliant color influenced younger artists like Seurat, who assimilated Chéret's formal approach in his late paintings, and Toulouse-Lautrec, who developed the potential of the poster medium still further. Henry van de Velde, a leader in the decorative arts movement, acknowledged Chéret's contribution to the poster style of Art Nouveau, and thus to the visual environment of our own time.

The triumph of iron architecture at the Paris World's Fair of 1889 is communicated by Seurat's homage to the Eiffel Tower—itself the product of an entrepreneur-engineer-artist—just as three years earlier he had painted *La grande jatte* as a testament to contemporary fashions.[184] Some years later the painter Delaunay would spend many hours contemplating the Eiffel Tower as a symbol of modernity, finding in its individuated parts a metaphor for the fragmented universe.

French entrepreneurs, architects, and engineers led the world in the appreciation not only of iron in architecture but of concrete as well.[185] Coignet and Lambot pioneered in *beton armé*—reinforced concrete—which changed the face of modern architecture. Hennebique, one of the ablest entrepreneurs of the last century, established an audacious organization for the construction of buildings in this material and developed his system throughout the world.[186] His reinforced construction permitted the filling of structural concrete frames with sheets of glass only and also solved the problem of providing adequate daylight in multistory factory blocks. Thus the architectural developments of the twentieth century—the most conspicuous signs of entrepreneurial ecology—were made possible by the innovations of French entrepreneurs.

EXCHANGING
ROLES

Sometime in 1918 Nathan Wildenstein, the director of the world-famous gallery, received this message from the widow of the author of the vicious tract *La France juive*: "Monsieur, je suis la veuve d'Edouard Drumont, le farouche antisémite. J'éspère que vous n'en serez pas moins impartial. J'ai des tableaux à vendre, veuillez, je vous prie, venir des voir. . . ."[187] This ironic note sums up in a nutshell the curious relationship between the artist and the entrepreneur in the modern period. The Jew, notorious symbol of the *arriviste*, the very embodiment of the bourgeois spirit from which the artist purportedly sought liberation, was none other than the patron who guaranteed the artist's aspirations. At the same time that the artist wished "épater le bourgeois," he was bound to him in a symbiotic relationship.

But just as the anti-Semite needs the symbolic Jew to exist, so the artist needed the symbolic bourgeois to exist: the mythical symbols here become the mainsprings of mental activity. In the latter case, the myth was energized by the fundamental inferiority assigned to the businessman in the French social structure. Landes has characterized the main forces contributing to this state of mind: the aristocratic emphasis on nonmaterialistic values and the issue of birth, the scornful literature and art about anything smacking of bourgeois business and money, and the fact that the bourgeois himself swallowed the myth of noble superiority and modeled his existence along aristocratic lines.[188]

The French attitude toward business was reflected for a long time in the educational system: until relatively recent times there was nothing comparable to the London School of Economics, for example, the best talents almost invariably turning to the traditional honorific careers of law, medicine, or government. Except in the large family firms, this was also true of the children of entrepreneurs who often rejected positions in their fathers' business in favor of artistic careers. As reflected in literary and artistic opinion, the entrepreneur, or any moneymaker, epitomized crass philistinism. Ironically, then, the artists, who often espoused democratic social change, found themselves as bedfellows of the aristocrats in their antipathy to the businessman and his pragmatic values. This often led the artist into a contradictory position, since he could neither sustain the nobility-of-birth concept nor accept bourgeois materialism. But given a choice, he might prefer—as Couture and Gauguin did—the "natural" taste of the aristocracy for the fine arts.[189] The artist thus aligned himself with the aristocrat in condemnation of the businessman.

As Landes suggests, this general anticapitalistic climate helps to explain the traditional French emphasis on quality as against quantity, the preference for handicraft over machine work, the loathing of anything relating to speculation and easy money. These attitudes have analogues in the world of art: the academically minded artist laboriously contrived his canvas and opposed the sketchy works of the Impressionists on the grounds that they resembled the products of mass production and industry. This charge is not without foundation: but insofar as the Impressionists deliberately set out to record images of modernity, their abbreviated procedures are more immediately expressive of the age than the polished products of the academicians.

The period of the Impressionists coincides with the emergence of refined methods of selling and publicizing paintings. The *refusés* —those systematically rejected by the official Salon juries for their novel techniques and themes—then had some assurances that speculative ventures would supplement the patronage of their *mécènes*, including Durand-Ruel himself. But this dependence on the business world flatly contradicts the artist's opposition to the bourgeois class—a contradiction often expressed in the relations between artist and dealer. The Impressionists constantly requested financial support from Durand-Ruel, and even developed the technique of playing him off against his rival Petit. In the end they were dependent on Durand-Ruel for any sort of steady income, and their importunate requests smack of "bourgeois" proclivities.[190]

A close look reveals that the hostility between the two groups also originated from a self-perpetuating myth. Just as the world created the "money-grubbing" Jew, first by disenfranchising him and then by restricting his entry into the trades and professions, so nineteenth-century society created the myth of the artist in conflict with the bourgeois community. Despite Courbet's close personal relationship with his patron Bruyas, the artist, in his depiction of their encounter on the road, identifies himself with the "Wandering Jew" and casts Bruyas in a somewhat subservient role, thus reversing the conventional version of the theme and falsifying the equality of his and Bruyas' actual positions.[191] Evidently, the myth of confrontation stimulated the creative activity of artists who were in fact utterly reliant on bourgeois patrons. Courbet, for all his aggressive display of radicalism, enjoyed the support of such fashionable entrepreneur-collectors as the duc de Morny. Although his patrons are somewhat exalted in *The Studio*, the rampant anti-Semitism of that work continues the assault on the spirit of commerce—i.e., on the entrepreneurial ventures that alone could pay for Courbet's labor. Bruyas' career shows that the collector felt obliged to emancipate himself from a "money-grubbing" status, and after having failed to combine art and business, he forsook banking altogether for a lifetime of artistic indulgence. In the modern period, middle-class children drop out of the father's firm to pursue "pure," nonmaterialistic values, thus translating the oedipal conflict into the patron-artist, bourgeois-genius, Gentile-Jew antagonisms. One social critic, after observing that sons of Jewish entrepreneurs like Hirsch, Uhlmann, and Worms were turning to painting, concluded that art was now a business like any other![192]

On the other hand, the businessman-patron sustained the mythical cleavage for his own ends: he insisted on "patronizing" the artist whom he looked down upon as an impractical idealist. He saw the artist's survival as dependent on the businessman's pragmatic concerns, and he could rationalize his work-a-day occupation as the necessary prop of the castle-builders. He could even forgive the anti-Semitic rantings and bitter denunciation of bourgeois capitalism as predictable components of the artist's utopianism. In the end, only the hard-headed entrepreneur could advance creative activity by keeping the artist from starving. This paternalistic attitude is clearly marked in the banker Benoît Fould, who laughed at Jalabert's guilt for having overcharged on a commission.[193]

Actually, the businessman, and especially the Jewish businessman, was as much an outsider as the artist in nineteenth-century French society. The two groups not only sprang from the same social stratum, but they were both relegated to the marginal fringe—except in those cases where extreme wealth overcame all prejudices. Yet anti-Semitism among artists was common even when the artists were dependent on Jewish patrons for support.[194] It was easy to identify the Jewish financier with bourgeois capitalism, but apparently the artists refused to recognize that, like themselves, Jews swelled the ranks of the utopian reformers. There was a large contingent of young Jewish intellectuals in the Saint-Simonist sect, sons of assimilated business families in Paris or of the Sephardic Jewish community in Bordeaux.[195] Among them were Emile and Isaac Péreire, Olinde Rodriguez, and Gustave d'Eichthal. Simultaneously rationalist and romantic, they yearned for a system that could embrace their values, and in the meeting with Saint-Simon a perfect relationship was formed. They carried over into their business ventures the idea that the credit system was the heart of the social mechanism and that their methods did not serve primarily personal ends, but social ideas, too—the exploitation of nature and the amelioration of man's lot in this world. Contemporary artists also accepted this utopian vision and flocked in large numbers to the public lectures sponsored by Saint-Simon's disciples. At the same time, the Saint-Simon program attracted artists and businessmen because it relieved them of their borderline status and radically advanced their social position.

In fact, there are numerous points of similarity between the artist and the entrepreneur. Both groups are essentially in business for themselves, and their choice of profession entails risk-taking.[196] If an artist must await the conclusion of his work to see what he has been about, whereas the entrepreneur is guided throughout by a "design," both often face an unpredictable confluence of phenomena that require improvisation and sustained imagination under pressure. In this connection it may be worthwhile to mention a providential meeting between Eugène Delacroix, the titular chief of romantic painting and Jules Mirès, the king of nineteenth-century finance, at a dinner party in 1854.[197] A poor Jew from Bordeaux, Mirès managed to acquire control of newspapers, banks, railroads, and gas companies, and for a long time had everyone gasping until his arrest for irregular stock transactions. At the time of their encounter, both men were audacious pioneers at the height of their popularity and they hit it off immediately. Delacroix recorded in his journal that Mirès was "très original, très sensé, très spirituel," terms of a romantic flavor attesting to the authenticity of their expression. He quoted Mirès as saying that "the artist was a variety of madman," but Delacroix concluded that the artist had the advantage over other types since he had no need for the presence of mind or fixity of resolution required by generals, administrators, and financiers. But elsewhere in his *Journal* he claims that these are the very qualities needed to produce masterpieces or to see work through its final stage.[198]

Here indeed was a meeting of minds, for if any entrepreneur of the period was a variety of madman it was Mirès, whose financial empire would topple a scant few years later from his extravagant ventures. On the other hand, Delacroix was a speculator on the Bourse, and one of his great patrons, Adolphe Moreau, served also as his stockbroker. A diary entry of 1858 records that Delacroix requested Moreau to buy and sell a number of shares that day on the Bourse.[199] The painter, who assumed risks in his bold paintings, was as much a gambler as Mirès, whose financial enterprises may be likened to audacious creations.

There are many cases of role switching among entrepreneurs and artists in the nineteenth century.[200] Among the most stunning are those of Gauguin and his patron Arosa. A successful *agent de change* during the boom years of the 1870s who sometimes cleared several thousand francs in a day, Gauguin became, like so many of his colleagues, a victim of the Union Générale crash in 1882. The following year he turned to painting for his livelihood, and while the literature heralds this event as a daring departure from vulgar material concerns, the records show otherwise.[201] A letter from Pissarro, a Jew who spurned his father's business to become an artist and an early supporter of Gauguin, reflects astonishment at the latter's mercantile attitude. He wrote to his son Lucien about Gauguin's desire to paint in Rouen: "He is naive enough to think that since the people in Rouen are very wealthy, they can easily be induced to buy some paintings. . . . Gauguin disturbs me very much, at least he gives that impression. I haven't the heart to point out to him how false and unpromising is his attitude; true, his needs are great, his family being used to luxury, just the same his attitude can only hurt him. Not that I think we ought not try to sell, but I regard it a waste of time to think *only* of selling. . . ."[202]

Pissarro also notes that Gauguin painted some tapestry designs, still another means, along with his ceramic objects, by which Gauguin hoped to improve his finances. Gauguin's interest in applied arts reflected the same entrepreneurial urges he expressed in Copenhagen when he sold tarpaulins or, late in life, when he edited a newspaper in Tahiti. When Gauguin switched professions, he transferred to his new profession both the energy and the set of expectations that had theretofore been reserved for his business affairs. All his life he engaged in bold adventures; making money and making art were manifestations of the same restless existence.[203]

Gauguin's initial protector, Gustave Arosa, was also a jack-of-all-trades. His family belonged to the world of high finance: he was an *agent de change,* his brother Achille was a financier, and his son-in-law Calzado was the director of the Banque Bertin, where Arosa introduced Gauguin. But Arosa was also an artist in his own right and an important art collector. In addition, he experimented with a novel process of reproducing paintings and founded for this purpose a firm, which displayed its examples in the Exposition Universelle of 1878. Arosa's outstanding pottery collection undoubtedly provided the seeds of inspiration for Gauguin's attempts in ceramics.[204]

Equally surprising are the entrepreneurial proclivities of the one-time art dealer, Vincent van Gogh, who is nevertheless taken as the paradigm of the self-sacrificing creative artist. His correspondence, however, contradicts the conventional view: in one letter to Theo he noted that he was "concentrating on making my pictures have some market value." As a painter he thought it essential to always have "some stock of goods to do business with," and conceived a project for a confraternity of artists working for Goupil's through his brother, Theo. In order to fund the project he initiated an elaborate decoration about which he wrote: "I am going to try to please the public, so that a few pennies may come into our community." He was a perennial hustler: he took work on consignment from Bing, and he wanted to pay for a Gauguin painting by allowing the artist to stay the first month in Arles rent-free. In other letters he identifies the dealer with the artist, comparing their risks. At one point, he told Theo: "I wish I could manage to make you really understand that when you give money to artists, you are yourself doing an artist's work, and that I only want my pictures to be of such a quality that you will not be too dissatisfied with *your* work."[205] Of course, none of van Gogh's entrepreneurial ventures succeeded, and perhaps he would have been a failure in any professional venture; but my point is that if we ignore his commercial proclivities we distort his empirical personality—and the history of art.

The situation could also be reversed: Rodolphe Julian, a fairly successful genre and portrait painter, had an even greater "genius for affairs."[206] In 1868 he established the famous Académie Julian, which had a phenomenal development, its several branches opening their doors to those who wished more preparation for the Ecole des Beaux-Arts or who sought a more informal atmosphere. Julian hired leading academic painters to run his academy but allowed more freedom than did the Ecole. Students worked in the mode appropriate to their taste, and Julian's casual methods made his academy an international cynosure of art students. By the mid-1880s the school registers numbered over 400, rivaling the Ecole, which suffered a marked decrease in enrollment during this period.[207]

The Académie Julian inspired critics to contrast the evils of a state-controlled institution like the Ecole with the advantages of a privately owned institution like Julian's. Certainly, the Académie Julian represented a superb example of capitalist enterprise; a corporation, Julian was its chief executive and his teachers major stock holders. But a major reason for its spectacular success was the fact that the teachers sat on Salon juries and systematically awarded prizes to Julian's students. Bolstered by this kind of support, neophytes no longer needed the prestigious Ecole. Eventually, Julian's students formed a power bloc; they got all the best places and won a significant proportion of the medals. As George Moore remarked: "The more medals, the more pupils, and so the studio waxed prosperous. . . ."[208]

Julian's school is significant for the number of distinguished artists who passed through its curriculum. It was here that Serusier, Denis, Vuillard, and Bonnard formed the group that would eventually become the Nabis; later, future Fauves like Derain, Puy, and Matisse would work at Julian's. The American Robert Henri and the German Louis Corinth studied there, and in the twentieth century, Marcel Duchamp and Robert Rauschenberg are counted among its alumni. The list of outstanding painters and sculptors who trained at Julian's is endless.

Edouard Michelin planned to become a painter and began his career at the Ecole des Beaux-Arts. At thirty he was one of Bouguereau's brightest disciples. He exhibited at the Salons in the 1880s, and at the Salon of 1885 he received critical raves for his work *Pilgrims at Emmaus*.[209] But in roughly the same period the family rubber factories were in decline, and Michelin was called upon to take over the helm. He told Bouguereau that his new job was just temporary; fortunately for the pneumatic tire industry, Michelin changed his mind and decided to stay on permanently.

As previously mentioned, the entrepreneur and the artist sometimes combined conspicuously in the same person, as they commonly did in the applied arts at the time of Art Nouveau. Emile Gallé, the famous glass designer, opened a glass works in Nancy in 1874, and his designs had preeminent success when they were exhibited in Bing's shop.[210] But even before Bing opened his shop on the rue de Provence, a reviewer of the 1889 World's Fair had heralded Gallé's work as an *"art nouveau"*: "L'évolution que faisait prévoir, en 1878, la première Exposition des oeuvres de M. Gallé s'est accomplie: un art nouveau a éte crée, art bien personnel et véritablement original. . . ."[211] Gallé eventually became so pressed that he had to employ numerous craftsmen in order to meet the demand; although this meant repeating his designs, he compensated for this by increased production and wider distribution.

There is, then, ample evidence of artist-entrepreneur role exchange in this period, and I would now like to present the following thoughts. There are two fundamental constraints on our development—the inevitable exigencies of material survival and the need to create. What is the condition that leads to the extreme dissociation of the two from the point of view of the artist? Why does he insist that the representatives of the "survival" class are driven by an essentially trivial and inhumane materialism and that they are indifferent to the art object except insofar as it can be negotiated as an interchangeable commodity? On the other hand, why does the businessman try to ridicule the artist and insist that he is an impractical dreamer? In fact, as we have seen, the artist has to hustle and the entrepreneur has a need for a creative expression that is not reducible to a standardized commodity.

The way to promote progress in the world is to get businessmen to think like artists and artists to think like businessmen. Indeed, this study has shown, it is hoped, that that is what has been going on all along. But why then did the two groups behave as if there was not this other aspect of their personality? Why have they been so exclusive in the definition of their vocation? How did the ideology of exclusive vocation prevail, when in the real world artists and entrepreneurs are often found performing each other's jobs and even converting to the other's profession? What we must do is expose the mythology and readily admit that life consists in a very fundamental way of both the entrepreneurial and aesthetic modes.

NOTES

1. A. Habaru, *Le Creusot, terre féodale* (Paris and Brussels, 1934), pp. 12, 34 ff; G. Duveau, *La vie ouvrière en France sous le Second Empire* (Paris, 1946), pp. 130, 361-62, 393.

2. See J. Guiffrey, "Le legs Thomy-Thiéry au Musée du Louvre," *Revue de l'art ancien et moderne* 11 (1902): 113-14.

3. See A. Darcel, "La collection Louis Fould," *Gazette des Beaux-Arts* 6 (1860): 266 (hereafter referred to as *GBA*); C. Blanc, "La galerie Delessert," *GBA*, 2e. pér., 1 (1869): 105.

4. F. Haskell, *Patrons and Painters* (London, 1963), pp. 6 ff; A. Hauser, *The Social History of Art*, 2 vols. (New York, 1951), 2: 879.

5. J. R. Taylor and B. Brooke, *The Art Dealers* (New York, 1969), pp. 30-31.

6. For general references to this taste, see A. Thibaudeau's preface to Blanc, *Le trésor de la curiosité*, 2 vols. (Paris, 1857-58), 1: cxii, cxvii viii, and 2: 533, 595 ff.; G. Reitlinger, *The Economics of Taste: The Rise and Fall of the Picture Market, 1760-1960* (New York, 1964), pp. 138-39, 184; P. Dorbec, *L'art du paysage en France* (Paris, 1925), p. 90.

7. Thoré-Bürger (W. Bürger was the pseudonym of T. Thoré), "Les collections particulières," *Paris Guide* (Paris, 1867), pp. 536 ff.

8. See L. Gonse, "La galerie de M. Schneider," *GBA*, 2e. pér., 13 (1876): 494-96, 511-28. See also *Catalogue des tableaux anciens, dessins, et aquarelles composant la collection de feu M. Schneider* (Paris, 1876). This last work contains essays by Haro, Blanc, Saint-Victor, and d'Escamps.

9. Delaroche's portrait is reproduced in M. Delaborde and J. Goddé, *Oeuvre de Paul Delaroche* (Paris, 1858), no. 55. The work is presently in the collection of Mme Charles Schneider, Paris.

10. Gonse, "Galerie de M. Schneider," p. 494.

11. Reitlinger, *Economics of Taste*; R. L. Herbert, *Barbizon Revisited* (New York, 1962), pp. 18-19.

12. Blanc, "Galerie Delessert," pp. 115 ff.; second article, p. 213; L. Lagrange, "La galerie de M. le Duc de Morny," *GBA* 14 (1863): 290 ff.; second article, p. 398. Also E. Beaumont-Vassy, *Les salons de Paris et la société parisienne sous Napoléon III* (Paris, 1868), pp. 302-33; M. Chapman, *Imperial Brother: The Life of the Duc de Morny* (New York, 1931), p. 114. Meissonier soon became for some the test of an entrepreneur's net worth: in *L'argent*, Zola has Saccard stand before a Meissonier, "qu'il estimait à cent mille francs." See E. Zola, *L'argent* (Paris, 1891), p. 109.

13. Thoré-Bürger, *Musées de la Hollande*, 2 vols. (Paris, 1858-60). The critic helped promote Vermeer and Hals revivals.

14. M. Taine, *Philosophie de l'art dans les Pays-Bas* (Paris, 1869). Taine made his first visit to the Lowlands in the late fifties. For an exhaustive study of Taine's thought on Holland, see R. Wiarda, *Taine et la Hollande* (Paris, 1938). For Montégut, see E. Montégut, "Impressions de voyage et d'art," *Revue des deux mondes* 77 (October 1868): 956 ff.; 78 (November 1868); 78 (December 1868): 428 ff.; 79 (February 1869): 617 ff.; 80 (March 1869): 458 ff.; 81 (June 1869): 555 ff.

15. E. Fromentin, *Les maîtres d'autrefois* (Paris, 1876), pp. 271 ff. See the brilliant analysis of this study by Jacques Foucart in the Livre de Poche edition of 1965.

16. There is a rich literature devoted to the Péreires: see among others, M. Castille, *Les frères Péreire* (Paris, 1861); V. Frond, *Panthéon des illustrations françaises au xixe siècle* (Paris, 1869), vol. 1 (nonpaginated biographies); and A. Péreire, *Autour de Saint-Simon* (Paris, 1912).

17. I. Péreire, *La question des chemins de fer* (Paris, 1879), p. 11; R. E. Cameron, *France and the Economic Development of Europe, 1800-1914* (Princeton, 1961), pp. 206-7.

18. B. Gille, "La fondation du Crédit Mobilier et les idées financières des frères Péreire," *Bulletin du Centre de recherches sur l'histoire des entreprises*, no. 3 (June 1954), pp. 10 ff.

19. Castille, *Les frères Péreire*, p. 41.

20. Ibid.

21. Thoré-Bürger, "Les cabinets d'amateurs à Paris. Galerie de MM. Péreire," *GBA* 16 (1864): 193-213, 297-317. See also *Galerie de MM. Péreire. Catalogue des tableaux anciens et modernes des diverses écoles* (Paris, 1872).

22. Thoré-Bürger, "Van der Meer de Delft," *GBA* 21 (1866): 313. This piece was dedicated to Champfleury.

23. S. Meltzoff, "The Revival of the Le Nains," *Art Bulletin* 24,(1942): 260.

24. Champfleury, "Nouvelles recherches sur la vie et l'oeuvre des frères Le Nain," *GBA* 8 (1860): 322; Champfleury, *Documents positifs sur la vie des frères Le Nain* (Paris, 1865), p.14. Champfleury especially admired the Pourtalès example, which had passed through the collection of Cardinal Fesch. See Champfleury, *Catalogue des tableaux des Le Nain qui ont passé dans les ventes publiques de l'année 1755 à 1853* (Brussels, 1861), pp. 32-33.

25. See L. de Laborde, *De l'union des arts et de l'industrie. Exposition universelle de 1851. Travaux de la commission française sur l'industrie des nations* (Paris, 1856), pp. 204-5. Rousseau, Corot, and Diaz were especially favored by entrepreneur-patrons: Rousseau early had the backing of the banker Paul Casimir-Perier, and later, Emile Péreire and Frédéric Hartmann, the Alsacian textile magnate, became his patrons. See *Herbert, Barbizon Revisited*, pp. 23, 28; A. de Lostalot, "La collection Frédéric Hartmann," *GBA*, 2e. pér., 23 (1881): 456. Hartmann also supported Millet, apparently his favorite painter.

26. See S. O. Simches, *Le romantisme et le goût esthétique du* xviiie *siècle* (Paris, 1964), pp. 2–3, 20.

27. A. Vollard, *Renoir: An Intimate Record* (New York, 1934), p. 25.

28. *Collection de MM. Péreire. Catalogue de tableaux anciens des diverses écoles et principalement de l'Ecole Espagnole* (Paris, 1868), nonpaginated preface. The Péreires essentially salvaged parts of the precious Musée Espagnol, which had inspired so many French painters in the years immediately preceding the 1848 revolution. See T. Gautier, "Le Musée Espagnol," *La presse*, 24 September 1837; I. H. Lipschutz, *Spanish Painting and the French Romantics* (Cambridge, Mass., 1972), pp. 123 ff., 219 ff., appendix A; R. Ford, "Sale of Louis-Philippe and Standish Spanish Pictures," *Athenaeum* (London) 14, 21, 28 March and 4, 11, 18 June 1853.

29. Thoré-Bürger, "Galerie de MM. Péreire," p. 208. Here again the taste of the ruling class is decisive: during the reign of Empress Eugénie, everything Spanish enjoyed enormous popularity, and the entire French culture was saturated with Spanish influences.

30. Ibid., pp. 196–99; *Galerie des tableaux anciens et modernes*, no. 26. The replica of *Oedipus* was painted especially by Ingres for Emile Péreire in 1864. Also H. Delaborde, *Ingres, sa vie, ses travaux, sa doctrine* (Paris, 1870), pp. 212, 268; H. Lapauze, *Ingres, sa vie et son oeuvre* (Paris, 1911), pp. 97, 352.

31. Delaborde and Goddé, *Oeuvre de Paul Delaroche*, no. 76; Thoré-Bürger, "Galerie de MM . Péreire," p. 195. It was judged the best portrait in the London World's Fair of 1862. See also, *Dictionnaire universel des contemporains* (Paris, 1880), s.v. "Emile Péreire," by G. Vapereau. Emile owned several works by Delaroche and supported his favorite pupils, like Gendron and Jalabert.

32. C. Vendryes, *Catalogue illustré des oeuvres de W. Bouguereau* (Paris, 1885), pp. 14–16; E. Reinaud, *Charles Jalabert, l'homme, l'artiste, d'après sa correspondance* (Paris, 1903), pp. 136–37. The Péreires also commissioned Cabanel to decorate their mansion: see Thoré-Bürger, "Galerie de MM. Péreire," p. 195; Castille, *Les Frères Péreire*, p. 41.

33. The Salon, which provided exhibition facilities to a relative minority, was up until the Franco-Prussian War the primary institutional mechanism through which collectors purchased contemporary art. The bankers Jacques Laffitte and Benjamin Delessert obtained their contemporary pictures in this way, and clearly the Péreires commissioned Cabanel on the basis of the artist's smashing success at the Salon of 1857. See *Catalogue de la collection de tableaux et objets de curiosité de M. Jacques Lafitte [sic]* (Paris, 1834), p. iii; Blanc, "La Galerie Delessert," p. 215. The shift is symbolized in the next decade by Isaac Péreire's purchase of a work by Théodore Rousseau from the dealer Durand-Ruel. L. Venturi, *Les archives de l'impressionnisme*, 2 vols. (Paris and New York, 1939), 2: 158.

34. Blanc, *Trésor de la curiosité*, pp. 548 ff., 552.

35. A. Boime, *The Academy and French Painting in the Nineteenth Century* (London, 1971), chaps. 4, 5, and 9.

36. J.-B. H. Capefigue, *Histoire des grandes opérations financiers*, 4 vols. (Paris, 1855–60), 4: 249 ff.; D. S. Landes, "French Entrepreneurship and Industrial Growth in the Nineteenth Century," *Journal of Economic History* 9 (May 1949): 55 ff.

37. Blanc, "Galerie Delessert," pp. 105 ff., 201 ff.; *Notice sur la collection de tableaux de MM. Delessert* (Paris, 1846).

38. B. Delessert, *Notice sur Marc-Antoine Raimondi, graveur bolonais*, 2 vols. (Paris, 1853–55); *Catalogue raisonné d'une belle collection d'estampes d'anciens graveurs italiens, allemands, flamands et hollandais . . . qui composaient le cabinet de M. B[enjamin] D[elessert]* (Paris, 1852), nos. 36–182.

39. This was known immediately to his audience: see E. Chesneau, *L'art et les artistes modernes en France et en Angeleterre* (Paris, 1864), p. 190 n. Delessert possessed a proof of this engraving, *Jugement de Paris*, a work the catalogue entry described as "la plus parfaite de *Marc-Antoine*." It also noted that another proof had been recently sold at auction for 3,517 francs. See *Catalogue raisonné*, no.123.

40 *Catalogue des objets d'art et de haute curiosité . . . qui composent les collections de feu M. le Comte de Pourtalès-Gorgier* (Paris, 1865); *Catalogue des tableaux anciens et modernes, dessins, qui composent les collections de feu M. le Comte de Pourtalès-Gorgier* (Paris, 1865); A. Jacquemart, "La galerie du Comte Pourtalès. Objets d'art et de curiosité," *GBA* 17 (1864): 377 ff.; F. Lenormant, "La galerie du Comte Pourtalès. Antiquités grecques et romaines, " in ibid., pp. 473 ff.; E. Galichon, "La galerie Pourtalès. Les peintures italiennes," *GBA* 18 (1865): 5 ff.; P. Mantz, "La galerie Pourtalès. Les peintures espagnoles, allemandes, hollandaises, flamandes, et françaises," in ibid., pp. 97 ff. For an informative discussion of Delaroche's portrait of Pourtalès-Gorgier posed before part of his collection, see N. D. Ziff, "Paul Delaroche: A Study in Nineteenth-Century Painting" (Ph.d. diss., New York University, 1974), pp. 221 ff.

41. Once the *Orlando* aroused the envy and admiration of French artists; now it is given simply to "Italian School. XVIIth Century." Its present home is the National Gallery, London.

42. See G. M. Ackerman, "Gérôme and Manet," *GBA*, 6e. pér., 70 (1967): 163 ff.

43. E. C. Corti, *The Rise of the House of Rothschild* (New York, 1928), p. 257; J. Bouvier, *Les Rothschild* (Paris, 1967), p. 279; G. Seligman, *Merchants of Art: 1880–1960* (New York, 1961), pp. 48 ff. The Rothschilds also advanced loans to the government for maintenance of the French Academy at Rome. See Archives Nationales, F21:602, *bordereau* dated 6 November 1867.

44. Seligman, *Merchants of Art*; D. Cooper, ed., *Great Private Collections* (New York, 1963), p. 168.

45. Seligman, *Merchants of Art*, p. 55. The Baron Robert developed an interest in the Impressionists—particularly Renoir; his son, Baron Elie, extended this interest and has ventured into the realm of the avant-garde. Cooper, ed., *Great Private Collections*, pp. 168 ff.

46. E. Beaumont-Vassy, *Les salons de Paris et la société sous Louis-Philippe 1er* (Paris, 1866), pp. 328 ff.; J. Boudet, ed., *Le monde des affaires en France de 1830 à nos jours* (Paris, 1952), pp. 714, 717.

47. H. de Chennevières, "Le legs de la Baronne Nathaniel de Rothschild au Musée du Louvre," *GBA*, 3e. pér., 23 (1900): 5 ff.; P. Leroi, "Le Baron Alphonse," *L'art* 64 (1905): 259 ff.; J. Guiffrey, "Le Legs Arthur de Rothschild au Louvre," *Les arts*, no. 27 (March 1904), pp. 2 ff. Alphonse, a member of the Académie des Beaux-Arts, was a genuine *mécène*, and systematically aided the younger academically trained painters. He bequeathed a major portion of his collection to provincial museums and donated a magnificent Reynolds portrait, *Master Hare*, to the Louvre. Boudet, ed., *Mondes des affaires*, p. 730; *Histoire des collections de peintures au Musée du Louvre* (Paris, 1930), p. 106. The grandchildren also endowed public institutions: Henri left his collection to the state, and Edmond left 30,000 engravings and 3,000 drawings to the Louvre. Boudet, ed., *Mondes des affaires;* Paris, Louvre, Cabinet des dessins, *François Boucher: Gravures et dessins provenant du Cabinet des dessins et de la collection Edmond de Rothschild au Musée du Louvre* (Paris, 1971), pp. 5–6. Adolphe, son of the founder of the Naples branch, bequeathed his large collection of religious objects to both the Louvre and Cluny, including the exquisite Reliquary of the True Cross. See F. Marcou, "La donation Adolphe de Rothschild au Musée du Louvre, *GBA*, 3e. pér., 27 (1902): 265 ff.;

H. Frantz, "The New Room at the Louvre. The Adolphe de Rothschild Collection," *Magazine of Art* 26 (1902): 493 ff. The Rothschilds have always been especially generous to the Musée de Cluny: see Baron James among the list of Cluny benefactors in A. du Sommerard, *Les arts au Moyen Age en ce qui concerne principalement le palais romain de Paris, l'hôtel de Cluny issu de ses ruines, et les objets d'art de la collection classée dans cet hôtel*, 2 vols. (Paris, 1838), 2: 439. See also M. Schwab, "La collection Strauss au Musée de Cluny," *GBA*, 3e. pér., 5 (1891): 237 ff.

48. See J. Claparède, *Dessins de la collection Alfred Bruyas* (Paris, 1962), nonpaginated introduction; P. Borel, ed., *Lettres de Gustave Courbet à Alfred Bruyas* (Geneva, 1951), p. 9.

49. Paris, Louvre, *Catalogue de la collection Isaac de Camondo* (Paris, 1964); *Catalogue de la collection Isaac de Camondo*, 2d ed. (Paris, 1922), nonpaginated preface; G. Migeon, *Le Comte Isaac de Camondo* (Paris, 1913), pp. 3 ff.; E. Molinier, "Un don au Musée du Louvre: la collection du Comte Isaac de Camondo," *GBA*, 3e. pér., 17 (1897): 89 ff.; P. Jamot, "La collection Camondo au Musée du Louvre," *GBA*, 4e. pér. 11 (1914): 387 ff.; 12 (1914–16): 53 ff., 441 ff. Also the series of articles by Vitry, Dreyfus, and Migeon in the June 1914 issue of *GBA*, pp. 441 ff, on separate parts of the collection.

50. See R. Koch, "Art Nouveau Bing," *GBA*, 6e. pér., 53 (1959): 179–81; E. de Goncourt and J. de Goncourt, *Journal*, 4 vols. (Paris, 1956), 2: 1072–73; Molinier, "Camondo," p. 103; Migeon, *Camondo*, pp. 6 ff., 20.

51. For brilliant exposition of the influence of *japonisme* on French art, see the recent catalogue *Japonisme: Japanese Influence on French Art, 1854–1910* (The Cleveland Museum of Art, 1975), with essays by G. P. Weisberg, P. D. Cate, G. Needham, M. Eidelberg, W. R. Johnston.

52. Vollard made some sarcastic observations on Camondo, but Vollard was fond of poking fun at the amateurs and collectors who patronized him. In fact, Camondo was an early admirer of Cézanne and was very excited by Vollard's purchases of the artist's work from the sale of Père Tanguy's collection. See A. Vollard, *Souvenirs d'un marchand de tableaux* (Paris, 1937), pp. 126 ff.; Vollard, *Renoir*, pp. 178 ff.

53. Boudet, ed., *Monde des affaires*, p. 68.

54. See "Nécrologie," *La chronique des arts*, 15 April 1911, p. 119; Migeon, *Camondo*, p. 21; F. Fénéon, *Oeuvres plus que complètes*, 2 vols. (Geneva, 1970), 1: 346.

55. Goncourt and Goncourt, *Journal*, 2: 1072–73, 1118–19; 4: 114, 593.

56. For the early career of Cernuschi, who worked for a time in the Crédit Mobilier, see N. W. Senior, *Conversations*, 2 vols. (London, 1878), 2: 212 ff. See also G. Migeon, "Le Musée Cernuschi," *GBA*, 3e. pér., 18 (1897): 217 ff.; Boudet, ed., *Monde des affaires*, p. 42; *Larousse du xxe siècle* (Paris, 1929), 2: 90; *La grande encyclopédie* (Paris, n.d.), 10:63.

57. O. Monod, *Le Musée Guimet*, 2 vols. (Paris, 1966), 1: 1–3; *Larousse du xxe siècle*, 3: 916; *La grande encyclopédie*, 19: 594.

58. See the extensive account of Cognacq's life in P. Cabanne, *The Great Collectors* (London, 1963), pp. 99 ff. For a general history of department stores in France, see H. Pasdermadjian, *Le grand magasin* (Paris, 1949), pp. 2 ff.

59. L. Bénédite, "La collection Chauchard au Musée du Louvre," *GBA*, 4e. pér., 5 (1911): 89 ff.; "Nécrologie," *La chronique des arts*, 19 June 1909, p. 195; J. Guiffrey, *La collection Chauchard* (Paris, 1911); Boudet, ed., *Monde des affaires*, pp. 728 ff.

60. Vollard, *Souvenirs*, pp. 135 ff.; Guiffrey, *Collection Chauchard*, pp. 13 ff.

61. Guiffrey, *Collection Chauchard*, pp. 3–4.

62. See *Succession de Mme Ve. Boucicaut. Diamants, mobilier, tableaux* (Paris, 1888).

63. Boudet, ed., *Monde des affaires*, p. 728.

64. For information on Bader, I am grateful to the present director of the Galeries Lafayette, M. Max Heilbronn. See his correspondence to me dated 31 March and 10 May 1973. See also Vollard, *Souvenirs*, pp. 139–40.

65. Venturi, *Archives de l'impressionisme*, I, 39; R. Gimpel, *Journal d'un collection-neur, marchand de tableaux* (Paris, 1963), p. 103. The restaurant was located on L'Abbaye de Thélème, 103.

66. *Exposition universelle internationale de 1878 à Paris. Catalogue officiel* (Paris, 1878), 2: 336; *Didot-Bottin* 1870; Auriant, "Duranty et Zola," *La nef* 3 (July 1946): 51–52.

67. Auriant, "Duranty et Zola," p. 52; F. J. "Le dernier article d'Ernest Hoschedé," *L'art français*, 11 April 1891, nonpaginated.

68. Auriant, "Duranty et Zola," p. 51.

69. *Vente judiciaire des tableaux modernes et anciens, meubles et curiosités composant la collection Hoschedé* (Paris, 1878), nos. 64–72; Auriant, "Duranty et Zola."

70. J. Rewald, *History of Impressionism* (New York, 1961), pp. 374, 378. Hoschedé also supported a few academic painters who adopted some of the features of realists and Impressionists, including Paul Baudry (who painted portraits of Hoschedé and his wife Blanche), Carolus-Duran, Jean-Jacques Henner, and Alphonse de Neuville. See C. Ephrussi, *Paul Baudry* (Paris, 1887), p. 242; Bertall [pseud.], *La comédie de notre temps*, 3 vols. (Paris, 1874–76), 2: 335. At the Montgeron residence Manet painted a portrait of Carolus-Duran, who lived near by. After Hoschedé's death, his widow married Claude Monet.

71. E. Hoschedé, *Impression de mon voyage au Salon de 1882* (Paris, 1882), pp. vi ff.; Hoschedé *Brelan de Salons* (Paris, 1890), preface.

72. F. J., "Dernier article." The title of Hoschedé's piece was "Les femmes peintres et sculpteurs," *L'art français*, 7 March 1891.

73. See A. Alexandre's preface to the *Catalogue des tableaux anciens . . . et tableaux modernes . . . composant la collection de feu M. Henri Rouart* (Paris, 1912), pp. i ff.; *Catalogue des dessins et pastels anciens et modernes composant la collection de feu M. Henri Rouart* (Paris, 1912); J.-E. Blanche, *Propos de peinture, de David à Degas* (Paris, 1927), pp. 245 ff.; P. A. Lemoisne, *Degas et son oeuvre*, 3 vols. (Paris, 1946–49), 1:74. Henri was the director-engineer of a large metallurgical establishment in Paris and owned several patents on his discoveries. He apparently had wide-ranging investments and once sent a representative to the United States in the hopes of setting up a glass-blowing enterprise there.

74. Rewald, *History of Impressionism*, pp. 302, 312, 315, 391, 423, 469.

75. P. Acker, "Une ville industrielle alsacienne, Mulhouse," *Revue des deux mondes*, 6e. pér., 8 (1912): 430 ff.; C. Fohlen, *L'industrie textile au temps du Second Empire* (Paris, 1956, pp. 69–70. A grandson of the founder also became a painter: see H. Juillard-Weiss, "Note sur Josué Dollfus et ses oeuvres," *Bulletin de la société industrielle de Mulhouse* 74 (1904): 183 ff. The Dollfus descendants established a strong liberal tradi-tion; Jean's father—also named Jean—advocated free trade and did much to improve the lot of his workers. We may further note here that since the problems of color and design are central to the textile industry, it is not surprising to find textile manufacturers deeply involved in the fine arts. In addition to the Dollfus family, the Hartmann brothers from Munster, Fritz (or Frédéric, see n. 25) and Alfred, identified closely with artists and assembled notable collections. Alfred, who practically worshipped the landscapist Français, joined the artist on painting expeditions and owned eighty-one examples of his work. See Fohlen, *L'industrie textile*, p. 302, n. 60; Georges Lafenestre's preface in *Collection de M. Alfred Hartmann. Catalogue des tableaux modernes et aquarelles*

remarquables . . . (Paris, 1899), pp. iii ff.; A. Gros, *François-Louis Français* (Paris, 1902), pp. 71, 158 ff., 174.

76. A. Michel, "La collection Jean Dollfus," in *Catalogue de tableaux modernes dependant des collections de M. Jean Dollfus* (Paris, 1912), pp. 6 ff.; Duveau, *Vie ouvrière*, p. 183; *The Illustrated Catalogue of the Universal Exhibition (The Art Journal)* (London, 1868), pp. 254-55.

77. A. Alexandre, "La collection de M. Jean Dollfus," *Les arts 3* (1904); Michel, "Collection Jean Dollfus," p. 9; L. Hanson, *Renoir: The Man, the Painter, and His World* (New York, 1968), p. 151.

78. The Haviland material was drawn from J. d'Albis, "Histoire de la fabrique Haviland de 1842 à 1925," *Bulletin de la Société Archéologique et Historique de Limousin* 96 (1969): 193 ff.

79. A. de Lostalot, "M. Félix Bracquemond, peintre-graveur," *GBA*, 2e. pér., 30 (1884): 155 ff.; G. P. Weisberg, "Felix Bracquemond and *Japonisme*," *Art Quarterly* 32 (1969): 57 ff.; Weisberg, "Felix Bracquemond and Japanese Influence on Ceramic Decoration," *Art Bulletin* 51 (1969): 277 ff.

80. C. Gray, *Sculpture and Ceramics of Paul Gauguin* (Baltimore, 1963), pp. 5-6.

81. *Collection Ch. Haviland, tableaux modernes* . . . (Paris, 1922), nos. 9, 27-31, 41-42, 45, 50-55.

82. A. Joubin, "Jacques Doucet," *GBA*, 6e. pér., 3 (1930): 69 ff.; M. Dormoy, *Jacques Doucet* (Abbeville, 1931); J.-F. Revel, "Jacques Doucet, couturier et collectionneur," *L'oeil*, no. 84 (December 1961), pp. 44-51, 81, 106.

83. *Catalogue de Jacques Doucet*, 3 vols. (Paris, 1912); Goncourt and Goncourt, *Journal*, 3: 1270-71.

84. "Un temple de l'art moderne. L'appartement de M. J. D.," *Femina*, January 1925, pp. 29-32; "Collection d'un amateur," *La chronique des arts*, January-March 1918, pp. 90-91; Joubin, "Jacques Doucet," pp. 74 ff.

85. He also bequeathed to the Université de Paris the present Bibliothèque Littéraire Jacques Doucet.

86. Gimpel, *Journal d'un collectionneur*, p. 399.

87. See Poiret's autobiography, P. Poiret, *King of Fashion*, trans. S. M. Couset (Philadelphia and London, 1931). Also Man Ray, *Self-Portrait* (Boston and Toronto, 1963), pp. 120 ff.

88. *Catalogue des tableaux modernes* . . . *de la Collection Paul Poiret* (Paris, 1925); see nos. 46-47 for Poiret's own works. Occasionally, these artists might go too far, even for Poiret: he found Matisse's *Blue Window* too advanced after having commissioned it, and it passed into the Folkwang Museum of Karl Osthaus near Essen. A. H. Barr, *Matisse: His Art and His Public* (New York, 1951), p. 166.

89. Poiret, *King of Fashion*, pp. 159, 161 ff.

90. Boudet, ed., *Monde des affaires*, pp. 636 ff.; D. Bourdet, "Les fées," *Art et style*, no. 5 (October 1946), pp. 29-33; A. Fage, *Le collectionneur de peintures modernes* (Paris, 1930), p. 96.

91. Boudet, ed., *Monde des affaires*, p. 637.

92. *Exposition universelle de 1867. Rapport du jury international*, ed. M. Chevalier (Paris, 1868), 2: 27. Art Books, then as now, represented a special branch of the book industry. See H. Havard, "Les livres d'art au Champ-de-Mars," *GBA*, 2e. pér., 18 (1878): 1070 ff.; L. Gonse, "Publications artistiques de la librairie H. Quantin en janvier 1880," *GBA* 2e. pér., 22 (1880): 544 ff.

93. H. Girard, "Le livre, l'illustration, et la réliure à l'époque romantique," in *Le romantisme et l'art* (Paris, 1928), pp. 290 ff.; Boudet, ed., *Monde des affaires*.

94. J. Adhémar, *Les lithographies de paysage en France à l'époque romantique* (Paris, 1937), pp. 54 ff., H. L. Seaver, "The Golden Book of Landscape Lithography," *Print Collector's Quarterly* 5 (1915): 445 ff.; E. Maingot, *Le Baron Taylor* (Paris, 1963), pp. 33 ff. It should also be noted that Taylor was instrumental in setting up an extended form of patronage under the aegis of various relief organizations for artists; it anticipated group shows and artists' cooperatives. See Maingot, *Baron Taylor*, pp. 86 ff. His efforts earned him the cherished nickname "Père des artistes."

95. Adhémar, *Lithographies de paysage*, pp. 59, 69.

96. Seaver, "Landscape Lithography," p. 458.

97. Girard, "Le livre," pp. 303–6; R. Hesse, *Le livre d'art du XIXe siècle à nos jours* (Paris, 1927), pp. 7, 15–16.

98. Mention should also be made of the founding of the *Gazette des Beaux-Arts* in 1859, an art periodical that not only opened a new market to artists but also made a major contribution to the field of art history through its scholarly articles and influence on contemporary artists. Its original owner, Maurice Cottier, was an ideal nineteenth-century type: entrepreneur, painter, and collector all rolled into one. See H. Avenel, *Histoire de la presse française depuis 1789 jusqu'à nos jours* (Paris, 1900), p. 490; P. Mantz, "La galerie de M. Maurice Cottier," *GBA*, 2e. pér., 5 (1872): 375 ff.; L. Gonse, "Maurice Cottier," *GBA*, 2e. pér., 24 (1881): 465–67. The *Gazette*'s first editor, the great critic and art historian Charles Blanc, functioned as an entrepreneur in carrying out his monumental *Histoire des peintres de toutes les écoles*, a project issued in 631 sections and comprising 14 volumes. Blanc employed a legion of art historians and artists to execute the gargantuan task in the years 1849-76. The numerous illustrations were wood engraved. For general statistics on the industry at mid-century, see E. Texier, *Tableau de Paris*, 2 vols. (Paris, 1852–53), 2: 269–70.

99. M. Cloche, "Un grand éditeur du XIXe siècle, Léon Curmer," *Arts et métiers graphiques*, no. 33 (1933), pp. 28–36; G. Blanchard, "Curmer, ou la leçon d'un grand éditeur romantique," *Le courrier graphique*, no. 117 (1962), pp. 42–51; Hesse, *Livre d'art*, pp. 17 ff.

100. Cloche, "Léon Curmer," p. 28. For Curmer's direct involvement with his writers and artists, see H. de Balzac, *Correspondance*, 5 vols., ed. R. Pierrot (Paris, 1960, *et seq.*), 3: 489–90, 542, 622–24, 695, 743–44, and 762; Gros, *François-Louis Français* pp. 100 ff.

101. Cloche, "Léon Curmer," p. 31.

102. See A. Parménie and C. Bonnier de la Chapelle, *Histoire d'un éditeur et de ses auteurs, P.-J. Hetzel (Stahl)* (Paris, 1953); Bibliothèque Nationale, *P.-J. Hetzel* (Paris, 1966); Hesse, *Livre d'art*, p. 17.

103. Parménie and Bonnier de la Chapelle, *Histoire d'un éditeur*, pp. 25–26.

104. *L'art et l'industrie de tous les peuples à l'exposition universelle de 1878* (Paris, n.d. [1878]), p. 235. See A. de Laberge's general review of the illustrated art books of the period, pp. 227 ff.

105. Rewald, *History of Impressionism*, pp. 384–85, 419; "Mouvement des arts. Succession de M. Georges Carpentier," *La chronique des arts*, 20 April 1907, pp. 138–39.

106. Vollard, *Renoir*, pp. 88 ff.

107. Vollard, *Souvenirs*, pp. 304 ff.; U. E. Johnson, *Ambroise Vollard, Editeur* (New York, 1944); D. Bland, *A History of Book Illustration* (Berkeley and Los Angeles, 1969), pp. 329 ff. Vollard's role as dealer will be discussed below.

108. For French newspaper growth, see Avenel, *Histoire de la presse française*, chaps. 7, 8, and 9; Boudet, ed., *Monde des affaires*, pp. 420 ff.

109. Avenel, *Histoire de la presse française*, pp. 364 ff.

110. E. Zola, *Salons*, ed. F. W. J. Hemmings and R. J. Niess (Geneva, 1959), pp. 15 ff. We may note too that Cézanne included the newspaper portrait of his father as a reflection of the elder Cezanne's taste.

111. See R. Moulin, *Le marché de la peinture en France* (Paris, 1967); H. C. White and C. A. White, *Canvases and Careers* (New York, 1965). chaps. 3 and 4.

112. Champfleury [pseud.], *Oeuvres posthumes* (Paris, 1894), pp. 32 ff.

113. See M. Guicheteau, "Essai sur l'esthétique spontanée du marchand de tableaux," *Revue d'esthétique* 5 (1952): 53 ff. A refreshing article, this piece is sympathetic to the art dealer and attacks the conventional image.

114. D. Adamson, *The Genesis of Le Cousin Pons* (London, 1966), pp. 97 ff.

115. A. Toussenel, *Les juifs, rois de l'époque. Histoire de la féodalité financière*, 2 vols. (Paris, 1847), 1: i.

116. See T. R. Bowie, *The Painter in French Fiction* (Chapel Hill N.C., 1950). pp. 13–14; R. J. Niess, *Zola, Cézanne, and Manet: A Study of L'Oeuvre* (Ann Arbor, 1968), pp. 39, 50 ff., 399–400; Bibliothèque Nationale, Dossier of ms. notes "Zola-L'Oeuvre," pp. 348-61.

117. Gimpel, *Journal d'un collectionneur*, pp. 61-63. Zola's research notes, however, do reveal certain practices of the period: he observed that Sedelmeyer kept a special work aside with which to lure clients, apparently a device common to several dealers. See Bibliothèque Nationale, "Zola-L'Oeuvre," pp. 356-57; Gimpel, *Journal d'un collectionneur*, p. 277; E. Bonnaffé, "Physiologie du curieux," *GBA*, 2e. pér., 22 (1880): 32.

118. Bibliothèque Nationale, "Zola-L'Oeuvre," p. 349; T. Duret, "Quelques lettres de Manet et de Sisley," *La revue blanche* 18 (1899): 437; Alexandre, *Collection de feu de M. Henri Rouart*, p. vii.

119. E. Bernard, "Julien Tanguy, dit le 'Père Tanguy,' " *Mercure de France* 76 (1908): 600 ff.; Vollard, *Souvenirs*, p. 36. Tanguy, like Balzac's Magus, slept in squalid quarters and gave up all the room he could "to his beloved pictures." See C. Waern, "Some Notes on French Impressionism," *Atlantic Monthly*, April 1892, p. 541.

120. A. Level, *Souvenirs d'un collectionneur* (Paris, 1959), pp. 81 ff.

121. Venturi, *Archives de l'impressionisme*, 2: 166; *Exposition universelle de 1867. Rapports*, p. 139; E. Delacroix, *Journal*, 3 vols., ed. A. Joubin (Paris, 1950), 1: 330, 333, 345, 424, 490; 2: 447; 3: 143 et passim; *Collection MM. Haro. Tableaux anciens et modernes* (Paris, 1892); *Collection de M. Haro père. Catalogue des tableaux, anciens et modernes* (Paris, 1897).

122. See the extract of Goupil's biography by Henry Lauzac in *The Complete Letters of Vincent van Gogh*, 3 vols. (Greenwich, Conn., 1958), 3: 579-81; "The Art-Publications of MM. Goupil, of Paris," *The Art-Journal* 2 (1856): 7-8. Also the informative articles by Rewald, "Theo van Gogh, Goupil, and the Impressionists," *GBA*, 6e pér., 81 (1973): 1-64, 65-108. In 1875 Goupil was succeeded by Boussod and Valadon, but the name Goupil was retained in the new designation, and most people continued to refer to the firm as "Goupil." The business continued to wax prosperous, with a main gallery at 2, place de l'Opéra, its printing shop at 9, rue Chaptal, and another gallery at 19, boulevard Montmartre.

123. For Goupil's dealings with artists, see Reinaud, *Charles Jalabert*, pp. 128, 136, 140, 146, 226; C. Stryienski, *Charles Landelle* (Paris, 1911), pp. 14, 103, 104–5; Boussod, Valadon & Cie, *Half a Century with Jozef Israels* (The Hague, 1910). Landelle signed a contract with Goupil in the 1840s stipulating that the artist had to give the firm first look for reproduction of his work before taking it elsewhere. In 1871 Goupil paid Landelle 39,000 francs for his share of the sale of replicas and reproductions. Evidently, Goupil's

policy was to form close—almost familial—relationships with its artists: Jalabert moved into Goupil's newly constructed building on the rue Chaptal in 1858, Gérôme married the boss's daughter, and Israels was treated like a member of the family. Thus Theo van Gogh's close affiliation with the younger generation of artists may have originally been inspired by company policy.

124. E. Saglio, "Exposition de tableaux modernes dans la galerie Goupil," *GBA* 7 (1860): 46 ff. Goupil's importance to the art world is seen as early as 1848, when a group of artists dependent on the firm supported its petition to the provisional government for a subsidy to prevent its collapse amid the current economic crisis. See Archives Nationales F²¹:32, Dossier "Goupil et Cie, 1840–1849." On the other hand, the heirs of Vernet, Scheffer, and Delaroche sued Goupil in the 1870s for unfair monopolization of reproduction rights. Goupil made a fortune reproducing works by these artists in the national collections, and the heirs claimed a share of the profits in accordance with legitimate precedents. But Goupil, who had strong ties with the government, appealed to the Beaux-Arts administration for its intervention, and it promptly called in a government lawyer who ultimately won the suit in Goupil's favor. The sordid character of the episode is typified by a letter from the director of Beaux-Arts to Goupil asking the dealer to cover the government's expenses in the case. Archives Nationales F²¹:297, Dossier "M. Goupil."

125. E. Molinier, "La collection Albert Goupil," *GBA*, 2e. pér., 31 (1885): 337 ff.; H. Lavoix, "La collection Albert Goupil: l'art oriental," *GBA*, 2e. pér., 32 (1885): 287 ff.

126. *Complete Letters of Vincent van Gogh*, 1: 153, 157, 203-4, 208-9, 210, 214 et passim. Van Gogh made extensive use of Goupil's *Cours de dessin* and *Exercises au fusain*, created specially for the firm by the artists Gérôme and Bargue. It was Tersteeg, the manager of the Hague branch of Goupil's, who gave van Gogh the publications. Ibid., pp. 220, 235-36, 237. Also A. Boime, "A Source for van Gogh's Potato-Eaters," *GBA*, 6e. pér., 69 (1966): 249 ff.

127. See J. Bailly-Herzberg, "French Etching in the 1860s," *Art Journal* 31 (Summer 1972): 382-86; G. P. Weisberg, *The Etching Renaissance in France: 1850-1880* (Utah Museum of Fine Arts, 1971), pp. 9 ff.

128. For Durand-Ruel, see Venturi, *Archives de l'impressionisme*; Cabanne, *Great Collectors*, pp. 63 ff.

129. See Bouvier, *Le Krach de l'Union Générale (1878-1885)* (Paris, 1960); Cameron, *France and the Economic Development of Europe*, p. 198; Cabanne, *Great Collectors*, pp. 76-77; Venturi, *Archives de l'impressionisme* 1: 60, 66; ibid., vol. 2: 210 ff.

130. Fénéon, *Oeuvres plus que complètes*, p. 352; Bibliothèque Nationale, "Zola-Oeuvre," p. 355.

131. Vollard, *Souvenirs*, pp. 240, 279.

132. Gimpel, *Journal d'un collectionneur*, p. 188.

133. Cited in Johnson, *Ambroise Vollard*, p. 39.

134. Vollard, *Souvenirs*, pp. 320 ff.

135. D.-H. Kahnweiler, *Mes galeries et mes peintures. Entretiens avec Francis Crémieux* (Paris, 1961).

136. Ibid., p. 25.

137. Ibid., p. 35.

138. See *Catalogue des objets d'art et de haute curiosité composant l'importante et précieuse collection Spitzer*, 3 vols. (Paris, 1893), prefaces by E. Bonnaffé and E. Molinier; A. de Lostalot, "La vente des collections Spitzer," *GBA*, 3e. pér., 9 (1893): 331 ff.; Bonnaffé, "Le Musée Spitzer," *GBA*, 2e. pér., 23 (1881): 281 ff.; E. Müntz, "La collection de tapisseries de M. Spitzer," *GBA*, 2e. pér., 23 (1881): 377 ff.; Seligman, *Merchants of*

Art, pp. 14, 70; G. Reitlinger, *The Economics of Taste: The Rise and Fall of the Objets d'Art Market Since 1750* (New York, 1963), pp. 120 ff. Many of the items in Spitzer's collections wound up in the collections of J. Pierpont Morgan and the Metropolitan Museum of Art.

139. *Catalogue des objets d'art*, 1: p. xiii. Even the academy supported this trend, although it differed from some critics as to how this unity should come about: see Académie des Beaux-Arts, "Rapport sur l'ouvrage de M. le Comte de Laborde Intitulé: De l'union des arts et de l'industrie," *Séance publique annuelle . . . 2 octobre 1858* 13 (1854-1858), pp. 10 ff.

140. See the thirteen articles on the collection written by Müntz, Popelin, Blondel, Piot, Garnier, Darcel, Bonnaffé, Beaumont, and Le Breton, published in the *Gazette des Beaux-Arts* during the years 1881-88.

141. J.-E. Blanche, *Les arts plastiques* (Paris, 1931), pp. 451-53; Koch, "Art Nouveau Bing," 179 ff.; Goncourt and Goncourt, *Journal*, 2: 1073-74, 1138, 1194; 3: 269, 523; 4: 893 et passim. See also the informative articles by Weisberg in *The Connoisseur*: "Samuel Bing: Patron of Art Nouveau," vol. 172, October and December 1969, and vol. 173, January 1970; "Samuel Bing: International Dealer of Art Nouveau," vol. 176, March and April 1971, and vol. 177, May and July 1971.

142. E. Chesneau, "Exposition universelle. Le Japon à Paris," *GBA*, 2e. pér., 18 (1878): 386. For general references on the Japanese influence in France, see L. Gonse, "L'art japonais et son influence sur le goût européen," *Revue des arts décoratifs* 18 (April 1898): 97 ff; E. Scheyer, "Far Eastern Art and Impressionism," *Art Quarterly* 6 (1943): 117 ff.; C. Lancaster, "Oriental Contributions to Art Nouveau," *Art Bulletin* 34 (1952): 297 ff.; *Japonisme: Japanese Influence on French Art*.

143. *Complete Letters of Vincent van Gogh*, 2: 600-601, 611, 613, 614. Both Vincent and his brother Theo had business arrangements with Bing.

144. S. Bing, *Artistic America, Tiffany Glass, and Art Nouveau*, intro. R. Koch (Cambridge, Mass., 1970).

145. Laborde, *Exposition universelle de 1851*, pp. 2-3, 51, 408, 455, 695 ff.; Académie des Beaux-Arts, "Rapport sur l'ouvrage de M. le Comte de Laborde," p.6. Laborde, who spoke for a wide segment of his society, dreamed that everyone might become an artist and that "les artistes se fassent industriels, que les industriels se fassent artistes." He also suggested the novel idea of having public places decorated and operated by great artists: "On ira au *Café Delaroche*, à la salle de *Concert Ingres*, au *Théâtre Delacroix.* . . ."

146. The Ecole des Beaux-Arts—wrested from the academy's control by the decree of 13 November 1863—was the most severely affected institution. The reforms introduced into its curriculum were imbued with the ideas of Laborde and enlightened entrepreneurs. See *Réorganisation de l'école impériale des Beaux-Arts, documents officiels extraits du Moniteur officiel* (Paris, 1864); A. Boime, "The Pedagogical Reforms of 1863 and the Evolution of Nineteenth-Century French Art," *Art Quarterly* (forthcoming). See also Archives Nationales F²¹:613, a published approbation from provincial artists and architects welcoming the reforms and requesting that the administration publish the new courses "qui par leur nature élevée sont destinés à donner à l'enseignement des arts un nouvel essor."

147. A. Dupuis, *De l'enseignement du dessin sous le point de vue industriel* (Paris, 1863), pp. 10, 26-27, 31-32, 34, 65 ff.; M. E. Cavé, *La couleur* (Paris, 1863), p.5; *La femme aujourd'hui, la femme autrefois* (Paris, 1863), pp. v-vi, 2, 26, 40, 211; "Procédé pour faciliter l'étude des arts du dessin, par M. Roulliet, Commission (1843)," in Archives Nationales F²¹:497; A. Roulliet, *Principes de dessin* (Paris, 1863), pp. 3, 5; A. Etex, *Cours élémentaire de dessin*, 2 vols. (Paris, 1853), 1: p. viii; Etex, *Beaux-Arts Cours public fait à*

l'association polytechnique pour les élèves des écoles et pour les ouvrières (Paris, 1861), pp. 18, 21–22, 27–28, 225, 256; Dossier "M. Gélibert, Paul," in Archives Nationales F²¹:297; M. Lecoq de Boisbaudran, "Education de la mémoire pittoresque" (first published in 1848 and reedited in 1862), reprinted in *L'éducation de la mémoire pittoresque et la formation de l'artiste*, ed. L.-D. Luard (Paris, 1953), p. 32. I am preparing a comprehensive work on these teachers and their methods.

148. All these teachers rejected the conventional method that initiated neophytes in slavish copying of engravings and forced concentration on the mastery of individual parts of the body. Their aim was to make the student immediately aware of the "ensemble" of a subject, and they advocated more spontaneous drawing techniques and simpler approaches to form.

149. F. de Tapiés, *La France et l'Angleterre* (Paris, 1845), pp. i, 81 ff., 86 ff., 286, 367 ff., 481 ff.; A. de Beaumont, "Les arts industriels en France et l'exposition de 1863," *Revue des deux mondes*, 15 October 1863, pp. 986 ff.; C. D'Henriet, "L'enseignement populaire des arts du dessin en Angleterre et en France," *Revue des deux mondes*, 1 September 1868, pp. 193 ff. A revealing letter from D. Potonié—a hardware entrepreneur—to the emperor, dated 17 April 1854, states: "Nous devons faire notre Exposition aussi bien ou mieux que les Anglais" (Archives Nationales F²¹:519). Also C. P. Kindleberger, *Economic Growth in France and Britain, 1851–1950* (Cambridge, Mass., 1964), p. 2.

150. Archives Nationales, F²¹:643, letter from Belloc, director of the Ecole de dessin, to the minister of the interior, 13 March 1844, and "Rapport du 26 octobre 1844 au Monsieur le Ministre Secrétaire d'Etat au Département de l'Intérieur"; F²¹:563, Texier's "Note à Son Excellence Monsieur le Ministre d'Etat sur l'administration des Beaux-Arts." Of course, the rivalry was especially keen on the English side, and the title "School of Design" owes its origin to the French Ecole de dessin. See W. Dyce, "Report to the Board of Trade on Foreign Schools of Design for Manufactures" *Art-Union* 2 (1840): 143–44; Q. Bell, *The Schools of Design* (London, 1963), 47, 68, and 68 n; J. Steegman, *Consort of Taste, 1830–1870* (London, 1950), pp. 144. 224; *Official descriptive and illustrated Catalogue of the Great Exhibition* (London, 1851), 3: 1168–69.

151. Cameron, *France and the Economic Development of Europe*, pp. 60–61.

152. E. Barrault, *Aux artistes. Du passé et de l'avenir des beaux-arts. (Doctrine de Saint-Simon)* (Paris, 1830), esp. 76 ff.; *The Doctrine of Saint-Simon: An Exposition*, trans. G. G. Iggers (Boston, 1958), pp. xlv, 15 ff., 172–73, 240–41; G. Weill, *L'école saint simonienne, son histoire, son influence jusqu'à nos jours* (Paris, 1896), pp. 6, 47, 119, 121, 174, 300–301.

153. *Reminiscences of Rosa Bonheur*, ed. T. Stanton (London, 1910), pp. 8 ff.; 58 ff.; M. Kolb, *Ary Scheffer et son temps* (Paris, 1937), p. 104; Weill, *Ecole saint-simonienne*.

154. Chevalier in Delacroix, *Journal*, 1: 452–53; Talabot in L. Soullié, *Les ventes de tableaux, dessins, et objets d'art au XIXᵉ siècle (1800–1895)* (Paris, 1896), p. 284. For Talabot's involvement with the Saint-Simonists, see Baron Ernouf, *Paulin Talabot, sa vie et son oeuvre* (Paris, 1886), pp. 3 ff.; *Rosa Bonheur*, p. 69. Mention should also be made of the art patronage of Adolphe d'Eichthal (who especially admired Delaroche), a regent of the Banque de France, whose brother Gustave was a prominent Saint-Simonist.

155. J. Peyronnet, "Ecole Polytechnique," *Paris Guide*, pp. 180–81; Cameron, *France and the Economic Development of Europe*, p. 46.

156. *Notice historique sur l'ancien prieuré de Saint-Martin des Champs et sur le Conservatoire national des arts et métiers* (Paris, 1882), pp. 29 ff.; F. B. Artz, "L'enseignement technique en France pendant l'époque révolutionnaire (1789-1815)," *Revue historique* 196 (1946): 280 ff.; Cameron, *France and the Economic Development of Europe*, pp. 46–47.

157. *Ecole centrale des arts et manufactures, destinée à former des ingénieurs civils, des directeurs d'usines, des chefs de manufactures, etc.* (Paris, 1829), pp. 11 ff. The aim of the school was to provide students with a "véritable encyclopédie des arts et manufactures" and to develop their understanding by making them undergo the whole process of creation from the sketch conception to material realization. See also A. Perdonnet, "Ecole centrale des arts et manufactures," *Paris Guide*, pp. 186 ff.; Cameron, *France and the Economic Development of Europe*, p. 50.

158. See Archives Nationales, F²¹:659, [Ecole Polytechnique] *Bulletin des lois, No. 338: Loi relative à l'organisation de l'Ecole polytechnique du 25 frimaire an* VIII, "Relativement au dessin"; F²¹ 660: *Prospectus de l'Ecole polytechnique, 1832–1833*. This last document begins: "L'Ecole polytechnique est destinée, en général, à propager les sciences, mathématiques, la physique, la chimie et les arts graphiques." One of the conditions of the entrance exam was to copy a print of a nude. See also *Programmes de l'enseignement de l'Ecole royale polytechnique* (Paris, 1834): "Programme de l'enseignement du dessin de la figure et du paysage," pp. 45–46; *Notice historique . . . sur le Conservatoire national*, pp. 37 ff., 61–62; and *Ecole centrale des arts et manufactures*, pp. 20, 27–28, 35–36, 100. Also, *Exposition universelle de 1878. Rapports du jury international*, intro. J. Simon (Paris, 1880), pp. 480 ff.; Artz, *Enseignement technique*, pp. 276–77.

159. A. Etex, *Les souvenirs d'un artiste* (Paris, 1877–78), p. 22; Archives du Musée de Compiègne, Liogier to Couture, 28 August 1873; P. A. Lemoisne, *Gavarni, peintre et lithographe*, 2 vols. (Paris, 1924–28), 1: 4.

160. G. Pinet, *Léonor Mérimée* (Paris, 1913), p. 37. Mérimée, the school's first drawing instructor, was an early supporter of the applied-arts movement, and belonged to the Société d'encouragement pour l'industrie nationale. For Cogniet and Charlet see J. Claretie, *Peintres et sculpteurs contemporains*, 2 vols. (Paris, 1882–83), 1: 381; M. de La Combe, *Charlet, sa vie, ses lettres* (Paris, 1856), pp. 372 ff.

161. *Ecole centrale des arts et manufactures, Prospectus* (Paris, n.d. [ca. 1829]), pp. 7, 11, 15, 38 ff.; *Exposition universelle de 1878. Rapports*, p. 480.

162. Archives Nationales F²¹: 644, "Rapport générale sur l'Ecole royale gratuite de dessin et de mathématiques" (n.d. [ca. 1830]).

163. Archives Nationales F²¹: 644, Laemlein's brochure, "Application de l'art à l'industrie" [ca. 1868].

164. See F. B. de Mercey, *Etudes sur les Beaux-Arts*, 3 vols. (Paris, 1855–57), 3: 192–93. De Mercey, director of Beaux-Arts in 1855, was instrumental in organizing the Exposition Universelle that took place that year. He wrote: "En plaçant sous les yeux de nos chefs d'ateliers, de nos ornemantistes et de nos dessinateurs industriels les meilleures productions des arts de chaque peuple, elle devait rechauffer leur imagination, éclairer leur goût, stimuler leur intelligente activité, imprimer enfin à leurs produits ce caractère d'originalité et ce cachet de noblesse et de haute distinction qui double leur valeur et qui fait la gloire d'un peuple."

165. *Illustrated Catalogue of the Universal Exhibition*, p. xii. This was a widely held English view; see also *Reports of Artisans Selected by a Committee Appointed by the Council of the Society of Arts to Visit the Paris Universal Exhibition* (London, 1867), p. 96.

166. *Illustrated Catalogue of the Universal Exhibition*, pp. 22, 153; *L'art et l'industrie de tous les peuples à l'exposition universelle de 1878*, pp. 255, 331; Boudet, ed., *Monde des affaires*, p. 539. Later, Christofle introduced the Japanese style into his silver products. See L. Falize, "Exposition universelle de 1889. Les industries d'art, l'orfèvrerie," *GBA*, 3e. pér., 2 (1889):215. Since 1842 Christofle had pioneered in the use of the galvanoplastic, or electroplating, process—a rapid and relatively inexpensive means to

reproduce three-dimensional objects. For Christofle's biography, see Frond, *Panthéon des illustrations francaises*, vol. 2. Other references to the employment of sculptors in industry may be found in Falize, "Exposition universelle. Les industries d'art au Champ-de-Mars," *GBA*, 2e. pér., 18 (1878): 220 ff.; L. G., "Post-Scriptum," *GBA*, 2e. pér., 18 (1878): 256; Falize, "Exposition universelle de 1889."

167. The Union centrale more than bore out Blanc's prediction and did become a regenerative force in the art world, stimulating pedagogical reform (one of its competitions inspired Goupil's drawing course) and the improvement of industrial design, as well as contributing to new stylistic directions such as the taste for *japonisme*. See C. Blanc, "L'Union centrale des beaux-arts appliqués à l'industrie," *GBA* 19 (1865): 193 ff.; T. Labourieu, *Organisation du travail artistique en France* (Paris, 1863) (a manifesto of the new association by one of its founders); D'Henriet, *Enseignement populaire*, pp. 205 ff.; Archives Nationales F²¹:298, P. Sedille, *L'industrie d'art à l'exposition de l'union centrale* (Paris, 1869); C. Bargue and J. L. Gérôme, *Cours de dessin*, 3 vols. (Paris, 1868–70), 1: 3 ff.; A. Ottin, *Rapport sur l'enseignement du dessin à l'exposition universelle de Paris en 1878* (Paris, 1879), pp. 5 ff., 92 ff. Two pioneers behind the development of the Union centrale generally ignored by their contemporaries were the sculptor Jean Feuchère and his pupil Jules Klagmann. Eventually, the Union centrale amalgamated with another agency, the Société du Musée des arts décoratifs, to form the Union centrale des arts décoratifs. See S. T. Madsen, *Sources of Art Nouveau* (New York, 1955), p. 139.

168. A. André, *Renoir* (Paris, 1928), p. 13; G. Moore, *Reminiscences of the Impressionist Painters* (London, 1906), p. 38; Vollard, *Renoir*, p. 130. See also the artist's own writings, "L'art décoratif et contemporain," *L'impressionniste*, 28 April 1877, reprinted in Venturi, *Archives de l'impressionnisme*, 2: 326 ff.; "Lettre d'Auguste Renoir à Henry Mottez," in Cennino Cennini, *Le livre d'art*, ed. V. Mottez (Paris, n.d.), p. xii.

169. G. A. Sala, *Notes and Sketches of the Paris Exhibition* (London, 1868), p. 236. See also *Illustrated Catalogue of the Universal Exhibition*, p. 314; *Exposition universelle internationale de 1878 à Paris. Catalogue officiel* (Paris, 1878), 2: 195 ff.

170. For the wallpaper industry, see J. Desfossé, *Exposition universelle de 1855. Note pour MM. les présidents et membres du jury international concernant l'établissement de Jules Desfossé, fabricant de papiers peints à Paris* (Paris, 1855), pp. 1 ff.; M. Aldrophe, "Papiers peints," *Exposition de 1867, Rapports*, 3: 221 ff.; *Exposition universelle internationale de 1878*, pp. 181 ff.; H. Clouzot and C. Follot, *Histoire du papier peint en France* (Paris, 1935); Paris, Musée des arts decoratifs, *Trois siècles de papiers peints* (Paris, 1967).

171. For fans, see M. Duvelleroy, "Fabrication des éventails," *Exposition de 1867. Rapports*, 4: 322 ff.; *Illustrated Catalogue of the Universal Exhibition*, p. 45.

172. *Exposition de 1867. Rapports*, 3: 230; *Illustrated Catalogue of the Universal Exhibition*, p. 231; *Exposition universelle internationale de 1878*, pp. 158, 166. Carrier-Belleuse, who made designs for a number of different industries, functioned as an entrepreneur himself and carried out numerous commissions. See A. Ségard, *Albert Carrier-Belleuse* (Paris, 1928), pp. 41–42, 44, 46–47.

173. *Illustrated Catalogue of the Universal Exhibition*, p. xii.

174. Ibid., p. 297; Falize, "Exposition universelle. Les industries d'art au Champ-de-Mars," pp. 238 ff., and second article, p. 604.

175. T. Couture, *Méthode et entretiens d'atelier* (Paris, 1867), pp. 254 ff.

176. Cameron, *France and the Economic Development of Europe*, p. 207. Emile lived in an apartment over the railway shops on the site of the present Gare St. Lazare, where he could be close to the work and could personally supervise the crews.

177. Adhémar, *Lithographies de paysage*, p. 29, Note 2; F. Bonhommé, *Histoire pittoresque de l'industrie* (Paris, 1836–?).

178. J. Robert, *Album de Salon de 1840* (Paris, 1840), nonpaginated.

179. Goncourt and Goncourt, *Journal*, 2: 1022, 1230.

180. Boudet, ed., *Monde des affaires*, pp. 470 ff.; C. Martin, *Histoire de l'Algérie Française* (Paris, 1963), pp. 53 ff.; J. Alazard, *L'Orient et la peinture française au XIXe siècle* (Paris, 1930). The office of the Governor General of French Possessions in North Africa was established in 1834, and Delacroix had made his voyage two years earlier; but it was the prior activities of French entrepreneurs that had led to the office and also to the diplomatic mission to Morocco of which Delacroix was a party. The governments of the July Monarchy and the Second Empire made great efforts to get Frenchmen to invest in Algeria, and here again the trail of the artists (both avant-garde and conservative) was mapped out by entrepreneurial ventures.

181. Boudet, ed., *Monde des affaires*, p. 506. The European colonists in the South Seas represented a continual point of conflict for Gauguin, but at the same time he was dependent upon them for sustenance. See B. Danielsson, *Gauguin in the South Seas* (London, 1965).

182. Chroniqueuse [pseud.], *Photographs of Paris Life* (London, 1861), pp. 64 ff., 324 ff.; N. W. Senior, *Conversations with Distinguished Persons during the Second Empire, from 1860 to 1863*, 2 vols. (London, 1880); Boudet, ed., *Monde des affaires*, pp. 457, 467; M. Allem, *La vie quotidienne sous le Second Empire* (Paris, 1948), pp. 281 ff.

183. A. Ségard, *Les décorateurs*, 2 vols. (Paris, 1914), 1: 213 ff.; Boudet, ed., *Monde des affaires*, p. 410.

184. M. Schapiro, "Seurat: Reflections," *Art News Annual*, 1964, pp 40–41, 102. Seurat trained in one of the municipal drawing schools committed to the alliance of art and industry, and it may very well be that his systematic approach and subject matter derive in part from this early experience. See G. Coquiot, *Seurat* (Paris, 1924), p. 27.

185. N. Pevsner, *The Sources of Modern Architecture and Design* (New York, 1968), pp. 15–16.

186. P. Collins, *Concrete: The Vision of a New Architecture* (London, 1959), pp. 26 ff., 60, 64 ff · Boudet, ed., *Monde des affaires*, pp. 168–69.

187. Gimpel, *Journal d'un collectionneur*, p. 23.

188. Landes, "French Entrepreneurship and Industrial Growth," pp. 54 ff.

189. Archives du Musée de Compiègne, "Portrait d'un caste," in *Répertoire des oeuvres de Thomas Couture, Peintre, 1815–1879: Album de dessins*, no. 56.137, inscription below drawing *La noblesse*; J. de Rotonchamp, *Paul Gauguin, 1848–1903* (Paris, 1925), p. 259. Baudelaire early recognized the paradoxical alignment of the aristocrat against the bourgeois; see Charles Baudelaire, *Art in Paris, 1845–1862*, ed. and trans. J. Mayne (London, 1965), pp. 39–40.

190. White and White, *Canvases and Careers*, pp. 127–28; I. L. Zupnick, "The Social Conflict of the Impressionists," *College Art Journal* 19, (Winter 1959–60): 147.

191. See the brilliant discussion of this work in L. Nochlin, "Gustave Courbet's *Meeting*: A Portrait of the Artist as a Wandering Jew," *Art Bulletin* 49 (1967): 209 ff. Nothing more tellingly establishes Courbet's true position than the fact that in his self-portrait in *L'atelier* he sports the same jacket worn by Bruyas in *Le rencontre*.

192. Bertall, *Comédie de notre temps*, pp. 297–98.

193. Reinaud, *Charles Jalabert*, p. 165.

194. Ibid., pp. 94–95, 136–37; Archives du Musée de Compiègne, *Quelques lettres (brouillons) et notes de Couture*, no. 9, draft for a letter to MM. Golsmit (should read "Goldschmidt"). Jalabert's patrons included Benoît Fould, the Péreires, and a number of

other Jewish families. But the classic case is that of Degas—a notorious anti-Semite—and his benefactors May, Camondo, and others.

195. Ironically, van Gogh best exemplifies the entrepreneur-artist: he looked upon his works as marketable commodities and communicated with Theo as if he were a business partner. See *Complete Letters of Vincent van Gogh*, 2: 577, 579, 582, 600–601; 3: 58. At one point Vincent writes: *"It is no easier*, I am convinced, to make a good picture than it is to find a diamond or a pearl: it means taking trouble, and you risk your life for it as a dealer or as an artist. Then once you have some good stones, you must . . . boldly fix your price and stick to it."

196. Delacroix, *Journal*, 2: 148–49. For Mirès, see J. Mirès, *A mes juges* (Paris, 1861); Senior, *1860 to 1863*, pp. 168 ff.; Boudet, ed., *Monde des affaires*, pp. 35–36, 38; Cameron, *France and the Economic Development of Europe*, pp. 131–32, 258, 285, 291.

197. Delacroix, *Journal*, 3: 248–49, s.v. "Hardiesse," an entry for his projected dictionary; also 320–21, *"Finir* demande un coeur d'acier."

198. Ibid., p. 217.

199. See G. Weill, "Les juifs et le Saint-Simonisme," *Revue des études juives* 31(1895): 261 ff.; A. Szajowski, "The Jewish Saint-Simonians and Socialist Antisemites in France," *Jewish Social Studies* 9(1947): 3 ff.

200. After being introduced to a financier who wrote a popular musical comedy, the perplexed Goncourts recorded this 1857 entry in their journal: "Ce temps est étrange: on vous présente un homme d'affaires, c'est un vaudevilliste. Il y a un mélange d'états incroyable, c'est la confusion des métiers," Goncourt and Goncourt, *Journal*, 1: 353.

201. C. Chasse, *Gauguin sans légendes* (Paris, 1965), pp. 19 ff.; M. Bodelson, "Gauguin, the Collector," *Burlington Magazine* 112 (1970): 594, 597; Boudet, ed., *Monde des affaires*, p. 68. Gauguin did not quit, but lost, his job in 1883 with the Agence financière d' Assurance. The Agents de Change (Gauguin's professional designation) were severely hit because they sold on a wide margin, and it was the Compagnie des Agents de Change that had to be bailed out by the few remaining solvent institutions. The Agents de Change, much like stock brokers working for Merrill Lynch, aggressively pushed the shares of *Union Générale*. See Bouvier, *Le Krach de l'Union Générale*, pp. 11, 177.

202. C. Pissarro, *Letters to His Son Lucien*, ed. J. Rewald (New York, 1943), p. 44. Van Gogh also observed this attitude: *Complete Letters of Vincent van Gogh*, 3: 40.

203. Pissarro, *Letters*, pp. 35–36; Gray, *Paul Gauguin*, pp. 5 ff.; Danielsson, *Gauguin*, pp. 75–76, 186 ff., 208, 214 ff.

204. Rotonchamp, *Paul Gauguin*, pp. 16 ff.; Chassé, *Gauguin sans légendes*, p. 15; *Tableaux modernes composant la collection de M. G. Arosa* (Paris, 1858); *Album de la collection de M. G. Arosa. Tableaux modernes* (photocopy in Frick Reference Library) (Paris, 1878); *Exposition universelle internationale de 1878*, p. 78; Gray, *Paul Gauguin*, pp. 22 and 57. Evidently, Arosa's process proved to be a commercial failure, and to recoup some of his losses he was forced to sell part of his extensive pottery collection in 1878.

205. *Complete Letters of Vincent van Gogh*, 3: 38–39, 40, 60, 64, 74, 89. He writes Theo again: "At present I do not think my pictures worthy of the advantages I have received from you. But once they are worthy, I swear that you will have created them as much as I, and that we are making them together."

206. G. Moore, *Impressions and Opinions* (New York, 1891), pp. 249 ff.

207. Archives de l'Académie Julian, rue de Berri, *L'Académie Julian* (Paris, n.d. [ca. 1906]), bound together with *Opinion de la Presse sur l'Académie Julian. Enseignement libre*; R. I. Homer, *Robert Henri and His Circle* (Ithaca, 1969), pp. 40 ff.

208. Moore, *Impressions*, p. 261.
209. *Catalogue du Salon de 1885*, no. 1778.
210. Madsen, *Sources of Art Nouveau*, pp. 19 ff.
211. E. Garnier, "Exposition universelle de 1889. Les industries d'art," *GBA*, 3e. pér., 2 (1889): 578–79.

ABOUT THE AUTHORS

Charles P. Kindleberger is professor of economics
at the Massachusetts Institute of Technology.

David Landes is professor of history at Harvard University.

Maurice Lévy-Leboyer is professor of history
at the University of Paris-Nanterre.

Albert Boime is professor of art at the State
University of New York at Binghamton.

Edward C. Carter is associate professor of history at
the Catholic University of America.

Robert Forster is professor of history at the Johns Hopkins
University.

Joseph N. Moody is professor of history at the College of
New Rochelle.

THE JOHNS HOPKINS UNIVERSITY PRESS

This book was composed in Baskerville text and Baskerville Bold display type by Jones Composition Company from a design by Susan Bishop, and printed on 60-lb. Warren 1854 regular paper. It was printed and bound by The Maple Press Company.

LIBRARY OF CONGRESS CATALOGING IN PUBLICATION DATA

Main entry under title:

Enterprise and entrepreneurs in nineteenth- and twentieth-century France.

"Four essays . . . given as lectures in a series sponsored jointly by The Catholic University of America and The Johns Hopkins University in the spring of 1973."
Includes bibliographical references.
CONTENTS: Kindleberger, C. P. Technical education and the French entrepreneur.—Landes, D. Religion and enterprise.—Lévy-Leboyer, M. Innovation and business strategies in nineteenth- and twentieth-century France. [etc.]
1. Businessmen—France—History—Addresses, essays, lectures. 2. Entrepreneur—History—Addresses, essays, lectures. I. Carter, Edward Carlos, 1928–   II. Foster, Robert, 1926–   III. Moody, Joseph Nestor, 1904–

HC275.E56   338'.04'0944   75-36936
ISBN 0-8018-1717-X

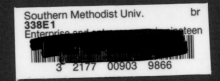

Blatherskite

Blatherskite

MARIAN POTTER

William Morrow and Company
New York   1980

Printed in the United States of America.

1 2 3 4 5 6 7 8 9 10

Library of Congress Cataloging in Publication Data

Potter, Marian.
    Blatherskite.
    Summary: A talkative 10-year-old, living in rural Missouri in the 1930's, becomes the heroine of her family and community by putting her wagging tongue to good use.
    [1. Country life—Fiction.   2. Missouri—Fiction]
I. Title.
PZ7.P853Bl   [Fic]   80-18450
ISBN 0-688-22249-8
ISBN 0-688-32249-2 (lib. bdg.)

1

Maureen had great confidence in the United States mail, although she had never received anything unexpected at the postal window. After school she ran ahead of her brothers toward the store. The sign above the wide porch read, *General Merchandise, S. P. Stackhouse, prop.* In smaller letters below were the words, *U. S. Post Office, Dotzero, Missouri.* Maureen was proud of Dotzero's post office, which was as good as any in a big town or even a city. Lots of places back in the hills, off the railroad, didn't have post offices.

"Wait for me," she called to Mit and Walter. "I'm going to ask for mail."

"Won't be any. We've got to get over our bridge. The creek will be up from the rain," Mit said. He was the oldest and thought he knew everything.

"There might be something . . . no telling what." As Maureen opened the door, Walter started to follow her. He was seven, three whole years younger than she, and tagged after her a lot. Maureen knew that if he came into the store, he'd get fidgety and not let her talk to Mrs. Stackhouse. "Stay out here on the porch, Walter. I'll only be a minute."

Maureen wasn't sure of the meaning of *prop.* on the store sign. If Mr. Sterling Price Stackhouse was the prop of general merchandise, then Mrs. Stackhouse must be the prop of her husband. She was his store clerk *and* the Dotzero postmistress, both at the same time.

Mrs. Stackhouse wasn't much taller than Maureen, but she was a lot wider. Her head showed just above a pile of overalls on the dry-goods side of the store. When she saw Maureen, she hurried to the postal window and stepped up on a stool to reach a mail pigeonhole.

"Any mail for McCracken?" Maureen asked the routine question.

Mrs. Stackhouse puffed for breath as she looked carefully at an envelope. "Well, yes. It's from St. Louis, came in on Number 3 this morning. It could be from your Uncle Millard." She tapped the letter in the palm of her hand as she came out from behind the postal window.

Studying Maureen's thin cotton dress and worn slippers, she said, "Tell your mother we have two new bolts of gingham and some heavy Buster Brown laced shoes."

"Oh, I will." Maureen tugged at her garters to pull up her cotton stockings. "She'll be in to pick out dress

6

goods. Right now I'm wearing out these patent-leather slippers and this summer dress before I outgrow 'em."

"We've got in some new barrettes, too, a whole card of nice ones."

Maureen brushed back her short black hair. "I'll have to get one. I lost mine at morning recess playing Prison Base."

"How did Dotzero School go today?" Mrs. Stackhouse asked. "I didn't see hide nor hair of a Sansoucie going up that school hill."

"They came the first day; then they quit. I sure miss walking to school with Rose Sansoucie," Maureen said. "Sansoucies and us are the only ones living across Lost Creek. Rose said they have to save their shoes for colder weather, said the little kids might come barefoot, but she wouldn't."

"Sansoucies are laying low," Mrs. Stackhouse said, with a knowing nod. "How's Alma Huckstep doing with her teaching?"

"All right, far as I know. But when it rained so hard today, there wasn't much school. There was so much thunder over the schoolhouse we felt as if we were under a washtub. It was dark, too. So I just talked out loud."

"Talked out loud! Can't she keep order?"

Mit stuck his head in the door. "Maureen! Come on! We've got to get over the creek."

Maureen held out her hand for the letter, which Mrs.

Stackhouse gave her as if she hated to release it. "How are your kinfolks getting along in St. Louis?"

"Tol'able, just tol'able." Maureen used her grandmother's expression. She wasn't sure what it meant, but she wanted to try it out. "We haven't heard from them for a long time. I don't remember for sure when. Easter maybe. They didn't come to Dotzero all summer. Of course, my cousins have to go to school just about all the time up there. I sure am glad—"

"Let us know how they are," Mrs. Stackhouse interrupted. "Lots of city folks are having it harder than peach pits."

Out on the porch Maureen studied the envelope. It was Uncle Millard's handwriting. The postmark read St. Louis, Missouri, September 21, 1936. Mit snatched the letter from her and put it in the pocket of his denim jacket. "I'm in charge of anything first class."

He set a fast pace down the narrow, muddy road beside the railroad track. It wasn't easy to keep up with him, especially for Maureen who talked steadily the mile and a half to Lost Creek. "Declarative, imperative, exclamatory, interrogative," she recited. Then she explained to Walter, "Those are sentences, and if you don't say things that way, then you just haven't said anything. I learned that today listening to Mit's language class."

When she had told all she knew about the types of sentences, she continued to chant the words: *declara-*

8

tive, imperative, exclamatory, interrogative. Interroga-tive was good for five running hops.

At the creek, a plank footbridge lurched in the churning water, blood red from the wash of hillside clay. "We can't get home over our bridge." Mit yelled to be heard over the roar of the water. "We'll have to cross on the railroad trestle. You hung around the post office too long, blabbing to Mrs. Stackhouse. You'd be there yet if I hadn't shagged you out." He turned onto a path that led through dry weed stalks up a steep railroad embankment.

Maureen watched him. Mit wouldn't coax. He'd scramble up that bank and expect Maureen and Walter to follow.

They looked up. It was an awful distance from the red water up, up to the trestle. Dotzero School, even McCrackens' house could fit under that bridge with room to spare. It had no sides. Worse yet, it had no bottom except steel supports and crossties. Maureen's head felt light when she looked up and saw the ragged gray clouds and dark sky between the ties. If the Sansoucie kids had been along, she would have been braver, just to give them courage.

There was no other way. She and Walter would have to climb up and walk across those ties. Looking up didn't make Maureen nearly as sick as looking down from the bridge through the open spaces high over the swirling water. That's when Walter got dizzy and some-

9

times couldn't take another step. He would walk slower and slower, then stop, like a rundown toy, right in the middle of the trestle. Maureen would have to urge him on and talk him across.

She started up the bank, but Walter lagged and looked back. Across the swift water, the opposite bank was only a few feet away. He shivered in his damp jacket. "Wait, wait a minute," he pleaded.

"Come on. Step on it, Walter," Mit ordered, "and don't look at me with those hound-dog eyes."

Walter caught up with Maureen and grabbed her sweater, trying to hold her back. "Dad will come with the mules and take us across."

"Dad's got work today, remember? He has maybe three days with the railroad extra gang that's laying side track."

Maureen shifted her heavy school books from one arm to the other. As she was three grades ahead of Walter and had more books, she liked to bring lots home. Now she wished she had left them at school. It was hard enough to take care of herself on the bridge without the burden of books. "Milton, carry my books." She used his name, which sometimes pleased him; her voice was pleading and pitiful.

"You brought 'em; you carry 'em." Mit wasn't going to give in on anything.

Maureen looked up at the tall signal beside the track.

10

The trestle was on the main line of the Missouri Pacific Railroad, and they never knew what might be coming. If the red-and-white signal arm at the top was straight up, no train was within a five-mile block of track. If a train *was* coming, the signal arm fell to the side to show a red light. The arm was straight up.

"There's nothing in the block, nothing coming," Mit announced.

Maureen turned to look at Walter. "No use to expect anybody to help us, Walter. You're seven, going on eight. You're not supposed to be afraid to cross the trestle after first grade. The railroad company has built this high bridge, so we might as well use it." Maureen was afraid to cross the trestle too, but she knew that once across the relief would be worth the fright.

At the bottom of the cindery embankment, Maureen stooped to pick a cluster of purple berries from a tall weed. Mit kicked down a shower of track ballast. "Keep moving," he shouted.

"I'm getting some pokeberries to make Walter some pokeberry ink. It will be good enough ink for him to learn to write with. He ought to get so he—"

"Shut up, Maureen, and come on." Mit stepped onto the bridge.

Pokeberries could be messy. Maureen tossed them aside and climbed the embankment. Carefully she fitted her speller, reader, arithmetic and language books

11

on top of her big geography book and clasped the load to her chest for better balance. With a choppy stride, stepping on each tie, she started across.

Walter followed, brave as long as he could look down between the ties and see the tops of willow trees on the bank below. A few more steps put him over surging water. He stopped.

"Put one foot down and then the other." Mit demonstrated stepping high. "First thing you know, you're over the trestle. Don't look down at the water. Look at Maureen's heels. Step when she does."

"I have to look down," Walter wailed.

"If you don't, you might fall right smack-dab between the ties," Maureen warned.

"Hush up, Reen Peen," Mit ordered.

"Don't call me that," she muttered through tense lips.

"Don't scare Walter then," he retorted. "You can't fall between the ties, Walter," Mit called to him. "If I took a sledgehammer and tried to drive you through the space between the ties, I couldn't do it."

Walter knew it was true. But it was also true that he was fearful. He had to force his short legs over the few inches of open space between the firm timbers that supported the track.

Mit was across. He tested his pitching arm throwing bits of gravel ballast from beside the track. Walter was sure taking his time, so Mit shouted to him, "If you look down now, you'll see the sandbar this side of the bank. Don't take the rest of the day."

Two more steps and Maureen would be on solid ground. "There might be an extra freight or a signalman's speeder coming, and it would knock us to smithereens," Maureen shrieked.

Mit pinged gravel at her feet. "Stop scaring him, Reen Peen."

"Well, once there was a fellow—tramp maybe—and he forgot to look at the block signal to see if anything was coming, and he got out on the middle of the bridge, and sure enough here came the Sunshine Special. He had to jump off into Lost Creek, only he didn't make it."

Walter's steps quickened. Firm ballast filled the awful space between the ties, and he took a deep breath. "I walked the trestle," Walter said, beaming. His smile was so broad that his eyes became sparkling slits.

"You did fine, Walter," Mit assured him.

"I walked it when I was little like him, huh, Mit?" Maureen asked.

"I don't remember. If you did, nobody was scaring the daylights out of you. You probably blabbed, blabbed all the way across."

Mit had sure turned mean since he was thirteen and in the eighth grade. He ran ahead up the lane beside the bottom field where McCracken corn had been cut

13

and gathered into shocks. A path that was a shortcut led from the lane up the hill.

The path was red as it crossed the bank of wet, slippery clay. Then it turned grayish as it threaded its way through limestone rock ledges. Maureen and Walter took care to walk on each natural rock step, for Maureen had assured Walter that those steps brought good luck. A person was likely to have good luck anyhow, but sometimes it had to be helped along.

Mit paid no attention to the steps. Someday he might be sorry. He just wouldn't listen.

Mit was first to reach the little frame house, which showed a few traces of white paint on its gray, rain-soaked clapboards. Tisket, their fox terrier, raced from the yard to greet him. She acted as if he'd been gone a couple of years.

Maureen put her books on the back porch and went to the tire swing that hung from a branch of the oak tree in the front yard. There was a puddle of water in the worn spot under the swing. But it didn't matter. Maureen's slippers were already wet as sop.

As she pumped herself up in the swing, she looked at the McCracken house, which she considered very stylish. Three dormer windows extending from its rust-streaked metal roof made it different from a plain, pointed-roof house, the kind that Walter drew. She had been trying to teach him how to draw a house with dormer windows, but it wasn't easy.

She was glad that her home was more than a house, that they had a farm, too. McCrackens didn't have to live out of a paper sack, running to the store all the time. The fenced garden was located on the south side of the house, where the sun warmed it in early spring. Turnips, cabbage, and butter beans would grow there until frost. The chicken house and run were nearby, so the tubs of chicken manure they used for fertilizer didn't have to be carried far. The whole south side of the chicken house was a big window to let the sun pour in and keep the hens warm and laying all winter.

Orchards were different. They belonged on the north. Maureen could see only one row of trees at the top of the north slope below the barn and the pigpens. Winter snow would melt there last, and the apple trees wouldn't bloom until spring had really come.

The loft under the spreading tin roof of the barn was crammed with hay. This time of year, in fall, no daylight showed through the hayloft, which was a good thing. Maureen could see cracks of light, however, between the thick, gray boards of the lower part of the barn where there were stalls for Fox and Jack, the mule team, and Molly, the milk cow.

The lane up from the cornfield and from Lost Creek separated the house yard from the barnyard, and fainter wagon traces led to the three fields east of the house. The one next to the barn lot grew pasture for the stock. The middle ridge field was planted in corn, in case the bottom field was flooded out. Hay was cut three times a summer from the south field. Maureen had a special path across it and a place to crawl under the barbed-wire fence to get to Sansoucies' and visit her friend Rose.

The woods of cedars, oaks, walnut, and hickory-nut trees spread above the farm like a dark frame on a picture.

Maureen liked to swing and look at the whole place. The clustered buildings seemed to keep each other company.

"Maureen, get in here!" Mit yelled from the back door.

She slid out of the swing. She knew she had to go in and change her wet shoes.

2

Maureen waited until Dad was home and the family was eating supper to start her account of crossing the trestle. She saw that Mit only half listened; maybe her story needed more action.

"It was raining cats and dogs, pitchforks and saw-logs"—Maureen waved her arms—"and our plank foot-bridge was bucking around like an outlaw horse." She got up from the table to demonstrate.

"Maureen, sit down and be mannerly. You haven't been excused from the table," Mama reminded her.

Maureen slid back into her place opposite Dad and Mit. Though everybody said those two looked alike, said Mit was the spitting image, the very spit of Cleve McCracken, Maureen thought there was considerable difference. For one thing, Dad's hair was streaked with gray, although he said it had been coal black when he was a kid like Mit. Then there were those forehead wrinkles over Dad's gray eyes. Mit had gray eyes, too, but Maureen didn't think he'd ever have wrinkles.

Maureen wished folks said she looked like someone in her family, but they didn't. They just said she was an O'Neil, whatever that meant. Certainly it didn't mean her appearance. O'Neil had been Mama's name before she was married, but Maureen didn't look like her. Mama's wavy hair was the color of sorghum syrup. She complained that Maureen's black hair was straight as a mule's tail. Wisps of it were always getting into her eyes. Maureen thought her eyes were fine for seeing, but not much for looks. They were sort of green, not big and brown like Rose Sansoucie's eyes.

Mama said Maureen had always been long-legged as a newborn colt. Maureen didn't mind that, for she was a fast runner, always chosen first to play Wolf Over the Ridge or Prison Base. She wondered if long legs had anything to do with being an O'Neil.

"Mama, what does it mean to be an O'Neil?"

"Well, some were kings and some were ne'er-do-wells. My goodness, what a change of subject." Mama shivered a little.

"Are you cold, Mama?" Maureen asked.

"No, I'm still thinking about you kids crossing the railroad trestle. It makes me downright nervous. There must have been hard rains south of Dotzero. I didn't think the creek would come up so fast. I was out looking for mushrooms when the rain drove me inside, and there was a stack of *Capper's Weeklies* from all summer. So I got to reading this continued story. If I'd realized

18

there was high water, I'd have tried to hitch up Fox and Jack and meet you with the wagon."

"No need for you to try to handle that team, Mama," Mit said. "We got over the trestle all right. I checked the block signal."

"Walter did fine and dandy," Maureen said, "except he thinks he's skinny as a case knife and might fall through."

"I'd say Walter is shaped more like one of those little round cedar trees in the upper pasture," Dad teased.

"Still and all, we need a bridge. I worry so about you kids crossing that trestle," Mama said. "So does Pat Ash, working down there at Dotzero depot."

"Need a lot of things. Bridge ought to be at the top of the list," Dad agreed. "Especially in these hills where we get fast runoffs."

After all the chores were done and the supper dishes cleared from the oilcloth-covered kitchen table, Mit and Maureen spread their school books out. Maureen tried to concentrate on her long-division problems, but none of them came out even, which discouraged her. Only when they came out even could she be sure they were correct.

She traced her pencil around the carving on the back of her kitchen chair. Was the design a tassel or a palm tree in a cyclone? She couldn't decide.

There was no carving on the bench against the wall

19

near the cookstove. Plain as a plank, it had been made by some jackleg country carpenter, according to Dad. *Capper's Weekly* papers and some books were stacked at one end of it. On the other side of the cookstove, the woodbox left just enough room for the door to the cellar to swing open. Maureen surveyed the kitchen— Mama's worktable, the tall cabinet, the coal-oil stove used only in summer but always smelling of kerosene. For her, it was a comforting room.

She decided to read aloud to Walter from Hurlbut's *Story of the Bible*, which lay on the bench. They both liked it, although she had to be careful about the pictures she showed him in that book. Walter hated one of an Israelite slave being beaten and had ripped it halfway out of the book.

Maureen settled Walter on the bench beside her and read about the man who found his lost sheep. Then she read about the woman who swept out her whole house looking for a lost coin.

"Rattle, rattle, rattle," Mit objected. "I've got to study a poem and know it by heart. Miss Huckstep thinks it's better to have poems in your head than money in the bank."

"Maureen, read to yourself," Mama ordered.

"Well, I would, but it wouldn't do Walter any good. He hasn't had most of these words, because Miss Huckstep thinks the second grade ought not to learn anything except the second-grade reader, and if I was to—"

20

"Maureen talking machine, you cause me all kinds of trouble. Look at this composition I wrote last night." Mit held up a paper spotted with red marks. "These are all places I should have spelled Depression with a capital *D*."

"It's not my fault Depression is so bad you have to spell it with a capital *D*," Maureen protested.

"I might have thought of it and looked it up in *Capper's Weekly* if you hadn't been talking a blue streak."

"Well, anyhow, Miss Huckstep gets some funny notions," Maureen went on. "Like today, when second grade colored the black cats they drew. She didn't put Walter's up over the blackboard; said he didn't make the color lines all go the same way. That made Walter feel bad. So I just went up to her desk and told her that it was a kitten just been licked by the mother cat, fur every whichway. And she told me to—"

"Stop, babbling brook!" Mit held his head. "See. Now you almost made me forget the letter we picked up." He took the wrinkled envelope from his pocket and handed it to Mama.

She opened it and moved closer to the lamp. Mama read aloud, "Dear Lillian and Family. I wish I could write you better news, but I guess the luck of the O'Neils is running low. I never saw things so bad as they are now in St. Louis. I was laid off last spring, didn't get a lick of work for three months. Now I have got temporary work in a box factory, but it won't be for long.

We can't do much to help ourselves here in the city. There's no space to grow a garden, not even a decent lettuce bed. City rents are high. Work or no work, the landlord comes on rent day expecting his money. I was wondering if we could bunk for a while in the old smokehouse there at the home place. I can still carpenter, or wood butcher, ha ha, and could put in a rough floor and some windows. Used to be good land on the railroad right-of-way where we could put in a crop of potatoes come St. Patrick's Day. And there ought to be enough coal fall off the engine tenders for winter fuel. I know your house is small but thought the annex, ha ha, might be available. With love from your brother Millard. P.S. Don't bother to worry Ma any about this."

"The old smokehouse!" Maureen exclaimed. "It's torn down."

"Everybody knows that, parrot," Mit mumbled.

Dad's gray eyes were troubled. "Nothing left but a grease spot where hams used to drip. Millard went off to the city years ago, when wages were good. Now he expects everything to be the same here."

Mama reread the letter to herself, then said, "Even if the building stood, it would be a hard row to hoe for Millard and Cora and that family—nine children, no stock, no tools. Fox and Jack are the only power around here except elbow grease. Millard's family is used to electricity now. Still, we have to do what we can." Mama

22

folded and refolded the letter. "Cleve, how are we going to answer this letter?"

Mama seemed cold again, and Dad checked the cookstove. The supper fire was almost out. When he poked split wood into the stove, sparks shot up. "Man is born to trouble as the sparks fly upward," he quoted. "That was the preacher's text last Sunday. Sure is gospel truth."

Maureen could see one of Dad's black moods coming on. Sometimes they lasted a whole day, even two days. It was just awful when Dad got all out of heart and didn't talk to them. The best thing to do was to try to get him thinking about something interesting.

"Well, say, do you know what I found out today? I found it right in the geography book we have now in fifth grade. It's printed across the map of where we live here in Missouri. It says St. Francois Mountains. Did you know that, Dad? Did you? Did you know we lived in the St. Francois Mountains? Mountains with names, just like the Rocky Mountains or the Cascade Mountains or any of them? Did you know?"

Dad shook his head.

"Be still, Maureen." Mit spoke in a low voice. "Dad's got other things to think about, and so have I."

"I think it's pretty important to know where you live and that you live in the St. Francois Mountains. Did you know that, Mama?"

"Just old, hardscrabble south Missouri hills, far as I

23

know." Mama sighed. "Names don't make living here any easier in these times. Now be still, Maureen, and let me try to think what we could offer. Eleven. That's a lot of people."

"It's no wonder you didn't know you were living in the St. Francois Mountains. Miss Huckstep didn't know it either; never even told us. I had to go to her desk and show it to her on the map."

"Right during our civics class," Mit said.

"And why did Miss Huckstep call Maureen a cracker box?" Walter asked.

"Cracker box?" Mama looked puzzled; then she smiled. "She must have said chatterbox."

Dad chuckled. Walter's comment had headed off his black mood. Everybody was always ready to laugh at her, Maureen brooded. Even Walter, telling on her like that. Here she'd gone and got the mail, helped Walter over the trestle, tried to tell them all something interesting, and all they ever did was tell her to stop talking.

Maureen didn't say good-night to Walter when Number 41, his bedtime train, went by and Mama led him off upstairs. But soon after Mama came down and started to work on her letter, Maureen heard him call.

"Somebody! Somebody come!" Walter yelled.

Without a word, Maureen got the broom and started upstairs. She liked to have the broom for protection on the dark stairway and in the upstairs hall.

Mama had left the coal-oil lamp burning low in the

24

room Walter shared with Mit. Walter made a little lump under the covers of his single bed in the corner.

"Okay, Walter, is it in the closet again?"

"Yes." Walter uncovered his eyes.

A few minutes later Maureen was back downstairs, well satisfied with the job she had done. "I can drive that spook out better than anybody. Walter said so," she announced to the others.

"It's your fault it's there," Mit stated. "I've heard all those scary yarns you tell him."

"I just go up there and fling open the closet door, and I whack around like this." Maureen demonstrated beating with the broom. "And I say, 'Get out of here! Out! Out! Don't you ever come back to pester Walter Lee McCracken again. And if you do, you'll be sorry.' I looked over at Walter, and I could tell by his eyes that he wasn't scared anymore and was smiling. So I said, 'You know there's nothing there just like there wasn't last night,' and he said 'Yes, but I want it chased out anyhow.' And I said, 'Now, Walter, if you would just—"

"Blatherskite!" Mama tore a sheet from Mit's ink-paper tablet. "Blatherskite! You're right, Mit, a person can't think with Maureen's rattling. How can I write Millard a sensible answer?"

All at once Maureen felt very tired. Well, all right, she'd never talk to them again. Maybe then they'd be happy. That's what they wanted.

Wordlessly she went to her little room at the end of

25

the upstairs hall and got undressed. After she was in bed, she brooded on all the names they called her—talking machine, parrot, babbling brook, blatherskite.

At last Maureen fell into a troubled sleep and felt herself falling, falling into rushing muddy water. She awoke on the floor beside her bed, struggling in her quilts. Maureen started to cry out that she'd had that dream again, the one where she fell off the bridge, but then she remembered her plan. Instead, she untangled the quilts and climbed silently back into bed.

3

The next morning Maureen looked out her dormer window at the white fog that lay like a roll of soft cotton along Lost Creek. If the water had not run down yet, it would be a job to get Walter over the trestle.

In the kitchen Mama put a plate of fried salt pork and eggs on the table in front of Dad. Then she hurried to strain the pail of foaming milk that he'd brought in. Mit had already given Fox and Jack their oat measure and turned them out to pasture. Walter found the rubbers Mama insisted they wear to school. Through all, Maureen remained silent. Nobody noticed.

When they were ready to leave for school, Mama handed Mit a letter. "Get this in the morning mail. Maybe God should have broken my arm when I was writing last night, but I went ahead and told Millard if worst came to worst there in the city, they could move in here with us." She pointed to the row of pegs over the woodbox. "We might have to hang some of you kids on nails."

Maureen said not a word. She just nodded good-bye.

Mama was right; they needed the rubbers. Along the bank of Lost Creek the layer of mud covering the sand came up in sheets with each step. Walter's tracks were almost as big as Mit's. Clusters of torn leaves caught far up in the willows on the bank showed how high and swift the water had been.

The sun burned through the fog, and under their footbridge shallow water glided smoothly over clean gravel. Walter pointed to the sparkling stream. "Is it the same creek as yesterday?"

To Maureen, Lost Creek seemed like a person who had gotten over a tantrum and was trying to be extra nice. She started to share this observation. "Say, I was just thinking. . . ." Suddenly she stopped.

"Thinking what?" Walter asked.

"Nothing."

"We know it's nothing," Mit said, "but finish it anyhow."

Maureen glared at him and was glad to hear a train whistle for the Dotzero crossing. The freight came on with a roar, casting its shadow over them as it thundered across the trestle. Mit and Walter couldn't hear Maureen call off the names of the passing cars: Missouri Pacific, M K and T, Illinois Central, C and E I, Denver and Rio Grande, Missouri Pacific, Missouri Pacific, Frisco, Pennsylvania. She liked the names of the railroad companies. They were a regular geography lesson.

28

She was also glad to know that her voice still worked.

"I counted five fellows bumming rides on that freight," Walter said.

"Men riding freights are common as pig tracks. I counted six. You missed one, Walter. How many did you count, Maureen?" Mit asked.

She didn't answer that question or any of the others they pestered her with. She was strong, firm, quiet. Much as she wanted to tell Mrs. Stackhouse of the offer to Uncle Millard, she kept on the road to school while Mit ran off to mail Mama's letter. Still, it was hard to resist Walter when he took hold of her hand and implored her to tell him what was wrong.

Mit was back in no time, for he never stopped to be friendly to Mrs. Stackhouse. "Don't beg her to talk, Walter," he said gleefully, when he heard Walter's appeal. "Just be thankful old Reen Peen is not running off at the mouth. She was vaccinated with a phonograph needle. Reen Peen, Reen Peen, used to talk till her face got green." Delighted with his chant, Mit repeated it.

Maureen flung down her books and covered her ears, but Mit only chanted louder. Finally Walter helped her pick up the books, and they went on, with Mit tormenting her all the way. When they reached the edge of the Dotzero School playground, Maureen knew she had to stop him. The whole school would hear her own brother teasing her. They would all start calling her Reen Peen.

She scooped up a handful of mud from the roadside ditch and drew back her hand in warning. Mit danced around, yelling louder. Something grasped Maureen and shook her—it was her own anger—and the mud flew.

Mit dodged. It wasn't a good throw. Only a little mud spattered on his jacket. Maureen got the worst of it; her hand was a mess. First she tried to wipe it off on the wet grass, then on the skirt of her cotton dress.

That day at school was the longest Maureen had ever put in. Though she knew the answer to almost all of Miss Huckstep's questions to the fifth grade, she didn't raise her hand. She did turn in all her written work, hoping it would show Miss Huckstep how smart she really was. Several times she saw Miss Huckstep looking at her in a puzzled way, and Maureen just nodded when she asked her if she felt all right.

Maureen missed her friend Rose. If only she had been at school, Maureen could have talked to her a little at recess.

When the long, long day finally ended, Maureen didn't even go into the store to ask for mail. So far no one except Walter seemed to care one whit that she'd given up speaking. Mit raced ahead, prancing and whistling as if he had some great news to tell.

He had to wait, for there was company when they got home. At the yard gate, they recognized the old Durant sedan that belonged to Mrs. Wiley. She lived in Beaumont. Grandma lived in Beaumont too, and sometimes she rode along when Mrs. Wiley came to see about all the places she owned between Dotzero and Post Oak.

Maureen loved company. With anticipation, she hurried through the kitchen and across the hall to the sitting room, where Mama was serving cookies and coffee. A sharp-eyed woman in an ugly brown dress sat in the best rocker by the stand table. Mrs. Wiley always looked the same. Her thin gray hair was combed back so tight it was a wonder she could bat her piercing eyes.

Grandma sat in a straight chair by the door and kissed Walter and Maureen as they came in. She would have kissed Mit as well if he hadn't dodged.

Mrs. Wiley looked the children over. "Lillian, you've got your work cut out for you. Sister, there, how old are you?"

Maureen ducked her head shyly and didn't answer.

"What's the matter, Maureen? Cat got your tongue?" Grandma asked. That was something you said to a little bit of a kid. Maureen stuffed a sugar cookie in her mouth to keep from answering.

"I'm seven," Walter volunteered.

Mrs. Wiley turned her attention to Mit. "Now a boy that age, he'd eat like a threshing hand. Bottomless pit, trying to fill him up."

As if to prove her right, Mit took more than his share

31

of cookies and fled from the sitting room. Walter chased after him.

Maureen pulled a footstool into a corner, hoping she wouldn't be noticed. If she couldn't take part in the conversation, she could at least listen and observe.

Although Mrs. Wiley and Grandma had been friends a long time, they were not much alike. Grandma O'Neil wore flowery dresses with lace collars and kept her hair frizzed in a permanent. Mrs. Wiley, on the other hand, wasn't a bit stylish, even if she did live in a brick house in town. People said she was land poor. They said she was as close as the bark on a tree with money, held on to a dollar until the eagle screamed, still had every last cent and every last acre her husband left her.

Mrs. Wiley came out from Beaumont in summer to chase blackberry pickers off her land. All year she drove over back roads to collect cash rent from the tenants of the ramshackle houses on her lands. One of those houses, on the nearby Wiley place, was where the Sansoucies lived. Mrs. Wiley had just come from there.

"I allowed I could ford the creek today." Mrs. Wiley put her coffee cup down with a clatter. "I put up with it just as long as I could. They haven't paid me a cent, not one red cent, for a year, and the place is getting run down with that big family. How can I make repairs? You know that place is special to me, being the old home place of my husband's people. He'd turn over in his grave if I let it go to ruin."

"Sansoucies might have some pigs to sell later on," Mama ventured.

"I've heard about those pigs for a year," Mrs. Wiley stated flatly. "I know times are hard. Nobody knows that better than I do, with the taxes I have to pay on my land. But I'm going to keep it free and clear—Sansoucies or nobody can change me on that—so I had no choice except to tell them they had to move out, and right away."

Maureen was dismayed. Rose was her best friend and the only girl her own age she had to play with on their side of Lost Creek. She didn't know what she'd do without Rose, who was quiet and didn't mind how much a person talked.

Conversation in the sitting room drifted to the possible size of the Sansoucie store bill, the disgracefully low market price of hogs, the number of quarts of canned food in the cellar. Maureen kept thinking of Rose and of all the Sansoucies. No matter how often she went there, she was always treated like company.

When Grandma asked if they had heard from Uncle Millard, Maureen kept silent, although she could have added much to Mama's statement that times were hard in the city, just as they were in the sticks.

At their departure, Mama followed the visitors to the yard gate. Maureen was still waving vigorously at the Durant lurching down the lane when Mama returned to the porch. She put her hands on her hips. "Well,

33

Maureen, I never! Young lady, I've got some hash to settle with you. I was so outdone! You know Grandma is getting hard of hearing. Out there at the gate, what do you think I heard Mrs. Wiley holler at her?" Mama popped out her eyes, turned down her mouth, and spoke in a harsh voice, imitating Mrs. Wiley. " 'Now that middle one, the girl, is she right bright? Didn't appear to be.' "

Maureen was silent. "You can't blame her," Mama declared. "You come in with your school dress as muddy as if you'd fallen in the pigpen, won't say how do or anything, and then just sit while we're visiting, listening with your mouth open fit to catch flies. I was just flabbergasted. Of course, your grandma stuck up for you, said you were sharp as a tack most of the time, a regular blatherskite. But, still, I felt ashamed of one of my own young ones."

Maureen broke away and raced across the yard to the tire swing. She didn't feel very good either. Her good friend would have to move away. The plan to make her family appreciate her wasn't working very well. Her silence suited Mit fine. But it bothered Walter, who didn't understand it, and it had made Mama ashamed of her.

Maureen went over these injustices as she swung back and forth. One thing sure, she wasn't going to give up. She'd make her family sorry they were mean

34

to her and called her names. At least, today had been different in one way. Other visits she'd been bawled out after company left for getting wound up, talking too much, and showing off.

4

By Saturday morning Maureen had such a tight feeling in her chest that she felt as if she were about to explode. She hoped her voice was still working, although she had learned from listening to Mit's hygiene class that muscles got weak and useless from lack of exercise.

After breakfast, the chances were that everyone would clear out and leave her alone in the kitchen. She sat down on the worn linoleum in front of the door that led to the cellar and waited. In the door's lower panel the wood grain formed a face. Maureen had named it Peloponnesus, a word she'd heard listening to Mit's geography class. When she had a chance, she would test her voice on Peloponnesus; she frequently talked things over with him.

Mit and Walter got instructions for the Saturday job Dad had given them. "There's a break in the upper side of the pasture fence by the sassafras tree," Dad had said. "Take your hammer and nails, some scrap wire, and mend it. Walter, you're straw boss on the job. I'll hitch up Fox and Jack to haul wood. When you finish, come help me load."

That took care of them. Mama said nothing could keep her in the house on such a sunny fall morning. She'd clean the hen house, the worst job on the place. It wouldn't seem so bad on such a good day.

As she took her barn jacket down from the peg near the cellar door, she stumbled over Maureen. "I declare, you'll cause me to fall and break a hip. Now if you can't help, don't hinder." Mama was never very definite about assigning chores.

As soon as the house was still, Maureen stared at the lower panel of the door. The distorted face in the wood was framed by lines that looked like long, flowing hair. "I have to tell you about Rose, Peloponnesus," she began. "She's going to have to move away, and I'll miss her and all the Sansoucies, miss them worse than pay-day. You don't find people like them every day. They treat company like family and family like company. But they're going, no two ways about it. I don't know when I'll ever again have a friend living right close, because we're here across Lost Creek.

"I've been thinking about a bridge and how you get one." Maureen nodded to Peloponnesus. "That's right. You know we need it. For a while there, it looked like we'd never get it, but then I just worked it out, and

37

we'll soon have it. No more walking that trestle." Her voice was fine.

She talked for quite a while as she imagined the bridge with concrete sides, wide enough for two cars or wagons to pass, high enough for any flood. She told of all the families that would come across it to visit the McCrackens. They included everyone she knew in Dotzero and an imaginary family with girl triplets her own age.

"And I'll tell you something else, Peloponnesus," she continued. "Everybody in our family was just dumbbellfounded that I got us that bridge. Well, they said it was just like some kind of magic how I got it."

"Ah, ha! Dumbbellfounded!" Mit lunged across the kitchen and seized Maureen by the shoulders. "So you *can* talk! Even got us a bridge. Who were you talking to, Maureen?"

"Nobody."

"You're talking to yourself. Only crazy people talk to themselves."

Maureen tried to shake off his grip. "You're supposed to be fixing the fence."

"I forgot my nails here in the kitchen."

"Dummy, you only had to remember three things, and you forgot one," Maureen jeered.

"Well, this way I heard you got us a bridge." Mit shook her and shrieked with laughter.

38

Anger gripped Maureen, and she jabbed Mit in the stomach with her elbow. He let go of her shoulder. She beat at his face with both fists. Wham! Her head rang from a terrible, jarring slap.

Tears almost blinded Maureen as she grabbed Mit around the neck in what she hoped was a choking hold. "I've got you in a hammerlock," she said panting.

"Oh, no, you haven't, blatherskite bridge builder." He tried to shake her off the way Tisket shook a rat. She held on.

They struggled across the hall into the sitting room. Mit forced Maureen's head down onto the floor and held her there by the back of the neck. With his other arm across her back, he tried to flip her over. "A beautiful half nelson! A beauty!" he yelled.

"I'll break that hold," Maureen muttered. "I'll get you in a hammerlock." She gathered all her strength and came up. Mit came up too. His foot hit the little stand table. Crash! Over went the table and everything on it.

Mit and Maureen stood apart, staring at the damage. Mama's cut-glass dish lay in four pieces. Maureen picked up the biggest piece and held it helplessly. Uncle Millard had given Mama and Dad that dish for a wedding present.

Mama had left her rubber boots on the porch, so they didn't hear her coming. She appeared in the door-

39

way in baggy overalls and her barn jacket. Her pretty hair was stuffed under Dad's old felt hat. Her face was smudged, and she smelled like the chicken house.

Although she was likely due for a switching, Maureen didn't think about herself for a second or so. She thought about Mama and how different she must have looked when Uncle Millard had given her that cut-glass dish.

"Can't I step out of this house for one minute?" Mama yelled. "I see the two of you managed to break just about the only nice thing I had."

"Mit started it. He jumped out at me and shook me around."

"Maureen jabbed me right in the gut, then tried to choke me to death."

"Clear out of here, both of you," Mama shrieked. "I don't want to hear any more."

"I wasn't doing one thing to him, Mama, wasn't even talking to him, and he comes and. . . ."

"Shut up, Maureen," Mama said with a sob. "Shut up and leave me alone for a while."

Maureen fled to the tire swing. She watched Mit as he started off, swinging his hammer as if nothing had happened. The accident was all his fault, too. He'd started it, but Mama wouldn't listen to her. Mama had told her to shut up, first time she'd spoken for two days.

Maureen's head touched the side of the tire, and her ear felt sore. That was from Mit's slap. She remembered

40

a story his class had read about Thomas A. Edison, who went deaf after he was slapped.

If she went deaf, Mit would be sorry. They'd all be sorry. She listened to a train whistling far off for the Dotzero crossing. Did it sound fainter than usual? Making her deaf would be one awful thing for Mit to have on his conscience, even for a little while.

5

Maureen braced her feet in the bare spot under the swing to give herself a push. Nobody had given her a job. Mama wanted to be left alone. Walter didn't need her. He was getting to be like Mit, too big for his britches, fixing fence and loading wood. Tisket was off chasing rabbits.

Maureen heard faint, faraway shouts. The Sansoucie kids were playing. She wouldn't hear that much longer. She'd better get over there and play while she had a chance. Saturday had started wrong, but there was no use in wasting the rest of it.

Without asking permission, Maureen slipped out the yard gate to her path through the hayfield. When she got to the Wiley place, her cotton stockings and dress hem were itchy with sticktights. But she had no time to pick off the hitchhiking burrs; they would have to wear off. The Sansoucies were playing a game of Prison Base with much yelling.

"Rose, Rose," Maureen called. "I've come to play."

Rose swung a toddler onto her hip and left the game to come greet Maureen. Though Rose was small for her age, she could do something Maureen couldn't do. She could run and carry a little kid at the same time. Of course, the kids were trained to hang on. That helped.

"Maureen, I'm proud you came early." It was nice to see Rose's big smile. "I've finished my Saturday work, much as we can do in our house. Nothing to do now but mind the least ones. You got done early too, huh?"

"I was going to help all day long, but Mit caused Mama's cut-glass dish to get broken."

Rose sucked in her breath. "Oh, that was so pretty."

"I didn't like it much, looked like cat scratches to me, but Mama liked it. And she just broke up, worse than the dish, and told me to shut up before I had a chance to say anything. And Mit smartin' out all the time, so I thought I'd come over here." She studied her friend for a moment. "Rose, you look different."

Rose smoothed her hair. "Mom gave us all haircuts. She said she didn't want us looking like bur-oak acorns when we went anywhere. Do you think she botched the job?"

Rose's hair looked as if it had been cut with a knife and fork. "It'll grow out," Maureen said.

The other children motioned and called to the two girls.

"If you want to play Prison Base, you can be on my side." Rose shifted the little one to her other hip. "I get an extra player because I have to pack this one. Or would you want to get the little ones together and play house?"

"Prison Base!" Maureen raced toward Rose's team. The more running and shouting, the better Maureen liked the game.

Afterward they played Wolf Over the Ridge, Rotten Egg, and Lemonade. Then Rose suggested Antony Over. The low Wiley house was just right to throw a ball over the roof for the team on the opposite side to catch. They played until the ball rolled down the roof and lodged in the rusting roof gutter.

Maureen knew she shouldn't stay to eat at noon. There was little enough of the cold biscuits and mashed turnips for the Sansoucies. But they invited her politely and even opened a quart of canned blackberries because she was company.

After dinner the little kids took naps, and Maureen and Rose had a chance to hunt hickory nuts without having to drag babies along.

Finally, in late afternoon, Maureen knew she had to go back across the meadow. It had been so pleasant talking to Rose as they searched among the big, golden hickory leaves that Maureen had almost forgotten the misery of the morning. She felt her ear; it was still sore. She wondered what Mama would say about her being gone all day. Whatever it would be, Maureen decided not to hear very well, if at all.

44

As Maureen came to the back porch, Mama raised the shade on the kitchen-door window. "Now where have you been, Maureen? I called and called you to come take your bath right after Walter. We've all had ours. You'll have to have yours later in fourth water."

Everybody was in the kitchen. There was hardly room for the washtub that was pushed near the stove. Maureen preferred a switching to a bath in that cold, gray water, so she decided to ignore Mama's order.

Mama looked like a different person with clean clothes and just-washed hair. She started to peel potatoes. "I hope nobody faints from hunger before I get supper on the table. I'm late starting, but I had a lot to do outside and could have used some help from Maureen. Even so, I stayed out as long as I could. Took a walk over by the Wiley cemetery. You know that rose of Sharon bush there? I picked a bouquet for the stand table so it wouldn't look so bare." She didn't look at Maureen.

"Funny thing about that bush," Dad said. "Without fail, it blooms every fall. Money runs out, people go broke, stand in breadlines. Old Hitler and old Mussolini take over across the water. The whole world changes, and that bush blooms just the same."

Mama nodded. "That's a good thing for you to remember, Cleve, when you get down-in-the-mouth."

Mit's face was soap shined, and his wet black hair was combed back in a pompadour. "Maureen, you didn't

45

tell us where you were. You sure made yourself scarce. We needed you to open field gates when we hauled wood."

"What?"

"Where were you this afternoon when we needed you?"

"What?"

"What, what, stick your nose in a coffeepot. Pull it out when it gets red hot," Mit chanted.

So far Mit wasn't overly concerned that she couldn't hear thunder. Walter began to pester her with questions she didn't answer. He finally gave up and announced that Maureen was now both deef and dumb. Nobody thought one thing about it except to laugh because Walter said *deef* instead of *deaf*.

At supper Maureen had to listen to Dad and Mit brag about what a help Walter had been. Walter smiled until his eyes shut. After she'd finished eating, Maureen got right up from the table and started stacking dishes.

"I'm glad to see you're going to do dishes without a fuss," Mama said. "Be sure to fasten the chicken-house door when you pitch out the dishwater. Did you hear me?" she asked in an exasperated voice.

Maureen didn't answer; she stared blankly at Mama.

"What's the matter with you, Maureen?" Mama demanded. "I cleaned the chicken house by myself, not one lick of help from you. You had enough pep, though, to break my bowl. Now the least you can do is see that all the chickens have gone to roost and then fasten the door."

There were a lot of dishes and pans for just five people. It was dark when Maureen finished, and she went to bed without taking a bath.

When she came downstairs the next morning, she knew something was wrong. In the kitchen, Mama was tight-lipped and unsmiling.

Dad called from the back porch, "The waste of it, to see a young laying hen mauled like this. She was just full of eggs, Lillian. Come look at this." Maureen followed Mama outside. Dad pulled a cluster of little yellow spheres from inside the back of a hen. "I'll dress this one. The other two were so mutilated there's no use to try to dress them to cook. Total loss." He looked up at Maureen. "When I went to turn the chickens out, I found them up in the plum trees around the yard. Three hens were dead inside the open door of the chicken house. A 'possum or weasel got them."

"You didn't mind last night, Maureen. I told you to shut the door. Why didn't you?" Mama asked. "Why can't you take some responsibility, be dependable?"

Maureen took a deep breath. "I was going to, to do something for all of us, responsible like, and I was just thinking about it and how I could do it and all, and sometimes I can't figure out how anything is going to work unless I talk about it, and when I talk everybody tells me to shut up all the time. So I wasn't bothering

47

anybody, just kind of thinking out loud, and like I tried to tell you, along comes Mit, and he starts tormenting me and aggravating me and he gets me so mad. Then he lams me up the side of the head, kerwhack. He hit me so hard that my head rang just like a bell. And I saw stars and I couldn't hear very well, only nobody would listen to me if I tried to tell them. All day yesterday I couldn't hear very well on account of this busted eardrum or whatever it is, and so when you said that to me last night, I couldn't hear you for sure, and. . . ."

Maureen stopped talking. Mama's lips were moving; she was saying something. Maureen couldn't hear one word. A scared feeling grew in her stomach like an expanding balloon. What was Mama saying? She couldn't hear!

Then came the far-off sound of the Sansoucies shouting at play. Tisket barked; a train whistled. From the top of the stairs Walter called, "Maureen, come help me find my Sunday shirt."

Maureen sighed with relief.

"I see you haven't learned to read lips yet." Mama still looked stern. She didn't say anything about a switching. Maybe she couldn't think of any punishment bad enough to pay for killing three laying hens.

Maureen thought over her deaf act. It sure had been a dumbbell thing to pretend. Even if she were really deaf, she would want her family to be proud of her, not sorry. Now she had to prove that she could be a dependable, responsible middle kid, the kind Mama wanted. She'd start with the hens.

"I'll pay you back for the hens, Mama."

"I won't hold my breath," Mama said.

6

Monday morning Maureen was surprised and pleased when the Sansoucie children came trooping across the meadow to join the McCrackens for the walk to school.

Maureen stayed close to Rose as they crossed the footbridge. "I hope you come all week," she said. "We're going to have a spelling match and a ciphering match on Friday."

"Only coming today," Rose said in her gentle, low voice.

"Don't worry when you see your desk is empty," Maureen assured her. "I took your pencil, your tablet, and your box of colors and put them in my desk so nobody would steal your pink crayon. Pink, that's the one they either steal or borrow and use up."

"Much obliged for taking care of my things. I'll soon get them out of your way." Rose stopped to let the other children go ahead. "I hate to tell you this, but we're going to move. We came to school today to get stuff from our desks and to tell Miss Huckstep good-bye. My dad found a place in Cold Spring school district. We can live in the tenant house, and he'll get some work from the farmer that owns it."

"Mrs. Wiley is the meanest person I know, and I know a lot of mean people," Maureen stated angrily.

Rose shrugged. "We've got nothing against her. We might be better off at Cold Spring. My mom says she can't do anything to make the Wiley house pretty. She papered the walls with clean newspaper, but it didn't help much. Still, I'd like to stay here where Miss Huckstep is teacher. I had aimed to come to school regularly whenever we could get across the creek. I won't have any friend at Cold Spring."

"How about me?" Maureen asked with self-pity. "You'll have enough kids around for lots of good games, but I won't. After you move, I can't jump wide rope unless I tie one end of the rope to a post and beg Walter to turn the other. I can't depend on Mit for anything except torment."

During recess Maureen stayed close to Rose, and at noon they took the tin lard buckets that held their lunches and went to eat at the edge of the playground. Maureen couldn't help but see that Rose had only two biscuits that were not even buttered, just stained with a little berry jelly.

She offered Rose part of her chicken sandwich, explaining that McCrackens had an extra lot of chicken due to a sort of accident. Rose said she didn't like chicken. Maureen knew that couldn't be, and finally she talked her into taking some.

At four o'clock, when the school day was done, Miss Huckstep had cards prepared showing what grades the Sansoucie children were in. "Give these to the teacher at Cold Spring School," she said, as she handed Rose the cards. "Enroll right away, and be sure to go to school every day."

"Yes ma'am," Rose said politely.

The two girls went together down the hill to the store, but Rose waited on the porch while Maureen went in to the postal window.

"We got *Capper's Weekly*." Maureen held up the newspaper when she came out. "No letter, though. I was expecting mail from Uncle Millard. Mama wrote and told him the family could live with us if the box factory closed down. Must be still going. Don't you want to ask for mail, Rose? You never know what you might get. All you have to say is 'Any mail for Sansoucie?' "

Rose shook her head. "My dad said for us not to go into the Stackhouse store."

"Why?"

"Last time my dad was in there to do some trading, Mr. Stackhouse was right overbearing."

It was Saturday before Maureen saw the Sansoucies again. She had just thrown kitchen scraps out to the

52

chickens when she saw the whole Sansoucie family coming across the field. With long strides she ran to meet Rose, who walked ahead of the rest.

"Maureen, we've all come to tell you folks goodbye." Rose gestured back to the other children and to her parents who carried the smallest ones. "But I wanted to be first to ask you to come visit us at Cold Spring whenever you can."

"Oh, I will," Maureen promised. "It's not very far. And maybe you can come stay all night with me sometime. There's plenty of room until Uncle Millard, Aunt Cora, and all my cousins come."

Mr. Sansoucie came up and held out his hand to Maureen. "Sure looked natural, you galloping across that meadow, Maureen. We're much obliged to you for being company to our kids." He shook her hand just as if she were grown up.

Dad had described Mr. Sansoucie as wiry, and Maureen agreed. She felt he could be bent every whichway and not break. Rose's mother wouldn't break either. She was too soft. Her voice, her flesh, her handshake were all soft. She tried hard to make soft things that looked pretty.

"Mom, can we give Maureen her keepsake present now?" Rose asked.

"We made two, one for you and one for your mother," Mrs. Sansoucie said, as she handed Maureen folded cloths. "It's new goods of a chick-feed sack, the last bag we bought. Rose hemmed them, and I crocheted trim for the ends to make fancy hand towels. Or dresser scarves, if you want to use them for that."

"Oh, they're nice. Thanks a lot. I never had a keepsake present before."

"I see your dad and mom out by the lot gate," Mr. Sansoucie said. "I better get up there for the last of my borrowing from the McCrackens. We can't move unless we borrow Fox and Jack and the wagon."

Mrs. Sansoucie gave Mama her present, and Mr. Sansoucie told Dad how much obliged they were for all the McCrackens' help. Then he asked to borrow the team and wagon.

"You're welcome to them," Dad said, "but I'd better drive the mules across the ford when you're ready. There are some washed-out holes there, but I know where the water is shallow and the gravel firm."

"It'll be mighty lonesome over here on this side of the creek with you folks gone," Mama said. "Maureen and Walter won't have any children to play with. Of course, Mit is getting up now to where he doesn't have much time for play. It's easy to learn to play, harder to learn to work, I've found. Mit's a lot of help to Cleve."

"We'll miss good neighbors," Mr. Sansoucie said, "but we never cared much for the Wiley place. The chimney is so unhandy. It takes too much pipe to set up a heating stove."

In late afternoon all the Sansoucies, in the wagon

54

loaded with furniture, stopped at McCrackens'. As Dad
drove off toward the ford, Maureen and Walter waved
and waved, the way they waved at passenger trains.

"There go all my friends in one wagon, Walter."
Maureen had finally stopped waving, and she had an
empty feeling. "Maybe we ought to go over to the
Wiley place and see how it is with everyone gone."

They set off across the meadow with Tisket following. The Wiley place looked so lonesome that Tisket
whined at the sight. Maureen and Walter skirted the
sagging yard fence where hummocks of dry grass and
weeds from bygone summers had made the ground un-
even. With an awful squawk, something flapped up,
just missing their faces. Walter almost fell into a nest
full of eggs.

"Sansoucies missed one of their hens. No wonder,
she's hidden her nest. And she's off schedule, too, setting in the fall," Maureen said. "You never can tell
about a Rhode Island Red."

While the hen clucked and fussed nearby, Walter
touched one of the warm eggs. He asked about the
nesting habits of various birds and fowl—guineas, geese,
penguins.

"Walter, everything that has wings lays eggs," Maureen asserted blithely.

"Do angels lay eggs?"

Maureen looked at him sharply. "Walter Lee Mc-
Cracken, you just better watch out, asking things like

that." Still, she pondered the question. Maybe Hurlbut's *Story of the Bible* might tell. Or she could talk it over with Peloponnesus.

The children cupped their hands around their eyes and looked through the windows into the small, vacant rooms. Most of the walls were covered with yellowed newspaper. "That's where their stove was, and over in that corner is where we played school on rainy days." Maureen moved to another window. "Somehow this house doesn't seem empty," she said.

She ran across the bare yard to the cistern pump and gave the handle a turn. "Look, they left this. I heard Mrs. Wiley say, like as not, they would take everything that wasn't nailed down. This is kind of loose, so watch out." She turned the handle until water splashed out from the pump spout. *"Helen, Helen, Helen.* That's what cistern pumps say, don't you think, Walter?"

A tall metal case covered the pump wheel and its chain with the little copper cups that brought water up from the cistern. A lid like an old-time soldier's hat fit on top of the case. Maureen pried it off and looked down into the black shaft. The wheel and cups took up most of the space, but the water below mirrored a bit of the sky. Her own head was reflected in the water, and something else floated there too.

"Walter," she called, "you won't believe what I've found. Just what you were asking about. An angel's egg. They lay their eggs in water, like frogs do, you know, and there's one here in the Wiley place cistern. Want to see it?"

Walter's eyes came just to the top of the pump case. "You're an awful chunk," Maureen said, as she strained to lift him so he could see down the cistern shaft. "If we had asked Peloponnesus, he could have told us where to find it. But I guess we managed to find it by ourselves."

Walter saw the reflection of Maureen's head and part of his own. Then he saw a bright sphere floating. Maureen jiggled the pump handle. Far down in the cistern the metal cups on their chain moved. So did the sphere.

"That's a ball, Maureen, a red rubber ball." Walter's voice echoed in the cistern. "Red rubber ball, red rubber ball," he shouted in order to hear the echo.

Maureen dropped him with a jolt. "You're the one wanted to know about an angel's egg. I find you one. Now you won't believe it."

"Would so, too, if you found me a real one, but I know that's a ball. Sansoucies had a red one. Somehow it got into the cistern."

Maureen thought of the Antony Over game when the ball had stuck in the roof gutter. Rain might have washed it into the downspout, which led into the cistern. Still, it was interesting to think it could be an angel's egg.

"Now, Walter," she said, "there are a lot of wonderful things going on in the world, and I don't want you to miss any. You will if you decide that something that could be wonderful is just an old rubber ball, so once in a while. . . ."

"Maureen, Mit says a lot of the stuff you tell me is just malarkey, that you should go tell it to the Marines. Mit says you are the worst blatherskite—"

"Mit says! If he knows so much, you can just go and tag along after him and get him to chase things that aren't there out of your closet at night." Maureen turned and stomped off across the yard. At the broken gate she glanced back. Walter looked very small beside the vacant house. But he knew his way home. He had to learn that she wouldn't put up with any old thing. He was getting more and more like Mit and wouldn't listen.

Now she had no one at all. Maureen sniffed back tears. After a while she began to go over the names and ages of the departed Sansoucies. Then she talked to herself about a still larger imaginary family. As she wandered along the edge of the meadow, she gave them all names and ages. When there was any trouble, they could all depend on the middle child, a girl Maureen's age who was most reliable.

By the time she reached home Maureen felt better. Smoke drifted from the chimney, which meant that Mama had started the supper fire and would nab her and make her help if she wasn't careful. Then Maureen remembered the hen and the hidden nest. She burst into the kitchen, ready to tell Mama about the discovery.

Mama was rolling out biscuit dough. "Maureen, you didn't ask to go over to that empty house. Walter has been home for a long time. He had to come alone. You should not have left him over there by himself, playing around that old cistern. He could have been snakebit around the house foundation or run a rusty nail into his foot."

"But he didn't, and anyhow Tisket was with him, Mama."

"I never thought you would go back on Walter." Mama shook her head.

"I didn't. He got smarty over at the Wiley place, where it's just so lonesome. If you find an old rag or worn-out shoe or anything, it makes you feel like bawling because you knew them and don't know when you will ever see them again or have anybody to play with besides Walter. Anyhow, I'm dependable about replacing those hens. I've got one, and when the chicks hatch out, won't be any time until I'll have the other two, even have two to spare."

Mama put her hands on the sides of her head, flattening her pretty hair. "What *are* you talking about?" she asked.

"I've got to get some corn and take it back over there for this old biddy hen the Sansoucies left. She hid her nest outside the chicken house and has four eggs. I'll coax her into a basket with corn and bring her and the

59

eggs here and put them in the hen house so the varmints won't get them. Then I'll take care of them and raise them."

"It's a wonder that hen didn't come out of the brush and flop down to have her legs tied, the Sansoucies move so often," Mama said. "You know she belongs to them, and you know the story about counting unhatched chicks. When a hen gets broody in the fall, she goes into a late molt, runs around half feathered, stuffs on corn all winter, and won't lay until spring. Still, the Sansoucies ought to have her." Mama looked out the kitchen window. "There will still be daylight after supper. I'd like to walk over to the Wiley place myself. You can't manage a setting hen alone."

Mama was worse than Walter. If there was something you wanted to skip over, not think about, she wouldn't let you leave it out. Maureen knew Mama was right that the hen and chicks to come weren't McCrackens'. There went her scheme to be responsible and replace their lost chickens. Still, she thought, brightening, if she helped the real owners get them back, that was an even better kind of responsible.

7

At school a few days later Maureen announced that all four eggs had hatched. Miss Huckstep seemed so interested that Maureen started to repeat the story of the hidden nest.

"We understand, so you need not tell it again," Miss Huckstep interrupted. "If you want to surprise the Sansoucies with their poultry, I'll take you over there Saturday. I've wondered if they enrolled in Cold Spring School."

Maureen hadn't expected to see the Sansoucies again for a long time. It just showed what good luck came from stepping carefully on the stones of the shortcut path. Maureen reminded Walter of this as they waited for Miss Huckstep to arrive in the Huckstep family Model A Ford.

Miss Huckstep knew just how to ease a car into Lost Creek ford: slowly enough to keep the coils dry, then quickly down on the gas, to keep from miring in the loose gravel. Maureen and Walter sat squeezed on the front seat beside her, holding a basket of peeping baby chicks across their laps. The mother hen had put up a squawking fight, but now lay quietly at their feet with her legs tied together. On the back seat lay a bag of wheat and a bag of cracked corn for the chicks. Mama had sent squash, potatoes, and onions for the Sansoucies.

"We're much obliged to you for taking us, Miss Huckstep," Maureen said. "I think I could walk it, but not with an old Rhode Island Red about to flog me with every step. I don't know about Walter. His legs aren't as long as mine. By rights, he ought to come, though. He helped find the nest."

Miss Huckstep checked the block signal and crossed the railroad track at Cold Spring. After they passed the school, they rode by a farmhouse with a big barn. The tenant house would be close to it.

As they steered around a thicket matted with honeysuckle vines they saw the place. Rose and her sisters were hanging wash on the line, and they seemed like familiar movie stars in a new picture show. When the car stopped, the Sansoucie children were startled and started to run inside.

Maureen jumped out. "It's me, Rose. I promised I'd come visit."

"Maureen! You've come already." Rose smiled. "You kids go tell the folks Miss Huckstep is here."

"We've brought you a present," Maureen said lifting the hen out of the car.

The visitors were soon surrounded by all the Sansoucies, who thought their hen had been carried off by a fox.

"Leave it to Maureen to get here to see us and bring extra, besides," Mrs. Sansoucie said. Maureen could see the tenant house had many handy things, including a proper hen coop, where the Rhode Island Red was soon scratching and clucking to her brood. "She'll feel at home in no time, the way we did. You folks come in and see our place," Mrs. Sansoucie invited.

Maureen looked at the low house, which seemed to be held up by a huge trumpet creeper vine that grew to the roof. The surrounding sheds appeared even more interesting. Much as she liked to visit, she decided to stay outside.

"There must be great places to hide for I Spy," she said to Rose.

"Best of any place we ever lived," Rose assured her. "So we can play that to start. I'll be It. Remember, you're not playing, Bud." She spoke to a glum-looking boy sitting by the woodpile.

"Why can't he play, Rose?"

"He's not to run and rip and wear out his shoes in case we go to school."

There were so many good games to play, and later on so many places to explore with Rose, that Maureen did not go inside at all while Miss Huckstep talked with Mr. and Mrs. Sansoucie. The visit was over too soon.

"There's lots more to show you. When are you coming again?" Rose asked.

"Some of these days. You never can tell about Walter and me. At least, I know you're not gone for good now. I'll think of you over here, yelling and playing and wearing out the grass in another yard."

Rose's brown eyes were serious. "I think finding our hen was a good sign."

"Well, yes, and how about Miss Huckstep bringing us here on her Saturday? She's an extra good teacher."

"I know," Rose agreed. "She's better than most."

The road to Cold Spring was so narrow that Miss Huckstep pulled far to the side when they met another car. "I'm glad you kids had the chickens to take. We'll have to think of some other reasons for visits. I don't believe I got very far with my urging."

"We'd like to come anytime, wouldn't we, Walter? Maybe after Mama gets every last thing all canned, jellied, pickled, squeezed out, dried, she'll come too. She likes to get away from home, get a change of scenery. What would we be urging?"

Miss Huckstep laughed. "If you'd let me get a word in edgewise, I'll tell you. I'm trying to get the Sansoucies to go to school. They haven't started, and it's a downright shame. They're smart."

"Especially Rose," Maureen agreed.

"You have to keep right after them to get them to go

64

to school. I wasn't doing very well myself at Dotzero."
Miss Huckstep steered to miss a deep rut. "Cold Spring
is worse. The teacher is Lorene Stackhouse."

"Stackhouse!" Maureen exclaimed.

"Yes. Sterling Price Stackhouse is her uncle. She was
in my high-school class, and she was the last one of us
hired to teach a school. I just have my doubts that the
Sansoucies will set foot in a school taught by a Stackhouse. Of course, you might be able to talk them into
it, Maureen."

"Well, I'll try, but sometimes my folks claim I talk
too much," Maureen admitted.

Miss Huckstep reached over and gave her a pat.
"You'll have to learn to use that gift of gab the right
way."

All during the next week, Maureen was anxious to
stop at the post office and tell Mrs. Stackhouse about
her visit to Cold Spring, but Mit dashed in ahead of her
every day and asked for their mail. Finally she had a
chance the day Mit stayed home from school to help
Dad haul corn. Besides asking for mail, she had to get
a box of salt for Mama.

"Are you sure that's all?" Mrs. Stackhouse asked, as
she added the item to the McCracken bill.

" 'Tis for now. Even with Walter to help pack, I
can't carry too much across our footbridge. Might lose
my balance. Mama will be coming in to get a lot of

65

things." Maureen looked across at the dry-goods side of the store. "She'll be getting dress goods and a lot of stuff. She could hitch up Fox and Jack and come in the wagon, but she says she'd rather be in hell with her back broke than try to handle that stubborn pair.

"She claims Mit hasn't got the patience to drive them. They mind my dad, but he's either working on the railroad extra gang, which is lucky, or, if he doesn't have work, he's hauling corn for Fox and Jack. And then he says mules are like people, ought to have a day of rest once a week. But sometimes it doesn't make much sense to me. We have Fox and Jack so we can plant corn and cut hay. And we have to grow corn and hay to winter Fox and Jack. So. . . ."

"Whoa, Maureen, back up a little. I want to know about the Sansoucies. You said you visited them at Cold Spring. So they've moved away from Dotzero?"

"Oh, yes, they were asked to move, because Mrs. Wiley wanted cash rent. I told Rose I thought Mrs. Wiley was mean, but I never let on to any of 'em that I knew they had to move. Rose didn't say anything, so I didn't either. Never opened my mouth about it because I thought, well, might make 'em feel bad."

"I wouldn't worry about their tender feelings. They've got enough gall." Mrs. Stackhouse raised her voice. "Sterling, it's just the way we thought. They moved without a word about their store bill."

Mr. Stackhouse brought an account pad to the counter. He pushed his felt hat back on his head and adjusted his glasses the better to read the figures. "You can't get blood out of a turnip, and a good bit of it is my fault. I let this run on too long. But when them little peaked-faced young uns come in here with their dad, I just weighed up a few more beans."

"Yes, you should have shut them off before you did. We've got our own bills to think about," Mrs. Stackhouse said.

"Walter and I would never have got over there with that old hen if it hadn't been for Miss Huckstep. The Sansoucies left a hen, only there were five chickens when we went, because Miss Huckstep. . . ."

"Miss Huckstep, now how is she anyhow?" Mrs. Stackhouse seemed especially interested. "How is her term of school going?"

"Tol'able I guess. We're going to have a ciphering match every Friday. Miss Huckstep says the kids in eighth grade will pass their final examination if they come to school regular."

"Well, I declare." Mrs. Stackhouse puffed heavily from climbing up on the store step stool. "I guess Alma Huckstep is a born teacher. Like as not, she'll be an old maid."

"No, she won't." Maureen was emphatic.

Mr. Stackhouse chuckled. "Can't never tell for sure."

"Yes, you can so too. About her anyhow."

Mrs. Stackhouse reached high to arrange cans on a

67

shelf. "I know she's been going with Jim Nolan, the carrier on Dotzero rural route. But that could go on for a long time. He's got a mother to keep house for him. I've asked him about Alma, but I can't get a word out of him. Alma Huckstep could wait around for him and end up an old maid."

Maureen was pleased to have news. "No, she won't, because they are married already. Secretly married."

"Are they now?" Mrs. Stackhouse purred. "I wouldn't be too sure of that if I were you, Maureen."

"I saw it printed out, right in the St. Louis paper, little bitty print. I was at the Sansoucies' when they lived at the Wiley place where they had papered their kitchen with newspapers. One day we were playing school and didn't have any books. I was teacher, and I gave one of the kids the big print to read. He was slow, so while he was stumbling around reading that big print from the newspaper on the wall, I read the little print under marriage licenses, and I saw it. I told Mama about it."

"And what did she say?" Mrs. Stackhouse purred another question.

"She said if Miss Huckstep never said anything about getting married, then as far as she knew, there wasn't anything to it, and for me just to be still and forget about it."

"In that case, I guess you're right. Alma won't be

an old maid." Mrs. Stackhouse seemed very pleased, considering she wasn't even kin to Miss Huckstep.

Maureen felt important. Both Mr. and Mrs. Stackhouse were paying attention to what she had to say. It was a good opportunity to ask Mr. Stackhouse something she had wondered about. "There are lots of bridges over creeks and rivers. Almost every place has a bridge. Why don't we have one over Lost Creek for a wagon or a car so we can go places even if it rains?"

"Who's up there, Maureen, on the other side of Lost Creek, except you folks and the hoot owls? Even the Sansoucies loaded up and pulled out. Just not enough people up there in your neck of the woods."

As business was slack, Maureen stayed and chatted for a long time with Mr. and Mrs. Stackhouse. It sure would be nice to have a mother and father like them who really listened, she thought. Finally Walter got so fidgety that Maureen had to tear herself away and go home.

8

Maureen came home full of talk and was glad when Dad and Mit finished their chores and joined the family in the kitchen. Mama had just started supper.

"I thought we would never get out of that store," Maureen reported, "because there were Mrs. Stackhouse and Mr. Stackhouse acting like they were downright lonesome, wanting to know about everything."

"Sterling Price Stackhouse must know where he can get information." Mama put the biscuits in the oven.

"Price? Why does he have that name?" Walter asked. "Is Price his maiden name?"

Walter was puzzled when everyone laughed, so Maureen had to explain. "Of course not. He was named after General Sterling Price. That was a general in Missouri in the Civil War. I learned that from Mit's history class. His nickname was Pap. Pap Price, that's what they called him. Once I heard men talking on the store porch about when Pap Price and Abe Lincoln had their war, like there were only two people in the war."

"You're getting off the track," Mama reminded her. "You were telling us about all the attention you got at the store today."

Maureen felt wonderful. She was getting attention at home, too. "Yes, they told me the sawmill might shut down and some people move from Dotzero. And they asked me again about Uncle Millard and how his family was getting along. I told them they were having it hard, couldn't have a cow or chickens or anything there in the city, and that Mama had written and told them they could crowd in with us."

"That's family business. You don't need to advertise it." A gloomy look came over Dad's face.

"Appears Stackhouses were uncommon nosey even for them," Mama said. "Didn't they give you any news?"

"Yes, they said the Sansoucies moved and left a big store bill."

Dad sighed. "Not much news in that."

Maureen thought for a second. "And Mr. Stackhouse thinks we don't have a bridge because it's only us and the hoot owls up here, and Mrs. Stackhouse said it's a bad situation. In case any of us get sick, probably a doctor wouldn't even come. And if the house caught fire, the place would just have to burn to the ground, couldn't get any help."

"Now wasn't she a big ray of sunshine?" Mit was annoyed.

"I didn't let that bother me any," Maureen declared.

71

"Something else did, though, and I got to wondering. What is Miss Huckstep's name?"

Mama clattered stove lids. "You know her name. Why are you asking?"

"Because of what I saw printed in that paper. Mrs. Stackhouse got my goat, talking about her going to be an old maid. Kept going at it, she did. So I just up and told them about Miss Huckstep being secretly married."

Dad groaned. "Blatherskite! You didn't do that!"

Mama sank into a kitchen chair. "Of all people to tell. You might as well put it in the *Beaumont Banner* as to tell those two."

"I said it was a secret. Secretly married, that's what I said."

"Lotta good that will do," Mit muttered.

"Why is it so secret?" Maureen asked.

"Now you wonder why." Mama sounded disgusted. "Now you realize there might be a reason. You should think before you speak. Learn to bridle your tongue."

"Pretty hard to bridle a galloping horse," Mit chimed in.

"Maureen's tongue is tied in the middle and loose at both ends." She'd heard Dad say that before.

"Right now everybody is talking but me . . . and Walter."

"Cracker box," Walter ventured.

"But you don't tell me *why* it's a secret marriage."

Mama put wood in the stove, then opened the oven

72

door to check her biscuits. "She's a married woman, Maureen, secretly but legally married. Her man is a rural mail carrier, drawing regular pay. One job to a family these days, if you're lucky. Schoolboards don't hire married women."

"So you see, Miss Flap-jaw Blabbermouth, you'll cause Miss Huckstep to lose her job. She won't be hired next year." Mit pushed aside the books Maureen had brought home and sat down on the kitchen bench. "It won't matter to me. I'll be through the eighth grade and finished at Dotzero, but you're liable to have Lorene Stackhouse for a teacher."

"How do you know so much?" Maureen yelled.

"That's not hard to figure. Mit's right." Mama was always saying that. "Sterling Price Stackhouse will try his best to get elected school director and hire his niece. Dotzero district pays its taxes and gives the teacher $100 a month. Cold Spring can only pay $60."

Maureen felt miserable. She didn't know about taxes. Mit's civics class hadn't gotten to them yet.

The next morning Maureen had to go to school just as any other day. Miss Huckstep acted as if nothing had happened, and Maureen tried to do the same. But she had trouble looking directly at her. As Maureen bent over the neatest arithmetic paper she had ever prepared, she was sure Miss Huckstep's eyes were on her. Maybe she wouldn't finish the term, Maureen thought.

73

Mit might not graduate. Sooner or later Miss Huckstep would learn Maureen McCracken was the one who blabbed something that was none of her beeswax. It sure wasn't much of a way to thank a person who had taken her and Walter to visit their friends. She'd never intended to cause her teacher to lose her job.

Miss Huckstep kept all the grades busy during the morning and didn't holler but a time or two. At noon Maureen looked in the window from the playground and saw Miss Huckstep eating alone at her desk. She looked as tired as a hired girl. Miss Huckstep was just getting the hang of teaching, which wasn't easy with the Stackhouses waiting to see if she would botch the job.

Maureen realized bitterly that the Stackhouses had pumped her like a cistern. They had told her about the sawmill and people moving, about why there was no bridge. They had given her more news than the *Beaumont Banner*. But all the time they had wanted something from her. It was just the way Mama said: any dog that brings you a bone will take a bone.

After school Maureen surprised Walter. She stopped on the store porch and pushed him toward the door. "Go in and ask for mail."

"You want *me* to ask?"

"Yes, and if Mrs. Stackhouse is puffing around and pretends not to see you, speak right up. Loud."

"You ask; I'll wait."

"I'm not setting my foot in that store. I'm not going

in the U. S. post office. The Stackhouses made me so mad that I can't even talk to them."

"You must be *really* mad, Maureen."

"I am, and I'm not talking to people who are tricky to a person just trying to be friendly. Now go on before Mit gets too far ahead."

9

Mild autumn was going fast, and nobody could stop it. Darkness came now before Mit and Dad finished the evening chores. Soon there was ice in the ditch along the school road. Mit stamped right over the frozen ruts in the heavy, high-topped, laced boots he wore for school and chores.

Two of the brightest birds, the blue jays and the cardinals, stayed all winter. They hopped among the brown leaves still clinging stubbornly to the oak trees.

As Walter's cheeks reddened like coals in the cookstove, his teeth chattered, but his feet stayed warm. He appeared to have regular bird feet. Maureen hopped like the birds trying to warm hers. They were always numb when she got to school and ached as they slowly warmed in the room heated by a jacketed wood stove.

Maureen's other problem was that she wore thin cotton gloves. She'd paid no attention to the rock steps the day it snowed, and she'd been repaid with the bad luck of losing her wool gloves when her coat brushed them off the toilet seat down the hole of the school privy.

She and Walter couldn't keep up with Mit in his boots as they climbed the windy hill to school. Maureen took off her thin gloves and blew on her hands. "Mama says I have to get along with these sleazy things all winter, but I think she's knitting me some new ones for Christmas. I saw some red gloves about my size on her knitting needles, but I didn't say one thing, Walter, not one word. Making me gloves after I didn't take care of my good ones, that's what you call the spirit of Christmas. I wish I could get Mama a gift, a present to make up for her hens and for the cut-glass bowl."

"We had this story in our reader about some people so poor they couldn't buy even a tree at Christmas. That's what it said. But there are Christmas trees around everywhere." Walter pointed to a little cedar on the hill. "They're in the pasture and in the woods. Why would anybody want to pay money for one?"

"Walter Lee McCracken, everybody doesn't live in the St. Francois Mountains where cedar trees grow. People like Uncle Millard's family probably do well to have a tin Christmas tree."

"Maureen, you know those Christmas cards with pictures of houses with fireplaces and doors with wreaths on them? Do city people pay cash money for those wreaths?"

"When we get home, we'll ask Peloponnesus."

When Mama was out gathering eggs that evening, Walter and Maureen sat on the kitchen floor facing the cellar door. Maureen stared at it for quite a while before she whispered, "Every last one. That's what he says. City people have to buy every last one of those wreaths unless they have a Christmas tree growing in their yard and can hack off some limbs and make one. But most of them, if they have a tree, they baby it and don't hack anything off. That's not all. You know how Mit horsed around and broke Mama's cut-glass bowl? Peloponnesus says there's a way we can make some money and buy another bowl for Mama for Christmas."

"How?"

"Make wreaths and sell them to city people."

"We don't know any city people," Walter pointed out, "except our kinfolks and they wouldn't buy any."

"Don't worry. Peloponnesus told me how to handle that. You've got to help me make wreaths."

Walter agreed, but soon wished he hadn't as he carried armloads of prickly cedar branches, which Maureen had cut with Mama's garden pruners.

Mama let them work in the sitting room as long as they kept up the fire and cleaned the mess when they finished. The sitting room, usually cold and unused in winter, became a cozy workshop, fragrant with cedar.

Maureen took extra wire hangers from Mama's closet

78

and bent them into rings. Then she wired on bunches of cedar. Walter was not much good at this part of the operation, but Mit helped sometimes.

A week later Maureen admired the six finished wreaths, which were full and fat and trimmed with blue cedar berries. She felt very useful and dependable.

She explained to Walter her plan to reach city folks, and he was with her at Dotzero depot on Saturday. Walter had two wreaths; Maureen held four. Train Number 3 pulled in at 10:52 A.M. The train conductor bought a wreath from Maureen. Neither the engineer, fireman, nor brakeman wanted any.

While Pat Ash, the station agent, loaded lumpy pouches of mail into the mail car and cans of cream into the express car, Maureen and Walter walked beside the passenger coaches. Around the big, solid wheels, steam hissed out into the cold air.

Maureen held up a wreath. To her surprise, a woman motioned her aboard. She slipped up the car steps. Walter watched her walk the length of the car and come down the steps at the other end. She held her remaining wreath up to frame her smiling face.

During the next week, they made three more wreaths to replenish their stock. Saturday found them waiting again at Dotzero for Number 3. Number 6, the fast passenger train, was due first; Maureen and Walter intended to stay right on the station platform while it thundered through.

Maureen braced herself for the rush of air, but there was none. Number 6 sighed to a stop on the sidetrack. The train conductor swung down the steps of a coach, tipped his gold watch out of his pocket, and glanced at it as he hurried across the main track to Dotzero depot.

Maureen motioned Walter to follow her, and she swung up the same car steps. She spindled three wreaths on his arm, pointed to a coach door, and went in the opposite direction.

The name *Osage* shone in gold letters on the heavy door Maureen pushed open. She knew a named car was a Pullman where people rode all day, then made up their seats as beds and slept all night.

Maureen sold her wreaths right away. As she turned back down the aisle, she felt a sudden jerk, then a slight motion. She raced to the door and pulled it open. Looking down over the covered steps, she saw railroad ties jerking by in a blur. She stared out helplessly as familiar landmarks flowed by; the section house, Dotzero School, the store with Mrs. Stackhouse on the porch.

The train gathered speed. It plunged into the total darkness of Tunnel 19, and choking smoke and stinging cinders poured in. Somebody grabbed her. Daylight flashed again. It was Walter.

"Where did you come from?" a voice shouted over the roar of the train. Maureen stared at brass buttons

80

holding a dark-blue coat closed over a fat belly. She dared look up no higher.

"We come from Dotzero," Maureen shouted. "It's no wonder you wouldn't know because Number 6 usually just tears right through Dotzero, like we didn't have a post office or anything."

"Dotzero!" the voice thundered.

"Yes, that's where we live, and it's not a nothing kind of a place either, the way some people think. My dad, he works on the railroad extra gang sometimes. He says he's extra on the extra. Well, he told us how our town got that name. When they were building the railroad, they had to plan it out so's they would know where the railroad was going. They had these surveyors that did arithmetic, and one of them put a dot and a zero down on the paper and said they had to start somewhere, so they called that place Dotzero, and that name stuck. That's where we come from, Dotzero." Maureen was hoarse from shouting.

"For crying out loud, get on out of here. This is a Pullman." Maureen got brave enough to look at the conductor's round, red face. He was eyeing Maureen's worn shoes and Walter's handed-down mackinaw. "I'm the Pullman conductor. People that ride Pullmans travel in style and comfort."

"Oh, I know that," Maureen shouted. "None of your rough travel on a Pullman. I know about the Pullman

81

strike and everything because I listened to my brother Mit's history class. Then I listened to—"

The conductor opened the heavy door of the car and gave them a push. "Get out of here before you talk my arm off. See the regular conductor in the coach."

"Not going to see him unless he sees me first," Maureen mumbled, as she nudged Walter toward an empty seat by the window and slid in beside him. "That almost worked. I thought maybe I could keep talking until we stopped at Beaumont, and then we could get off. Oh oh, Walter, here he comes. Try to disguise yourself as an innocent, paying passenger.

Another big man in a blue coat with brass buttons stopped at their seat. "No seat check here? I must've missed you two at our Poplar Bluff stop. Tickets?" He held a big hand right under Maureen's nose.

She jabbed Walter in the ribs with her elbow. "Can't you hear the conductor? Stop looking out the window and pay attention. Give him our tickets."

Walter stared at Maureen in disbelief. "I don't have any tickets."

"You do so! I gave them to you because you have better pockets than I have."

He looked at her, mystified. "We haven't got any tickets."

"Haven't got any tickets! What would we be doing on the train if we didn't have any tickets?"

"I don't know," Walter admitted.

Maureen glanced out the window. Farms flew by. She recognized them as places near Beaumont. She turned back to the conductor and smiled. "Well, I'll have to help him look through all his pockets. He always gets the jitters when we ride on a train to our grandma's." Maureen started digging into the pockets of Walter's mackinaw. She was glad to hide her hands, which were dirty and sticky with cedar sap.

Walter had sold his wreaths too, and the conductor looked at their empty basket. "Is that all the luggage you have?"

"Yes, we always take our basket empty," Maureen explained, "because our grandma, she spoils us and gives us all kinds of stuff to bring back. Toys and everything."

Maureen started on Walter's overall pockets. The conductor stood there, tapping his big fingers on the back of the seat in front of them. He should be walking through the car, calling Beaumont station, Maureen thought. But the train continued at full speed, its whistle wailing at the crossings. They were Beaumont crossings! Flash! That was the Beaumont depot; there was the shoe factory, the feed store, the high school.

"Don't you stop at Beaumont?" Maureen asked, looking up at the conductor.

"Beaumont! This train hasn't stopped at Beaumont for two years. This is no galloping goose on a pumpkin vine, girlie. This is Number 6."

Maureen nodded. "And the company can't go stopping a big fifty-three hundred engine like this one at a place no bigger than Beaumont. Sometimes I listen to the eighth grade at our school. I heard them say it costs two dollars and thirty cents just to stop a big engine like this and start it up again. So where do you stop next?"

"St. Louis Union Station."

Maureen tried to hide her shock. It was seventy-one miles from Dotzero to Union Station. She and Walter had never been to St. Louis. Uncle Millard lived there, but she didn't know where in that big city. She pushed Walter to his feet. "Stand up, so I can search your back pockets. Mr. Conductor, I know I can find our tickets, but it'll take a while. If you come back in a little bit, maybe I'll have them."

"You better." The conductor walked slowly down the aisle.

"Stop it! Quit looking in my pockets." Walter was furious. "You know we didn't buy any tickets from Pat Ash. You're just a big fat blatherskite liar."

"Be quiet! Do you want everybody on this coach to hear you? No matter what I say, don't you dare say anything different. See all those icicles hanging off the rock out there? That's how cold it is. You want to be put off the train out in the middle of nowhere, cold as it is? Besides, this might be our only chance to see St. Louis."

"Mama will be worried," Walter said, a little calmer.

"Won't either. She's reading that new book Miss Huckstep lent her. *Gone with the Wind* is real thick. You know how she is when she gets her nose in a book. She won't know we're gone. Anyhow, we've got no choice. Now sit up straight; here he comes."

Maureen's forced laugh sounded more like a grunt. "He finally told. I like to never got it out of him. He kept taking those tickets out of his pocket, taking them out, to see if he still had them. Then he put them in his mouth so's he would know he had them, and he got to chewing on them and got them all disgusting. And he thought I'd be mad, and he swallowed half of one and thought it wouldn't be any good, so then he just threw the rest away as we got on the train."

Walter looked out the window so he wouldn't have to face the conductor.

"He looks like a pretty big boy to do a thing like that." The conductor made a hole in a little pink card with his punch and clipped it in their window shade. "I'll chance it; the run is nearly over. Do you know what a spotter is?"

"Oh, sure. If there is one on the train, and he comes and asks me, why I'll tell him the Gospel truth like I told you. I don't want to cause you to get fired for letting us stay on because we couldn't cough up the tickets. I know nowadays it's hard to get a job. Because of talking I might have caused my teacher to lose her job, only I don't know for sure. My Uncle Willard has this job in a box factory, but he might get laid off. . . ."

"Shut up; he's gone."

Maureen looked at the broad blue back going down the aisle. The conductor put his big hand on the back of each red-plush seat as he passed it.

10

Maureen sat up straight and tried to look confident. "I'm sorry I had to make you seem so dumb, Walter."

Walter sniffed. "Made me seem worse than Tisket when she was a pup, chewing up things."

The railroad right-of-way narrowed to a strip between high bluffs and the broad Mississippi River. Great jagged ice flows hung like inverted church steeples from the cliffs. On the other side of the track chunks of mud-stained ice swung in the eddies of the wide river.

First Walter pressed his face against the window, trying to see the top of the cliffs. Then he turned to stare in awe at the width of the Mississippi. Since he was only seven, going on eight, Walter hadn't thought of something that had already occurred to Maureen. If they got to the big city, how would they get home?

Bluffs and river disappeared. Except for the wail of its whistle, Number 6 ignored the towns that were getting bigger and closer together.

"I think we just went through Vicinity," Walter announced.

"Vicinity?"

"We hear it on the radio, weather for St. Louis and Vicinity."

Maureen didn't try to straighten him out. She was too fascinated by the row after row of identical houses. Maybe Uncle Millard and his family lived in one of them. There was no way to tell.

They raced by flat-roofed factories, warehouses, acres of livestock pens. Walter pointed to a building where dark smoke poured from one tall chimney and white smoke poured from another. "What's that place?"

"Factory, I guess."

"I think it's where they make the sky," Walter said.

There was a flow of railroad tracks. Then the train slowed and eased to a stop. The car darkened. They moved backward into the big, dim train shed of Union Station.

Everyone hurried off the train. Maureen and Walter hurried along with them just as if they had some place to go. They passed the Pullman car *Osage*. It seemed to Maureen about a year since she had boarded that car in Dotzero.

"Are we going to Uncle Millard's house?" Walter asked.

Maureen thought of the miles of streets and houses they had seen from the train window. If she had mailed

Mama's letter to Uncle Millard, she might have memorized the address, but Mit had been in charge. Maureen didn't see how anybody found anything in such a mess of streets. "Walter, if we spend all our time looking up kinfolks, we won't see anything of the city. We have to make the most of our chance."

It was two o'clock by the big station clock. Walter complained that he was hungry—he was getting to be a bottomless pit just like Mit—but Maureen was too excited to eat. They strolled around a little open store looking at candy bars, magazines, and all kinds of souvenirs and dit-dats.

A broad stair led to a room bigger than a barn, where the marble floors were as slick as the ice on Lost Creek. Maureen forbad Walter to skate or to act in any way as if he had never been in a big railroad station.

They ventured out into the cold streets. Strings of colored lights on lampposts and storefronts glowed in the murky, smoke-filled air. Maureen didn't know there were so many colored lights in the world. As they strolled about, she looked back frequently to make sure she could see Union Station's high, pointed tower.

The December sun disappeared behind a tall building, and Maureen's feet soon got as cold on the city sidewalks as they did on frozen country roads. As they went back to the station, Walter whined with hunger and pointed to a man selling apples near the wide, arched entrance. They spent a nickel of their wreath money for one. It was a lot for just a single apple. Maureen thought of all the apples from their home orchard in their cellar and wondered how many apples were in a bushel of juicy Winesaps.

"Are we getting only one apple?" Walter asked.

"That's all for now. Let's go back out there by the train shed where we came in."

Maureen gazed up at the big board, which listed train numbers. Sure enough, there it was—Number 41, Walter's bedtime train. She felt as though she had found an old friend. They walked by the numbered gates until they came to the one for train Number 41, south to Cliff Cave, Beaumont. Dotzero wasn't listed; it didn't need to be. Anyone going to Dotzero knew Number 41 stopped there. It left in a half hour, and people were already getting on. A man in a trainman's uniform looked carefully at the ticket of each person passing through the gate.

"Give me the core of that apple, Walter. We can't buy another one. We'll have to use our money for tickets."

It wasn't as if Maureen didn't know how to stand in front of the window and buy a ticket. She'd seen Mama buy a ticket to Beaumont from Pat Ash often enough. But standing at this window was different.

"We're both half fare. How far can we get for fifty-five cents?" Maureen's voice was squeaky with nervousness.

A crabby-looking man pushed back his green eye-shade. "Oh, now, that's a new one. Which way are you going? We sell tickets to stations here. Find out where you're going."

Maureen thought of a station near St. Louis. "Cliff Cave. How much are two half fares to Cliff Cave?"

"Sixty-eight cents." The man put two tickets on the counter and held his finger ready to take the payment.

"What's the station before Cliff Cave?" Maureen asked.

"Look here, I'm selling tickets. This is not the information desk. Find out from your folks where you're going."

They found the big circular information desk, but it was very busy. The clerk looked out over their heads. Maureen watched the big clock; Number 41 would leave in seven minutes. At last, she was noticed. The station north of Cliff Cave was Coke. The information clerk took a long time to look up the half fare in a big book. It was twenty-six cents.

The ticket seller took his time too. Finally Maureen and Walter ran through the crowds, holding their tickets ready for the gateman to punch. The train conductor called all aboard as they climbed on. The brakeman tossed his little landing step up behind them and Number 41 jerked to a start.

They ducked into the first empty seat they came to on the coach.

"We don't know anybody in Coke," Walter reminded Maureen.

"I know, but we had to have tickets to get by that gateman. At first I thought I'd take the blame this time, Walter, and tell the conductor I went into the toilet and accidentally dropped the tickets down the hole the way I did my good gloves. It could happen. That's such a little bitty place in there. But anyhow, we're on and headed home."

Number 41 was a snail compared with Number 6. It eased along through what seemed to be endless city. Once it sighed to a full stop near a roofed, open pavilion. Streetlights illuminated dark forms partly wrapped in newspapers on counters under the roof.

Walter pointed. "What's that?"

"I think it's a place where they sell garden truck and the like in summer." Maureen cupped her hands around her eyes to see better from the lighted car. Suddenly she realized the dark shapes were men, lying on the counters. They had wrapped themselves in newspaper to try to shut out the cold.

"What are those things doing there? What are they?" Walter asked.

"Men with no homes, no place else to go, trying to get a night's sleep. You know, we hear about them on the radio, but I didn't know there were so many. Only a few tramps come to our door in Dotzero."

The train pulled out, and papers blowing in the

wind were all Maureen could see. As she sat back in her seat, she knew she would never forget the homeless men. She didn't know how to help them, but she did know she would always remember them, even if she lived to be older than Grandma.

When the conductor stopped at their seat a little while later, he didn't open his mouth. He just took their tickets, scribbled a number on a little card, and put it in the clip on their window shade.

The train was only a few stops out of St. Louis when the brakeman stuck his head in the car and called, "Coke, Coke station, next stop."

Maureen pulled Walter far down in the seat. "Stay down. It's like I Spy. Stay down."

Number 41 stopped briefly at Coke, then at Cliff Cave, Pevely, and Sulphur Springs. After they left Hemitite, the conductor came through the coach. He glanced at their seat check and stopped. "What's this? You kids got carried by. Why didn't you get off at Coke? Didn't you hear the station called?"

"Carried by? Now how could that be? We were sitting right here all the time, didn't go get a drink or anything," Maureen said. "But it won't matter. We can go on down the line."

"Oh, yes, it does matter, matters a heap. Your tickets are for Coke."

"Coke or some other place, about the same to us." Maureen shrugged. "By rights, we ought to have our

93

railroad pass, but I forgot it. My daddy works for the railroad."

The conductor studied them. "I seem to remember you kids from someplace, but I never saw you on my train before. What's your dad's job?"

The conductor didn't wait for an answer, however. He had to rush and see if anybody got off or on at Victoria.

"We're getting down the line, Walter," Maureen whispered. "Every stop puts us closer to Dotzero."

In no time the conductor was back at their seat, waiting for an answer to his question.

"Our dad works on the railroad extra gang, not steady, but it sure comes in handy. Last summer they painted bridges. There's a bridge right close to our house. It hasn't got any sides, just steel across to hold the ties and the track spiked to the ties. And is it ever scary walking across that thing!" Maureen paused for breath.

"Extra gang is not working for the railroad," the conductor broke in. "That's a separate contract job. So you've got no pass and no ticket either beyond Coke."

"Oh, I know it's not like regular railroading, not like Pat Ash's job. He's agent at Dotzero. I guess you know. He's the only person I know who's got just six letters in his entire name. There's a storekeeper at Dotzero named Sterling Price Stackhouse. Let's see, how many

94

letters is that?" She counted them. She told the conductor everything she could think of concerning Mr. and Mrs. Stackhouse, including the information that they were sometimes nosey. That took them as far as Beaumont.

After Beaumont, the conductor wouldn't listen anymore. He took a pad out of his pocket. "Tell me your father's name and where you live. That's all."

"Cleve McCracken. We live at Dotzero."

"That's the next stop. Get off my train."

No one else got off Number 41. Pat Ash was the only person there. His lantern and the lamp in the depot window gave some light, but even so it seemed awfully dark after the train pulled out.

Footsteps crunched on the track ballast, and a flashlight shone in Maureen's face. "Where in the name of sense have you been?" Mit demanded. "Man alive, are you going to catch it this time!" Remembering his manners, Mit turned and called, "Much obliged, Mr. Ash, for telling me you saw them here this morning."

As they trudged home Mit grumbled but held the flashlight so they could see the road. "You had everybody worried sick, and you are really going to get it."

All at once, Maureen felt so tired she could hardly put one foot in front of the other. "Did Mama finish her book?" she asked wearily.

"Yes, about suppertime. Then she realized you were

off on a wild-goose chase and had taken Walter with you. Mama says she is going to wear you out with a peach-tree switch, soon as she gets hold of you."

"Where's Dad?" Walter sounded tired too.

"Home now after calling and tramping all over our place and the Wiley place, too. He's out of heart, besides. Thinks you might have got killed on the track. I've been looking and asking all over Dotzero. Pat Ash told me he'd seen you at the depot this morning; said maybe you went on the morning train to see Grandma. You're sure going to get it for not asking."

There was no use wasting strength and breath on hardheaded Mit. Maureen decided to save both until she got home. Mit yoo-hooed before he got to the door to let Mama and Dad know they were found. By the kitchen lamp, Maureen saw that Dad looked as weary as she felt. She'd never seen his forehead wrinkles so deep. His eyes looked as if they were full of cinders.

Mama sat on the edge of a kitchen chair. Her mouth made such a straight line that her lips didn't show.

Maureen took a deep breath. "Well, we've been to St. Louis, Walter and I have. Nobody can ever say that Maureen and Walter Lee McCracken lived in the St. Francois Mountains of south Missouri and never even went anywhere or saw anything, didn't go to the city that was real close.

"We got along pretty well, considering we didn't plan it or anything. If we had, then I would have worn my Sunday dress, and Walter could have worn his Sunday shirt."

Mama was still sitting on the edge of her chair. Maureen felt she might suddenly fly at her like a broody hen and flog her.

"You see, last week this woman motioned for me to get on the train when it was stopped at Dotzero and sell her one of our wreaths. She was real pretty and rich, and she had her hair rolled all around her head like a big link of baloney. I got the idea then of selling on the train. This morning Number 6 stopped on the siding at Dotzero, and we got on to sell wreaths, and the first thing I knew we were moving."

Maureen had her second wind now; her weariness was gone. She told of the coach conductor's demand for tickets. First she stood, taking the part of the gruff conductor. Then she sat and meekly squeaked her own lines. Mama relaxed enough to sit back in her chair.

"Wasn't any use spending the whole time in the depot," Maureen continued. "I wanted Walter to see something so he could tell Miss Huckstep about it. He's too bashful at school. So out we went on the street. Oh, Mama, you should have seen all the beautiful Christmas lights in the store windows, on the light posts, all the colors just everywhere.

"We went on and on down this street to a big building spread out bigger than a circus tent. In front of it there were two big bears somebody had carved out of

97

a big rock. But they looked real soft. We touched them, didn't we, Walter, because they looked so soft? But they were stone, all right. Did you ever see them, Mama?"

"No, never did. Never saw the Christmas decorations either. Lots of things I haven't seen, but someday maybe I'll get to take a trip out West. That's where I'd like to go." There was a faraway look in Mama's eyes. Her mouth no longer looked like a line.

"I think you'll go, Mama. You never can tell what's going to happen."

Dad shook his head. "I guess you proved that today. How did you get home?"

"Here's this ticket seller. He's real sour." Maureen put on Mit's cap as a prop. She played all the parts of the scenes at the ticket window, information booth, and train gate. "It was dark when the train left St. Louis, but we saw these men wrapped up in newspapers to keep warm. Wasn't just a few either, but a lot of them. I couldn't count how many. That's where they were trying to sleep. I'll never forget those men."

Walter shivered. "I'm glad I'm home and can sleep in my bed. Was there anything left from supper?"

"That's another thing. If you travel, you ought to take a lunch, a box of fried chicken and some apples," Maureen advised.

"That was quite a show you put on for us, Maureen. Now I guess it's time for after-theater refreshment."

Mama got up and buttered slices of bread for everybody. "Kettle's hot, Cleve. I'll make you a cup of tea."

"I'd be much obliged." He didn't look so worried now.

Mama poured boiling water into the brown teapot. "You and Walter did have quite an unexpected day. So did we. I was ready to give you a good switchin', but now that I've heard your story I get the feeling you won't pull a stunt like that again."

"I won't for sure, Mama. I had hopes of earning enough money to get you another bowl, but we didn't clear a thing. Anyhow, I guess the best part about that bowl was that Uncle Millard gave it to you a long time ago. Nobody can smash that."

"Now that's about enough from you, blatherskite." Mama almost smiled. "You and Walter get up to bed."

Maureen was still awake when Mit clumped upstairs in his high boots. He stopped at her door. "You got off easy this time, but someday, Reen Peen, you're going to get into something you can't talk yourself out of."

Maureen had given Dad the idea of sending a bushel of big Wolf River apples to Uncle Millard's gang for Christmas, and the covered basket went out from the Dotzero depot by railway express with Pat Ash's assurance that it would be delivered in good condition to Uncle Millard's door, wherever that was.

Dad worried about Uncle Millard and his family. When he sat by the heating stove in the evenings, he often said he wished they lived closer so he could haul them a load of wood.

"They know they can come here," Mama reminded him. "That's what I told them in my letter. We could all warm by the same fire."

Maureen hoped Dad wouldn't get one of his black moods. If it came on near Christmas, it might last until Groundhog Day. She stopped daily at the post office to see if there was a Christmas card or any word from Uncle Millard. Though she had forgiven the Stackhouses long ago, she now guarded her talk. Any reports she gave them of school included high praise for Miss Huckstep.

Clearly this year was not one to hint for Christmas presents. So Maureen didn't say one word about gifts, although she and Walter looked at the toy section of the Sears Roebuck catalog until the pages came loose.

At Walter's request, Maureen read aloud the description of his favorite cowboy suit: heavy duck trousers with imitation leather, metal rivet trim, fringed yoke, cotton twill shirt, red banana handkerchief.

"That's bandanna handkerchief," Mit corrected. "Now pipe down. Walter can read that to himself. I've got to learn all these parts by heart for the Christmas program."

Maureen had already memorized her recitation. Miss Huckstep had picked a very long one for her, so it must be that she still didn't know Maureen had blabbed to the Stackhouses. Otherwise, she would have given her just a short baby piece. Or maybe Miss Huckstep knew and had forgiven her for being such a blatherskite.

Even so Maureen wished she had as many parts in the Christmas program as Mit, who got to be the father in every dialogue. There were not many big kids left at school since the sawmill had closed and two more families had moved away.

Mit had all his parts down pat when the time came for their afternoon program, which would close Dotzero School for Christmas vacation. Maureen knew her

101

recitation so well that she had to put on the brakes to keep from saying it too fast. At the end of the program, Miss Huckstep handed out an extra-good treat of a bag of candy and an orange for each pupil.

That night sleet rattled the dormer window by Maureen's bed. When Dad came in the next morning with a pail of Molly's milk, he pronounced the day a real bone snapper.

Mama wanted to go with them to cut the Christmas tree, but she was afraid she'd fall and break a hip. Nothing could have kept Maureen indoors, though. She and Walter slid and fell keeping up with Mit, who cracked the ice with his heavy boots as they searched for the best Christmas tree.

They were deep in the woods when the sun broke through gray clouds. Sunlight on the ice-covered trees was more beautiful than all the colored lights Maureen and Walter had seen in St. Louis.

Mit was so particular. Maureen's feet and fingers were aching with cold by the time he agreed that a full, well-shaped cedar, greener than most, would do. They slid and dragged it home and set it up in the sitting room. As the room warmed from the heating-stove fire Mit had built, the cedar gave off the exciting fragrance that always meant Christmas to Maureen.

By Christmas Eve the tree was trimmed with foil-covered stars, strings of popcorn, and fifteen yards of paper chains made by Maureen and Walter. As she

102

looked at the decorated tree, Maureen wished that Rose could see it.

Christmas morning Mama covered the oilcloth on the kitchen table with their Turkey red cloth, and Maureen put a bowl of cedar twigs and blue berries in the center of the table. Then she and Walter went in the wagon with Dad to meet Grandma, who was coming to Dotzero on Number 3.

They could smell the roast chicken before they opened the kitchen door. There was sage in the dressing, whipped cream on the baked apples, and vanilla sauce on the suet pudding. For a while after dinner Maureen had a very tight feeling around her middle. She didn't want to move.

"I haven't eaten that much for a month of Sundays." Grandma folded her napkin. "It makes me feel guilty, though, when I think about Millard and Cora and all those little ones. Wonder what kind of day they're having. They're always on my mind. In my last letter, I sent them a postal money order for Christmas. It won't help much, but I can't write checks now since my bank failed. Sometimes I feel like my courage has failed too." Grandma fell silent.

Maureen looked at Dad. His smile had faded and a worried look had come into his eyes. It was time to cheer everyone up. Maureen recalled the Christmas program and recited her piece at both slow and fast speeds. She also recited a longer piece she had made up, which she thought was better. Since she had memorized all the dialogue, she took all the parts and did two complete dramas.

At that point Mama mentioned the sunshine outside and told her and Walter to go out for some fresh air.

Walter climbed into the tire swing. "The tree in the house is just a cedar tree with paper stuff hung on it. Why does it feel like a different day, not a regular Wednesday?" he asked.

"Because it's Christmas, and it's Christmas because you feel different, and don't you forget it, Walter."

"Do you think Santa Claus couldn't get across Lost Creek?"

"Now just watch out what you're saying, Walter Lee McCracken. Santa Claus doesn't keep track of everything, writing it all down like a store bill—who wants what and how much and all. Christmas puts trimming on winter, just the way we put trim on that tree. Remember, there may be lots of kids running around in new cowboy suits today, but they don't have real live mules like our Fox and Jack. They don't have a cow like Molly either. Her cream is so thick you can hardly pour it out of a pitcher."

A hen cackled in the chicken house. "That hen just laid an egg," Walter observed. "Uncle Millard doesn't have any chickens."

"Well, of course not. They haven't got a cellar full of apples either. That's what worries Grandma. We'd

104

need a big house for Uncle Millard's family." Maureen jerked the tire swing to a stop. "We can make our play-house bigger. Do you remember the one we built last summer, over there by the gate? It's not too cold to work outside. We'll make it big enough for us and our cousins, too, in case they come."

They brushed dirt and dried grass off the rows of rocks that marked the rooms of their summer play-house. Carrying more rocks from the hillside into the yard was hard work. Then came the easy part of placing them side by side to outline the floor plan of added rooms. Anything aboveground was left to the imagination.

When it was time for Grandma to leave to catch the train back to Beaumont, Mama and Dad came outside with her. As they waited for Mit to bring the wagon around, Mama looked at the playhouse. "My goodness! Have you kids been packing more rocks into the yard?"

"Not just rocks," Maureen explained. "We're build-ing more rooms on the playhouse, in case Uncle Mil-lard's family come. You see, here's the kitchen—"

"I'll see later, Maureen. Come now and tell your grandma good-bye."

Grandma kissed everybody and cried and said she thought it was her last Christmas. She missed Millard and his family and thought something terrible was amiss because they had sent her a cheerful card but hadn't come to see her.

It was enough to put Dad into a black mood, but instead his gray eyes twinkled. "Don't worry, Grandma. We'll build a couple of rooms on the house the way Maureen and Walter have enlarged their playhouse. Millard's family can move here to Dotzero, and we can all celebrate Christmas together next year."

12

It hadn't come out even like a long-division problem that was correct, but still Maureen felt she had made up somewhat for the broken bowl and the slain hens. She considered her demonstration of building on to a house her Christmas present to her entire family, including Uncle Millard.

Dad was really serious about adding two rooms to the McCracken house. The day after Christmas he bargained with the extra-gang boss for scrap lumber left from a job, and he got it dirt cheap. Although they didn't tell Grandma, not wanting to get her hopes too high, Dad and Mit began hauling the lumber while the good weather held. When the McCracken hogs were sold, there should be enough cash for the needed windows, doors, hardware, and roofing.

Maureen and Walter continued to equip their playhouse. They searched the Wiley place for salvageable junk. That's where they were when they learned Grandma was sick.

Maureen was breathless from running when she told Mama. "Walter and I chased right home to tell you about Grandma. We were over by the Wiley house, and *chug-chug* up the lane comes Mrs. Wiley in her Durant. Walter wanted to hide, and I wouldn't let him. Makes it look like we were meddling around there, which we weren't. You know if you act as if you've done—"

"About your grandma, Maureen?"

"Well, I was just as polite as you please, said howdy and all. Then I shut up tight as her pocketbook and listened to her. And do you know what she is thinking about doing? She told me, out and out. She's thinking about tearing down the Wiley house. She said she didn't want tramps and such using it, making fires, maybe setting her woods afire. And she said her husband that's up in the cemetery would rather know it was torn down than that it fell down, and besides, if there was no house, the taxes would be lower."

"You haven't got to the part about your grandma."

"She didn't either for a long time, did she, Walter? All at once, she looked at us as if she just figured out who we were. She stared at me with her bug eyes as if I didn't know *b* from a bull's foot, didn't know how to pound sand in a rathole—"

"Maureen!" Mama was getting impatient.

"—and she says, 'Now you tell your mama this.' And she turns to Walter and says, 'If your sister doesn't get it straight, you tell your mama—'"

"Tell me what?" Mama demanded.

"That Grandma has come down with the flu so bad it might go into pneumonia."

"Bad news and more of it. Your grandma would never pull through pneumonia, frail as she is." Mama bit her lip. "I'll just have to get ready to go to Beaumont and stay with her until she is better."

"Can we go too?" Walter asked.

"You might catch the flu. Then I'd have three down with it. You're better off here at home, where Maureen will be needed anyhow."

"For what, Mama?"

"Oh, for lots of things." Mama looked at the kitchen clock. "Now let me think. Maybe I'll have time to catch Number 32 if I get a move on. It's a good thing I've finished the ironing and have clean things to pack." She gathered up a stack of clothes from her worktable and left the room.

Maureen picked up the slip and blouse Mama had dropped and followed her into the hall. "Do you have to go away now? It's still Christmas."

"Sickness doesn't pick a time. You'll have plenty to do." Mama opened the door to the cold sitting room. "You can take down the Christmas tree for starters. It's dry enough to set the house afire."

Maureen and Walter shook with cold as they unwound paper chains from the tree. "Nope, it's *not* still Christmas," Maureen said. "It's over, and this is an

109

awful job. It's like working to pay for a dead horse."

By the time Mama was ready to leave, the Christmas tree lay in the yard, bits of tinsel blowing from its twigs. When Dad and Mit finally showed up with the wagon, they took Mama and her suitcase to Dotzero. Maureen looked after them sadly.

The first few days Mama was gone, Maureen and Walter kept each other company. Dad and Mit were usually away, either hauling lumber or hunting. All during small-game season, Mit was allowed to use the twenty-gauge shotgun.

The extra Christmas food didn't last long. Mit was always hungry. Two days after Mama left, Maureen watched him and Dad put on their heavy mackinaws, ready to go out into the morning cold.

"Will you be home for dinner?" she asked.

"Yes, about noon. It takes a half day for Fox and Jack to make the trip for lumber. You're chief cook," Dad said, hurrying out the door.

"What shall I cook, Dad?" Maureen called after him.

"How about rabbit? There's half a dozen, skinned and dressed, hung up on the back porch."

Maureen and Walter watched the wagon go down the hill toward Lost Creek. The house was lonesome without Mama, so they stayed outside and got chilled to the bone playing in the tire swing. After they waved at Number 3 going by, Maureen knew the time had come to stir up the fire and fix dinner.

The rabbit carcasses hung in a stiff row from the porch rafter. The dark-red flesh was covered with a bluish membrane. They were frozen hard.

Walter looked up at the skinned rabbits. "I'm glad they didn't hunt for anymore today. We've got enough."

"Yes, and because I'm a girl instead of a boy like you, I'm supposed to know how to cook a froze rabbit."

Maureen sulked for a moment and then determinedly brought a chair from the kitchen, climbed up on it, cut down the biggest rabbit, and took it inside. Even with Mama's sharpest knife, she had trouble severing the joints. But she knew it had to be cut in pieces, or she could never get it in the skillet. She hacked and pulled on the icy meat until she had six pieces—four legs and the body cut in two. Her hands were freezing.

She poked kindling into the coals in the cook stove. Over the crackling fire, the lard in the skillet melted to hot, clear liquid. Maureen stood back and tossed the cold meat into the skillet. The hot fat spattered, and she jumped in pain as it hit her hands.

After a bit she got closer and with a big cooking fork turned a piece over in the skillet. Sure enough, it was brown on one side. Maybe it wouldn't be so hard to cook rabbit after all.

When Mit and Dad returned at noon, stamping their

111

feet from the cold, the pieces were nicely browned on both sides. Maureen felt proud as she placed them on a platter. Besides rabbit, there were some of Dad's drop biscuits left over from breakfast, a crock of skim milk, and a quart of canned blackberries.

Mit took the biggest piece from the platter and eagerly bit into the meat. A shocked look came over his face. He spit out black pellets and held his jaw. "It's full of shot! I almost broke a tooth."

Dad spit out his bite. "You should have dug out the shot with a sharp knife, Maureen. And you didn't get this near done. It's downright raw and cold next to the bone."

Maureen turned a piece on the platter. "It's brown all over, like cooked meat."

"It's awful," Mit howled. "I'm hungry, and it's raw and full of shot."

"It takes a while to tenderize game. I guess you didn't cook it long enough," Dad explained.

"If I had cooked it anymore, it would have burned," Maureen argued.

Mit got up from the table. "Reen Peen can't do anything right. She can't do any work at all, just blab, blab. That's all you can get out of old Reen Peen."

"You should have told me yesterday," Maureen defended herself. "Then I could have brought the rabbit inside and let it thaw out."

Mit snorted. "Lotta good that would have done."

"Would so too, because I tell you froze rabbit is something hard to handle. Walter and I feel bad anyhow to think about how this bunny used to be hopping around, soft and all."

"You eat plenty when Mama's here to cook it."

Maureen took a deep breath. "Well, but then—"

"Stop chewing the rag, both of you. I should have known that cooking rabbit right would be too hard for Maureen." Dad finished his biscuits and blackberries, got up from the table, and turned on the radio. "I want to hear this livestock report. I've been holding off selling our hogs in hopes the price would go up to something more reasonable. Then if Sterling Stackhouse can get his truck across the creek, I'll have him haul those porkers to market."

Dad wanted absolute quiet when he listened to the noon livestock market report broadcast from National Stockyards, Illinois. Mit, not able to complain aloud, made sickening faces and held his stomach as if he were starving.

"When rabbit is all cooked up with onions and brown gravy, it's different," Maureen whispered. "But for all I know that rabbit I cooked was the one Tisket chased every evening last summer in the orchard. It was a regular pet."

"Baloncy bulls are steady," the radio announced.

"And when that rabbit ran by, I'd say to it, 'Rabbit, Rabbit, you're looking mighty thin.'" In a louder voice, Maureen spoke for the rabbit. "'Yes, sir, yes, sir, but I'm cuttin' through the wind.'"

"Turning now to the hog market . . ." the radio reported.

"Simmer down. I want to hear this." Dad moved closer to the radio.

Maureen put her words to a tune, singing out, "'Mr. Rabbit, Mr. Rabbit, your coat's mighty gray.'" She no longer felt bad about the dreadful dinner.

"Light hogs of medium quality, three cents a pound, a record low," the radio crackled.

"'Oh, yes, sir, it's made that way.'" Maureen sang and jumped like a scared rabbit.

"Great heavens above!" Dad yelled. He swung his big hand. Its full force landed on the side of Maureen's head. "Can't you be still? You drive a person to distraction!" Cold air fanned into the kitchen as Dad went out and slammed the door.

Maureen was stunned from the blow and from the fact that Dad had hit her. Even Mit looked a little shocked. Without a word, he followed Dad.

Maureen held back tears as long as she could. Then she huddled on the floor in front of Peloponnesus and cried. Without looking up, she reached for a towel from the kitchen rack. As she wiped her eyes she felt the roughness of its lace trim. She had grabbed her Sansoucie keepsake towel, which was displayed on the rack for show. Maureen stared at the pattern of coarse pink lace and thought of her friends at Cold Spring.

She replaced the towel on the rack and saw Walter sitting on the linoleum in a warm patch of sunlight, which shone from the south window. On such an afternoon, the Sansoucies would be out playing for sure.

"Can you hear all right?" Walter asked.

"Yeah, I can hear, but he should not have hit me like that when Mama is gone and it's lonesome." Maureen stared at Peloponnesus. After much nodding, she turned again to Walter. "Peloponnesus says we can't do anything about the hog market, but we can do something for ourselves. He says there is no use staying here the rest of the day in this kitchen full of dirty dishes. Walter, without asking, we're going to hightail it over to the Sansoucies."

"Not me!"

"I'd catch it worse if I let you stay by yourself. I'll tell Dad I made you go with me, which is Gospel truth. I am."

The old wagon road, not good enough for cars, was the shortest way over the two hills and through the one hollow to the Sansoucies. Maureen walked fast. Walter and Tisket trotted along behind her. They passed the Cold Spring School, which had faded paper Santas pasted in the windows.

It seemed that in no time they could hear the Sansoucies playing in the distance. That sound was better than music to Maureen. A big game of Prison Base came to a halt so that both sides could give them a welcome, which made Maureen feel very important.

Rose grasped Maureen's hands. "I knew you'd come again the way you promised."

"No school, so we thought we might as well visit. Only we can't stay very long because it gets dark so early now. And we're walking this time," Maureen said.

While new sides were being chosen, Maureen told Rose they had walked by the school. "Did you make one of the Santas in the window?" she asked.

Rose marked the thawed ground with the toe of her worn shoe. "We haven't gone yet."

"You better start, Rose, right after vacation. If you don't, you might not get promoted."

"I know, and then I'd be too big for my class and not want to go to school anymore. I want to go now, but Lorene Stackhouse is the teacher, and my folks think she might have it in for us. Then, too, we don't have decent clothes."

When the children went into the house later to warm themselves by the heating stove, Maureen had the entire Sansoucie family as an audience for her description of her trip to St. Louis. They listened as if she were the "March of Time" radio broadcast.

At the end of the story, Mrs. Sansoucie took up her

116

crocheting. "I don't see how you could take the risk of getting on that big train. I'd be scared of a train wreck."

"How about the conductor? He gets on it everyday, just about every day of his life," Maureen pointed out. "But he's not so brave. He might be afraid to live out here on this farm the way you do."

"How did you know what to do in that big depot with all them trains?" Mr. Sansoucie wanted to know. "I wouldn't know what to do in a place like that."

"Oh, I read the list of Missouri Pacific trains and found Number 41. Then I read the signs on the gates. And, of course, I could read all the other signs in the station and out on the street, too. I could have read the thick book that gave the ticket costs, but they wouldn't let me see it. It's mighty handy to be able to read."

"Yes, I guess it is," Mrs. Sansoucie agreed. Maureen watched her pull one loop of thread through another. That's all there was to crocheting, but she was making a pretty pattern.

Walter nudged Maureen and pointed to the west window.

Maureen nodded. "We've got to get home. It'll soon be sundown."

Mr. Sansoucie studied the evening sky for a few minutes. "Yes, and a cold night coming. I'm proud you came to see us. I wish we still lived neighbors. We've had to move so much that our kids are getting

117

behind in their books, but they're starting at Cold Spring next week. You can tell Alma Huckstep that."

When Maureen and Walter started home, Rose went with them as far as Cold Spring School, carrying one of her little sisters. She looked at the one-room white building and then smiled shyly at Maureen. "I'd be braver starting here if I had you to talk for us, Maureen." Her smile widened. "But we're coming, even if our clothes don't look like a Sears order. We're coming. You heard my dad say so."

Rose stood on the road waving until she was little more than a speck on the horizon. After they had turned around for the last time, Maureen and Walter ran down the first hill. As they started up another, Maureen stopped and felt her eyetooth.

"Does your jaw still hurt?" Walter asked.

"No, but I think I might have got a tooth knocked loose."

"Dad didn't have hardly any dinner," Walter reminded her.

"You think I don't know anything? And he heard that hog market report, too, even if it wasn't still enough to hear a pin drop. He was counting on cash from our hogs to get stuff we need to finish the rooms. Now there won't be enough. So I got this awful slap."

"We ran away, and he'll be extra hungry for supper." Walter's eyes were as sad and serious as a hound's.

"He can't be as mad as he was, Walter. I'm not as mad at him either."

When they came to the brow of the last hill, Walter pointed down to Fox and Jack, standing in the barn lot. "They're back before us."

Maureen listened at the back door. "I hear Dad whistling," she whispered. Then she flung open the door. "We're back, and I think we did some good, too. Miss Huckstep thinks it's a downright shame that the Sansoucies don't go to school. So we went over there because I didn't want to be miserable a whole afternoon of Christmas vacation, and that's what I was, Mama gone and all, so we went to visit the Sansoucies. Maybe I talked them into going to school. Their dad said they would go."

Maureen watched Dad stir batter in a crock. "What are you making? Want me to do that? I'll do whatever you say."

"I'm making us some flapjacks for supper. A couple of eggs would make them rise right off the griddle. Run out to the hen house and gather the eggs before they freeze. Then we'll have to get all these dishes washed after supper. I saw Mrs. Wiley on the road. She tells me Grandma is much better. Mama's coming home tomorrow morning."

"Oh, I'm glad to hear that."

"So am I," Walter agreed.

119

"I was glad to hear it myself," Dad said. "Kind of saved the day. Sitting in the wagon, watching the mules' ears flop, I had time to think. We'll manage somehow, cash or no cash. We've always managed."

Maureen picked up the round-bottomed egg basket and motioned Walter to follow her. Outside she swung the empty basket over her head. Although Dad had not said so, Maureen thought he was sorry he had slammed her on the side of the head. He had kept himself out of a black mood even though his only girl blabbed during the livestock report and couldn't cook rabbit.

"Walter, I wanted you to come along because we might find an angel's egg. Sometimes about sunset, if there's a pink one like tonight, you might find one right in a hen's nest. Look for one. It'll be real big."

13

That very night Walter woke everyone up crying because of a terrible pain in his stomach. Mit said that came from eating raw rabbit and being dragged up hill and down dale by Maureen. Dad was ready to go to the Stackhouses' store and call Dr. Varney in Beaumont. Then, just at daybreak, Walter fell asleep. He was still sleeping peacefully when Mama came home from Grandma's. Maureen imitated Walter's cries, but she was not sure she had convinced Mama of how sick Walter had been.

He got better, but he didn't stay better. Every week or so he would get a gut pain that just about bent him double. Then it would go away, and Walter soon would be out running on hard, frozen ground and skating on the ice of Lost Creek.

One day the wind blew warm instead of chill, and rain fell. Everything was soft and wet. The road to Dotzero was muddy as a hog wallow. Ice broke loose, and water rose in Lost Creek. Mit, Maureen, and Wal-

121

ter just made it across their footbridge after school. The February thaw had come.

Walter's cries woke the family again that night. Mama felt his forehead and said that he was burning up with fever. The pain had never been so bad.

The kitchen clock struck five when Dad decided to start for the store to call Dr. Varney. As Maureen and Mama followed him downstairs to the kitchen, Maureen remembered that Mrs. Stackhouse had said it would be hard for them to get a doctor. "Will Dr. Varney come?" she asked anxiously.

"He'll come if I can get hold of him. He knows he'll get paid sooner or later. McCrackens are good pay," Dad said. "He won't have a twenty-mile round trip for nothing."

Mama walked the floor. "It rained all night, and it's still raining. The Dotzero road is a loblolly of mud. Even if he slid over the road, Dr. Varney couldn't cross Lost Creek in that new, low car of his."

Dad lighted the barn lantern. "Fox and Jack can ford it. After I telephone, I'll wait at Dotzero and bring Dr. Varney here in the wagon. We'll get him here to see Walter."

Mama looked out the kitchen window. "It's still pitch dark, Cleve. I dread for you to go into the ford."

"It'll soon be dawn, Lillian, and I know the current. You get back upstairs to Walter."

Mama sponged Walter's face and chest with cold

water to try to bring the fever down. Then Walter asked Mit to play the French harp to make the waiting easier.

Maureen felt useless. She had to do something, so she went downstairs and put on her coat, then found her rubbers and Mama's umbrella. Tisket followed her to the creek ford where the footbridge was underwater. They waited in the rain for the wagon to return.

Tisket heard it first and barked. When the flopping ears of the mules came in view, Maureen thought they were a beautiful sight. Through them she could see two big, dark figures hunched against the rain on the wagon seat. Dad watched the water surging around the wheels as Fox and Jack forded the creek. He didn't notice Maureen. By the time she ran up her shortcut path, Dr. Varney was already in the house. In his big, dripping slicker, he seemed to fill the whole kitchen. Maureen thought that being someone like Dr. Varney whom folks were always glad to see must be wonderful. She wished she could be a person like him.

Dr. Varney pushed different places on Walter's stomach. When he pressed one spot, Walter yelled with pain.

Dr. Varney sat down beside the bed. "You say he's had these attacks before? How many?"

"First one was right after Christmas." Maureen started to count on her fingers. "And then. . . ."

Mama touched her shoulder. "Be quiet, Maureen."

123

"But I remember. The next one was on the way home from school. . . ."

"Shut up," Mit hissed.

"I'd say about five, Doctor, but this is the worst," Mama said. "He's been in pain since about midnight."

Dr. Varney led the way into the hallway. "I believe he has appendicitis. We've got to get him to the hospital at once. If surgery is postponed, the appendix will rupture. That is very dangerous."

Dad's face looked bleak and strained. "You saw that creek ford. The ambulance couldn't get here. We'll have to take him out by wagon as far as Dotzero."

Dr. Varney shook his head. "Slick, rutty road in a slow wagon is not good. Any jarring is dangerous. You folks are so cut off here without a bridge. We've got to get that boy to St. Louis and into a hospital." He spoke very quietly.

"I know something we could do," Maureen announced.

"Pipe down," Mit whispered. "Dangerous! You heard what the doctor said. Do you want Walter to know how sick he is?"

"Number 6, that fast train Walter and I rode to St. Louis, will go right by our house." No one seemed to hear Maureen or notice when she slipped downstairs. As she put on her soggy coat, she spoke to the cellar door. "Peloponnesus, you know how bad Walter is, and you know I've got to help him, so wish me luck."

124

At the railroad bridge, Maureen checked the block signal to be sure no train was coming. She'd never crossed the trestle alone. Now she had to get over it by herself in the pouring rain.

She gritted her teeth and stepped onto the bridge. Tisket whined and followed. "Go back, Tisket. I'll do well to take care of myself."

She was over in no time. It was only a mile and a half to Dotzero, and she was a fast runner. As she ran, she repeated: *declarative, imperative, exclamatory, interrogative.* She ran until her side hurt and her throat was dry.

Maureen could see Pat Ash in the depot bay window, which faced the track. She ran right through the waiting room into the agent's office. "Mr. Ash," she panted. "You have to stop Number 6 at the trestle by our house. Walter has appendicitis. Dr. Varney says we have to get him to the hospital in St. Louis. Stop the train, and we'll put Walter in the express car the way you do a veal calf. It's the fastest way to get him there."

"Hold on, Maureen. I can't just up and stop a fast train. Do you think I'm president of the railroad, some bigwig or official? I'm just the agent here at Dotzero."

"You can *try*, Mr. Ash," Maureen pleaded. "We're good pay for shipping Walter. If you don't even try, you'll be sorry you didn't. Number 6 won't jolt him like a mule wagon would."

Telegraph instruments rattled on Pat Ash's table.

125

There was a telephone by his desk, too, but it wasn't like the one at the store. The agent drew it out on its adjustable rack. Curved wires over his head held the receiver to his ear, leaving his hands free to write down the train dispatcher's orders.

"Dispatcher. Dotzero. I've got a girl here, wants Number 6 stopped at Milepost 72, Bridge 43. Yes, that's what I told her. Oh, I'd say about ten or eleven years old."

Pat Ash flinched and covered the mouthpiece with his hand. "He's cussin' a blue streak. I knew he would. Says he doesn't know what I'm talking about."

"I'll tell him." Maureen took the receiver off Pat Ash's head and put it on her own damp hair. She'd never talked on any kind of telephone before, let alone one with a mad train dispatcher on the other end. "Mr. Dispatcher, this is Maureen McCracken. My brother Walter, he's eight now, has got this appendicitis about to bust. Lost Creek is way up so the ambulance can't get across to our house, and the wagon is too rough on the mud road. We might not get Walter out in time. But if you stop Number 6, Walter could go right to St. Louis and to the hospital. We'd get him on real fast so it wouldn't mess up your railroading."

There was some awful cussing, then Maureen heard very clearly, "Where's Ash?"

Maureen handed him the receiver. He wrote, repeated, and spelled out the numbers of a train order. "Train number 6, s-i-x, stop Bridge 43, f-o-u-r t-h-r-e-e, Milepost 72, s-e-v-e-n t-w-o, pick up express, emergency patient for St. Louis isolated by high water, depart 11:09, e-l-e-v-e-n n-i-n-e."

Pat Ash looked at his pocket watch. "Here's a copy of the train order the dispatcher's giving Number 6 at Arcadia. You've got very little time to run back and tell your folks to have Walter on the right-of-way. Make sure you check the block signal at the trestle."

Maureen ran back faster than she'd come. She had to get across the trestle before Number 6 came into the block. She was almost at the bridge when she saw the wagon coming slowly down the rainswept hill. She yelled and waved her arms. They saw her; Mama waved back. Maureen called out her message, but she knew she couldn't be heard for the roar of Lost Creek.

Mit hopped off the wagon and was soon scrambling up the railroad embankment. He came toward her across the trestle. "What are you trying to do, Maureen, yelling like that? You want to scare Fox and Jack into a runaway? Get over this bridge before Number 6 comes into the block."

Maureen panted for breath and pointed to the milepost on the opposite side of the bridge. "It's going to stop for Walter, over there." She handed Mit the crumpled copy of the train order.

127

He read it, then without another word to her he turned back and bounded across the trestle ties, two at a time.

Maureen tried to follow him, but suddenly the thought of being high over swirling water made her so dizzy that she couldn't set foot on the bridge.

Number 6 came into the block. From the safety of the right-of-way, Maureen saw that Mit had reached the wagon. She watched Dad and Dr. Varney hold the ends of a blanket so that it formed a stretcher and carry Walter up to the track as carefully as if he were a setting of angel's eggs.

Number 6 whistled for a crossing. It seemed to be coming as fast as ever. No, there was a difference. It was easing to a full stop. Hands reached out of the express car to take hold of Walter's blanket. Dad climbed up into the car. Maureen had a glimpse of the top of Walter's head; then the train, Walter, and Dad were gone.

Mit drove the mules across the ford and stopped at the foot of the embankment below Maureen. She wished he would come up and carry her down piggyback, but she knew that was out of the question.

Somehow she got down the bank, and Mama helped her into the wagon. "Maureen! How did you do that? A big, fast train! Did you get Pat Ash to stop it?"

"I guess so, but now I feel powerful weak."

"Well, no wonder!"

128

"When I had to cross the bridge to help Walter, I didn't have trouble, but just now I couldn't get back across it to save me."

Mama hugged Maureen, wet as she was. "It's like the sermon text on Sunday. 'Perfect love drives out fear.' "

Maureen began to cry. "I do love Walter, even when I tell him things I make up. I didn't even get to tell him good-bye."

"You did a very remarkable thing for your brother, Miss Maureen," Dr. Varney said. "Don't worry now. You folks get me back to my car at Dotzero. I'll call the hospital from the store and have an ambulance meet the train. All of you get in the dry. I don't want to be called back across Lost Creek to treat pneumonia."

"We'll get across before the water gets higher," Mama said, excited with relief. "This is a young team and fractious at times, but we'll make it."

14

Walter's operation was just in time. If Maureen hadn't stopped the fast train, he never would have made it. Everyone agreed on that, so Maureen didn't have to say so herself. Whenever she was praised, she warmed with pride and satisfaction.

As jam-packed as it was, Dad had stayed at Uncle Millard's until Walter was ready to come home from the hospital. Besides losing his plump apple cheeks and getting a scar on his stomach, Walter was just the same. He wasn't a bit stuck up because he'd had an operation.

At school Mit didn't grumble about the number of times Maureen told of stopping Number 6. Miss Huckstep let her repeat the story frequently, as long as she said blankety-blank-blank for the train dispatcher's swearing. Walter was her best audience. His cheeks were thinner, but he still smiled his eyes shut when Maureen described her run in the rain. She included great leaps to show him how she crossed the trestle.

They had Walter home, and now Dad wanted to bring Uncle Millard's family to the farm, too. He had seen with his own eyes how bone-hard things were for them. The box factory had shut down. Aunt Cora got a day's work now and then trimming hats in a factory.

Maureen made herself keep still as Mama and Dad talked of Uncle Millard's family. "We could get by now, especially with summer coming. Some of the kids could sleep on the floor," Mama said.

Dad nodded. "So I told him, but he won't bring his gang, bag and baggage, and pile in on top of us. You know Millard is stubborn as a Missouri mule, stubborn as Fox and Jack put together. He's proud, too. Years back he left the farm and Dotzero and said no more cornbread living for him. He'd be ashamed as a whipped dog to come back empty-handed now."

"When we're ready to frame up the rooms, he could help," Mama suggested.

"It'll be many a day before we get to that. Hospital bill will take the cash, farming and extra-gang work will take the time." A gloomy look came over Dad's face.

"Cleve, it's spring, Walter was spared to us. I'm going to put in extra garden. I believe Millard's gang will be here to eat it by the middle of the summer."

Maureen liked to imagine their yard and hillside noisy with many cousins, playing games she directed.

131

The Sansoucies could come and stay all day. Summer would soon arrive; there were already lots of signs of spring.

A patch of waxy, white flowers bloomed at the edge of the cindery railroad embankment. On the way home from school the next day, Maureen stopped to pick some.

"You'd better get on home and help Mama," Mit ordered.

"I'm just getting a couple of bloodroot flowers to give Walter some freckles." Reddish fluid oozed from the flower stems, and Maureen dotted some on Walter's nose. "He still looks kind of peaked."

"Someday Walter won't stand still for you, Maureen." Mit was forever predicting a day when a lot of awful things would happen. Maureen thought he was grouchy because he hadn't been able to miss a single day of school to help Dad plant potatoes. He had to study for his eighth-grade examination. Then he'd be through. Someday she would miss Mit at school, but Maureen wasn't going to tell him and make him a worse swellhead than ever.

Right now she was glad it was spring. Creek willows were leafing out the color of lettuce. Beside the shortcut path, a little shad tree had burst into bloom, like popcorn in a hot skillet. With white patches flashing, a mockingbird flew up to the peak of the dormer window and began imitating all the birds of the St. Francois Mountains.

"Now, Walter, you take that mockingbird. Suppose you never heard one and I told you there was a bird with a little bitty brain and that it could sing like any other bird, even *meow* like a cat. You'd say it was a big fib, couldn't be. But you hear it, so you know it's true."

Walter, tuckered out, just nodded and trudged on.

When they reached home, Maureen wandered off alone across the pasture toward the Wiley house. Spring beauties, bluets, and Johnny-jump-ups misted the short spring grass. She remembered the wild pansies and raced over the flowery carpet to the clay bank where they had bloomed the year before. There they were, blooming away. Maureen picked some of the flowers, which looked like extra-large lavender violets. She especially liked the ones with two velvety, dark-purple upper petals.

At home she showed them to Mama. "Look at these. It's just the way you said. These wild pansies are right where they were last year, same as ever."

"Spring and the sun haven't failed us yet." Mama pointed to tomato seedlings growing in an old dishpan on her worktable. They were all slanting toward the south window. "I sure liked working outside all day. I got the ground ready to put in extra garden for Millard and the family."

"When school is out, I'll help," Maureen promised. "Garden dirt isn't like house dirt, is it?"

"Not one bit." Mama was sure of that.

At school Miss Huckstep made them work even though they were on the last chapters of their textbooks. She didn't act like a teacher who wasn't returning. Maybe she still didn't know that Maureen had spilled the beans to the Stackhouses. If her big mouth had caused Miss Huckstep to lose her job, Maureen didn't know how she would ever make it up to her.

There was always a basket dinner on the last day of school. Usually there was a program given by the graduating eighth grade, too. But this year only a dinner was planned for the closing day in April. Two more families had moved away, which left Mit the only one finishing eighth grade. Miss Huckstep just handed him his diploma and made jokes about his being the best in his class.

It was warm enough to eat outdoors, so long boards were set on carpenter's horses to make a table. Miss Huckstep helped Mama set out baked beans, potato salad, and the cured ham she'd brought. "Alma, I want you to know we think you did a first-class job your first year of teaching, and, regardless of anything, we hope you get your school back." Mama lowered her voice. "I see Sterling P. Stackhouse, our new school director, is taking an interest. He's right here ready to tie into the eats. What does he say about next term?"

"I can't tell what's going on." Maureen could hardly hear Miss Huckstep. "I wrote out my application and gave it to him a month ago. Every day I go into the store to give him an opportunity to tell me if I'm hired for next year. He just hems and haws something about a confused situation. So it leaves me uncertain. Sometimes I think he's waiting to see if his niece, Lorene, gets her school back at Cold Spring. If not, he'll get her in here."

Miss Huckstep unwrapped a stack of paper plates. "Of course, he may have another reason not to hire me. Yesterday I got a letter at the post office addressed to Miss Alma Huckstep. Mrs. Stackhouse held on to it as if it belonged to her and asked me twice if that name was correct. It was her way of telling me she knows I'm married to Jim Nolan. She's been trying to get it out of him for a long time. They found it out somehow. I guess you know it too, Mrs. McCracken."

Maureen's throat felt dry, and she swallowed hard. Miss Huckstep knew she talked a lot in school. Now she'd find out Maureen had talked out of school, too.

Mama poured lemonade. "It was bound to come out, Alma, in a little place like Dotzero. But there's no law against a married woman teaching, and we're for you."

Mama could have put the blame right on Maureen, but she smoothed things over. Still, it might be the last day Miss Huckstep would be a teacher. School wouldn't be the same without her. Maureen watched Mit fill his plate. He wouldn't be at Dotzero School next year

135

either. She imagined a dark, rainy fall morning when she would have to get herself, Walter, and all of Uncle Millard's kids across the trestle without Mit.

If it had not been the last day of school, Maureen would have felt terrible. As it was, she didn't eat nearly as much as she should have, given an opportunity like the basket dinner.

15

Nobody expected Grandma to be ailing in summer after the flu and pneumonia season was over, but that's what Mama reported when she came home from Beaumont one day.

"I'll just have to go back prepared to stay a few days," Mama explained, as Maureen watched her pack a suitcase for herself and Walter. "Grandma is in a slump. Walter and I won't be gone long, just for a while to check up on your grandma. At her age, you can't tell. She might get weak, fall, and break a hip." Mama away was lonesome enough; now she was taking Walter. Since he'd almost died of appendicitis, Mama couldn't stand to have him out of her sight.

"Now, Mit, Dad will need your help. Maureen, do your best while we're gone."

"Even if Maureen does her best, we'll likely all starve," Mit predicted gloomily. "Time for a meal, Maureen's wandering around talking to herself or else

137

to the cellar door. I guess it doesn't matter, though, because she can't cook anyhow. When you're gone, Mama, Dad and I come in hungry from working hard and there's nothing on the table but the dirty dishes from the last meal we had to cook for ourselves."

"Oh, now, Mit, Maureen might surprise you," Mama said.

Maureen's eyes opened wide. Mama had hopes for her. Well, she'd surprise Mit and Dad with meals on time, and what's more she'd have a surprise for Mama, too, when she came home.

Much as Mama liked to work outside, she spent many hot summer days in the kitchen, canning fruits and vegetables. When other women told of how many quarts they had canned, Mama always had the most.

In her absence, Maureen decided to take over the canning job. When Mama returned, she would go down in the dim cellar and see jars of golden fruit filling a whole shelf. She'd be just dumbbellfounded at how hardworking and responsible Maureen had become.

Maureen knew just where to start. She'd seen early seedling peaches falling from a tree by the pigpen into the rank weeds below. She would can every last one of them.

After Mama and Walter had left to catch the train to Beaumont, Maureen was glad to have something to do so she wouldn't miss them so much. She tramped down the weeds and picked a half bushel of very small peaches. Some of them looked wormy and rotten on one side, but no matter. She could cut out the blemishes and they'd can up fine.

Tired and hot after that job, Maureen went into the cool sitting room and lay down on the floor. She was just dozing off when she began to itch. No wonder! Little black fleas jumped up from the rag carpet to gnaw on her. That was Walter's doing. If he wasn't watched every minute, he'd let Tisket into the sitting room to keep him company while he looked at pictures and tried to read Hurlbut's *Story of the Bible.*

Mama had left food to heat up for supper. That was about all Maureen could manage, what with scratching all her fleabites. At bedtime, she shook out her night-gown, but there were fleas in her bed all the same. She itched and scratched all night long.

When Maureen looked in the mirror in the morning, she knew she had more than fleas. The little blisters on her face and hands were from poison ivy. She had not noticed the three-leafed vine among the weeds when she'd picked up the peaches. Worse yet, she had spread the rash to all the fleabites she had scratched.

Well, that was the kind of thing you had to put up with when you kept house full-time, and the peaches still had to be canned. She'd finish the job after she put flea powder on the carpet.

139

It was a miserable morning. The sting of sweat made Maureen's irritated skin itch terribly. When she scratched, the blisters broke into red, swollen blotches.

The peaches were miserable too. By the time she peeled them and cut out the rot and the worms, there was hardly anything left. She was crying when Dad and Mit came in for noon dinner.

"I haven't got it ready yet," she wailed. "I didn't want these peaches to go to waste after I picked them up to can. Some I just have to throw away. I've got more to throw out than I have to kee-e-e-p," Maureen said, sobbing.

Dad examined her swollen hands and face. "You don't look in very good shape, Maureen. You've got an awful dose of poison ivy."

"I know. I got it yesterday, picking up these peaches. I didn't see it out there; the weeds were so thick and big. I wanted to have a lot of peaches canned up so Mama would be proud of all the work I'd done. But it was hot and then I got into a mess of fleas that must've just hatched out of the sitting room car-r-r-pet."

"That's what I call a peck of trouble." Dad looked at the basket of peaches and at the bucket of peelings, swarming with gnats. "But that's no peck of good peaches."

"I just have to go ahead and can some," Maureen insisted.

Dad looked at her eyelids. "Your eyes are about swollen shut with poison and cryin'. You might can us some little white worms if you can't see."

"I've got to show Mama." Maureen jerked with sobs.

"Now I'll show you what we're going to do with all this." Dad emptied the sloppy peelings on top of the little hard peaches. Through the narrowing slits of her swollen eyelids, Maureen watched him stride across the yard and barn lot and dump the whole mess into the pigpen.

What a wonderful thing to do! It made Maureen feel much better. She didn't even mind when Mit grumbled that now they had no peaches and no dinner either.

Dad mixed powdered sugar-of-lead and water in a little jar. He took a clean cloth from the rag bag and handed it to her. "Use this instead of your fingernails. Remember, it's poison, but I know I can trust you. Sop some on when you get to itching. I think the coolest place for you to be is out on the back porch. Stay out of the sitting room for a while."

It was cooler on the porch. The medicine made her more comfortable, but Maureen was disappointed that she hadn't reached her goal of the day. There would be no glowing shelf of canned peaches to show Mama. Mit was right. He and Dad would have to cook their own supper.

The salty tears that rolled down her cheeks hurt her irritated skin. She must stop crying. After all, Dad had trusted her with a jar of poison. That showed she was dependable. Maureen thought of her father's long strides across the yard and barn lot to heave those ornery peaches over the fence to the pigs. She would have smiled to herself if her face hadn't been so swollen.

16

The poison-ivy rash was drying up by the time Mama and Walter returned from Beaumont. Mama seemed to think that Maureen had gone out on purpose as soon as her back was turned and got herself plastered with itchy blisters. Maybe Mama didn't half listen to Maureen's explanation because she was still worried about Grandma, who had a bad case of being all out of heart. Mama considered that worse than tonsillitis or croup.

"I think it's because she'll be seventy her next birthday," Mama explained. "Three score and ten, that's a life-span according to Scripture. She kept quoting that text, saying it was the Gospel truth.

"She's far from well," Mama continued, "but I just had to get home, take care of our big gardens, do the canning, cook for the men. It's lucky school is out. That's where you come in, Maureen."

"What?"

"We've got a special job for you." Mama moved over to make room for Maureen beside her on the porch

143

bench. "Dr. Varney says Grandma shouldn't be alone just now. We want you to stay with her in Beaumont."

"Beaumont! I don't know any kids at all in Beaumont. Here I've got Walter. I wouldn't have anybody to play with in Beaumont."

Mama brushed Maureen's hair back from her eyes. "There won't be much time for play."

"But that's what I'm figuring on doing this summer. There are lots of things I want to show Walter. We're looking for something special, besides. He can't swim, so I'm going to teach him at least to dog-paddle this summer."

"We need you in Beaumont, Maureen."

"Can I go barefoot there?"

"No, best not in town, not an O'Neil."

"Can Walter go with me?"

"With my only girl away working, I'll need somebody here for company." Mama looked around the yard as if trying to see where Walter was. "He's had that operation. I need to keep tabs on him."

Maureen gazed at the cool woods above the sunny fields, then at the big barn backed by a fringe of orchard trees. "I want to stay at our farm, Mama, where I hear the bobwhite quails first thing in the morning and the whippoorwills last thing at night. Beaumont is all shoes and sidewalks."

"It's a lot to put on a girl your age, I know that. I like to be out in the cool parts of the summer days my-

144

self." Mama walked to the end of the porch for a better view of her gardens. "I wouldn't ask you to go if it wasn't important, Maureen. You have the spunk to be away from home to help. You got yourself in a pickle boarding the train, but you got yourself and Walter home. You talked to the dispatcher and stopped a big train for Walter. We're used to depending on you. You'd be staying with your own grandma."

Maureen fidgeted for a moment, then slid off the bench. "All right. I'll find Walter and tell him summer is not going to be the way we thought."

Walter was in the pasture, dragging a heavy hoe. "Dad gave me this pay job. I get a penny for every twenty-five thistles I cut down." Walter beamed. "I've already got one penny, and I'm starting on another."

"Walter, I hate to tell you this," Maureen said with a serious face, "but I have to leave home. I've got a sort of no-pay job in Beaumont staying with Grandma. It takes somebody dependable, so I ought to be glad I've got a chance at it. I won't have any time to play this summer vacation."

As Walter stared at her, Maureen left him and watched for her chance to slip into the kitchen and sit before the cellar door. "I won't be here again for I don't know when, Peloponnesus. For some reason I feel uneasy about staying with my own grandma. She's nice to me, brought me two barrettes for Christmas, and always sticks up for me because I'm an O'Neil and all. Still, it

145

will be just me and Grandma there in Beaumont. I won't have you or Walter to talk to. And then in no time, summer will be over and I won't have had any time to play or for Rose to come stay all night, or to learn if Miss Huckstep will be teacher, or to find an angel's egg. . . ." Maureen stopped, for someone was coming.

That was the last chance she had to talk to Peloponnesus. Mama kept her busy ironing all the dresses she was to take to Grandma's.

The day she left, Mama and Walter went along on Number 40, the early-morning train. They planned to stay in Beaumont all day and make sure Maureen was settled in at Grandma's. Mama cooked dinner, and the day was a nice one. But the scared, uneasy feeling almost overwhelmed Maureen when Mama and Walter walked down the street toward the Beaumont depot and she was left alone with Grandma.

Everything about Grandma's house was old. It smelled old—old dried-up varnish on old wood, old air in the rooms, old houseplants outgrowing their old pots and shutting out the light from the old windows.

Maureen soon discovered that Grandma liked to stay huddled up inside, but she escaped to the old front-porch swing whenever she could. As she pushed herself back and forth, she thought of Walter. Like as not, he would stop looking for an angel's egg. He would hoe down thistles and come to believe that the most wonderful thing in the world was a jar of copper pennies. Tisket would get ticks in her ears, and nobody would pull them out. Dad might slip into a black mood if she weren't there to prevent it. Maureen sorely felt she was more needed at home.

When she went inside and raised a window shade in the sitting room, Grandma pulled it down again so the sun wouldn't fade the carpet. Even in the afternoons, Grandma didn't wear any of her nice flowered dresses. Washing would fade them, too. Instead, she wore something she called a "wrapper." Maureen agreed that it was the color of brown wrapping paper.

Meals were awful. Grandma said nothing tasted good. There was no use cooking; she couldn't choke anything down. At first Maureen didn't feel like eating much either, but she soon grew hungry.

Eggs, biscuits, milk, and oatmeal—that's what a person was supposed to have for breakfast. Yet Grandma was sopping a store doughnut in coffee and then complaining about gas on her stomach. When Maureen was sent to the Kroger store, she bought oatmeal instead of the doughnuts Grandma had ordered. The next morning she followed the directions on the box and served Grandma a dish of hot oatmeal.

"Where are my doughnuts?"

"We're going to have oatmeal for a change. Now I'll tell you how I know about oatmeal, all the vitamins, minerals, and all that. I learned it listening to the eighth

147

grade. They have health. We don't have health in fifth. Now if you take minerals. . . ."

"Minerals!" Grandma snorted. "I'm not used to eating rocks and such."

She did take a couple of spoonfuls, however. Then she put her spoon down.

Maureen continued to talk. "Grandma, did you know Mit made the highest grade on the eighth-grade examination? Miss Huckstep said it was real good. Do you know Miss Huckstep?"

"One of Joe Huckstep's girls, I think. There was a raft of those Hucksteps. Her mother was a . . . never mind, I'll think of it directly. Now if you talk to me, speak up."

Maureen spoke louder. "The one I know, her name is Alma. She's right smack in the middle of her family. She told us that. There are four older than her and four younger. Now first there's Nathan. His nickname is Tate. He got that because the little kids couldn't say Nathan."

Grandma sighed, picked up her spoon, and took another bite of oatmeal. By the time Maureen had listed all the names, nicknames, and a few characteristics of each Huckstep, Grandma had finished her oatmeal.

Since they hadn't had eggs for breakfast, Maureen decided to fry some for noon dinner. Grandma watched her tap the egg on the edge of the stove to break it. Maureen had seen Mama do that many times. Then she stood back from the skillet, which held melted lard, and threw the egg in. Hot fat spattered on her hands while the yolk of the egg broke and ran over the white.

"Don't throw it in that way, as if you were killing a snake. Move the skillet over here, away from the hottest part of the stove."

Maureen grabbed the hot iron handle of the skillet. She shrieked, then jumped up and down with pain.

"No need to blister yourself." Grandma took hold of the hot handle with a crocheted pot holder shaped like a pair of drawers. "Cooking is not much fun if you're forever burning yourself. Always use a pot holder."

As soon as Grandma sat down to her egg and toast, Maureen began to tell her about the Sansoucies. "First chance I get, I'm going over to Cold Spring to see if they went to school the way they said they would. Rose wanted to go. Besides, I like to go there to play some good running games." Maureen gave the rules and ways to win all her favorite games.

While she talked, Grandma ate a pretty good dinner.

Supper didn't go as well, though. Maureen tried to make vegetable soup. While the vegetables cooked up to mush, the meat on the soupbone was too tough to eat.

"How do you get them to come out even, Grandma? It's like long division. I always know it's right if it comes out even."

"Oh, that's as easy as weeding after a rain. You start the soupbone an hour or so ahead. Then you boil the vegetables a few minutes in that good beef stock the meat cooked in. I'd have supposed your mother would have taught you that, same as I taught her. Hasn't she taught you to cook, Maureen?"

"Guess not." Maureen thought for a few seconds. "Mama likes to garden and work outside, but she's not much for teaching. Of course, maybe I was not very good at listening," she added. "One thing I've wondered. If you were cooking a rabbit, how would you get it done inside before it burned outside?"

"That's as easy as falling off a log. You brown it first over a hot fire. Then you pull it away from the heat some or turn down the burner if it's a coal-oil stove. You put a lid on it so its own steam will help cook it. And you turn it now and then and let it cook until it's tender."

"Same with fried chicken?"

"Yes, except with chicken, first you dip it in batter and then roll it in flour."

"Tomorrow I'll make us some," Maureen promised. She felt good about learning to cook. To do things, she had to take time to learn instead of being mad because she wasn't born knowing everything.

Maureen had to think of something to talk about as well as something to cook every mealtime. As long as she kept talking, Grandma kept eating. Things were tasting better every day to both of them.

150

17

Days were improving. Evenings were still lonely, especially when the train whistles blew. Maureen thought of the trains that rushed below her house at Dotzero, with their whistles moaning. It was still light when Walter's bedtime train went by. She thought of him catching lightning bugs by himself. He probably didn't miss her reading Hurlbut's *Story of the Bible* to him in summer. She wondered if Grandma had that book.

There was a bookcase in the sitting room, but it contained more knickknacks than books. The few on the shelves had small print and no pictures. Under a stack of quilt pattern booklets, Maureen found a photograph album. She marveled that the Grandma she knew, with her low, hoarse voice and spindly legs, had ever looked like the young woman in the yellowed photographs.

Grandma found her studying the pictures when she came in to pull down the sitting-room window shades. "I appear different on the outside," she said, looking down at Maureen, "but I'm still the same person. It helps me if others remember that."

Maureen moved the books about on the shelf. "Have you got Hurlbut's *Story of the Bible?*"

"Got no such watered-down thing. I have the real Bible there on the table. It would be nice if you read me some Scripture, loud enough for me to hear. I quit going to church. Couldn't hear our new preacher." Grandma left the shades up and settled into a rocker.

No one except Walter and Miss Huckstep had ever asked Maureen to read before. Pleased, she opened the Bible and began.

"Not there," Grandma objected. "Too much slaying and slewing. I like Proverbs. Ecclesiastes, that's good too. Open the book right in the middle, and you'll find Psalms."

Maureen also liked the words of Psalms. Grandma was surprised at how well Maureen read. She set aside a time each day for Maureen to read Scripture.

At other times Grandma wanted neither reading nor conversation. She wanted to listen to news broadcasts on KSD. In a way, that was progress too. When Maureen had first arrived, Grandma wouldn't let her turn on the radio, although there was electricity in the house and no need to worry about running down the battery. She said she just did not want to hear "Fibber McGee and Molly" or "Guy Lombardo and His Royal Canadians" or anything.

Now Grandma turned up the volume and wanted everything as still as Dad did when he tuned in the livestock market report. Maureen heard about WPA and PWA and AAA and REA. It was like listening to the eighth grade at school; she learned a lot.

The letters that interested her most were PWA because she had seen them on a sign near Kroger's where men were building a curb. Grandma told her that towns all over the U.S.A. had PWA.

"How come we don't have it in Dotzero?" Maureen asked.

"Maybe because you never asked for it," Grandma allowed.

Maureen began to think. She was right there in Beaumont. Perhaps she could get PWA for Dotzero if she knew where to ask. The foreman on the curb job might help her.

Maureen needed a lot of nerve to talk to the man even if she did know about foremen from Dad's extra-gang job. He was the one that gave lots of orders and did little work. First she said howdy to him as she passed on her way to Kroger's. Then he began to chat with her and answer her many questions.

He explained that there was an awful lot of red tape involved in getting a PWA project. The application was enough to choke a horse. It had to show how many people were out of work, the need for the project, and the number of people to be served. The Beaumont

PWA office fielded it around for a while; then it went up to Jefferson City and even to Washington, D.C., itself.

Discouraged, Maureen was ready to give up the whole idea. She did use the information she'd learned to entertain Grandma at supper that evening, though.

That night Maureen dreamed of crossing the Dotzero railroad bridge. She was carrying one of Uncle Millard's kids piggyback. With all her strength she tried to lift her feet from the ties, but they wouldn't move. A train was coming. It whistled, and she could hear the bell clang as it came nearer and nearer. She awoke to hear the shrill whistle of a train engine at the Beaumont Main Street crossing.

Maureen told her dream to Grandma the next morning at breakfast. "I think it's a sign that we need a road bridge at Dotzero," Maureen said.

The Scripture reading from Ecclesiastes that day included the words, "A time to keep silent, and a time to speak." That was a second sign. Maureen knew she would have to speak for a bridge.

Carefully she got ready. She had a clean dress. Although her shoes were getting too tight, they looked fine with a little polish. She pinned wisps of her hair back with bobby pins while she tried out what she hoped was a smile rather than a grin before the dresser mirror.

On her way to the PWA office, she silently practiced her speech and kept on rehearsing it as she waited in the office for someone to notice her. After a long time, Maureen decided she could not sit forever in that waiting room, so she went into the inner office. The man in the white shirt at the big desk looked like the boss, so she marched up to him.

He looked up from a stack of papers. "What do you want, sister?"

"My name is not sister. It's Maureen McCracken of the Dotzero McCrackens. I want a bridge."

The man looked at her over the top of his glasses. He smiled and sat back in his chair as if he were ready to watch a good picture show. "Yeah, I remember Dotzero. Zero would be more like it. I used to fish down there on Lost Creek. Anybody still hanging around that place?"

"Yes, all us McCrackens and a big bunch of O'Neils moving in, too. All going to Dotzero School and have to cross Lost Creek to get there. If there was a bridge, folks from Post Oak could do their trading and catch the train in Dotzero. It would be a lot shorter for them than coming clear into Beaumont, wouldn't it? We need a bridge a lot more than you need a street curb in Beaumont. There's people out of work at Dotzero. They don't have to sleep under newspapers, but they can't pay the store bill or make an order to Sears or anything. They just sit on the store porch whittling on the benches and telling lies. Some of the kids haven't got decent clothes for school.

"So if they had work building the bridge. . . . It wouldn't have to be very wide, one-car wide would be enough. If ever two cars or a wagon got there at the same time, one could wait for the other, and it wouldn't need fancy banisters or anything. But it ought to be high, because Lost Creek comes up in a hurry.

"Everybody in Dotzero knows that. If we need a doctor now, we can't always get him across to tell us what sickness we have. Next time if it's anybody but Pat Ash at the depot, he might not stop the train the way he did for my brother Walter when he almost died with appendicitis. So instead of having everybody crying around at a funeral, we ought to have this bridge."

"Now hold your horses, Miss Maureen McCracken. All that may be so, but first an application form has to be filled out by a civic leader." The man in the white shirt laughed. "Of course, you wouldn't understand that term."

"Yes, I do. Eighth grade has civics, and I listen. It's somebody like Sterling Stackhouse, only he's no good. He wouldn't ask for a bridge unless all his kin and all his wife's kin got the jobs. I could fill it out. I've filled out orders to Sears."

The man shook his head. "I'm afraid that wouldn't work. But here's an application. You're all fired up.

You might get the community interested." He looked up at a map on the wall with a lot of pins stuck in it. "We don't have any projects down at that end of the county. More people and more needs elsewhere, I guess. Of course, we could make a stab at it and see if we get approval. There's a lot of red tape, you know."

Maureen nodded. Everybody was supposed to know about red tape, whatever that was.

Maureen was almost ready to turn off sizzling hot Main Street into a shaded walk when she recognized Miss Huckstep. Hot as it was, Maureen ran to meet her. "Miss Huckstep! I'm so glad to see somebody I know in Beaumont."

"I'm glad to see you, Maureen." Miss Huckstep moved into the shade of a store awning. "My, you look neat as a pin."

"You, too." Maureen admired Miss Huckstep's stylish ankle-length dress and her new hairdo, rolled in side sausages.

"I'm going to summer school. How is your grandma?"

"Perking up, Dr. Varney says. It's not as bad here in Beaumont as I thought it would be. I don't have to stay with Grandma every minute the way I did at first. This morning I went and got this." Maureen held out the application form. "Maybe you could fill it out. But first, tell me if you'll be our teacher again."

"I've not been hired, Maureen, but no one else has either, as far as I know."

157

The time had come. Maureen felt she had to confess. "I'm the one that did it. I told Mrs. Stackhouse you were secretly married. She made me. She stood right there in the U.S. Post Office and made me tell that secret. Well, she didn't torture me or anything like that. At home they said a married woman wouldn't be hired. I'm the one told it. Do you hold that against me?"

Miss Huckstep dabbed her face with her handkerchief. "I did hope to teach, because I liked working with you kids. I'm still hopeful, so I'm going to summer school to keep my certificate up to date. Of course, you did a little unnecessary talking."

"I know. I read Scripture to Grandma this morning. It said 'a time to keep silent and a time to speak.' It was a time to keep silent." Maureen creased the folds of the application.

"And that's not so easy for you, Maureen, so no hard feelings. Now let's see what you have here." She took the form from Maureen and studied it.

"It's for a bridge over Lost Creek, right by the railroad trestle where we have to ford now. And there will be eleven more when Uncle Millard's family comes."

"Yes, the number of persons served is important. A couple of blanks ask for that information. Okay, I'll fill it out and turn it in. If I get stuck, I'll call on you, Maureen."

158

18

Grandma looked nice in her pink voile dress as she talked to Dr. Varney in the sitting room. It was bright and cheerful there with the window blinds raised. A spindly straight chair creaked under Dr. Varney's weight, and Maureen wished he had sat in the oak rocker.

He shook pills from a bottle into a little white envelope. "I'll leave you a few of these, but you may not need them."

"Oh, I know I'm a heap better. Getting my strength back, Doctor. Before Maureen came, I wasn't even tol'-able well. I had a bad spell. Trying to eat alone, day in and day out, I just about got out of the habit of eating." Grandma's eyes twinkled. "I think Maureen talked me into eating. Wasn't much else I could do while she rattled on. What a blatherskite! She got to be a real good cook, too."

"Now I think you can take care of yourself. I know that's what you want to do. Let's try it." Dr. Varney

159

turned to Maureen. "Good young company can be better than medicine."

Maureen was pleased to be praised by Dr. Varney. Best of all, she knew she really had helped Grandma. They had helped each other.

A few days later Maureen went home to Dotzero on the train. There was nothing to it when she had a ticket.

Maureen was joyful as a fiddle tune just to be home. She pumped herself high and swung for a long time in the tire. It was good to go away once in a while, just for the happy feeling when she came home.

Maureen dramatized Dr. Varney's last visit for Mama and Walter. She took the parts of Grandma and the doctor, but left herself out. Naturally, she had said nothing while Grandma and Dr. Varney had bragged about her.

"We sent the right nurse," Mama said with a satisfied smile. "When Dad and Mit get home, you tell them how it went."

"You mean you *want* me to tell it again?" Maureen's cup was overflowing.

"Sure do. Everybody ought to know how you helped Grandma to take heart and be her old self again."

There were lots of changes at home. Mit's corn crop was waist high; spring chickens were frying size; potatoes, cucumbers, and green beans were ready to eat from Mama's garden. Walter seemed to have grown a little

160

too. Dad had worked more days than he expected on the extra gang.

"We're about to see our way clear to buy the nails, roofing, and hardware for our addition," he said. "What do you think, Lillian? Shall we go to Millard's for the day soon? We can take a mess of garden truck to him and see if he's ready to come help butcher wood?"

"Good a time as any," Mama agreed. "Maureen's here to look after things."

"I've made a deal with Sterling Stackhouse," Dad explained. "You know, he's always looking for a bargain in wood to heat the store. We'll get some supplies from him in exchange for good, dry firewood; it's been stacked, drying for months. He likes to get it well ahead."

"I'm glad we don't have to charge anything this time," Mama said. "I don't like the way he slaps that store-bill pad down on the counter. We don't need much now with the hens laying, garden growing, but we can get flour, coal oil, and a little dry salt meat, too."

"Mit can haul the wood on the day we go," Dad said. "Then he can wait for the train and bring us, the supplies, and the grub home in the wagon all together."

A few mornings later Maureen rose at dawn with Mama. She got her feet and dress wet with dew as she helped gather a little of everything in the garden.

161

On the porch, they washed the root vegetables, picked over the lettuce, and carefully packed all the produce into two big splint baskets. "I feel as if we're going on a picnic today instead of to St. Louis," Mama said.

"Won't you have a lot to carry to the train?" Maureen asked.

Mama lifted a basket. "Not as heavy as those school books you carry home, and the walk's no farther than the one you kids have made to school many a time. Of course, by the end of this long day, we'll be ready for a ride home in the wagon along with our building supplies."

Mama, Dad, and Walter got an early start for their hike to the Dotzero depot. Mit had morning chores to finish before he left. As she washed the breakfast dishes, Maureen felt dependable, downright important.

She straightened up the kitchen and swept the back porch. It was still too early to start Mit's dinner. There was no one in the kitchen to overhear, so she turned to the cellar door to tell Peloponnesus about the PWA bridge.

Maureen gasped. The door was solid green. Peloponnesus was painted over. In the excitement of coming home, she had not noticed this change before.

Mit had started to load the wagon. Maureen could hear the clunk of stovewood as he tossed it from the pile near the yard into the wagon.

162

"Mit, oh, Mit," she called, as she ran outside. "What happened? Who painted the cellar door?"

Mit leaned against the wagon and grinned. "Somebody spoiled that loony game of yours while you were gone. A fellow, down and out, came up from the track and stayed here for a while. He was a house painter, so Mama bought some cheap paint on sale, and he painted different places around the house to pay for his keep. Mama likes all those colors."

"Well, I don't, and nobody asked me."

"I thought you'd be too useful now to waste time talking to yourself, Reen Peen." Mit sneered. "You could help me load this wood right now."

Maureen carried a stick of wood to the wagon. She was not as strong as Mit and could not throw it in the way he did. She hadn't told anyone at home about the bridge application. Now she couldn't tell Peloponnesus. She longed to tell someone.

"Mit, do you know we're going to get a bridge across Lost Creek? Not just a footbridge, a regular car bridge."

"Ha, ha, you make me laugh." But Mit wasn't laughing.

"It's so. We are."

"You're still going to get us a bridge? Ha, ha, what a laugh."

"Somebody does everything, Mit, and I'll tell you what I did when I stayed in Beaumont." Maureen tried

163

her best, but she couldn't convince Mit that the bridge would ever come to be.

It was discouraging. Mit was so stubborn. Everyone else praised her for saving Walter and helping Grandma out of a slump. Not Mit! Now that he had finished eighth grade and was through with school, he thought he was smarter than anyone else.

Maureen tried to toss the big chunks of wood with all her strength. "So when I stayed in Beaumont, I sure didn't know I'd get us a bridge. Then I met Miss Huck-step. You never know what's going to happen. That's what I tell Walter. I don't know exactly when we'll get it, do you? When do you think?"

"Never, so what's the use rattling on about it? Give your tongue and my ears a rest." Mit pointed to a black cloud in the south. "We're going to get a hard rain. Hurry, let's finish! I'll harness Fox and Jack in the barn and bring them here to hitch up. You can go with me if you stop blabbing."

It was going to storm for sure. Even Tisket could tell. She whined and stayed underfoot as Maureen tried to help Mit fasten the harness trace lines.

The storm had turned into a steady downpour by the time Mit reined the mules to a halt at Lost Creek ford. He and Maureen stared at the little creek in amazement. Swift, muddy water overflowed the banks.

Maureen held on to the wagon seat. "It didn't rain that much. What made the creek so high? What do you think, Mit? Huh? What do you think? I tell you what I think. I betcha it rained all night down around Post Oak, and the water just got here. That's it. Don't you think so, Mit? Our footbridge is gone—plank, chains, stakes, and everything. You see that willow in the water? That tree is supposed to be on the bank. I remember that tree because Walter and I used to skip stones toward it."

Fox, the red mule, pawed and backed. "Whoa, whoa, Fox." Mit pulled on the reins. "Maureen, will you hush? Fox and Jack don't like this high water. Pipe down, or we're going to have trouble. I've got two loads of wood to haul. I want to get this one across now."

"We don't need to have trouble. Just let Fox and Jack back up, back all the way up the hill home. I'll fix us some dinner. We don't need to go plunging into that deep water. And if I were you, Mit, I wouldn't—"

"You're not me." Mit looked up at the black sky. "The longer we wait, the higher the water."

"I saw something like this in a picture show once. Grandma and I went to it in Beaumont. They made boats out of wagons. Of course, they didn't have a load of firewood. Maybe—"

"This is no picture show. Now shut up." Mit clicked his tongue and flipped the ends of the lines over the backs of the mules. They moved into the water.

The wagon went down with a hard jolt. Water rose halfway up the wheels. "It's all washed out!" Maureen

165

yelled. "It's way too deep. Turn them around! Turn them!"

"Can't," Mit muttered through clenched teeth.

"Then back them out, Mit. Back them out!"

"Shut up, can't you? Steady, Fox. Easy, Jack. Where's that shallow place?"

The wheels disappeared underwater. Just ahead of the mules, the current raced. Jack headed into it. Fox pulled back. Maureen was horrified to see the big rumps of both mules turn crosswise to the current. Jack thrashed in the harness, trying to swim. Maureen screamed. The wagon tipped, tipped, and went over. With chunks of heavy wood falling about her, Maureen went down into the swift, muddy water.

She tried hard to turn and get to the surface while she could still hold her breath. Which way was up? Something snagged her dress. With the strength and breath she had left, Maureen struggled free, pushed her head above water, and gasped for air.

She couldn't swim out of the swift current. All she could do was keep her head above water as she was swept downstream. Suddenly Maureen saw overhanging tree branches. She grasped a limb and with all her might pulled herself along it to the bank. She lay there, coughing up water.

When she had the breath to call, she screamed for Mit. His voice answered from someplace. Tree branches at the water's edge moved, and Mit came stumbling toward her. He was wild-eyed and appeared half drowned.

Far downstream, mules, harness, and wagon churned in the deep, strong current. "Whoa, whoa, steady Fox, Jack," Mit yelled. It was useless. He knew it. "They're drowning! Fox and Jack are drowning!"

Maureen saw Fox's red head come up and go down. Jack's black head didn't come up again. A few pieces of wood floated downstream. That was all.

"Fox and Jack are drowned, gone." Mit made a choking sound. "The wagon, everything gone. I'm not staying here, not after this. Maureen, you're good at talking. Tell Mama and Dad what happened to their team of young mules."

"Wait, don't leave me here by myself," Maureen pleaded.

Mit looked like a crazy person. He climbed on all fours up the railroad bank. Once he reached the track he started to run away from Dotzero two ties at a time.

The section crew filling in a track washout saw her first Cleve McCracken's girl, wet and crying about a drowned team and runaway brother. They took her to the depot to stay with Pat Ash. He brought an old coat from the freight room and put it around her to try to stop her shaking.

Maureen sat and cried while she waited for the train to bring Mama, Dad, and Walter. Train sounds, people

167

talking in low voices, Mrs. Stackhouse with soda water, clicking telegraph keys were all a jumble to her during the long afternoon.

Finally Pat Ash said, "It's in the block, Maureen. You better let me tell your folks."

She ran ahead of him to meet them as they got off the coach. They were shocked to see Maureen's torn, muddy dress and tearstained face. Dad grasped her shoulders. "What's wrong? Where's Mit?"

"Oh, it came! That awful day Mit talked about. It was today. Everything terrible happened!"

"What? What is it?" Mama cried.

"You folks better come sit down in the waiting room." Paul Ash led the way. "As you see, Maureen is all right, but there was a gully washer, the creek current shifted. . . ."

"Mit! Where's my boy?" Dad demanded.

"He's not drowned," Maureen said, sobbing.

"Oh, thanks be to God." Mama stumbled to a place beside Dad on the waiting-room bench.

"But the mules are. We don't have any more Fox and Jack." Maureen buried her face on Dad's shoulder.

"Near as I can tell, Mit must have miscalculated," Pat Ash explained. "The ford was washed out."

"Fox and Jack." Dad sounded stunned. "Good young mules, best in Dotzero. Just had them gentled down. I can't believe they couldn't swim out."

"Maureen says not, Cleve, says they pulled against

each other. Of course, scared as she was, maybe she's mistaken. They might have made it farther downstream."

"No, no, they didn't," Maureen insisted. "They're gone, and Mit's run away."

"He's probably home by now." Pat Ash tried to sound hopeful. "Or he will be by morning."

Mama stood up. "We'd better go see if he's there."

Dad didn't move. "Strange thing. I stepped off that train thinking everything was fine. The next second it's all changed. I guess I was born to be a poor man, never get ahead or be able to help Millard or anybody."

"Cleve, please don't talk that way," Mama begged. "We could have lost the children."

"I could get somebody to take you folks up to Lost Creek trestle," Pat Ash said.

Dad lifted Walter up onto his shoulders. "Much obliged, but we might as well start walking. We'll be doing a lot of it from now on."

19

Maureen awoke early the next morning and went at once to the boys' room. Mit's bed with the pillow plumped and the quilt unmussed was a dreadful sight to her. It meant that Mit had not come home during the night. He didn't come the next day either, nor the next.

Everyone around Dotzero was on the lookout for him. A farmer who lived three miles down Lost Creek found the carcasses of the mules. They were entangled in the harness, still hitched to a piece of the wagon. None of the families farming Lost Creek bottomland saw Mit, nor did anyone living near the railroad.

Maureen felt as if she had swallowed a stone. As each day passed, the stone felt heavier.

Mama stopped trying to drive away the black cloud of despair that overshadowed Dad. Instead of hoeing her garden, she sat idly on the porch staring down at the track. Sometimes she walked the floor, not talking to Maureen directly, but saying things like, "The good

Lord spared one of my boys and then took the other."

"Mama, Mit's not dead!" Maureen exclaimed. "He's off looking for work, maybe got something by now. He'll send us a postcard."

"It's terrible out on the road." Mama resumed her pacing.

Maureen thought of the homeless men she had seen from the train window, rows and rows of them wrapped in newspapers on a cold night. She tried to strengthen Mama's hope and her own, too. "But it's summertime. It'll be like camping out for him while he's looking for work. Maybe he'll go out West to the wheat harvest."

"Boys like him have it hard out on the road. I know." Mama started pacing again. "It's the young ones that come to the door to ask for a handout. The hard, older fellows wait on the track to take most of it. They figure most families can't refuse a youngster."

"I don't know why he ran away." Maureen sobbed.

"It was a lot to face. Mit knew we couldn't raise a crop, peddle apples or wood, or do anything without the team. We put too much on him, tried to put an old head on young shoulders. Now we're worn out with worry and got no help either."

"Well, when Uncle Millard comes," Maureen suggested, "then he. . . ."

"No more talk of that now. We wouldn't expect a bare-tailed possum to make a living in this Godforsaken place."

171

"Mama, our place is not Godforsaken! We live in the St. Francois Mountains."

"No more of that palaver, Maureen."

Their own hill, Godforsaken. Maureen hustled Walter outside so he wouldn't hear any more such talk. He was too little to get all out of heart. She urged him to keep searching for an angel's egg and even pointed out a white china doorknob in the trash pile for him to investigate.

Walter held up well enough except at night. Then Maureen could no longer drive the spook from the closet. Because Walter was afraid to sleep in the big room without Mit, Maureen slept in Mit's bed. Muddy water swirled through her dreams. Asleep and awake, she often saw the big haunches of the mules thrashing in the water. Mama thought dreams about muddy water meant bad luck. Apparently she was right.

Maureen wished Mama and Dad would come right out and blame her for the mules drowning and Mit's running away, just say that her jabbering had caused Mit to make a mistake. But they didn't. They just kept watching and looking anxiously whenever a man approached from the track to ask for something to eat.

As Mama didn't give her any jobs to do, Maureen often slipped away from Walter and wandered over the pasture and hayfield. She pretended she was talking to Mit. Yes, he was right. There would be no bridge. Without Uncle Millard's family, there would not be

172

enough people served. If Miss Huckstep had already sent in the form with the wrong count, it would land on the red-tape pile of requests containing lies.

Sometimes Maureen went as far as the Wiley place. She was poking around the yard there one day when Mrs. Wiley drove up. Maureen felt like ducking down behind the overgrown lilac bush, but instead she went to meet Mrs. Wiley and looked directly into her bright, sharp eyes. "I come over here every now and then to see if the house is torn down, but it's still here."

Mrs. Wiley pushed at the sagging fence. "Yes, but not for long. I'll give it a decent ending as it was the Wiley home place." She looked sharply at Maureen. "You're the one that helped your grandmother. She was telling me. Then I heard about your troubles. Any word from your brother?"

"Not yet, but he'll come up the hill home most any day now. He'll be back, but our mules won't ever be. Now we can't haul the lumber to build the rooms on our house for Uncle Millard and my aunt and nine cousins. They were going to move here from St. Louis because the box factory shut down in the city."

"Don't think the McCrackens and O'Neils alone have trouble." Mrs. Wiley shook her head. "You're not burdened with taxes on property as I am. No, indeed. I own most of the land in Dotzero School District, and I kept those taxes paid so that Dotzero School is in fine condition."

173

Maureen considered herself an absolute expert on Dotzero School. She could have told Mrs. Wiley about a broken windowlight and a loose floorboard under a certain desk.

"Whatever was required was forthcoming," Mrs. Wiley continued. "A drilled well, more windows, a woodshed, new fancy outhouses, maps, books—whatever those people in Jefferson City said that school had to have, my school taxes, all paid, provided."

Maureen wanted to tell Mrs. Wiley that she would like some new library books. But Mrs. Wiley was talking to her as if she were at least an eighth grader, maybe even a civic leader. Perhaps talking to somebody made Mrs. Wiley feel better. Maureen remembered the Scripture she'd read to Grandma. It was a time to keep silent. Maureen listened.

"Do you know what they say now?" Mrs. Wiley didn't wait for a guess. "They say we don't have enough pupils, claim Dotzero must be closed and the district go into Post Oak Consolidated. Of course, I know some have moved away, and for no good reason either, as it will be out of the frying pan into the fire. All the more attention for those, like yourself, remaining. But you should hear the arguments."

Mrs. Wiley flung up her hands in disbelief. "The children would have art and music and such." Mrs. Wiley snorted. "Wasting their time with daubs and scribbles. As for music, they get all the children tooting on horns. One or two can play a tune. The rest are just blowing their brains out. All that folderol costs money, don't forget. The school tax is much higher in Post Oak Consolidated District. It will bring me near ruin if the Wiley place and my other tracts go into that district and my tax bill goes even higher. Carting the children all over creation. I'm opposed to it." Mrs. Wiley's sharp eyes burned.

"Oh, I am too," Maureen agreed. "They have nine months of school at Post Oak Consolidated. They get scarcely any summer at all, not like Dotzero where we have eight months of school."

"High-handed I call it. Your folks must know of it, as the little tax you have to pay will also increase."

Maureen shrugged. "I don't know much about taxes. My folks haven't talked about taxes or about hardly anything much. Just thinking about Fox and Jack and the bridge we won't get and Uncle Millard can't come now, and worst of all, where Mit is."

"It's outrageous, just when he was big enough to help, start to pay for his raising, he ups and runs away. I thought it would put your grandmother back on the sick list. But, no, the surprising woman says she's coming to Dotzero for her birthday dinner, same as usual. I told her that if she had that much spirit, I'd drive her here myself and stay for dinner. I may look inside the house then, but not today."

Mrs. Wiley went to her car and just sat there behind

175

the wheel. She kept looking at the Wiley house. Maureen had started toward home when Mrs. Wiley called to her. "It's a crying shame about Millard and all those children. I know it's a great brood."

20

Maureen came home to find Mama still sitting on the porch. The *Capper's Weekly* that Maureen had brought earlier from the post office was on a chair beside her. She had not unfolded it to read one word of her continued story.

"Want me to do anything?" Maureen asked.

Mama shook her head.

"I saw Mrs. Wiley over at the old place. She says Grandma wants to come here for her birthday." Maureen put her arms around Mama. "Tell her No. I don't want to have a birthday dinner, same as usual."

"I know. I don't either." Mama sat up and straightened her shoulders. "You'll have to keep a stiff upper lip, Maureen. If Grandma wants to celebrate this birthday, we'll go ahead with it and put a good meal on the table. Anybody you want to ask?"

"Miss Huckstep, because maybe I'll never see her again."

"Never is a long time," Mama said. "I try not to

think of that word." Her voice softened. "I worry so about Mit. Then I reason that it's natural for young people to set out on their own. But he went too soon, went empty-handed, not even a change of clothes."

"I wish Mit would back up, get straightened out, come home, like a boxcar switched onto the right track," Maureen said.

That night Maureen dreamed of men wrapped in newspaper, lying on rafts that tossed on muddy water. The dream frightened her so that she fled crying into the next room to Mama's side of the bed.

"Sh-h-h, try not to wake Dad. He just got to sleep, and he has a day's work on the extra gang tomorrow. Every day counts. We've got to hold up for his sake. Think about what you are going to do tomorrow when daylight comes. I've found that helps."

Maureen went back to her bed and thought about going to the post office. She still had confidence in the U. S. mail and went everyday, hoping to hear from Mit.

The next morning Maureen and Walter waited at the postal window while Mrs. Stackhouse sorted the mail that Pat Ash had brought from the depot. Mrs. Stackhouse studied the address on a postcard. "You did get something here. It's not addressed to your folks, but to you, Miss Maureen McCracken. Postmarked yesterday, from . . . can't quite make that out." She turned the card over.

Maureen grabbed it from her fat fingers. She felt a

sickening wave of disappointment. The handwriting was not Mit's. It was an ordinary post-office card, no nice picture on the front. The card read: Dear Maureen, We are fine and hope you are the same. After you came to visit us, we went to school every day. We all passed. Come again right away. I know something <u>very important</u> to tell you. Your friend, Rose S.

On the porch, Maureen read the card twice to Walter. "You see how she's underlined very important?"

"Why didn't she write what it was?"

"Didn't have room maybe. Walter, we're going to the Sansoucies. This time we'll ask."

Mama said that if they wanted to make the long, hot walk on the back road to go ahead. One thing was sure, walking was the only way to get there.

Entwined with a blooming trumpet creeper and shaded by big maple trees the Sansoucies' house looked different in the summer. No one was playing in the bare, sunny part of the yard when Maureen and Walter arrived. At first, Maureen thought no one was home.

Then Rose came running from the shade. "I was looking for you, Maureen. I've got the kids pounding up rocks to make their own sandpile. You can help, Walter. The littlest ones are taking naps. C'mon, Maureen." Rose motioned and started walking away from the house. "We can't take the whole gang. I'll have to show you. It's by the tracks, not far from the water tank."

"What, Rose, what?" Maureen skipped to keep up.

"I think I saw Mit yesterday morning. It looked for all the world just like him, the glimpse I had before he took to the weeds and brush. I think he recognized us and didn't want us to see him."

As they headed for the track, Rose explained that the Sansoucie children had been picking blackberries along the railroad right-of-way. Berries were getting scarce, so they had gone farther from home than usual. "I didn't tell the other kids I'd seen somebody. They were scared because we weren't supposed to go that far and had seen a hobo fire. They wanted to get home."

Near the water tank, Rose stopped and pointed. "See that path off into the brush and briars? Hoboes stay down there, and when the engines stop to take on water, men come out and hop the freights."

"All right, Rose, wait for me here. I might do better by myself."

The weeds smelled rank as Maureen followed the path to a wide circle of trodden ground. Someone lay asleep near a pile of ashes and charred wood. It was Mit.

"Mit, oh, Mit, I've found you! Boy, am I glad!" Maureen shouted.

Mit roused and stared at her. His eyes were like burned holes in a blanket, and his black hair was dull with dust. He leaped to his feet.

Maureen grabbed him by the hand. "Mit, don't run

180

away again. Come home. It's just awful there now, as if somebody died, because you're gone."

"Fox and Jack died." He shook her hand loose. "Go ahead, blab to everybody that you saw me. But they won't find me. I'm getting out of here."

"Milton, won't you ever come home?"

"I'll be home when I can come leading a span of mules."

"Want me to blab that?"

Mit shrugged. "It's up to you."

"I won't, because Mama and Dad would feel worse. They don't care so much about the mules. Already they're getting used to no Fox, no Jack. They care because you ran away, acted as if they would hold losing the mules against you forever."

Maureen noticed that the toes of Mit's shoes were worn through and that his torn, dirty overalls hung on him. "You're skinny, Mit. Mama worries about how you're eating all the time. Where have you been?"

"I walked way up the other side of Beaumont, but there's no work there. So I came back here. Heard about this place at Cold Spring to hop a freight. I'm going to get out of here."

"Don't go, Mit. Dad's in such a blackness he might never come out of it. Mama's all out of heart. Walter pesters me all the time about when you're coming home. Tisket whines around. Grandma is holding up the best,

181

I guess." Maureen took a deep breath. "We're having a birthday dinner for her Sunday. It'll be real good. Different people are bringing things. She wants to bring something herself. Mama told her to bring deviled eggs. Only Grandma never says deviled anything. She calls them dressed eggs. Mrs. Wiley is going to drive Grandma to our house. She's bringing yeast rolls. Says they cost little and taste good, which they do.

"We'll fry up three or four spring chickens. They will be good with roasting ears just coming in and the first ripe tomatoes from Mama's garden. Miss Huckstep has a way of fixing new potatoes with creamed garden peas. She'll bring them and blackberry pie, maybe a meat loaf, too. Pat Ash is coming right after Number 3 so he can bring the ice cream packed down in ice that comes by express on the train.

"I'm going to make Grandma's favorite three-egg cake with chocolate frosting. I know how to do that now. So many hens are laying now that Mama will whip up a big angel-food cake and with the yolks left she'll make a sunshine cake. So there will be three kinds of cake. Which do you like best?" Maureen studied Mit closely.

Mit's eyes looked glassy. "Chocolate, only I won't be there, not with everybody saying, 'There's Mit Mc-Cracken, the one lost his Dad's good, young team.' "

"They'll be too busy eating to say any such thing. Everybody would be extra happy if you were home. Oh,

I forgot. We'll have homemade pickles, little sweet ones, and current jelly for the hot rolls, and Molly's butter, and crocks of sweet milk, and a couple pitchers of lemonade. It's this coming Sunday."

"What day is today?" Mit croaked.

"Thursday, so you might as well come now. Then we could all go home together."

Mit stirred the cold ashes with a stick. "No, guess I'll not come. Just go ahead and have your big feed."

Maureen hated to leave Mit there alone, but she knew she needed help to persuade him to come home. She pushed aside the weeds beside the path and returned to the track where Rose patiently waited.

"You saw him all right, but it's a wonder you knew him. He looks so different, Rose, and he says he's moving on. Walter and I can't stay to make sand. I'll have to get home and tell Dad where we saw Mit. I tried, but I don't know if I did any good or not."

A train whistled for the Cold Spring crossing. Rose and Maureen stood close to the right-of-way fence and watched the freight slowly glide into the water-tank siding. "I think Mit is still trying to get up nerve enough to hop a train," Maureen said, "so maybe there's time yet."

21

Walter's bedtime train went by, but Mama let him stay up and wait for Dad. He had been gone for hours to search for Mit. Mama was lighting the kitchen lamp when they heard footsteps on the porch. Lamplight shone on Dad's face; they did not need to peer into the darkness beyond the door to know he was alone.

"Any trace, Cleve?" Mama asked.

"Just a fellow at the hangout. He said a youngster like Mit had shagged out of there."

"I should have made him wait," Maureen said.

"You did your best, Maureen." Dad stroked her hair and brushed some wisps out of her eyes. "You couldn't hog-tie him. I can search every hobo jungle on the railroad, but I can't drag him home by the scruff of the neck. He's got to come round to it himself."

It was the most Dad had said for a long time.

Mama looked ready to cry. "I was so in hopes he would be here Sunday for Grandma's birthday. Wouldn't that have been a surprise?"

184

"I told him about it. I told him," Maureen repeated.

"We'll go through with it same as usual, even if we don't feel like it." Mama sighed.

On Sunday Mama wanted the plank table set out in the shade. Grandma and Mrs. Wiley were the first to come. Grandma didn't act like company. As spry and handy as a pocket in a shirt, she put an apron over her flowered dress and helped with dinner.

Maureen's last task was to make sure the number of seats and plates matched the number of people. She was careful to check that there was an extra setting, in case it was needed. Just before everyone sat down, she went to the edge of the yard for one more look toward the track. Mit was not coming. It was all Maureen could do to keep a stiff upper lip.

Grandma gave thanks for the food. She gave thanks for the years she'd had and for the ones she was expecting. Then she asked God to look after all of her family—in the big city and abroad in the world, wherever they were. It was enough to make a person bawl.

Jim Nolan sat beside Miss Huckstep, who was taking second helpings when she announced, "I want to tell you that I'll be teacher at Dotzero next term. That's what Sterling Stackhouse tells me. He and the like-minded board members have decided to let an old married woman teach."

Mama passed the chicken. "Why the change of heart?"

185

"His niece got rehired for one thing. For another, he's finally sure our school meets all the state requirements. Mostly, I think he's grateful to me for applying for the bridge. I'm happy to tell you that the project has just been approved. Mr. Stackhouse says it will bring him more paying trade."

Dad looked at Maureen with astonishment. "That bridge Maureen told us about? I never thought it would go through."

Mama laughed. "Maureen had that dream where she falls off the trestle once too often, so she spoke up and did something about it."

Miss Huckstep beamed at Maureen. "She learned to use her gift of gab."

Everyone was laughing and talking at once, glancing with admiration at Maureen. But she was silent; she knew the good news wasn't true. There were not enough children for a school at Dotzero. There were not enough people for a bridge.

Maureen looked up when she heard Mrs. Wiley clear her throat. She too wished to make an announcement. "I've been thinking of the Millard O'Neil family. They are welcome to move into the Wiley place, rent free, if they want."

Dad dropped his fork. "Do you mean that, Mrs. Wiley? That's uncommon generous."

"They would be better off here with the rest of you."

186

She waved her hand over the table. "Be able to raise food as you do. Of course, I'd expect some repair on my house in place of rent, nail up a loose board now and then."

"That's wonderful!" Mama smiled and cut more cake. "Now I'll have some good news to write to them."

Grandma took another piece of chocolate cake. She looked over and patted her friend's hand. "Mrs. Wiley, I never thought of you as an instrument of Providence, but in this case I believe you are."

There was enough food for everyone to take some home and still leave plenty. Mama wanted to let the dishes wait for a while so she could get out her tablet and write to Uncle Millard. Maureen had figured something out and was bursting to talk, but she decided to stay outside with Walter until Mama finished her letter. She was giving Walter his turn in the swing when she saw someone coming up from the track. She knew that walk; it was Mit.

Walter slid out of the tire and ran to grab Mit around the legs. Tisket had a fit of joy. Maureen was speechless.

"Anything left to eat? What's the matter, Maureen? Didn't you expect me?"

Maureen ran toward the house, shouting, "Mama, Dad, it's Mit! He's home! He came round to it!"

Mama began laughing and crying. She just about ruined a page of her letter with tearstains.

The dark expression left Dad's face as he looked at Mit. "You've taken a heavy load of worry off us, just the sight of you."

"I aimed to stay away until I could come back leading a span of mules." Mit grabbed Walter and tickled him. "Then I thought Walter would be grown up by then. I got so lonesome I even missed Maureen's blatherin'. And I got so hungry I could have eaten her cooking."

"You'll be surprised." Mama looked proudly at Maureen. "Things don't always stay the same."

"Then when Maureen and Rose bird-dogged around and found me, Maureen talked me into coming home," Mit continued.

"Maureen did that?" A big smile spread over Dad's face.

"It didn't work right away, but the closer Sunday came the hungrier I got."

Mama jumped up. "What am I thinking of?" She quickly started filling a plate for Mit. As she watched him shovel in food, she said, "You must have learned a lot out on the road."

"Learned there was a lot I didn't know. I can't do the work of a mule team, but I can earn my keep."

Mama filled his plate again. "There's a job for all of

us now. We've got to get the Wiley place fit to live in. Mrs. Wiley says Millard's family can live there rent free."

"Things *don't* stay the same! Mrs. Wiley! Are you sure?" Mit gulped down a glass of milk.

"Well, I can tell you why. . . ." Maureen began. Then she stopped. She could have gone on and explained what she had figured out. It was like a long-division problem that came out even. Mrs. Wiley had given the house to Uncle Millard's family so there would be enough kids in the district to keep Dotzero School open and her taxes down. But if Maureen told that, everybody would go back to thinking Mrs. Wiley was as close as the bark on a tree, mean, and kept kids from tooting horns at Post Oak Consolidated. Mrs. Wiley had saved the bridge and saved Maureen from a month of extra school. Besides, she was an instrument of Providence, according to Grandma. Maureen was grateful to her. It seemed one of those times it was best to keep silent.

"Tell what?" Walter asked.

"Why I want you to come finish your turn in the swing," Maureen said, pulling him away from the others.

"A lot of good things happened today, Maureen, but we won't ever find an angel's egg like Peloponnesus said. He's gone, painted out."

189

"Oh, no, he's not, Walter. Peloponnesus is under the paint. Things are not gone just because you can't see them."

Walter smiled until his eyes closed. "Okay, then I want to show you something."

Near the fence, Walter stooped beside a patch of bare earth. A smooth, rounded white form bulged from the ground. "Maybe this is it." He worked his fingers around the white bulge.

"Careful, careful, Walter."

His short fingers slipped under an edge. He pulled out a jagged shape resembling a broken bowl. They both stared at it.

"It has already hatched," Walter whispered.

Maureen sighed with satisfaction. "Just think, it hatched out here at the McCracken place on Lost Creek in the St. Francois Mountains during the Depression."

They gazed up at the last rosy clouds in the evening sky. One was shaped just like an angel Maureen had seen in the colored glass window of the Beaumont Methodist Church.